MYTH AND COSMOS

John Middleton
received his D.Phil. from Oxford in 1953. He has taught
anthropology at Capetown, Northwestern, and New York uni-
versities, and at present he is professor of African anthropology
at the School of Anthropology and African Studies, University
of London.

He has done field research in Uganda, Zanzibar, and Nigeria.
He is the author of *Black Africa* and *Lugbara of Uganda*, and,
with David Tait, he edited *Tribes without Rulers*. Dr. Middleton
also edited four other volumes of the Texas Press Sourcebooks
in Anthropology series: *Comparative Political Systems*, with
Ronald Cohen; *Gods and Rituals*; *Magic, Witchcraft, and Curing*; and *From Child to Adult*.

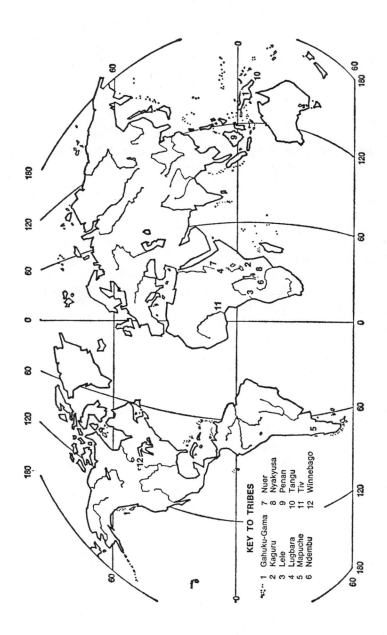

KEY TO TRIBES

1	Gahuku-Gama	7	Nuer
2	Kaguru	8	Nyakyusa
3	Lele	9	Penan
4	Lugbara	10	Tangu
5	Mapuche	11	Tiv
6	Ndembu	12	Winnebago

Texas Press Sourcebooks in Anthropology
were originally published by the Natural History Press, a division of Doubleday and Company, Inc. Responsibility for the series now resides with the University of Texas Press, Box 7819, Austin, Texas 78712. Whereas the series has been a joint effort between the American Museum of Natural History and the Natural History Press, future volumes in the series will be selected through the auspices of the editorial offices of the University of Texas Press.

The purpose of the series will remain unchanged in its effort to make available inexpensive, up-to-date, and authoritative volumes for the student and the general reader in the field of anthropology.

Myth
and
Cosmos

Readings in Mythology and Symbolism

Edited by John Middleton

University of Texas Press

Austin and London

Library of Congress Cataloging in Publication Data

Middleton, John, 1921–   comp.
    Myth and cosmos.

    (Texas Press sourcebooks in anthropology; 5)
    Reprint of the ed. published for the American Museum of
Natural History by the Natural History Press, Garden City, N.Y.,
issued in series: American Museum sourcebooks in anthropology.
    Bibliography: p.
    Includes index.
    CONTENTS: Middleton, J. Introduction.—Leach, E. R. Genesis as
myth.—Lévi-Strauss, C. Four Winnebago myths. [etc.]
    1. Mythology—Addresses, essays, lectures. 2. Symbolism—
Addresses, essays, lectures. I. Title. II. Series. III. Series: American
Museum sourcebooks in anthropology.
    [BL313.M48 1976]   291.1'3   75-43817
    ISBN 0-292-75030-7

Published by arrangement with Doubleday & Company, Inc.
Previously published by the Natural History Press in cooperation
with Doubleday & Company, Inc.

CONTENTS

INTRODUCTION

THIS VOLUME is concerned with some of the ways in which people conceive of their society and the world in which it is set. There seem to be certain virtually universal concepts which are used to do this: a belief in a Creator Spirit (or God), usually remote from men although believed to have been in contact with them at the beginning of the world; beliefs in various intermediaries between this spiritual power and men—deities, ancestors and so on; and beliefs in various human intermediaries who have the power to move from the sphere of ordinary mortals to that of the Creator Spirit—diviners, priests, prophets, shamans and others. People express these and related ideas in various ways—by myth, legend, folktale, by notions of time and space. They also express them in action, by sacrifice, prayer and the like; but in this volume we are concerned with the former only, with beliefs, concepts and symbols. Other ways are described in the two companion volumes of readings, *Gods and Rituals* and *Magic, Witchcraft, and Curing*.

The study of myth and cosmology has a long history. They have been studied by folklorists, interested mainly in motifs and their evolution and distribution; by psychologists, interested in what can be discovered from them about the individual psyche; by linguists; by historians of religion, interested mainly in the world religions; and lastly by anthropologists. The accounts in this volume are by anthropologists who, despite many differences in their views and aims, are nonetheless all concerned with a fairly similar set of problems and who all have a fairly similar viewpoint.

In general, anthropologists have approached mythology and cosmology from the point of view that they are cultural phenomena, or, in Durkheim's words, "collective representations" or "social facts." The underlying implication of this view is that myths and cosmological notions are not mere fairy tales, exotic and quaint expressions of a "primitive mentality." They are statements, made deliberately and consciously by the people who tell them. The popular notion that a "myth" is in some way "untrue" —indeed, that its untruth is its defining characteristic—is not only naive but shows misunderstanding of its very nature. Its "scientific truth" or otherwise is irrelevant. A myth is a statement about society and man's place in it and in the surrounding universe. Such a statement is, in general, a symbolic one, so that an important anthropological problem becomes one of understanding the reality that the statement is used to symbolize.

There have been two main ways in which anthropologists answer this problem. The earliest, exemplified by the "Intellectualists," Tylor and Frazer, was that myths express the half-forgotten origins of mankind and the natural and other disasters that occurred in history and pre-history. Although this approach has been outmoded for many years, it contains a very obvious truth of anthropological significance: that myths and cosmological notions are concerned with the relationship of a people with other peoples, with nature and with the supernatural. Against this is the more sociological approach, which starts with Mauss and Durkheim (for Mauss the central aim of anthropology was to understand the ways in which man conceives of his own experience) and is represented today most clearly by Lévi-Strauss and Leach. Myths are ways of explaining paradoxes, the paradoxes of social order within extra-social chaos, of the relationship of authority to power and the like. I have included several examples of this approach in this volume.

The later papers included are accounts of aspects of cosmological systems that are concerned with more specific matters: some of the culturally rich symbolic systems that have been described in recent years; an illuminating example of the social anthropological approach to folktales; and examples of notions of time, space and naming. I have had to omit much interesting and important material; in particular I am sorry to have included only two papers dealing with the Indians of the Americas, but little is obtainable outside the voluminous and fascinating accounts of the early American ethnologists and this is not easily reproducible without distortion in a collection of short pieces.

JOHN MIDDLETON

MYTH AND COSMOS

1   GENESIS AS MYTH

Edmund R. Leach

A DISTINGUISHED German theologian has defined myth as "the expression of unobservable realities in terms of observable phenomena" (Bartsch 1953). All stories which occur in the Bible are myths for the devout Christian, whether they correspond to historical fact or not. All human societies have myths in this sense, and normally the myths to which the greatest importance is attached are those which are the least probable. The non-rationality of myth is its very essence, for religion requires a demonstration of faith by the suspension of critical doubt.

But if myths do not mean what they appear to mean, how do they come to mean anything at all? What is the nature of the esoteric mode of communication by which myth is felt to give "expression to unobservable realities"?

This is an old problem which has lately taken on a new shape because, if myth be a mode of communication, then a part of the theory which is embodied in digital computer systems ought to be relevant. The merit of this approach is that it draws special attention to precisely those features of myth which have formerly been regarded as accidental defects. It is common to all mythological systems that all important stories recur in several different versions. Man is created in Genesis (chapter I, verse 27) and then he is created all over again (II, 7). And, as if two first men were not enough, we also have Noah in chapter VIII. Likewise in the

Reprinted from *Discovery*, May 1962, by permission of the author and the editor, *Discovery*. The original figures 1 and 3 have been omitted.

Readers should consult E. R. Leach, "Lévi-Strauss in the Garden of Eden," *Transactions of the New York Academy of Sciences* 23 (4), 1961: 386–96, for an earlier version of this paper.

New Testament, why must there be four gospels each telling 'the same' story yet sometimes flatly contradictory on details of fact? Another noticeable characteristic of mythical stories is their markedly binary aspect; myth is constantly setting up opposing categories: "In the beginning God created the heaven and the earth," "they crucified Him and two others with him, on either side one, and Jesus in the midst," "I am the Alpha and the Omega, the beginning and the end, saith the Lord." So always it is in myth—God against the world and the world itself for ever dividing into opposites on either side—male and female, living and dead, good and evil, first and last . . .

Now, in the language of communication engineers, the first of these common characteristics of myth is called *redundancy* while the second is strongly reminiscent of the unit of information—the *bit*. 'Information' in this technical sense is a measure of the freedom of choice in selecting a message. If there are only two messages and it is arbitrary which you choose then 'information is unity,' that is = 1 bit (*bit* stands for 'binary digit') (Shannon and Weaver 1949).

Communication engineers employ these concepts for the analysis of problems which arise when a particular individual (the sender) wishes to transmit a coded message correctly to another individual (the receiver) against a background of interference (noise). 'Information' refers on the one hand to the degrees of choice open to the sender in encoding his transmission and on the other to the degrees of choice open to the receiver in interpreting what he receives (which will include noise in addition to the original transmitted signal). In this situation a high level of redundancy makes it easy to correct errors introduced by noise.

Now in the mind of the believer, myth does indeed convey messages which are the Word of God. To such a man the redundancy of myth is a very reassuring fact. Any particular myth in isolation is like a coded message badly snarled up with noisy interference. Even the most confident devotee might feel a little uncertain as to what precisely is being said. But, as a result of redundancy, the believer can feel that, even when the details vary, each alternative version of a myth confirms his understanding and reinforces the essential meaning of all the others.

BINARY STRUCTURE OF MYTH

The anthropologist's viewpoint is different. He rejects the idea of a supernatural sender. He observes only a variety of possible receivers. Redundancy increases information—that is the uncertainty of the possible means of decoding the message. This explains what is surely the most striking of all religious phenomena —the passionate adherence to sectarian belief. The whole of Christendom shares a single corpus of mythology so it is surely very remarkable that the members of each particular Christian sect are able to convince themselves that they alone possess the secret of revealed truth. The abstract propositions of communication theory help us to understand this paradox.

But if the true believer can interpret his own mythology in almost any way he chooses, what principle governs the formation of the original myth? Is it random chance that a myth assumes one pattern rather than another? The binary structure of myth suggests otherwise.

Binary oppositions are intrinsic to the process of human thought. Any description of the world must discriminate categories in the form '*p* is what not-*p* is not.' An object is alive or not alive and one could not formulate the concept 'alive' except as the converse of its partner 'dead.' So also human beings are male or not male, and persons of the opposite sex are either available as sexual partners or not available. Universally these are the most fundamentally important oppositions in all human experience.

Religion everywhere is preoccupied with the first, the antinomy of life and death. Religion seeks to deny the binary link between the two words; it does this by creating the mystical idea of 'another world,' a land of the dead where life is perpetual. The attributes of this other world are necessarily those which are not of this world; imperfection here is balanced by perfection there. But this logical ordering of ideas has a disconcerting consequence —God comes to belong to the other world. The central 'problem' of religion is then to re-establish some kind of bridge between Man and God.

This pattern is built into the structure of every mythical system; the myth first discriminates between gods and men and then becomes preoccupied with the relations and intermediaries which link men and gods together. This much is already implicit in our initial definition.

So too with sex relations. Every human society has rules of incest and exogamy. Though the rules vary they always have the implication that for any particular male individual all women are divided by at least one binary distinction, there are women of *our kind* with whom sex relations would be incestuous and there are women of the *other kind* with whom sex relations are allowed. But here again we are immediately led into paradox. How was it in the beginning? If our first parents were persons of two kinds, what was that other kind? But if they were both of our kind, then their relations must have been incestuous and we are all born in sin. The myths of the world offer many different solutions to this childish intellectual puzzle, but the prominence which it receives shows that it entails the most profound moral issues. The crux is as before. If the logic of our thought leads us to distinguish *we* from *they,* how can we bridge the gap and establish social and sexual relations with 'the others' without throwing our categories into confusion?

So, despite all variations of theology, this aspect of myth is a constant. In every myth system we will find a persistent sequence of binary discriminations as between human/superhuman, mortal/immortal, male/female, legitimate/illegitimate, good/bad . . . followed by a 'mediation' of the paired categories thus distinguished.

'Mediation' (in this sense) is always achieved by introducing a third category which is 'abnormal' or 'anomalous' in terms of ordinary 'rational' categories. Thus myths are full of fabulous monsters, incarnate gods, virgin mothers. This middle ground is abnormal, non-natural, holy. It is typically the focus of all taboo and ritual observance.

This approach to myth analysis derives originally from the techniques of structural linguistics associated with the name of Roman Jakobson (Jakobson and Halle 1956) but is more immediately due to C. Lévi-Strauss one of whose examples may serve to illustrate the general principle.

Certain Pueblo Indian myths focus on the opposition between life and death. In these myths we find a threefold category distinction: agriculture (means to life), war (means to death), and hunting (a mediating category since it is means to life for men but means to death for animals). Other myths of the same cluster deploy a different triad: grass-eating animals (which live without killing), predators (which live by killing), and carrion-eating creatures (mediators, since they eat meat but do not kill in order to eat). In accumulation this total set of associated symbols serves to imply that life and death are *not* just the back and the front of the same penny, that death is *not* the necessary consequence of life (Lévi-Strauss 1955).

My Figure 1 has been designed to display an analogous structure for the case of the first four chapters of Genesis. The three horizontal bands of the diagram correspond to (i) the story of the seven-day creation, (ii) the story of the Garden of Eden, and (iii) the story of Cain and Abel. The diagram can also be read vertically: column 1 in band (ii) corresponds to column 1 in band (i) and so on. The detailed analysis is as follows:—

Upper Band

First Day (I, 1–5; not on diagram). Heaven distinguished from Earth; Light from Darkness; Day from Night; Evening from Morning.

Second Day (I, 6–8; col. 1 of diagram). (Fertile) water (rain) above; (infertile) water (sea) below. Mediated by firmament (sky).

Third Day (I, 9–10; col. 2 and I, 11–12; col. 3). Sea opposed to dry land. Mediated by 'grass, herb yielding seed (cereals), fruit trees.' These grow on dry land but need water. They are classed as things 'whose seed is in itself' and thereby contrasted with bisexual animals, birds, etc.

The creation of the world as a static (that is, dead) entity is now complete and this whole phase of the creation is opposed to the creation of moving (that is, living) things.

Fourth Day (I, 13–18; col. 4). Mobile sun and moon are placed in the fixed firmament of col. 1. Light and darkness become alternations (life and death become alternates).

Fifth Day (I, 20–23; col. 5). Fish and birds are living things corresponding to the sea/land opposition of col. 2 but they also mediate the col. 1 oppositions between sky and earth and between salt water and fresh water.

Sixth Day (I, 24–25; col. 6). Cattle (domestic animals), beasts (wild animals), creeping things. These correspond to the static triad of col. 3. But only the grass is allocated to the animals. Everything else, including the meat of the animals, is for Man's use (I, 29–30). Later at Leviticus XI creatures which do not fit this exact ordering of the world—for instance water creatures with no fins, animals and birds which eat meat or fish, etc.— are classed as 'abominations.' Creeping Things are anomalous with respect to the major categories, Fowl, Fish, Cattle, Beast and are thus abominations *ab initio* (Leviticus XI, 41–42). This classification in turn leads to an anomalous contradiction. In order to allow the Israelites to eat locusts the author of Leviticus XI had to introduce a special qualification to the prohibition against eating creeping things: "Yet these ye *may* eat: of every flying creeping thing that goeth on all four which have legs above their feet, to leap withal upon the earth" (v. 21). The procedures of binary discrimination could scarcely be carried further!

(I, 26–27; col. 7), Man and Woman are created simultaneously.

The whole system of living creatures is instructed to "be fruitful and multiply" but the problems of Life versus Death, and Incest versus Procreation are not faced at all.

Centre Band

The Garden of Eden story which now follows tackles from the start these very problems which have been evaded in the first version. We start again with the opposition Heaven versus Earth, but this is mediated by a fertilising mist drawn from the dry infertile earth (II, 4–6). This theme, which blurs the distinction life/death, is repeated. Living Adam is formed from the dead dust of the ground (II, 7); so are the animals (II, 19); the garden is fertilised by a river which "went out of Eden" (II, 10); finally fertile Eve is formed from a rib of infertile Adam (II, 22–23).

The opposition Heaven/Earth is followed by further oppositions —Man/Garden (II, 15); Tree of Life/Tree of Death (II, 9, 17); the latter is called the tree of the "knowledge of good and evil" which means the knowledge of sexual difference.

Recurrent also is the theme that unity in the other world (Eden, Paradise) becomes duality in this world. Outside Eden the river splits into four and divides the world into separate lands (II, 10–14). In Eden, Adam can exist by himself, Life can exist by itself; in this world, there are men and women, life and death.

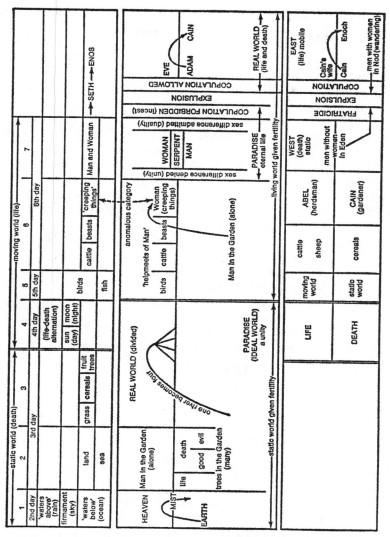

Figure 1. The first four chapters of Genesis contain three separate creation stories. Horizontal bands correspond to (a) 7-day creation; (b) Garden of Eden; and (c) Cain and Abel. Each story sets up opposition of Death versus Life, God versus Man. World is "made alive" by using categories of "woman" and "creeping thing" to mediate this opposition.

This repeats the contrast between monosexual plants and bisexual animals which is stressed in the first story.

The other living creatures are now created specifically because of the loneliness of Man in Eden (II, 18). The categories are Cattle, Birds, Beasts. None of these are adequate as a helpmeet for Man. So finally Eve is drawn from Adam's rib . . . "they are of one flesh" (II, 18–24).

Comparison of Band 1 and Band 2 at this stage shows that Eve in the second story replaces the 'Creeping Things' of the first story. Just as Creeping Things were anomalous with respect to Fish, Fowl, Cattle and Beast so Eve is anomalous to the opposition Man versus Animal. And, as a final mediation (chapter III), the Serpent, a creeping thing, is anomalous to the opposition Man versus Woman. Christian artists have always been sensitive to this fact; they manage to give the monster a somewhat hermaphrodite appearance while still indicating some kind of identification between the Serpent and Eve herself.

Hugo Van der Goes puts Eve and the Serpent in the same posture; Michelangelo makes Adam and Eve both gaze with loving adoration on the Serpent, but the Serpent has Eve's face.

Adam and Eve eat the forbidden fruit and become aware of sexual difference, death becomes inevitable (III, 3–8). But now for the first time pregnancy and reproduction become possible. Eve does not become pregnant until after she has been expelled from Paradise (IV, 1).

Lower Band

Cain the Gardener and Abel the Herdsman repeat the antithesis between the first three days of the creation and the last three days in the first story. Abel's living world is more pleasing to God (IV, 4–5). Cain's fratricide compares with Adam's incest and so God's questioning and cursing of Cain (IV, 9–12) has the same form and sequence as God's questioning and cursing of Adam, Eve and the Serpent (III, 9–19). The latter part of III, 16 is later repeated exactly (IV, 7) so Cain's sin was not only fratricide but also incestuous homosexuality. In order that immortal monosexual existence in Paradise may be exchanged for fertile heterosexual existence in reality, Cain, like Adam, must acquire a wife (IV, 17). To this end Adam must eliminate a sister; Cain a brother. The symmetry is complete.

CROSS-CULTURAL COMPARISON

The issue here is the logical basis of incest categories and closely analogous patterns must occur in all mythologies regardless of their superficial content. Cross-cultural comparison becomes easier if we represent the analysis as a systematic pattern of binary discriminations as in Figure 2.

Adam/Eve and Cain/Abel are then seen to be variants of a theme which can also occur in other forms as in the well known myth of Oedipus. The actual symbolism in these two cases is nearly identical. Oedipus, like Adam and Cain, is initially earth-bound and immobile. The conclusion of the Athenian version of the Oedipus story is that he is an exiled wanderer, protected by the gods. So also is Cain (IV, 14–15). The Bible also includes the converse of this pattern. In Genesis XXVIII Jacob is a lonely exile and wanderer under God's protection but (XXXII, 24–32) he is renamed Israel and thus given the status of a first ancestor with a territorial autochthonous base, and he is lamed by God. Although Jacob dies abroad in Egypt he is buried on his own ancestral soil in Israel (XL, 29–32; L, 5–7).

In the Oedipus story, in place of Eve's Serpent we have Jocasta's Sphinx. Like Jocasta the Sphinx is female, like Jocasta the Sphinx commits suicide, like the Serpent the Sphinx leads men to their doom by verbal cunning, like the Serpent the Sphinx is an anomalous monster. Eve listens to the Serpent's words and betrays Adam into incest; Oedipus solves the Sphinx riddle and is led into incest. Again, Oedipus's patricide replaces Cain's fratricide—Oedipus, incidentally, meets Laius 'at a cross roads.'

Parallels of this kind seem too close to be accidental but this kind of algebra is unfamiliar and more evidence will be needed to convince the sceptical. Genesis contains several further examples of first ancestors.

Firstly, Noah survived the destruction of the world by flood together with three sons and their wives. Prior to this the population of the world had included three kinds of being—'sons of God,' 'daughters of men' and 'giants' who were the offspring of the union of the other two (VI, 1–4). Since the forbears of Noah's daughters-in-law have all been destroyed in the Flood, Noah becomes a unique ancestor of all mankind without the implication of incest. Chapter IX, 1–7 addressed to Noah is almost the duplicate of I, 27–30 addressed to Adam.

Though heterosexual incest is evaded, the theme of homosexual incest in the Cain and Abel story recurs in the Noah saga when drunken Noah is seduced by his own son Ham (IX, 21–25). The Canaanites, descendants of Ham, are for this reason accursed. (That a homosexual act is intended is evident from the language "Ham saw the nakedness of his father." Compare Leviticus XVIII, 6–19, where "to uncover the nakedness of" consistently means to have sexual relations with.)

In the second place Lot survives the destruction of the world by fire together with two nubile daughters. Drunken Lot is seduced by his own daughters (XIX, 30–38). The Moabites and the Ammonites, descendants of these daughters, are for this reason accursed. In chapter XIX the men of Sodom endeavour to have homosexual relations with two angels who are visiting Lot. Lot offers his nubile daughters instead but they escape unscathed. The implication is that Lot's incest is less grave than heterosexual relations with a foreigner, and still less grave than homosexual relations.

Thirdly, the affair of the Sodomites and the Angels contains echoes of 'the sons of God' and 'the daughters of men' but links specifically with chapter XVIII where Abraham receives a visit from God and two Angels who promise that his ageing and barren wife Sarah shall bear a son. Sarah is Abraham's half-sister by the same father (XX, 12) and his relations with her are unambiguously incestuous (Leviticus XVIII, 9). Abraham loans Sarah to Pharaoh saying that she is his sister (XII, 19). He does the same with King Abimelech (XX, 2). Isaac repeats the game with Abimelech (XXVI, 9–11) but with a difference. Isaac's wife Rebekah is his father's brother's son's daughter (second cousin) and the relation is *not* in fact incestuous. The barrenness of Sarah is an aspect of her incest. The supernatural intervention which ultimately ensures that she shall bear a child is evidence that the incest is condoned. Pharaoh and Abimelech both suffer supernatural penalties for the lesser offence of adultery, but Abraham, the incestuous husband, survives unscathed.

There are other stories in the same set. Hagar, Sarah's Egyptian slave, bears a son Ishmael to Abraham whose descendants

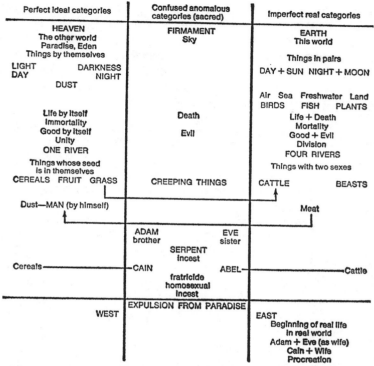

Figure 2. Incest categories have a logical basis in all myths. Similarity between myths is seen most clearly if they are analysed in a binary form as shown in this table.

are wanderers of low status. Sarah's son Isaac is marked out as of higher status than the sons of Abraham's concubines who are sent away to "the east country" (c.f. wandering Cain who made his home in Nod "eastward of Eden"). Isaac marries a kinswoman in preference to a Canaanite woman. Esau's marriage to a Hittite woman is marked as a sin. In contrast his younger and favoured twin brother Jacob marries two daughters of his mother's brother who is in turn Jacob's father's father's brother's son's son.

All in all, this long series of repetitive and inverted tales asserts:

a. the overriding virtue of close kin endogamy;

b. that the sacred hero ancestor Abraham can carry this so

far that he marries his paternal half-sister (an incestuous relationship). Abraham is thus likened to Pharaoh, for the Pharaohs
of Egypt regularly married their paternal half-sisters; and

c. that a rank order is established which places the tribal
neighbours of the Israelites in varying degrees of inferior status
depending upon the nature of the defect in their original ancestry
as compared with the pure descent of Jacob (Israel).

The myth requires that the Israelites be descended unambiguously from Terah the father of Abraham. This is achieved only
at the cost of a breach of the incest rule; but by reciting a large
number of similar stories which entail even greater breaches of
sexual morality the relations of Abraham and Sarah finally stand
out as uniquely virtuous. Just as Adam and Eve are virtuous as
compared to Cain and Abel, so Abraham's incest can pass unnoticed in the context of such outrageous characters as Ham,
Lot's daughters, and the men of Sodom.

I have concentrated here upon the issue of sexual rules and
transgressions so as to show how a multiplicity of repetitions,
inversions and variations can add up to a consistent 'message.' I
do not wish to imply that this is the only structural pattern which
these myths contain.

The novelty of the analysis which I have presented does not
lie in the facts but in the procedure. Instead of taking each myth
as a thing in itself with a 'meaning' peculiar to itself it is assumed,
from the start, that every myth is one of a complex and that any
pattern which occurs in one myth will recur, in the same or other
variations, in other parts of the complex. The structure that is
common to all variations becomes apparent when different versions are 'superimposed' one upon the other.

Whenever a corpus of mythology is recited in its religious setting such structural patterns are 'felt' to be present, and convey
meaning much as poetry conveys meaning. Even though the ordinary listener is not fully conscious of what has been communi-
cated, the 'message' is there in a quite objective sense. If the
labour of programming could be performed the actual analysis
could be done by a computer far better than by any human. Furthermore it seems evident that much the same patterns exist in
the most diverse kinds of mythology. This seems to me to be a

fact of great psychological, sociological and scientific significance. Here truly are observable phenomena which are the expression of unobservable realities.

NOTE

References such as (IV, 3) refer to the third verse of the fourth chapter of the book of Genesis (English Authorized Version) unless otherwise stated.

2 FOUR WINNEBAGO MYTHS: A STRUCTURAL SKETCH

Claude Lévi-Strauss

AMONG THE MANY talents which make him one of the great
anthropologists of our time, Paul Radin has one which gives
a singular flavor to his work. He has the authentic esthetic touch,
rather uncommon in our profession. This is what we call in
French *flair:* the gift of singling out those facts, observations, and
documents which possess an especially rich meaning, sometimes
undisclosed at first, but likely to become evident as one ponders
the implications woven into the material. A crop harvested by
Paul Radin, even if he does not choose to mill it himself, is always
capable of providing lasting nourishment for many generations of
students.

This is the reason why I intend to pay my tribute to the work of
Paul Radin by giving some thought to four myths which he has
published under the title *The Culture of the Winnebago: As
Described by Themselves* (Radin 1949). Although Radin himself
pointed out in the Preface: "In publishing these texts I have only
one object in view, to put at the disposal of students, authentic
material for the study of Winnebago culture," and although the
four myths were each obtained from different informants, it seems
that, on a structural level, there was good reason for making
them the subject of a single publication. A deep unity underlies
all four, notwithstanding the fact that one myth, as Radin has
shown in his introduction and notes, appears to differ widely in
content, style, and structure from the other three. My purpose
will be to analyze the structural relationships between the four

Reprinted from S. Diamond (editor), *Culture in History: essays in
honor of Paul Radin,* New York, Columbia University Press, 1960, pp.
351–62, by permission of the author and the Columbia University Press.

myths and to suggest that they can be grouped together not only
because they are part of a collection of ethnographic and linguistic
data referring to one tribe, which Radin too modestly claimed as
his sole purpose, but because they are of the same genre, i.e. their
meanings logically complement each other.

The title of the first myth is "The Two Friends Who Became
Reincarnated: The Origin of the Four Nights' Wake." This is the
story of two friends, one of them a chief's son, who decide to
sacrifice their lives for the welfare of the community. After undergoing a series of ordeals in the underworld, they reach the lodge
of Earthmaker, who permits them to become reincarnated and to
resume their previous lives among their relatives and friends.

As explained by Radin in his commentary (1949: 41, para.
32), there is a native theory underlying the myth: every individual
is entitled to a specific quota of years of life and experience. If a
person dies before his time, his relatives can ask the spirits to
distribute among them what he has failed to utilize. But there is
more in this theory than meets the eye. The unspent life-span
given up by the hero, when he lets himself be killed by the enemies, will be added to the capital of life, set up in trust for the
group. Nevertheless, his act of dedication is not entirely without
personal profit: by becoming a hero an individual makes a choice,
he exchanges a full life-span for a shortened one, but while the
full life-span is unique, granted once and for all, the shortened
one appears as a kind of lease taken on eternity. That is, by giving up one full life, an indefinite succession of half-lives is gained.
But since all the unlived halves will increase the life expectancy
of the ordinary people, everybody gains in the process: the ordinary people whose average life expectancy will slowly but substantially increase generation after generation, and the warriors
with shortened but indefinitely renewable lives, provided their
minds remain set on self-dedication.

It is not clear, however, that Radin pays full justice to the
narrator when he treats as a "secondary interpretation" the fact
that the expedition is undertaken by the heroes to show their
appreciation of the favors of their fellow villagers (1949: 37,
para. 2). My contention is that this motive of the heroes deserves
primary emphasis, and it is supported by the fact that there are
two war parties. The first one is undertaken by the warriors while
the heroes are still in their adolescent years, so they are neither

included in, nor even informed of it; they hear about the party only as a rumor (1949: 37, paras. 11–14), and they decide to join it uninvited. We must conclude then that the heroes have no responsibility for the very venture wherein they distinguish themselves, since it has been instigated and led by others. Moreover, they are not responsible for the second war party, during which they are killed, since this latter foray has been initiated by the enemy in revenge for the first.

The basic idea is clear: the two friends have developed into successful social beings (1949: 37, paras. 66–70); accordingly, they feel obliged to repay their fellow tribesmen who have treated them so well (1949: 37, para. 72). As the story goes, they set out to expose themselves in the wilderness; later they die in an ambush prepared by the enemy in revenge for the former defeat. The obvious conclusion is that the heroes have willingly died for the sake of their people. And because they died without responsibility of their own, but instead that of others, those will inherit the unspent parts of their lives, while the heroes themselves will be permitted to return to earth and the same process will be repeated all over again. This interpretation is in agreement with information given elsewhere by Radin: i.e., in order to pass the test of the Old Woman who rids the soul of all the recollections belonging to its earthly life, each soul must be solicitous not of its own welfare but of the welfare of the living members of the group.

Now at the root of this myth we find—as the phonologist would say—a double opposition. First there is the opposition between *ordinary life* and *heroic life,* the former realizing a full life-span, not renewable, the latter gambling with life for the benefit of the group. The second opposition is between two kinds of death, one "straight" and final, although it provides a type of unearthly immortality in the villages of the dead; the other "undulating," and swinging between life and death. Indeed one is tempted to see the reflection of this double fate in the Winnebago symbol of the ladder of the afterworld as it appears in the Medicine Rite. One side is "like a frog's leg, twisted and dappled with light-and-life. The other [is] like a red cedar, blackened from frequent usage and very smooth and shiny" (Radin 1949: 71, paras. 91–93; see also Radin 1945, especially the author's illuminating comments on pp. 63–65).

To sum up the meaning of the myth so far: if one wants a full life one gets a full death; if one renounces life and seeks death, then one increases the full life of his fellow-tribesmen, and, moreover, secures for oneself a state composed of an indefinite series of half-lives and half-deaths. Thus we have a triangular system:

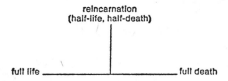

reincarnation
(half-life, half-death)

full life _____ full death

The second myth, entitled "The Man Who Brought His Wife Back from Spiritland," is a variation on the same theme, although there is a significant difference involved. Here too, we find a hero —the husband—ready to sacrifice his unspent life-span; not, as in the first myth, for the benefit of the group, but rather for the benefit of only one individual, his beloved wife. Indeed, the hero is not aware at first that by seeking death he will secure a new lease on life for both his dead wife and himself. Had he been so aware, and this holds equally for the protagonists in the first myth, the essential element of sacrifice would have been missing. In both cases the result is similar: an altruistic loss of life means life regained, not only for the self-appointed victim, but also for the one or more persons to whom the sacrifice was consecrated.

The third myth, "The Journey of the Ghost to Spiritland, as Told in the Medicine Rite," belongs, as the title suggests, to a religious society. It explains how the members of the Medicine Rite, after death, undergo (as do the protagonists of the other myths) several tests in Spiritland, which they overcome, thus gaining the right to become reincarnated.

At first sight this situation seems to differ from the others, since nobody sacrificed his life. However, the members of the Medicine Rite actually spend their lives in symbolic sacrifice. As Radin has shown, in *The Road of Life and Death* and elsewhere, the Medicine Rite follows the familiar pattern of letting oneself be "killed" and then "revived." Thus the only departure consists in the fact that whereas in the first and second myths the heroes are willing to die once and, so they anticipate, permanently, the heroes of the third myth (the members of the Rite) repeatedly, though symbolically, have trained themselves to self-sacrifice. They have, so to speak, mithridatized themselves against a full death by renouncing a full ordinary life which is replaced, in ritual practice, by a lifelong succession of half-lives and half-deaths. Therefore we are entitled to assume that, in this case too, the myth is made up of the same elements, although Ego—and not another person, nor the group as a whole—is conceived as the primary beneficiary.

Let us now consider the fourth myth, "How an Orphan Restored the Chief's Daughter to Life," a tale which has given Radin some concern. This myth, he says, is not only different from the other three, its plot appears unusual relative to the rest of Winnebago mythology. After recalling that in his book *Method and Theory of Ethnology* (1933) he suggested that this myth was a version, altered almost beyond recognition, of a type which he then called village-origin myths, he proceeds to explain in *The Culture of the Winnebago* (1949: 74 ff.) why he can no longer support this earlier interpretation.

It is worthwhile to follow closely Radin's new line of reasoning. He begins by recapitulating the plot—such a simple plot, he says, that there is practically no need for doing so: "The daughter of a tribal chief falls in love with an orphan, dies of a broken heart and is then restored to life by the orphan who must submit to and overcome certain tests, not in spiritland but here, on earth, in the very lodge in which the young woman died" (1949: 174).

If this plot is "simplicity itself," where do the moot points lie? Radin lists three which he says every modern Winnebago would question: (1) the plot seems to refer to a highly stratified society; (2) in order to understand the plot one should assume that in that society women occupied a high position and that, possibly, descent was reckoned in the matrilineal line; (3) the tests which in Winnebago mythology take place, as a rule, in the land of ghosts occur, in this instance, on earth.

After dismissing two possible explanations—that we are dealing here with a borrowed European tale or that the myth was invented by some Winnebago radical—Radin concludes that the myth must belong to "a very old stratum of Winnebago history." He also suggests that two distinct types of literary tradition, divine tales on the one hand and human tales on the other, have merged while certain primitive elements have been reinterpreted to make them fit together (1949: 74–77).

I am certainly not going to challenge this very elegant reconstruction backed by an incomparable knowledge of Winnebago culture, language, and history. The kind of analysis I intend to offer is no alternative to Radin's own analysis. It lies on a different level, logical rather than historical. It takes as its context the three myths already discussed, not Winnebago culture, old or recent. My purpose is to explicate the structural relationship—if any—which prevails between this myth and the other three.

First, there is a theoretical problem which should be noted briefly. Since the publication of Boas's *Tsimshian Mythology,* anthropologists have often simply assumed that a full correlation exists between the myths of a given society and its culture. This, I feel, is going further than Boas intended. In the work just referred to, he did not suppose that myths automatically reflect the culture, as some of his followers seem always to anticipate. Rather, he tried to find out how much of the culture actually did pass into the myths, if any, and he convincingly showed that *some* of it does. It does not follow that whenever a social pattern is alluded to in a myth this pattern must correspond to something real which should be attributed to the past if, under direct scrutiny, the present fails to offer an equivalent.

There must be, and there is, a correspondence between the unconscious meaning of a myth—the problem it tries to solve—and the conscious content it makes use of to reach that end, i.e., the plot. However, this correspondence should not always be conceived as a kind of mirror-image, it can also appear as a *transformation.* If the problem is presented in "straight" terms, that is, in the way the social life of the group expresses and tries to solve it, the overt content of the myth, the plot, can borrow its elements from social life itself. But should the problem be formulated, and its solution sought for, "upside down," that is *ab absurdo,* then the overt content will become modified accordingly to form an inverted image of the social pattern actually present to the consciousness of the natives.

If this hypothesis is true, it follows that Radin's assumption that the pattern of social life referred to in the fourth myth must belong to a past stage of Winnebago history, is not inescapable. We may be confronted with the pattern of a nonexistent society, contrary to the Winnebago traditional pattern, only because the structure of that particular myth is itself inverted, in relation to those myths which use as overt content the traditional pattern. To put it simply, if a certain correspondence is assumed between A and B, then if A is replaced by $-A$, B must be replaced by $-B$, without implying that, since B corresponds to an external object, there should exist another external object $-B$, which must exist somewhere: either in another society (borrowed element) or in a past stage of the same society (survival).

Obviously, the problem remains: why do we have three myths of the A type and one of the $-A$ type? This could be the case because $-A$ is older than A, but it can also be because $-A$ is one of the transformations of A which is already known to us under three different guises: A_1, A_2, A_3, since we have seen that the three myths of the assumed A type are not identical.

We have already established that the group of myths under consideration is based upon a fundamental opposition: on the one hand, the lives of ordinary people unfolding towards a natural death, followed by immortality in one of the spirit villages; and, on the other hand, heroic life, self-abridged, the gain being a supplementary life quota for the others as well as for oneself. The former alternative is not envisaged in this group of myths which, as we have seen, is mostly concerned with the latter. There is, however, a secondary difference which permits us to classify the first three myths according to the particular end assigned to the self-sacrifice in each. In the first myth the group is intended to be the immediate beneficiary, in the second it is another individual (the wife), and in the third it is oneself.

When we turn to the fourth myth, we may agree with Radin that it exhibits "unusual" features in relation to the other three. However, the difference seems to be of a logical more than of a sociological or historical nature. It consists in a new opposition introduced within the first pair of opposites (between "ordinary" life and "extraordinary" life). Now there are two ways in which an "extraordinary" phenomenon may be construed as such; it may consist either in a *surplus* or in a *lack*. While the heroes of the first three myths are all overgifted, through social success, emotions or wisdom, the heroes of the fourth myth are, if one may say so, "below standard," at least in one respect.

The chief's daughter occupies a high social position; so high,

in fact, that she is cut off from the rest of the group and is therefore paralyzed when it comes to expressing her feelings. Her
exalted position makes her a defective human being, lacking an
essential attribute of life. The boy is also defective, but socially,
that is, he is an orphan and very poor. May we say, then, that
the myth reflects a stratified society? This would compel us to
overlook the remarkable symmetry which prevails between our
two heroes, for it would be wrong to say simply that one is high
and the other low: as a matter of fact, each of them is high in
one respect and low in the other, and this pair of symmetrical
structures, wherein the two terms are inverted relative to each
other, belongs to the realm of ideological constructs rather than
of sociological systems. We have just seen that the girl is "socially" above and "naturally" below. The boy is undoubtedly very
low in the social scale; however, he is a miraculous hunter, i.e. he
entertains privileged relations with the natural world, the world
of animals. This is emphasized over and over again in the myth
(Radin 1949: 74–77; see paras. 10–14, 17–18, 59–60, 77–90).

Therefore may we not claim that the myth actually confronts
us with a polar system consisting in two individuals, one male,
the other female, and both exceptional insofar as each of them
is overgifted in one way (+) and undergifted in the other (−).

	Naturè	Culture
Boy	+	—
Girl	—	+

The plot consists in carrying this disequilibrium to its logical
extreme; the girl dies a *natural* death, the boy stays alone, i.e.
he also dies, but in a *social* way. Whereas during their ordinary
lives the girl was overtly above, the boy overtly below, now that
they have become segregated (either from the living or from
society) their positions are inverted: the girl is below (in her
grave), the boy above (in his lodge). This, I think, is clearly
implied in a detail stated by the narrator which seems to have
puzzled Radin: "On top of the grave they then piled loose dirt,
placing everything in such a way that nothing could seep through"

(1949: 87, para. 52). Radin comments: "I do not understand why piling the dirt loosely would prevent seepage. There must be something else involved that has not been mentioned" (1949: 100, n. 40). May I suggest that this detail be correlated with a similar detail about the building of the young man's lodge: ". . . the bottom was piled high with dirt so that, in this fashion, they could keep the lodge warm" (1949: 87, para. 74). There is implied here, I think, not a reference to recent or past custom but rather a clumsy attempt to emphasize that, relative to the earth's surface, i.e. dirt, the boy is now above and the girl below.

This new equilibrium, however, will be no more lasting than the first. *She who was unable to live cannot die;* her ghost lingers "on earth." Finally she induces the young man to fight the ghosts and take her back among the living. With a wonderful symmetry, the boy will meet, a few years later, with a similar, although inverted, fate; "Although I am not yet old, he says to the girl (now his wife), I have been here (lasted) on earth as long as I can. . . ." (1949: 94, para. 341). *He who overcame death, proves unable to live.* This recurring antithesis could develop indefinitely, and such a possibility is noted in the text (with an only son surviving his father, he too an orphan, he too a sharpshooter), but a different solution is finally reached. The heroes, equally unable to die or to live, will assume an intermediate identity, that of twilight creatures living under the earth but also able to come up on it; they will be neither men nor gods, but wolves, that is, ambivalent spirits combining good and evil features. So ends the myth.

If the above analysis is correct, two consequences follow: first, our myth makes up a consistent whole wherein the details balance and fit each other nicely; secondly, the three problems raised by Radin can be analyzed in terms of the myth itself; and no hypothetical past stage of Winnebago society need be invoked.

Let us, then, try to solve these three problems, following the pattern of our analysis.

1. The society of the myth appears stratified, only because the two heroes are conceived as a pair of opposites, but they are such both from the point of view of nature *and* of culture. Thus, the so-called stratified society should be interpreted not as a sociological vestige but as a projection of a logical structure wherein everything is given both in opposition and correlation.

2. The same answer can be given to the question of the assumed exalted position of the women. If I am right, our myths state three propositions, the first by implication, the second expressly stated in myths 1, 2 and 3, the third expressly stated in myth 4.

These propositions are as follow:

a. Ordinary people live (their full lives) and die (their full deaths).

b. Positive extraordinary people die (earlier) and live (more).

c. Negative extraordinary people are able neither to live nor to die.

Obviously proposition c offers an inverted demonstration of the truth of a and b. Hence, it must use a plot starting with protagonists (here, man and woman) in inverted positions. This leads us to state that a plot and its component parts should neither be interpreted by themselves nor relative to something outside the realm of the myth proper, but as *substitutions* given in, and understandable only with reference to *the group made up of all the myths of the same series*.

3. We may now revert to the third problem raised by Radin about myth 4, that is, the contest with the ghosts takes place on earth instead of, as was usually the case, in spiritland. To this query I shall suggest an answer along the same lines as the others.

It is precisely because our two heroes suffer from a state of *underlife* (in respect either to culture or nature) that, in the narrative, the ghosts become a kind of *super-dead*. It will be recalled that the whole myth develops and is resolved on an intermediary level, where humans become underground animals and ghosts linger on earth. It tells about people who are, from the start, half-alive and half-dead while, in the preceding myths, the opposition between life and death is strongly emphasized at the beginning, and overcome only at the end. Thus, the integral meaning of the four myths is that, in order to be overcome the opposition between life and death should be first acknowledged, or else the ambiguous state will persist indefinitely.

I hope to have shown that the four myths under consideration all belong to the same *group* (understood as in *group theory*) and that Radin was even more right than he supposed in publishing them together. In the first place, the four myths deal with extraordinary, in opposition to ordinary, fate. The fact that ordinary fate is not illustrated here and thus is reckoned as an "empty" category, does not imply, of course, that it is not illustrated elsewhere. In the second place, we find an opposition between two types of extraordinary fate, positive and negative. This new dichotomy which permits us to segregate myth 4 from myths 1, 2 and 3 corresponds, on a logical level, to the discrimination that Radin makes on psychological, sociological, and historical grounds. Finally, myths 1, 2 and 3 have been classified according to the purpose of the sacrifice which is the theme of each.

Thus the four myths can be organized in a dichotomous structure of correlations and oppositions. But we can go even further and try to order them on a common scale. This is suggested by the curious variations which can be observed in each myth with respect to the kind of test the hero is put to by the ghosts.

In myth 3 there is no test at all, so far as the ghosts are concerned. The tests consist in overcoming material obstacles while the ghosts themselves figure as indifferent fellow travelers. In myth 1 they cease to be indifferent without yet becoming hostile. On the contrary, the tests result from their overfriendliness, as inviting women and infectious merry-makers. Thus, from *companions* in myth 3 they change to *seducers* in myth 1. In myth 2 they still behave as human beings, but they now act as *aggressors,* and permit themselves all kinds of rough play. This is even more evident in myth 4, but here the human element vanishes; it is only at the end that we know that ghosts, not crawling insects, are responsible for the trials of the hero. We have thus a twofold progression, from a *peaceful* attitude to an *aggressive* one, and from *human* to *nonhuman* behavior.

This progression can be correlated with the kind of relationship which the hero (or heroes) of each myth entertain with the social group. The hero of myth 3 belongs to a ritual brotherhood: he definitely assumes his (privileged) fate as member of a group, he acts with and in his group.

The two heroes of myth 1 have resolved to part from the group, but the text states repeatedly that this is in order to find an opportunity to achieve something beneficial for their fellow tribesmen. They act, therefore, for the group. But in myth 2 the hero is only inspired by his love for his wife. There is no reference to the group. The action is undertaken independently for the sake of another individual.

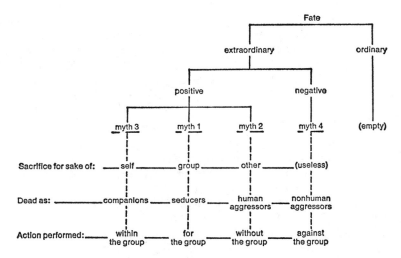

Finally, in myth 4, the negative attitude toward the group is clearly revealed; the girl dies of her "uncommunicativeness," if one may say so. Indeed she prefers to die rather than speak; death is her "final" exile. As for the boy, he refuses to follow the villagers when they decide to move away and abandon the grave. The segregation is thus willfully sought on all sides; the action unrolls against the group.

The accompanying chart summarizes our discussion. I am quite aware that, in order to be fully convincing, the argument should not be limited to the four myths considered here, but include more of the invaluable Winnebago mythology which Radin has given us. But I hope that by integrating more material the basic structure outlined has become richer and more complex, without being impaired. By singling out one book which its author would perhaps consider a minor contribution, I have intended to emphasize, in an indirect way, the fecundity of the method followed by Radin, and the lasting value of the problems he poses for the anthropologist.

3 SOCIAL IMPLICATIONS
OF SOME TANGU MYTHS

Kenelm O. L. Burridge

INTRODUCTION

THIS ESSAY attempts to examine some of the implications of four myths in which the similarities appear as significant as the variations.[1]

Tangu are settled in a knot of steep ridges some fifteen miles inland from Bogia Bay on the north coast of New Guinea in the Madang District. The total population of approximately two thousand souls is distributed through about thirty settlements grouped into four neighborhoods, each of which contains one or more major, and several minor, settlements. Few cultural features are exclusive to Tangu, and although they all speak the same language, this is also spoken by others farther inland.[2] Intermarriage with outside neighbors is fairly common; they have trading relations with selected peoples within their own milieu—including Manam Islanders, young men go to the coastal areas on contract labor—from whence they return to Tangu when their time is up, and many can speak pidgin English. Within Tangu there are groups organized on patrilineal, matrilineal, double unilineal, and ambilineal lines. Much of the content of their myths has common ground with the myths told in neighboring areas;

Reprinted from *The Southwestern Journal of Anthropology* 12 (4), 1957: 415–31, by permission of the author and the editor, *The Southwestern Journal of Anthropology*.

[1] This essay was first delivered as a talk to the Oxford University Anthropological Society. Fieldwork was carried out in 1952 under a scholarship with the Australian National University.

[2] There are some small differences as between neighborhoods of vocabulary and accent. Some general notes on the Tangu language are by A. Capell.

some of their dances are recognized as being imported while others which they regard as their own are danced elsewhere. Ascendent genealogies proliferate as the spokes from a hub, and although it is reasonable to suppose that Tangu are an amalgam of peoples who have come out from the hinterland and in from the coast,[3] they are, within the context of a larger culture area, a distinct entity.

The reminiscences of old men reveal that at about the turn of the century there occurred, in Tangu, a great plague or epidemic which, being associated with the activities of sorcerers, was followed by local migrations, a general scatter of the population, and much internecine fighting. Toward the end of this period, in the German era, labor recruiters and missionaries toured Tangu but did not stay there. After the war the mission renewed its contacts with Tangu, recruiters came again, and the Administration followed hard on their heels. It was about this time, Tangu say, that, taking their cue from the Europeans they had met, they first applied the name Tangu to the collectivity they represented.[4] By the early 'twenties the mission was taking to Tangu seriously, and the Administration was counting heads, collecting taxes, controlling migratory labor, and enforcing the peace—for which, Tangu say today, they were most grateful. During the last war the Japanese penetrated to Tangu and the resident missionary was forced to flee for his life. Later, the station he had built was virtually destroyed by allied aircraft. Later still, when the Japanese had been thrust out of New Guinea, Administration and mission returned to Tangu. With the help of Yali[5] the numerous small and scattered settlements were concentrated into larger groups. But with the peace there came further streams of ideas brought by those who had come into significant contact with Australian, Japanese, and American—including Negro—troops, and it was not long before Tangu became involved with cargo cult activities.[6]

3 "Objective" evidence for this statement exists.

4 It is hoped that the argument on this point will shortly be published.

5 Yali is the best known name associated with nativistic movements in New Guinea. *Vide* Burridge 1954a. For more information about Yali see also Peter Lawrence (1954).

6 Two articles by the present author give some idea of cargo cult activities in the area, viz. 1954a and 1954b.

THE MYTHS

During the ten years following the war—and especially in the Madang District—cargo cults had become very much a part of the Melanesian scene.[7] Tangu, however, are rather off the beaten track and they continued to lead their own lives in their own way. They cultivated their gardens, hunted, gathered, and planted palms and trees. By day their settlements are deserted and the population is scattered over the surrounding countryside engaged in the daily task of subsistence. Within their own terms Tangu are an empirically minded people, and in their cult activities[8] there is no evidence to show that they neglected subsistence for the sake of a greater and contingent reward. On the contrary, Tangu say— and the objective evidence supports their assertion—that cult activities were directed towards producing more to greater satisfaction. At the same time cargo cults were—impliedly or explicitly —anti-European, and the Administration suppressed them by force. Each of the four myths, or rather the four versions of what may be taken to be a single myth, presented below were elicited when conversation teetered delicately on the edge of my role as an assimilated investigator and the fact that I was a European. The preface to each version was that it was a secret, something known to Tangu, knowable to other black men in New Guinea, but not to a European. The latter not only did not know, but should not know of them.

It must be mentioned, too, that when the mission came to Tangu it saw with great clarity that if Christianity was to make any headway, the clubhouses, ritual and cultural foci especially significant for boys and girls passing through puberty, would have to go. They were abolished. And with the clubhouses went the organizing nexus of ritual life. Today, what remains of their religious life are their myths, a coherent belief in sorcery, Christianity, and some scattered remnants of ritual and belief with ethnographic but little or no sociological significance. Nevertheless, despite the hiatus between myth and ritual, most of the old

[7] For a full bibliography of the extant literature on cargo cults *vide* South Pacific Commission, 1952.

[8] 1954a: 244–45.

myths are still recounted, new myths are born,[9] and some of the
old stories are adapted to present circumstances. In this essay
the myth or myths selected are of the latter kind. They have a
nexus with cargo cult activities.[10] They are, or appear to be old
myths—but they have a special, contemporary twist. In their specific contexts, cargo cults are merely temporary; they break out
like a rash, and die away. They are symptomatic phenomena re-
flecting particular sets of circumstances. But the myths connected
with them continue to be told although there is presently no ritual
associated with them.

Version 1[11]

One day, the men of the village decided to go and hunt for a pig
by burning off a tract of ginger plants, and Duongangwongar, a
useless[12] character who had a mother but no father or mother's
brother, went with them. But when they arrived at the chosen
place the other men would have nothing to do with Duongangwongar, and they told him to go away.

Duongangwongar wandered off on his own. Presently, seeing a
pig-run entering a patch of *kunai* grass,[13] he followed it and was
confronted, almost at once, by a pig. Hastily setting arrow to his
bow string he took aim and fired. But he succeeded only in
wounding the pig.

The other men heard his cries for help and dashing out of the
ginger came into the *kunai* from all sides. They surrounded the
pig and killed it with their spears. Then, as each man withdrew
his spear from the body of the pig, he plunged it into Duongangwongar.[14] Duongangwongar fell dead. Satisfied, they placed the
body on a small platform and hid it in the roots of a tree. Then
they returned to the village.

Gundakar, the mother of Duongangwongar, asked where her
son was. The men said they did not know, they had not seen him.

That night Gundakar had a dream in which her son appeared

[9] E.g. the *Mambu* story (1954a: 245).
[10] 1954a: 252.
[11] See map and diagram (figs. 1 and 2).
[12] The Tangu word is *'mbatekas*. It may be translated as useless, bad,
evil, unfortunate, strange, unusual, peculiar, of unknown potential.
[13] Where pigs may usually be found today. They are not normally found
in ginger.
[14] Note here the identification of a "man" with a pig.

to her and told her he was dead and hidden in the roots of a tree.[15] So, next morning when she awoke, Gundakar went out to look for the body of her son.

As she walked out of the village a little bird, the spirit of Duongangwongar, settled on her shoulder and showed her the path she should take. By and by she found the tree where the body was hidden, and extricating it from the roots she put it into her string bag and returned to the village. Arrived there, she collected some yams, taro, bananas, mami, and sweet potatoes, and putting them into her string bag together with the body, she left the village.

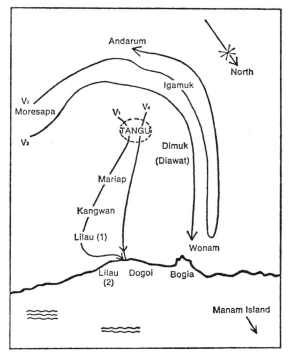

Figure 1. Diagrammatic sketch map to illustrate the journeys. V_1, V_2, V_3, V_4 respectively the starting points in the four narratives. Scale approximately 6 miles to 1 inch.

[15] This form of burial is not practised today. No man in Tangu will admit to having practised it except in the remote past when the story originated.

She came first to W'tsiapet[16] and asked if she might bury her
son. They refused. She went on to Amuk,[17] and they too refused
her, sending her on to Mariap. There they told her to go to Kangwan, and despite her pleas that she had taro to give them she
was ordered on to Lilau[18] on the coast. She rested by the sea,
but not until she came to Dogoi, where a man copulated with
her, was she able to bury her son. The man helped her. He dug a
hole, placed the body inside, and covered the grave with coconut
fronds. Eventually he married Gundakar and she bore him sons.
Meanwhile, the body of Duongangwongar rotted in his grave.

One day, when Gundakar was in the village alone and was in
need of some water, she went to her son's grave. She drew aside
the coconut fronds and, finding salt water and fish coming from
his nostrils, she filled her pot with the water and used it for
cooking the evening meal. Her husband and sons thought it good.

That night Gundakar's son grew tremendously. And next day
when her husband's younger brother (*Tuman*)[19] came to visit
them and saw his elder brother's (*Ambwerk*)[20] son grown so
much, he was surprised. "Your son has grown so big!" he exclaimed. "My own sons yet remain small: why is this?"

But nothing was said. And next day Gundakar collected the
skins of her yams, taros, and mami and flung them onto the garden plot which her husband had recently cleared and burned off.
Wonderfully, the skins took root, reached back into the soil and
became real tubers.

Then Gundakar returned to the grave of her son Duongangwongar and collected from his nostrils some water and one small
fish which she put in a pot and boiled for her husband and sons to
eat.

That night her son grew into a man.

Next day, *Tuman* was so surprised at the transformation that
he insisted on knowing how it was done. Gundakar turned to his
wife and told her what she must do. "Go to the grave of Duongangwongar," she said. "Take away the coconut fronds, draw
some water from his nostrils and take one small fish. You will

[16] W'tsiapet—the village of the storyteller.
[17] Amuk—in Tangu.
[18] Lilau used to be located inland from the coast a few miles. Now, the
villagers have moved down to the coast, leaving the former site deserted.
[19] *Tuman*—younger brother.
[20] *Ambwerk*—elder or eldest brother.

see there other, larger kinds of fish. Do not take them. Take only one small fish."

Tuman's wife repaired to the grave, removed the coconut fronds, and drew some water. Then, in the nostrils of Duongang-wongar she saw a large *ramatzka*.[21] She speared it.

At once there was loud rumbling in the earth like thunder. The water from Duongangwongar's nostrils came out in a seething torrent of foam and bubbling waves. The water which was the sea rose up and came between *Ambwerk* and *Tuman* who fled in different directions to escape.

Tuman, who had found safety in a low lying place, killed a small bird and after cooking the bones threw them into the sea. There was a small splash and a soft ssshhh . . . as of the water running over pebbles. Then *Tuman* killed a crested pigeon,[22] cooked the bones and threw them into the sea. There was only a small splash and the sea remained calm. So *Tuman* killed a horn-bill and did as he had done with the other birds. The surface of the waters rippled. He killed a cockatoo and surf flecked the waters. And he killed a cassowary, and when he threw the bones into the sea, the waves rose with a roar and tumbled on the beach.

Tuman was satisfied.

Pondering on the fate of his elder brother, *Tuman* plucked a leaf. He directed it to the village of *Ambwerk* and threw it on the waters. *Ambwerk,* who had found refuge on high land, saw the floating leaf, and picking it up, exclaimed "Oh! My young brother is all right. He has sent this leaf to me to find out how I am. I will send it back to him." So he threw the leaf back on the sea.

When *Tuman* saw the leaf floating back to him he knew that his elder brother was safe. So he took another leaf, and writing a message on it, despatched it to *Ambwerk*. The latter received the note and sent an answer in return.

Tuman felled a tree, hollowed it, and made a canoe. He set off to see his elder brother. *Ambwerk* saw *Tuman* in his canoe from afar off and he wondered what on earth it was. And when *Tuman* had beached his canoe and brought it to his village, *Ambwerk* looked at it and marvelled. "Who showed you how to make this?" he asked. "Surely you did not do it all by yourself?"

[21] A large eel-like fish found in the streams in Tangu.
[22] "Guria" pigeon.

Tuman answered, "I made it by myself. I thought of it on my own."

When *Tuman* had gone *Ambwerk* made a canoe of his own and went to visit *Tuman*. He returned to his village content. Immediately, *Tuman* started work on a boat. After he had had some practise in it, he went to his elder brother to show it to him. *Ambwerk* was surprised, and to his question *Tuman* replied, "I invented it myself. And I made it on my own."

When *Ambwerk* made a boat and went to visit his younger brother, *Tuman* complimented him on his craftsmanship. *Ambwerk* returned to his village content.

Then *Tuman* constructed a pinnace. He made an engine, fitted it, practised, and went off to show it to *Ambwerk*. *Ambwerk* was dumbfounded. Straightway he commenced work on a pinnace.

Tuman made a motor car, a motor bike, and a large ship with tall masts and a siren which went whoooo! *Tuman's* ship was so big that it broke his elder brother's jetty, and they had to secure it by ropes passed round coconut palms. Finally, *Tuman* made an aeroplane, canned goods, laplaps, and all sorts of other things. Each time he made something he went to show it to his elder brother. And each time *Ambwerk* copied him.

The story-teller's own comment at the end of his recitation was: "*Tuman* could use his head—like you."[23]

Version 2

A woman who had no husband left her daughter alone[24] in the village while she went to fish. A sorcerer came into the village, and after beating the child, killed her, and buried her.

When the woman returned to the village after fishing she could not find her daughter. "Oh where is my daughter?" she wailed. "I went to get some fish and she has disappeared!"

That night the woman had a dream, and in the dream she saw the burial place of her daughter. So, rising at dawn, she went off a little way into the bush. There she saw a bamboo thicket[25] which she recognized from her dream as the burial place of her

---

[23] Or, impliedly, "*Ambwerk* was rather unintelligent."
[24] Children left alone are especially vulnerable to sorcerers.
[25] Bamboo thickets are common enough inland but comparatively rare toward the coast from Tangu.

daughter. She dug in the earth, found the body, and put it into her string bag. She went off in the direction of Moresapa, came round by Sorkmung, thence to Dimuk and Wonam.

At Wonam, Damzerai, the man who had killed her daughter, came to her and asked what it was she had in her string bag.

"My daughter who is dead," replied Matzia, the woman.

Damzerai took pity on her and married her. He dug a hole and buried the body.

Very soon the body rotted and there was a rumbling in the earth like thunder; and Matzia, who had had another dream, hastened to the grave to have a look at her daughter. She saw the watery rottenness, and tasting it, she found it salty. She saw that there were fish there too, and she thought she would cook some of the fish and salt water for Damzerai. So, telling him nothing of how she had come by the fish, she put some in a bowl and gave it to Damzerai to eat.

Damzerai was sick. But after he had taken some lime and pepper he returned to his meal of salt water and fish, and this time he found it very good.

Matzia showed Damzerai the grave and what she had found there, and he thought it was a marvellous thing.

That night, their son—who had eaten the mixture—grew very large and fat.

Next day, Damzerai's elder brother came on a visit and was surprised to see how Damzerai's son had grown. "What have you given him to eat?" he asked. "My son is older than yours, and yet your son is much the bigger of the two."

"Eat some of this," said Damzerai. "We took it from the grave of my wife's daughter."

Dwongi, the elder brother, ate some of the food and thought it very good—so good that he took some home to his wife.

The following day Dwongi returned for more. They all had some of the fish and salt water, and then, while Damzerai and his family repaired to the garden, Dwongi went to the grave by himself and speared one of the larger fish. At once there was a thundering noise, and the sea spurted up out of the grave with a rush of foam, separating the two brothers.

Damzerai made an armlet of dried grass and threw it into the sea. It drifted to Dwongi who picked it up and examined it.

"My younger brother is alive!" he exclaimed. "He is somewhere over there!"

So Dwongi, *Ambwerk*, made a basket and threw it on the waters. It drifted to *Tuman*, Damzerai, who then knew that his elder brother was alive and well.

Tuman made a boat. *Ambwerk* made a canoe. *Tuman* set off in his boat but was sunk by a heavy sea. However, he swam back to land and decided to build himself a large ship. He fitted a large mast to his ship, and put in an engine, and then he went off to see his elder brother, warning him by a letter thrown on the waves that he was coming.

Ambwerk received the letter and said "Ha! I shall be seeing my young brother soon." And when *Tuman* arrived at the village of *Ambwerk* the two brothers shook hands. "Well met!" said *Tuman*. "I thought you might have died, and now I see for myself that you are alive and well."

"And I, too, thought you were dead," replied *Ambwerk*. "And now you have come to see me in your fine ship."

Tuman returned from whence he had come, and *Ambwerk* stayed where he was, on the top of Manam Island. *Tuman* made all the good things—clothes, knives, umbrellas, rifles, canned food, and so on. And he came again to see his brother. "You stay where you are," said *Ambwerk*, "and I will stay in my place."

So *Tuman* came to Tangu while his elder brother stayed on the top of Manam Island. And that is why some people have black skins that are dirty; that is why there are people like us.

Version 3

A widow had a daughter who was killed and buried by a stranger. Although the widow searched everywhere, and cried out aloud for her daughter, she could not find her anywhere. When night fell and the widow went into her hut to sleep, she dreamed that her daughter was buried in the cavity left by a tree that had been uprooted.[26] So she went to such a place, and lo! upon digging she found her daughter.

The widow put the body in her string bag and went to Moresapa. There they told her to go to Andarum whence she was forced to go to Wonam. At Wonam she married the younger of

[26] Nor is this form of burial found in Tangu.

two brothers, and after bearing two sons to her husband, she, her husband, and their sons returned to Andarum. The elder of the two brothers remained at Wonam with his wife and two sons.

Arrived at Andarum the woman went to the grave of her daughter. She removed the topsoil and found that the putrid flesh had turned into salt water and fish. She gave her husband and sons some of the fish boiled in the salt water. They were sick. But after they had chewed ginger for a few minutes they returned to their meal and found it good. That night the son grew big and strong.

Shortly afterward, the elder brother came from Wonam to visit them, and seeing the astonishing progress of his younger brother's sons, he asked what the secret was. They told him. *Ambwerk* went off to get some of the marvellous stuff. Unfortunately, however, he speared a *ramatzka* which was nothing less than the dead daughter herself. There was a thundering noise from underground and the sea spouted up, separating brother from brother.

(From this point on Version 2 is followed precisely.)

Version 4

Rawvend (whose alternative name is sometimes Niangarai) came to Biamp from Andarum via Mangigum, and he is the ancestor of all the men of Biampitzir.[27] Rawvend went off to Kangwan where he found a small pool. But actually he was looking for a convenient hole. He found one in Dogoi near where Lilau now is. So he killed his daughter, Samaingi, who had been sick and who was covered with sores. Having run her through with a spear, he buried her and covered the grave with coconut leaves. Samaingi rotted in her grave, and out of her putrid flesh came salt water and many fish. One of the fish was a *ramatzka*.

Tuman wanted to spear the *ramatzka*. But his mother prevented him, saying, "You must not shoot the *ramatzka*. Take the small ones only."

But *Tuman* did not heed her. He shot the *ramatzka* with his bow and arrow. There was a rumbling and a growling in the bowels of the earth, and the sea came rushing out. It came up around the Ramu valley; it came up the valley of the Iwarum; up and up and up it came until Rawvend said, "Enough!"

[27] Biampitzir, Mangigum—names of neighborhoods in Tangu.

Now the sea had divided people into two parties. Samaingi arose from her grave and went to Se-wen-de where she built the habitations of the White people and government men. And she, Samaingi, was also the ancestress of Chinamen and brown people —related to us black people.

Of the other party *Tuman* was on the mainland and *Ambwerk* was on Manam Island. *Tuman,* who was short of firewood, wrote a letter and sent it off on a log to *Ambwerk.* Then he wrote another and sent it off by a bird. And he chose a third messenger, a dog, which succeeded in reaching *Ambwerk,* and which also brought back some firewood for *Tuman.*

Tuman sounded his *kundu* drum, and *Ambwerk* replied on his slit-gong.[28] As a result of this interchange of signals *Ambwerk* and *Tuman* met at the grave of Samaingi, Rawvend's daughter. They decided to settle together. *Ambwerk* had paper; *Tuman* had yams and other tubers. Now, if it had been the other way around you white-skinned people would have foodstuffs, and we black-skinned people would have paper and all the other good things.

ASSESSMENT

Of the four versions the first was produced with the most confidence. The last, Version 4, may be regarded as the least reliable. The author made his delivery nervously and in a very muddled way. He was said to have been on the fringes of several cargo cults without having participated in them, and while Se-wen-de is a slang corruption of Seventh Day Adventist (Mission) there is also reason to believe—since I could find no other corroboration—that Rawvend may be a corruption of Yahweh or Jehovah. Versions 2 and 3 may be regarded as reliable.

Ignoring some of the discrepancies for the moment the basic plot of the story might run as follows:

> The scene produced for the listener is that of a mother and child without male protection. The child is killed and the body is hidden. Nevertheless, through a dream, the mother regains possession of the body, and placing it in her string bag, she sets out on a journey. The journey ends when she finds a place where she can bury the body and marry. After marriage and bearing sons the woman returns to

[28] Sounding the *kundu* drum is not so very common as a method of communication except within the near vicinity. Slit-gongs are usual.

the grave of her dead child and finds there salt water and fish, both of which are products of the putrefying body. The woman takes a small fish and some water and feeds them to her family. They find it good. More than that, the son quickly develops into manhood. This occasions the curiosity and envy of the husband's brother and his family. Letting them into the secret, the woman warns her relatives by marriage that they must not shoot the *ramatzka* fish. But the warning goes unheeded; the *ramatzka* is shot; the earth rumbles; and the sea rises up to divide brother from brother. Later, when the brothers get in touch with one another again, their relationship appears as a competitive one, and one of them emerges as much cleverer than the other. This explains why White men are different from, or are more masters of their environment than black men appear to be.

There are, here, a series of incidents involving four basic kinds of social relationship woven into a pattern of shifting roles. Parent and child where parent becomes wife (Version 4 *contra*); wife and husband where husband is also brother; brother and brother where the latent antagonism symbolizes the relationship between white men and black. The mother-child relationship is set in a context of helplessness. There are no husband, no brothers, no mother's brothers to care for them. In Version 1, from a patrilineal group, where the child is a son, his helplessness is less obvious and it is made more explicit. Version 3 comes from an ambilineal group, but as in Version 1, where the child is killed by those who are explicitly not in an amicable relation with him, the child (in Version 3) is killed by strangers who, in Tangu, are also enemies. Version 2, from a double unilineal group, follows the general idea, but the killer of the child later enters into an amicable relation with the mother by becoming her husband. In Version 4 the child is provided with a protector-father so that no one but he can kill her. And he does. This version comes from a locale where patrilineal and matrilineal peoples live in the same settlement; but since Rawvend is explicitly identified with Niangarai who, in another myth, brought forth human beings from the hole in the earth which he had made with a digging stick, a consistency may be elicited by the phrase, "The child of a creative element is killed." Each version provides an inner consistency by presenting situations in which it might be expected, almost inevitably, that the child is killed.

The dream[29] through which the mother finds her child is a normal Tangu technique for solving a problem or finding a way out of a dilemma. Whether antecedent or consequent, a dream contains information and an implied directive to action. Thus an "unsolicited" dream contains information to which thought must be given and action taken; and a man faced with a problem retires for the night with the hope that a dream will shed light on the matter and present him with a directive. At the same time, however, dreams may also be "tricks." A man who dreams that a pig has been caught in his trap visits his trap in high expectation of finding a pig there. If there is no pig, he says to himself "I have been fooled!" Nonetheless, even though a dream does not always

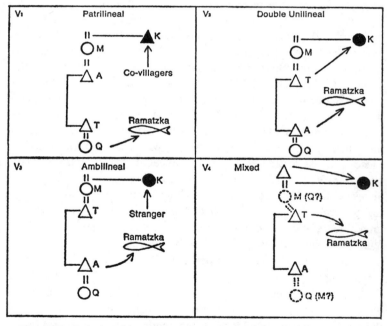

Figure 2. Relationships corresponding to the four versions. K, the child who is killed; M, the mother; Q, a wife; A, Ambwerk, elder brother; T, Tuman, younger brother; *arrow* indicates participants and direction of killing.

[29] *Vide* K. O. L. Burridge, 1954a: 246 and 1956.

solve the problem, it helps toward a solution, and Tangu feel that the information is always worth acting on.

The consistency of the dream in relation to "normal" observable Tangu life is followed through with the journey. The solution to the problem of the isolate mother-and-child is a husband. Among Tangu widows do not remain such for long. They become second wives, usually joining the household of a sister; they form unions with widowers; and if there is no man at home to take a widow, she travels until she can find one. During fieldwork I came across a woman and her two children living a precarious and animal-like life in the jungle. Her husband, who was dead, had been a noted sorcerer, and no one would have anything to do with her. When she could gather a sufficient reserve of food she journeyed to the nearest settlements to offer her services as a wife—and returned again to her lean-to in the forest. Tangu commented briefly, "She ought to go farther away where nobody knows of her past."

On another level the routes taken by the woman in the story reflect other factors. Routes 1 and 4 are the traditional paths taken by Tangu who, in the days before the European came, used to go down to the coast to fetch salt. They still use this route whenever they want to go down to the coast for whatever purpose. Then, as now, it was essential, when travelling far afield, to pass through a chain of settlements in which there were women standing as "sister" to the males of the party or "friends" of either sex. This not only ensured hospitality but also a certain amount of protection from sorcerers. The shorter and more direct route to the coast was in the possession of people who were bitter enemies of Tangu; and even today Tangu are most loath to take this route. The routing provided by Versions 2 and 3 are more difficult since they pass through country known to most Tangu only by hearsay. Direct contacts with people from Moresapa date only with the advent of mission and administration. The Diawat people (Dimuk) as well as those from Andarum are hereditary enemies. At the same time, however, the relation of enmity never prevented intermarriages. Wonam is the place where the Diawat people went for their salt, and it is possible that the salt found its way to Andarum through Diawat and the Igamuk area, where the people, Tangu-speakers, were at varying degrees of enmity and friendship with Tangu, Andarum, and Diawat. In addition, the existence of "sisters" in the named settlements mentioned in Versions 1 and 4 postulates an actual or putative descent line, from which it can be deduced that one can follow a genealogy through on the ground from settlement to settlement. In Tangu itself one can do this quite easily after inspection; but although Tangu can symbolize the process through myth, and they know the facts—or most of them—for themselves they do not make the connection in a coherent expressible way. Thus, by way of contrast, in my wanderings around these routes and elsewhere outside Tangu where conditions seem always to have been much more stable, a man told me—while we were discussing some of his own myths—that the travelling woman, or, in his particular case, a cassowary, revealed a matrilineal descent line. Similarly, the snake which travelled represented a patrilineal line. In short, uterine and penis lines of descent.

The marital relationship into which the story leads the reader or listener describes a normal and settled relationship in which the wife lives in her husband's village and bears him children. And from these norms of a relationship which every listener might be presumed to be familiar with, the story has the wife disturb the grave of her dead child—something most strange. For even though Tangu visit the graves of dead kinsmen fairly frequently, there is no record of any custom entailing a disturbance of the grave. And stranger still, coming from the nostrils of the rotting corpse are salt water and fish. This is the gift which, though there is an indication of reluctance—in Versions 2 and 3 husband and son are sick—both husband and son eventually find good. Indeed, so good is it for the boy that he grows big, or develops towards manhood, overnight. Evidently, this gift, a gift which raises the offspring of a union to adulthood, is the kernel of the marital relationship; and since the gift *does* seem strange, and is placed in the center of a familiar workaday relationship, one feels that the symbolism strikes deep and is only superficially related to a series of other items: the vital need for salt, the uterine line of descent providing safe conduct to the coast, fertility in terms of offspring in exchange for a husband's protection against marauders, the association of women with fishing (fish are not an important item of diet in Tangu), the duty of a wife to cook for her husband, economic coöperation in the household plot, the fertility of the crops, and a fair give-and-take within the household unit. Tangu social life today appears to provide no further clues as to the content of this gift, nor why it should bring the boy to manhood; nor can they themselves offer any deeper explanation of the symbolism. When taxed they say, "That is the story. She gave him a fish."

Moving in to the third relationship, the gift and its consequences arouse the envy of the husband's brother. He asks how it is done. He wants his own son to grow up as quickly. In Versions 2 and 3 husband is younger brother, *Tuman;* in Version 1 he is elder brother, *Ambwerk;* and in Version 4, since no marital tie is mentioned, it is not clear how the brothers would have stood to Rawvend or Samaingi. Where the husband is *Tuman,* it is *Ambwerk* who kills the *ramatzka* and who, later on, is presented as the denser of the two—in spite of the fact that in Version 2 it is *Tuman,* also husband, who committed the original murder. Although *Tuman* is not the husband of the "mother" (M, see diagram, Figure 2) in Version 1 it is he who, eventually, turns out to be the brighter. And there is a certain consistency in the fact that it is his (*Tuman's*) wife and not *Tuman* himself who kills the *ramatzka.* In Version 4 it is "mother" who tells *Tuman* not to kill the *ramatzka,* but it is left for the reader to decide for himself whether this "mother" is the mother of the brothers, or the mother of the slain child (K) and the wife of one of the brothers. At any rate *Tuman* has initiative even though the honors seem to be more evenly distributed. In addition, however, *Tuman* in Version 4 has common ground with *Tuman* in Version 2 in that while the latter is the murderer of K the child, the storyteller makes it explicit in Version 4 that when *Tuman* is killing the *ramatzka* he does not know that he is actually killing the child or its spirit or ghost. Thus the shift into the isolated interbrother relationship is occasioned by the act of the brother not married to the "mother" (Versions 2 and 3), or by his wife (Version 1). In Version 4 this detail is lacking.

As soon as the forbidden act is done, the sea rises up and separates brother from brother. The spousal and affinal relationships are dropped. M, K (and Q) (see diagram), have served their purpose. The story concentrates on the relationship between elder and younger brother, *Ambwerk* and *Tuman.* And in this setting—essentially rivalrous or competitive within friendship—*Tuman* appears as better equipped for meeting the hazards of this life. There is no question of luck here; he is fundamentally better endowed. He is cunning. He can think. He can invent things. Moreover, in Version 1 he does these things on his own—and in the vernacular this is doubly emphatic.[30] That is, he uses no ritual aids; he does not seek help from any spirit or godling, nor does any being or person outside of himself give him the inspiration. In other words the abilities of the successful brother reflect the claim made by Europeans that their own technical abilities are based in their own inventiveness, their own *nous*—which runs contrary to traditional modes of thought. For, in terms of the latter, most enterprises require ritual as well as pragmatic techniques to bring them to a successful conclusion.[31] The other brother does not lack in industry, and he has an honored position sitting on the volcano of Manam Island; but initiative, the ability to think for himself, is lacking.

In Version 4 the brothers make a pact of friendship based either on apartheid or coexistence or both. Nevertheless, while the story is being told, even the monotonous recitation of the things that *Tuman* does, working up the scale from a dug-out canoe through motor boats and steamships to an aircraft, hardly prepares one for the climax—"And that is why white men are different from black men," or, "That is why white men have all the good things of this world and we have only yams."

Stripped of cultural content and particular situational requirements, two things seem to spring from the inevitable death. First, associated with an exchange within the marital relationship, there is abundant life. Secondly, associated with a stupid act of disobedience—why kill the large *ramatzka* when a little fish would have done as well?—there is a flood which separates brother from brother. We have already commented on the first of these two factors; but taken together one might relate both elements to the peace, serenity, and easy moral relationships associated with the domestic household which is the smallest and most permanent coöperative group in Tangu, as compared with the actual or potential rivalrous or hostile relations to be found outside this circle. In isolation the second element has further significance.

[30] Supra Version 1: "Who showed you how to make it?" "I *myself* thought of it, etc. etc."

[31] *Vide* 1954a: 247–48. See also in this connection the Kilibob story (Lawrence, 1954: 16–17).

Mostly, white men are identified with younger brother, *Tuman*, who did not kill the *ramatzka;* or, as in Version 4, in spite of the fact that it is *Tuman* who has the initiative, with *Ambwerk* who also was not responsible for killing the *ramatzka*. Whether or not there is a "felt" kin relationship between the successful brother and white men, there is an obvious association with the abilities white men have. And these abilities appear to be directly related to some kind of innocence, for it was black men or their symbol which killed the *ramatzka*.

The expression of guilt[32] is vague or completely divorced from the relationship of elder and younger brother, but it is, on the other hand, brought into full focus when the shift is made into the relationship between white men and black. In fact Tangu attitudes within this relationship are characterized by humility,[33] aggression,[34] grievance,[35] and guilt.[36] And there is something else. In view of the extensive spread of legends in Melanesia concerning culture heroes or ancestors or a conquering people with white or reddish skins, it is an intriguing problem whether the association of the successful brother with white people was made before Tangu knew anything of the Europeans who first entered their lives, or whether it is a comparatively recent accretion to a much older story. If the first, then the myth was a potential reality which came true and served to bring their guilt home to them. Hence the sometimes abject humility of Tangu. If the second, then it not only reflects an actual dilemma which is made intelligible and supportable for Tangu by placing the root cause in the wrongful act of an ancestor or group symbol, but it also provides an example of the way myths move and adapt themselves to current circumstances.

[32] Versions 2, 3, 4, make it explicit.

[33] In the presence of Europeans, especially administrative officers, Tangu behave as though completely cowed. My own bare legs were objects of adoration: "They are so clean, so white, so lovely. . . ."

[34] "We will sweep the white men into the sea" (1954a: 245).

[35] "Why should white men have so much? Why should they treat us as dogs? Are we not human like they? Why will they not let us eat with them: we let them eat with us if they wish to."

[36] "Ah well, if he had not killed the *ramatzka* perhaps all would have been well."

CONCLUSION

It will be apparent to those whose main interests lie in mythologies that the gist of the myths recorded above is nothing if not familiar, and is echoed among many peoples widely separate both in time and in space. Yet, whatever meanings may be extracted from these myths either by comparative or psychological techniques—the gift within the marital relationship, for example, is excellent "archetypal" material—it is also true that they were obtained in a particular social context—from Tangu who themselves associated the myths with cargo cult activities. Due presumably to their history, and to the fact that the nature of Tangu society is disnomic, rather than anomic, today many cultural items are missing. It is quite possible, for example, that once upon a time they *did* bury their dead in the roots of trees, and that they *did* make some kind of medicine from the juices of rotting corpses. How far do these things matter? By attempting to "explain" the four stories by resorting to the internal evidence something significant is thrown up. The discrepancies of detail are matched by the congruence of ends—the idea that some kind of guilt explains the difference between white men and black men. If cargo cults express what is unsatisfactory in the relationship between white men and black men in terms of economic differences and political opportunity, the myths take the relationship deeper: moral attitudes are involved, a prime cause and a *rationale* of present circumstances are postulated. That the *rationale* is not wholly acceptable is evidenced by the existence of cargo cults. Yet, guilt is in itself so complex—entailing as it does variations of humility, aggression, and envy—that it leaves plenty of scope for, and may even demand, cargo cults.

4 SOME SOCIAL ASPECTS
OF LUGBARA MYTH

John Middleton

T HE LUGBARA are a Sudanic-speaking people of the Nile-Congo
divide and number 242,000, of whom two-thirds live in northwestern Uganda and the remainder in the adjoining area of the
Belgian Congo.[1] Their political system is a segmentary one, with
no form of centralized political authority. There is a system of
polysegmentary patrilineages, the largest series of which are the
exogamous units. Within the territorial section associated with
the agnatic core provided by such a lineage there is, or was, the
obligation to settle disputes by discussion between the parties
concerned so that feud was avoided, and it was only between
these sections that a permanent state of hostility could exist.
Each of these territorial sections consists on an average of some
4,000 people living in an area of some twenty-five square miles.
They, the largest of the groups called *suru* by Lugbara, and which
I refer to as maximal sections based on maximal lineages, are
the largest political units of the system. Like the three levels of
segmentation within them, they bear specific names, most of
which are found in all parts of Lugbara. I call these names clan-
names.

There are about sixty of these maximal sections in Lugbara. It

Reprinted from *Africa* 24 (3), 1954: 189–99, by permission of the International African Institute.

[1] Field-work among the Lugbara was carried out between 1949 and
1952, with financial assistance from the Worshipful Company of Gold-
smiths and the Colonial Social Science Research Council; field-work material has been written up with aid from the Wenner-Gren Foundation
for Anthropological Research, New York. I make grateful acknowledgement
to these bodies. I am also grateful to Professor E. E. Evans-Pritchard, Mr.
J. H. M. Beattie, and Dr. P. J. Bohannan for discussing drafts of this article.

was traditionally, and still is, rare for there to be much direct intercourse between members of other than neighbouring maximal sections; certainly those over ten miles or so away are usually beyond the range of direct contact. Lugbara is therefore not a single polity with definite boundaries. Nevertheless, even though Lugbara are not aware of the precise limits of their society, they conceive it in terms of a common culture and of common descent from the two hero-ancestors, Jaki and Dribidu, who entered their present country from an original home in the north. Jaki entered by what is now Kakwa country, to the north and north-west, and Dribidu by the Nile Valley, through what is now East Madi. Each, it is believed, underwent many adventures between their entry into the country and their deaths, Jaki on Mount Liru and Dribidu on Mount Eti, the two mountain masses that rise from the high Lugbara plains. During this time they wandered through the area begetting children by various women. Their sons were the founders of the original Lugbara clans which have segmented and so formed the present system of lineages. In most cases a clan is co-terminous with a maximal lineage defined as an exogamous group. But this is not always so, since some clans contain more than one maximal lineage, and it is then the maximal lineage and not the clan which is the exogamous unit. The distinction is that a lineage is a group defined by function—in this case, exogamy —whereas a clan is defined in genealogical terms only—its founder was a son of a hero-ancestor. Lineages are units of the political system, whereas clans are units in a conceptual system which gives validity and unity to Lugbara society as Lugbara themselves see it. Both are genealogical structures of many generations, usually between ten and fourteen. Genealogies validate the relations between territorial sections of varying span—maximal, major, minor, or minimal—each associated with a lineage, the relations being expressed in terms of a system of lineages genealogically linked. At the highest level they are interrelated to form a single conceptual system, Lugbara society, in terms of fraternal ties between the many sons of the hero-ancestors. It is significant that lineages of lower orders—major, minor, and minimal—are arranged in order of the seniority of their apical ancestors, but clans are genealogically equal. The former are units in the field of social relations of any given group, whereas the latter are units in the conceptual system which we may call Lugbara society, of which the total range includes the fields of social relations of all those groups that call themselves Lugbara.

Lugbara say that they are all of one blood, *ari alo*. This blood was created by *Adronga 'ba o'bapiri,* God the creator of men, when he created the two first beings on earth, the male Gborogboro and the female Meme, and domestic livestock. Meme had wild animals in her womb: the gazelle broke out and was followed by the other beasts. The name Gborogboro means 'the person coming from the sky' and Meme means 'the person with a big body'; some versions of this myth state that Meme was a man, while others say that the first beings on earth had other names which are usually given as the children of Meme. I do not wish to give the myth of creation at length in this paper; the precise order of appearance of the personages in it is not important. Gborogboro and Meme were man and wife, and Gborogboro is said to have given bridewealth for her, although it is not said to whom, since it is irrelevant in the context of the myth. After the animals had left Meme's womb God put children in it, according to some versions, but others say that the pair copulated in the human manner and so Meme bore a boy and a girl, who were brother and sister. Myths tell that these siblings produced another male and female pair, who did the same in their turn. The number and names of sibling-generations of this sort vary in the myths: Figure 1 shows a commonly accepted version.

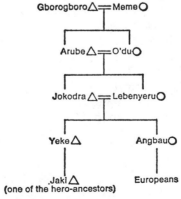

Figure 1. Diagram of Sibling-generations.

Some myths say that they did not copulate in the human manner but that the women became pregnant after goats' blood had been poured over their legs. All versions state that since they were siblings bridewealth was not given at these unions. The creation and these subsequent happenings occurred at a place called by Lugbara Loloi, to their north in the southern Sudan, 'a place near Juba'. Other myths tell of the separation of mankind from God in the sky, the separation of black and white peoples, the building of a Tower of Babel and the appearance of Lugbara and Kakwa and the diverse languages and tribes of men, and the creation of the outside world as it is today. All these events took place in the Sudan and are the subject-matter of distinct myths: they are not related to each other or put into any time sequence except in so far as the creation itself preceded all human activities and the various pairs of siblings followed one another in time (although their order varies and is not thought to be significant).

This corpus of myth culminates in the appearance of the two hero-ancestors, Jaki and Dribidu, coming to the present country of the Lugbara and there begetting many sons, who were the founders of the present clans, as I have already mentioned. They were not human as men are now: Dribidu means 'the hairy one', since he was covered with long hair over most of his body. He is also known as 'Banyale, 'eater of men', since he ate his children until he was discovered and driven out of his earlier home on the east bank of the Nile; he crossed the river at Gimara and came to the Lugbara highlands. The heroes came independently of one another—no fraternal tie is ever claimed for them—but the myths about them have close similarities. Both could do many superhuman and magical feats. They are both the subjects of long myths which tell how each found a leper woman who gave him fire on which to cook his meat; of how he cured her with medicine of which the secret is now lost, and made her his first wife. He lay with her and impregnated her, which resulted in war with her kin and the subsequent payment of seduction fine and bridewealth: the identity of her kin is not significant and so is unknown. Before this time there had been no fighting between men and, except in the case of the first created pair of humans, there had been no bridewealth. There is, of course, an intimate connexion for Lugbara between fighting and bridewealth, since most fighting is, or was, due to quarrels over such transactions.

The heroes were the first rain-makers, and gave the secrets of many magical medicines to their descendants.

The heroes were not normal human beings, but they mark the appearance of Lugbara society in the form which it has today. They married many women in various parts of the country and their sons married wives and begat children in the way that people do now. They transferred bridewealth at marriage and in turn their sons and sons' sons multiplied and became the founders of new lineage segments. Lugbara say that in this way the present-day lineages are descended from the founders of the original clans, with continual proliferation and amalgamation, and the moving away of individuals and families and their attachment to other lineages elsewhere. I do not wish to describe lineage segmentation here; it is sufficient to say that the ancestors who feature in genealogies, which are concerned with the descendants of the two heroes, are always regarded as having been normal human beings who behaved in the way in which men still behave, and men do so behave, of course, for the reason that their ancestors laid it down that they should. All special rights and mystical powers that are today possessed by certain men or certain lineages—for example, the power to control the rain or to possess certain magical objects—are validated by their having originated at the time of the heroes or of their sons, the clan founders. For Lugbara, society today is essentially the same as it was at that time.

The several accounts of the creation and the pairs of siblings, of the hero-ancestors, and of their descendants, differ in character. I have given them, very briefly, as though they were parts of a single history, in order to show the relationship between them. I have never heard Lugbara doing so: indeed, the differences in their nature make it unlikely that they would be told in any single situation. The accounts of the creation and the activities of the sibling-pairs before the heroes may be called mythical. Those of the descendants of the heroes are, for the Lugbara, genealogical and not mythical. Those of the hero-ancestors themselves present both mythical and genealogical features, that is to say they may be placed in either category on different occasions: the heroes, who mark the appearance of Lugbara society, are either at the end of the mythical period or at the beginning of the genealogical period, if we put them on a time-scale. This, of course, is to distort the significance of these accounts. The difficulty, as will be seen, is that our own myths and histories are placed on a time-scale and so all the concepts we use in this context contain a reference to non-recurrent measured time.

Using our own conceptual terms, the significant difference between the period before the heroes and that after them (the heroes appearing in both periods) is that in the latter the personages are ordinary human beings, behaving in the way in which people behave now, and are members of clans and so members of society; whereas in the former they behaved in a reverse manner and lived in isolation, in a world in which there were no clans. They committed incest, did not transfer bridewealth for their mates, and could do marvellous feats which men can no longer achieve. The first pair of siblings were called Arube and O'du, which mean 'maker of miracles' and 'miraculous omen' respectively. They are said to have been born with teeth and, although they are distinct personages in most myths, they are sometimes said to be one person called by different names by Lugbara and Kakwa in the days when both tribes spoke the same language; their respective sex varies. It is their non-human or contra-human characteristics that are important, and not details of name or parentage. It was with the appearance of the heroes and their begetting sons, who were the clan-founders, that human beings became social beings living in a society. Before that time they were not members of a society—there was no society, in fact —and they and their world existed in the Sudan, outside present Lugbara territory, a territory of which every part is associated in tradition with a particular clan. Before he entered present Lugbara country Dribidu was a cannibal, eating his own children. Once arrived in Lugbara the heroes became more or less human beings, but always retained some superhuman and magical powers. When they first met the leper woman they behaved as mythical figures, taking her without bridewealth: their later unions were proper marriages in the form that marriages take today. It is at this phase of the heroic period that social settlement began. The father of Jaki was Yeke, whose name means 'owner of the land', the man who first settled and farmed land. The fact that he is usually said to be Jaki's father is not significant, since he is sometimes given as his son; but even then he is never given as a clan founder but is still a mythical figure.

I refer to the attributes of the pre-heroic figures as 'inverted': the choice of this term will become clearer in a moment. Their inverted and superhuman attributes are significant as indexes of their asocial existence. Although I have done so, Lugbara do not put the pre-heroic and the post-heroic periods on a time-scale. The distinction that they make is between the non-existence and the existence of Lugbara society as it is today.

A similar use of myth can be seen in the accounts of the appearance of the Europeans in Lugbara. The ancestor of the 'red' people was Angbau, the brother of Yeke the father of Jaki, so that the red people have a parallel existence to the black people. But this is outside Lugbara society. Those Europeans who enter it are placed in a different category. Those who first entered Lugbara are called by various names, the usual one being *Ngilingilia,* the 'short ones'. They were cannibals (as are all Europeans even today except those well known to Lugbara), they could disappear underground, and they walked on their heads and could cover vast distances in a day by this means. As soon as they were noticed they began to walk on their legs, but if attacked would vanish into the ground and come up some distance away; they would then walk away on their heads. They were thus literally 'inverted'. I have heard it said that this is still the manner in which Europeans behave in their own country. Later came other types of European and Arab, who approached the edges of the country and took slaves and cattle: they are known generically as *Kutiria* or *Kotorea,*[2] although each set of *Kutiria* is also given a specific name. In 1900 came the *Berijiki* or Belgians, who set up a small post in central Lugbara; European administration of the area, however nominal, dates from this time. It is said that when they came everyone ran away. The *Berijiki* and their native troops, known as *Tukutuku* and notorious for their cruelty and reputed cannibalism, chased the fugitives and found one or two lineage heads and other men hiding in the grass outside the homesteads: these men were made 'chiefs' by the Belgians. Chiefs are the *atibo* (clients or servile persons) of the Europeans. Since the presence of *atibo* in a settlement is always explained by saying

[2] A form of the name given to Dongolan irregulars recruited by Emin Pasha from disbanded Nubian forces of the old ivory and slave traders. Emin was at Wadelai in the 1880's and some of his forces reached the Lugbara hills. See Stigand, 1923: 171.

that an ancestor found them 'hiding in the grass' outside the homesteads in no-man's land, without kin or possessions, so that they were not members of society, and took them in as 'his people', the appointment of chiefs is also explained in these terms. It is hardly necessary to add that, in fact, they did not run away nor were they found hiding, according to detailed accounts given me by people who were present in 1900. Other accounts say that since the Europeans came from outside society, as *atibo* come in time of famine, so were they taken in and welcomed by certain elders who acted towards them as 'fathers': they were then made chiefs by the Europeans who had rifles and used force against them. It is clear that either version explains the way in which the Belgians became part of Lugbara society. In 1910 most of Lugbara passed to the Sudan, and in 1914 to Uganda. It is said that Mr. A. E. Weatherhead, the first District Commissioner under the Uganda administration, could walk across the country at fantastic speeds: no sooner was it thought that he was safely away a hundred miles to the north, and people began to plan to attack his headquarters at Arua or to fight their neighbours, than he would suddenly appear in person among them. In addition, he is said to have walked among them without rifles: 'his words were strong' and he had an effect upon them that no other European, before or after him, has ever had.

Since those days Europeans entering Lugbara have had a place in Lugbara society and an expected role to play there. There are different categories of white-skinned people (*Adro*): some being *Mundu*, Europeans with authority ultimately backed by force, such as government officials and missionaries, and some not: but they are all given a fixed status. Lugbara can list most of their District Commissioners and missionaries since the days of Weatherhead. Other government officials are not remembered, but it is thought that there is some kind of genealogical tie between District Commissioners and between missionaries: I have often heard it said that certain Europeans were the sons of earlier figures. But all Europeans have been members of Lugbara society and they behave in the way that Weatherhead and his contemporaries behaved, according to the status given them.

For Lugbara time is periodic, reckoned mainly by generations of men, the seasons, the stars, the moon, and sun. All these phenomena occur at regular intervals and are not placed on a scale of non-recurrent time. Events that do not recur are not put on a measured comparative scale. Lugbara myth and genealogy are little related to historical time as we comprehend it. Genealogy is used to explain and to validate social relations which are significant at the present moment, by which I mean relations which are observed or expected in certain forms of behaviour between the groups or persons concerned. No Lugbara knows much of the genealogies of clans other than his own, since they are for the most part outside his field of everyday direct social intercourse; even within his own clan he will rarely know more than the names of the apical ancestors of major lineages other than his own. Genealogies deal with social beings as members of a given social field, and the ancestors are only significant, and so remembered, in so far as their existence and interrelationships validate the present composition of a group's social field. But these social beings are placed in society, and society itself is given meaning and validity, by myth. Myths, in Lugbara, deal with personages originally not members of society, beings whose relations to one another are asocial: not even Jaki and Dribidu are interdependent. Most of the values and sanctions concerned with social relations are supplied by the cult of the ancestral ghosts, and there is no ritual attached to the mythical figures. Inter-group relations are, or were, conceived in terms of fighting, which is said not to have existed at the time of the mythical figures. The myth themes end by certain personages entering into the society or forming a society and receiving a status within it. As the extent of the society increases and new persons are introduced into it, as were the Europeans and their chiefs, they are given identity and status in this way by means of myth. Mythical events are not set in any scale of non-recurrent time, and although it is known that certain genealogical figures lived before others their temporal relationships are not important. Mythical figures are outside society and genealogical figures are within it, and there are some personages—the heroes, the Belgians and the first District Commissioner—who belong to both myth and genealogical tradition. The two are thus intimately linked and obtain significance and validity from each other. But to set them into a scale of historical time-units is misleading, since events are related to each other not by their temporal relationships but by the social relationships of the personages whose activities compose myth and genealogical

tradition. These consist, not of isolated events each consequent
on the one preceding it, but of events of which the significance is
in the interrelationship of the actors.

The mythical, asocial phase of any one theme, whether that of
the creation and the ancestors or of the Europeans, is characterized by the inversion of social behaviour on the part of the personages concerned. The first Europeans were literally inverted,
walking on their heads. I use the same term for all the other
attributes of mythical figures and events which are the opposite
of those that Lugbara values decree as proper for members of
society. They together form a single complex of inverted attributes: physical inversion, cannibalism, incest, non-payment of
bridewealth, in a context that is not social, in which there are no
clans, no recognition of kinship ties—the significance of mythical
incest is that ties of siblingship have not yet been recognized,
not that they are recognized but ignored as in present-day cases
of intra-clan incest—and no fighting. Not all these attributes are
found together in any single myth, but nevertheless we may say
that one of the general characteristics of Lugbara myth is the
inverted character of its actors and events.

The same pattern, that of normal members of society, beyond
them certain people who present both normal and inverted attributes, and beyond them in turn people whose chief characteristic
is to be socially inverted, can be seen in the Lugbara system of
socio-spatial categories.

The country of the Lugbara is part of the high plateau which
forms the watershed between the Albert Nile and the southern
tributaries of the Uele. It is almost unwooded, and for the most
part densely populated. One can see across country for up to a
hundred miles or so in clear weather, and the homes and farms of
one's kin and neighbours can be seen spread around one's own
homestead; beyond them are visible the territories of clans with
which one has no direct contact at all. Lugbara see their society
around them on the earth as a series of socio-spatial categories,
which include both those groups with which a group is in direct
social relations and those beyond this range.

At the centre of a man's social life is his homestead, and beyond that the homesteads of his own family cluster, the group
under the domestic authority of an elder (*'ba wara*) the only
person with authority in the traditional Lugbara system. Beyond

that lie his group's *odipi* and *juru*. *Odipi* are those persons who are related agnatically or subsumed under an agnatic tie, as attached sororal kin may be. The range of *odipi* and their composition vary in different situations, sometimes including close agnates only, sometimes close agnates and attached sororal kin, sometimes distant agnates also. Even though their composition may vary, and with it the intensity of relations within the range of *odipi*, we may assume that since Lugbara use the one term for varying ranges of kin or quasi-kin they are put into one category. Beyond the range of *odipi* are *juru*. *Juru* are defined by reference to *odipi*: together they comprise the members of all those groups with which a person, as a member of a kin-group, has direct social relations, although the limit of *juru* cannot be very clearly defined. *Juru* do not stretch away interminably to the ends of the earth; they are people who, though unrelated by kinship or whose kin tie is temporarily insignificant in a given situation, are nevertheless in a social relationship. In the context of fighting one fights with arrows against *juru* and not against *odipi;* in that of marriage one marries *juru* and may not marry *odipi*. In these cases the range of *odipi* varies. One may fight people whom one cannot marry because they are related; one may not marry into one's maximal lineage but may fight, using weapons, with members of that lineage so long as they are of another major lineage. Territorially some *juru* will be closer than some *odipi*, but socially they are more distant. They are conceptual categories and not groups, although of course they refer to actual members of actual groups.

Juru thus extend to the limit of direct social relations. There is no point in trying to define this limit in terms of miles or the number of clans involved, since these vary so much for every group. But a group rarely has direct social relations with another group much more than seven or eight miles away, in the densely populated centre of the country, although individuals may have indirect ties of personal kinship acquired in trading or other expeditions over greater distances. At the limit of *juru* are those groups with very weak or only occasionally significant relationships, such as maternal kin of maternal kin, or distant agnates of people with whom one is in a state of hostility.

I have said that people rarely know anything of the genealogies of clans other than their own except the founding ancestors by

whom they are defined, and even then a man rarely knows the
names of the founders of clans at all distant territorially from
his own. This may be expressed in a different way by saying that
a man will know the ancestors of his group's *odipi* and something
of the genealogical traditions of his group's *juru,* although probably little more than the name of their clan founder when they
are of different clan affiliation.

From one's own homestead to the limit of *juru* people are
members of a group's field of direct social relations, and the
relations between people and groups within this field are validated by genealogical tradition. Beyond that other people are
living—one can see the trees on the ridges in their territories far
away across the open plateau; one can see the flame and smoke
of their field-burning in the dry season; one can often hear faintly
the drumming from their death dances. They may be Lugbara or
other peoples, Kakwa, Keliko, Ndu, and so on, but in the context
of social distance that is irrelevant—social ties cross tribal boundaries. What is relevant is that they are beyond the limit of direct
social relations and therefore not part of one's own social field,
and so not normal human beings. Lugbara attribute to these
groups certain attributes, the commonest of which is the possession of magical powers and medicines. Such people may turn
into snakes or trees at will; they possess strong sorcery-medicines
which they leave on paths for the unwary traveller. I shall not
describe any such people in detail here, but this situation is
found in every part of Lugbara that I know. There is always an
outer circle of people whose territories are visible but filled with
sorcery and magic and who are evilly disposed towards one's own
people, even though they are assumed to live in lineage groups
and to be descended from the same hero-ancestors as are one's
own kin. But this last point, of course, is irrelevant in this context; it only becomes relevant when they, in their turn, are compared to groups beyond them, who are even less like one's own
people and before whom the nearer strangers appear almost like
one's own kinsfolk.

Beyond the range of these hostile and strange groups whose
territories are visible are other groups whose names are known
and who are much feared for their reputed sorcery and evil practices, but whose land no one has ever reached. I once tried to
track down one such group called Mmua. However far to the

north-west in the Congo I went people still said that the Mmua lived farther away—in Vura it was said that they lived near Chief Avu's home, but Chief Avu said they lived away in Keliko, to the north, and a Keliko at Chief Avu's homestead maintained that they lived even beyond that in Logo country. It is not possible here to give in detail all the similar beings, since they would be numberless and their supposed identity is in any case irrelevant. Of such people beyond the bounds of society people say, 'How do we know where they come from or what deeds they do? We fear them and do not know them.' The most distant of these creatures are said to be hardly human in appearance, and they walk on their heads. Such are the Logo, the Mundu, the Lendu, and peoples beyond them. These people love to eat meat that is rotten, and 'bad' meat such as snakes, frogs, hyenas, and other night creatures. People such as the Pygmies, whom Lugbara call *alivuku* ('short people'), the Makaraka, the Mangbetu, and Momvu, and those peoples whom Lugbara know as Niam-niam, the Azande beyond the Logo, are all cannibals. They walk on their heads, have terrible methods of sorcery, and live in the thick forests beyond the open Lugbara plains in ways which Lugbara say men cannot understand.

Lugbara apply one conceptual scheme (which we can express only in the separate categories of space and time) to both of two situations: to the mythical and genealogical past and to the contemporary social environment. In mythical and genealogical distance any actual or comparative time-scale is irrelevant. Thus in the myths of origin and of the coming of the Europeans the same thematic pattern emerges. Similarly any actual or comparative scale of geographical distance is irrelevant in the spatial categories. The same thematic pattern is found in the socio-spatial categories of any group anywhere in Lugbara. It does not matter that for one group the beings with superhuman powers or inverted attributes live ten miles away and for another group they live twenty or fifty miles away. Only the anthropologist realizes the contradictions in this situation, in which groups only a few miles apart point to one another and make almost identical accusations of sorcery and inhuman attributes and behaviour.

These categories form a framework in which are set the relations of individuals and groups. But concepts of time and space denote extension in different dimensions. For Lugbara there are no fixed scales and no directions in this system of categories. Differentiation in time of the myths of origin and of the coming of the Europeans is irrelevant: the units or themes of each corpus of myth are arranged in the same pattern. Analogously the units of social distance are arranged in the same pattern round a focal point, but this arrangement is not expressed in terms of a common scale of distance measured in miles, nor is it oriented directionally or topographically. Lugbara use other categories, in this context, to refer to people to their north, or east, or in the centre of the country, and so on.

In both schemes of categories the essential distinction is between the close people—members of one's own field of direct social relations, validated by genealogical tradition—and the distant inverted people, who are outside the field of social relations and outside genealogical tradition. The former include one's *odipi* and *juru* and their ancestors; the latter the inverted beings on and beyond one's physical horizon and the mythical beings who feature in the myths of origin. The situation may be pictured as in Figure 2.

We may say that the former cover Lugbara society as it is significant for Lugbara themselves (apart from its significance for

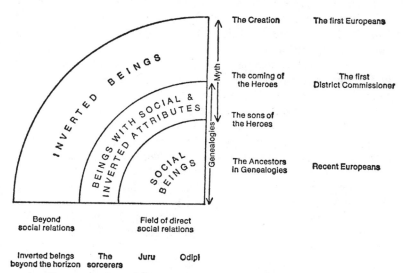

Figure 2. Lugbara Categories of Social Space and Time.

the anthropologist). Lugbara recognize their unique identity as Lugbara, defined in terms of descent from the heroes, as opposed to other peoples, both black and white, who are descended from their own heroes, though all are descended ultimately in one way or another from Gborogboro and Meme. Although Lugbara recognize the existence of a Lugbara people, in such a small-scale, almost fragmentary, society the groups which are beyond the range of direct social relations are not significant in everyday situations. There is no centralized political authority, all political relations being in terms of segmentary opposition. These relations, the composition and range of which are unique for every lineage, are validated by the genealogical tradition of descent from the sons of the hero-ancestors. Even the heroes themselves are given certain inverted attributes, especially in the context of events before Lugbara society was founded through their marriages, since they are significant primarily above the level of the direct external relations of a given group. It is only the ancestors of the clans and lineages within a group's field of social relations who are given a place in that group's corpus of genealogical tradition, and to whom are ascribed no inverted attributes at all. *Odipi* and *juru* and genealogical tradition are different for every group, but the same corpus of myth is held by all Lugbara. Likewise the inverted beings live far away, outside all groups of Lugbara society, the limits of which are defined by Lugbara in terms of mythical inversion.

5 DESCENT AND SYMBOLIC FILIATION

Sally Falk Moore

K INSHIP NETWORKS involve a paradox. On the one hand marriage links exogamic kin groups. On the other hand, it serves to link them only insofar as the ties of each spouse to his (or her) family of birth are maintained. This continuing connection with the natal groups is often represented by the bond between brother and sister, although it also appears in other forms.[1] As male and female of the same generation, their mutual involvement in their kin group makes them in some respects a counterpair to husband and wife. Since in many systems this sibling relationship serves structural ends, the brother-sister tie is seldom left simply to spontaneous expressions of devotion which might or might not be forthcoming. Instead it is reinforced with ritual, social, and economic obligations.

Some cultures also stress rather than minimize the incestuous overtones of the brother-sister relationship. Sometimes this preoccupation appears in the form of exaggerated prohibitions and avoidances. In other cases, it is woven through the conception of descent, as opposed to parenthood. It is this tying together of incestuous ideas and descent that is the subject of this paper, particularly with regard to brother and sister.

Common to a variety of descent systems are two means of prolonging the relationship between kin groups established by marriage. Both structural devices have the effect of stressing the

Reprinted from *The American Anthropologist* 66 (6, pt. 1), 1964: 1308–20, by permission of the author and the editor, *The American Anthropologist*.

[1] While brother and brother, or sister and sister, may effectively symbolize the descent group, same-sex pairs cannot epitomize the bridge *between* kin groups.

bond between brother and sister. One method is to repeat the affinal tie through cross-cousin marriage. This binds brother and sister twice over. The other structural device is to make the children of the marriage to some degree descendants of both kin groups, linking the two groups in their persons. (This may, but need not also involve a prohibition on cousin marriage.) Cognatic and double descent systems immediately come to mind. But unilineal systems may also trace descent in some form through both parents. Full membership in the patrilineage of the father and partial membership in the patrilineage of the mother is one way (Nuer). Or there may be a similar near doubling of membership in the matrilineages of mother and father (Hopi, Plateau Tonga). The tracing of descent through both parents in whatever manner extends the affiliations established by marriage at least another generation in the person of the common descendant. This also has the accompanying result that brother and sister have descent links of some kind with each other's children.

Both sorts of ongoing ties not infrequently place brother and sister together in a highly binding relationship to the progeny of one or both. This relationship is often represented in what might be called "the ideology of descent" as if it were a variety of mystical, sexless parenthood, a form of symbolic filiation.

Radcliffe-Brown thought brother-sister ties particularly associated with extreme matrilineality, while he believed that husband-wife bonds were more emphasized in cases of extreme patrilineality. He felt, however, that most systems fell somewhere in between (1952: 42). I plan to deal elsewhere with a full structural reappraisal of this Radcliffe-Brown thesis, but the present paper will focus on a single aspect of the problem: the representation of brother and sister as a symbolically parental couple in descent ideology. That this occurs in patrilineal and cognatic systems as well as in matrilineal ones will be plain from the materials examined. These include creation myths, on the theory that people model their mythical first family on their own kinship structure, and also include a few well known beliefs and customs relating to fertility and the procreation and well-being of descendants. Most of the myths collected here show incest explicitly. As would be expected, the kinship beliefs put the matter more delicately and indirectly, but the incestuous symbolism is unmistakable.

Any myth about the creation of man which postulates a single first family is bound to give rise to some incestuous riddles. There is the first man, or woman, or couple. They have children. Who marries the children of the first couple? Adam and Eve had two sons, Cain and Abel. Where did Cain's wife come from?

Many mythological methods exist to supply respectable mates for the original family. Sometimes spouses are simply found when needed. Cain's wife turns up conveniently in the King James version of the Bible, but Saint Augustine seems to have had no doubt that the sons and daughters of Adam and Eve married each other (Saint Augustine 1958: 350). In other myths many people emerge from the ground together and there is a kind of simultaneous creation of many ancestors for mankind. However, many peoples cheerfully and explicitly mate the first family to its own members. A number of such myths are listed below. These were collected and examined to discover which members of the family were most often partners in this original incest, and whether there was any observable correlation between the type of kinship system and the type of incest described. A few of the myths cited deal with the primary incest of the gods, a few others with an incest that began a particular lineage, but most of them tell of an incest from which mankind sprang. All but two are listed with the associated form of descent. The prevalence of brother-

SOME PEOPLES HAVING INCESTUOUS CREATION LEGENDS

People	Descent	Incest in myth	Reference
Greeks	Patrilineal	Brother-sister	Larousse 1960: 93
Hebrews	Patrilineal	Brother-sister	{ Saint Augustine 1958: 350 { Graves 1963: 17–18
Murngin	Patrilineal	{ Father-daughter { Brother-sister	Warner 1937: 528
Trobriand	Matrilineal	Brother-sister (implied)	Malinowski 1929: 497
Berber (Kabyl)	Patrilineal	Brother-sister	Frobenius and Fox 1938: 55
Ngona Horn S. Rhodesia	Patrilineal	Father-daughter	Frobenius and Fox 1938: 241
Maori	Ambilineal	Father-daughter	Best 1924: 115–18
Miwok	Patrilineal	{ Father-daughter { Brother-sister	Gifford 1916: 143–44
Baiga	Patrilineal	Brother-sister	Verrier 1939: 313, 331
Thonga	Patrilineal	Brother-sister	Junod 1913: 230
Chibcha	Matrilineal	Mother-son	Kroeber 1947: 908
Yaruro	Matrilineal	Brother-sister	Kirchhoff 1948: 462
Hawaii	Ambilineal	Mother-son	Dixon 1916: 26
Tahiti	Ambilineal	Father-daughter	Dixon 1916–26

People	Descent	Incest in myth	Reference
Celebes Minahassa		Mother-son	Dixon 1916: 157
Ifugao	Bilateral	Brother-sister	Dixon 1916: 170
Katchin	Patrilineal	Brother-sister	Lévi-Strauss 1948: 307
Mohave	Patrilineal	Brother-sister	Devereaux 1939: 512
Pawnee	Matrilineal(?)	Brother-sister	American Folk Lore Society 1904: 22
Tlingit	Matrilineal	Brother-sister	Krause 1956: 175, 185
Aleut	Patrilineal	Brother-sister	HRAF citing Veniaminov and Sarytschew
Alor	Bilateral	Brother-sister (implied)	Dubois, 1944: 105
Yurok	Bilateral	Father-daughter	Roheim (citing Kroeber) 1950: 273
Island Carib Dominica	Matrilineal	Brother-sister	Taylor 1945: 310
Veddas	Matrilineal	Brother-sister	Seligmann 1911: 74
Lakher	Patrilineal	Brother-sister	Parry 1932: 489
Garo	Matrilineal	Brother-sister	Playfair 1909: 84
Ba-Kaonde	Matrilineal	Brother-sister	Melland 1923: 156, 249-59
Cherokee	Matrilineal	Brother-sister (implied)	Mooney 1902: 240
Dogon	Patrilineal	Brother-sister	Griaule and Dieterlen 1954: 84-96
Abaluyia	Patrilineal	Brother-sister	Wagner 1954: 30, 35
Papuas of Waropen	Patrilineal	Brother-sister	Held 1957: 95, 299
Samoa	Ambilineal	Brother-sister	Mead 1930: 151
Lovedu	Patrilineal	Father-daughter Brother-sister Cycle of Kings	Krige and Krige 1943: 5, 10, 12
Tullishi	Double	Brother-sister	Nadel 1950: 351
Lozi	Ambilineal	Brother-sister	Gluckman 1950: 177, 178
Andaman Islanders	Bilateral	Brother-sister	Radcliffe-Brown 1933: 196
Japanese	Bilateral	Brother-sister	Etter 1949: 29
Ainu	Matrilineal	Brother-sister	Etter 1949: 20-21
Kei Islands SE Indonesia		Brother-sister	Dixon 1916: 156
Nambicuara	Bilateral	Brother-sister	Lévi-Strauss 1948: 369
Egyptians	Patrilineal	Brother-sister King Osiris	Frazer 1960: 421

Total number of peoples listed 42

Four peoples have more than one type of incest in their origin myth hence the disparity between the total number of peoples and the total instances of incest.

Descent	bro-sis	fa-da	mo-son
Patrilineal	16	4	
Matrilineal	10		1
Ambilineal	2	2	1
Bilateral	5	1	
Double	1		
Unknown	1		1
TOTALS	34	7	3

sister incest is striking, and the correlation of parent-child incest with descent rules quite suggestive. The examples examined have been culled from ethnographies, from the Human Relations Area Files, from indications in the Stith Thompson Index, from a picking over of the Handbook of South American Indians and other general sources likely to include such information. However, the list is a chance compilation depending upon library accessibility, and is in no sense complete. It is sufficient to suggest the wide appearance of the theme, and, perhaps, some gross correlations.

Some reservations should be made. For one thing, both myths and social organization change. Even assuming that myth is in some symbolic way a rationalization of a kinship system, it may be more or less durable than the social structure from which it sprang. There is also the related question as to what position the origin myth occupies in the total literature of a people. It may be an old story, part of an obscure heritage, seldom retold, but carried along, or it may have a good deal more vitality than that. This is a nuance which is not always discernible from the ethnographic literature. (For a penetrating discussion of these and related problems concerning the interpretation of myth, see Fischer 1963.)

It should also be said that though the relation of the form of the incestuous myth to the form of the social organization may be posed as a problem in correlations, it is not really suitable to treat it this way. Many, if not most, peoples do not have such a myth, but they have the same types of kinship structure as the peoples who have the myths. The inference to be drawn from this mythological material is that a fictive and symbolic incest is often a significant symbol of ancestry and descent. It may be found in many forms, of which origin myths are but one example. Hence the origin myths alert one to a kind of symbolism that appears in the ideology of some descent systems even in cultures in which this theme is not expressed in the particular form of a creation legend.

Lévi-Strauss has said that ". . . the purpose of myth is to provide a logical model capable of overcoming a contradiction . . ." (1955: 443) and that "mythical thought always works from the awareness of oppositions toward their progressive mediation . . ." (1955: 440). From this point of view these incestuous origin myths refer to a time when there were no people to explain how there came to be many people. They start with one family to show the source of all families. They tell of an ancient incest that sired the human race, yet plainly the descendants are forbidden to emulate their ancestors. Then and now are contrasted in a systematic way.[2]

Inspecting the table, it is clear that brother-sister incest is the one which most often takes place in the myths. This not only violates the incest prohibition; it also necessarily violates exogamic rules in any descent system. Where mythological parent-child incest occurs in unilineal systems, it, too, seems calculated to violate descent rules. The matrilineal Chibcha are descended from a mother-son incest, the patrilineal Murngin, Miwok, Ngona, and the Lovedu rulers from a father-daughter incest. The numbers involved here are too small to constitute a statistical proof, but they suggest a correlation with structure. It is interesting to note parent-child incest in the myths of three out of five ambilineal peoples and one out of six bilateral peoples. Presumably the structural resemblances of ambilineal systems to unilineal ones accounts for this difference, but the numbers are too small to warrant any firm conclusion.

Why should incest in origin myths be a common theme, and why should it tend so strongly to be sibling incest? And why should mythical parent-child incest tend to correlate with descent group exogamy? If one applies psychoanalytic theory, these myths can be regarded as a reiteration of Oedipal fantasies. The beginning of mankind then stands for the early wishes of the individual, and sibling incest is not more than a lightly veiled version of parent-child incest. This interpretation could account for the commonness of the incestuous theme in mythology. It might even superficially seem to account for the prevalence of the brother-sister over the parent-child type. *But it could in no way account for the correlation of mythological parent-child incest with descent.* Whatever element is unaccounted for in the parent-child cases, is logically unaccounted for in the sibling type, for one explanation must apply to all.

Thus even if one accepts psychoanalytic interpretations, they

[2] It has been objected that what is involved here and in Lévi-Strauss is not the juxtaposition of opposites, but of negatives. This well-taken point of logic undermines the form but not the substance of Lévi-Strauss' contention.

can only explain the general appeal of the theme of incest, not its particular variations or cultural applications. I agree with Murphy that ". . . the stuff of the unconscious tends to be expressed in cultural symbols where it serves some function in terms of social structure . . ." (1959: 97). The explanation of the variations must be sought in the cultural setting in which they are found.

In this matter Lévi-Strauss' approach to mythology (1955, 1962) is very useful. His conception of oppositions ties social structure to myth insofar as myths seek to reconcile what life is with what life is not. There is another string to his bow in "Le totemisme aujourd'hui." There he deals not with contrasts and negations, but with the replication of social structure in the classification of animals and plants. Hence mythological symbolism may either repeat or contrast with reality, as the case may be.

The incestuous creation myths do both. In them one finds a literary reconciliation of the incest prohibition and incest itself, both pushed discreetly into the primeval past. Descent postulates common ancestry. Man is of one kind. Thus all mankind has common ancestors. Ancestry is also the basis of the incest prohibition. But if all men are descended from one couple, then every marriage is distantly and vaguely incestuous. In this way the myth metaphorically and economically states both the unity of man, and that marriage is a substitute for incest.

Since the unified descent of mankind is best symbolized in a particular culture not only by incest, but by incest within the descent group, there may be a purely logical reason for the prevalence of the sibling incest theme against the parent-child type. Brother-sister incest conveys concisely for *any* descent system the same triple symbolism that parent-child incest conveys for particular ones, namely the fusion of descent, marriage, and incest. There may be an even simpler explanation. Since primary marriage most often tends to be within the same generation, brother-sister incest may be a closer symbolic replication of marriage than parent-child incest.

Robert Graves, like Frazer before him, interprets mythological sibling incest as an indication of a prior period of matrilineal land inheritance (Frazer 1960: 386; Graves 1963: 4). This seems a curious inference. As the table shows, sibling incest as an origin myth theme is as clearly associated with patrilineality as matrilineality. To treat legends of this type as accounts of early history is a naively literal approach. It is far more likely that these stories are a fictional validation of the present than an embroidered remnant of the past.

There is no better example than the Dogon of the French Sudan who state explicitly that their kinship system is based on their creation myth. So beautifully does their myth illustrate the sibling constellation and its symbolic content in descent ideology that it is worth making an excursion into Dogon cosmology. A patrilineal people having patrilocal kin groups, the Dogon prefer the marriage of a man with his mother's brother's daughter. Conventionally he also enjoys sexual relations with his mother's brother's wife. All this according to the Dogon has its precedents in the Beginning of Time.

The Dogon creation myth begins with the egg of the world. (I will spare the reader the rather orgasmic seven vibrations of the universe and some other cosmic upheavals.) The egg of the world is divided into twin placenta, each of which contains a "pair of twin Nommo, direct emanations and sons of God. . . . Like all other creatures these twin beings . . . were each equipped with two spiritual principles of opposite sex; each of them, therefore, was in himself a pair . . ." (Griaule and Dieterlen 1954: 86).

In Dogon belief every human being is the offspring of two pairs of Nommo like those in the original placenta, the father and the father's sister, the mother and the mother's brother. The ideal, but prohibited marriage, is conceived as that between brother and sister. Mystically, opposite sex siblings are conceived as parents of each other's children.

However, in the creation all did not proceed according to plan, "in one placenta . . . the male person emerged prematurely from the egg. Moreover he tore a fragment from his placenta and with it came down through space outside the egg; this fragment became the earth." Yurugu, for that was the name of this male creature, eventually went back to heaven to get the rest of his placenta and his twin soul. But unfortunately for him, "Amma (God) had handed over this twin soul to the remaining pair in the other part of the egg. . . . Yurugu could not retrieve her; and from that time on . . . (was) . . . engaged in a perpetual and fruitless search for her. He returned to the dry earth where . . . he procreated in his own placenta. . . ." However, this procreation with a symbolic maternal fragment did not produce people, but some sort of incomplete beings. "Seeing this, Amma decided to send to earth the Nommo of the other half of the egg . . ." (Griaule and Dieterlen 1954: 86). Mankind was then produced through the coupling of pairs of male and female twins.

The Dogon regard every male child as Yurugu with respect to his mother. He is her brother, her ideal husband. But since the normal incest prohibitions apply, the wife of the maternal uncle is taken as a sexual partner as a substitute for the mother. The boy is allowed to commit whatever thefts he pleases in his mother's brother's household, as these are regarded as a symbolical search for a wife. This comes to an end when the maternal uncle provides a wife, usually one of his daughters. "Clearly there is a correspondence here between the maternal uncle's daughter, his wife, and his sister, who is the mother of the nephew. The marriage is thus in some sense a reenactment of the mythical incest. It is also . . . regarded as a caricature and is thus a kind of defiance hurled at Yurugu . . ." (Griaule and Dieterlen 1954: 93).

The Dogon lay out their villages, their fields, their houses, in a pattern that is in keeping with the creation myth. No vestigial tradition, the myth has tremendous vitality and importance. The patriline is thought to follow the original orderly creation of Amma, the uterine group to represent the checkered career of Yurugu. While there is much else that is interesting about Dogon belief, three of its elements are of particular relevance here: first that brother and sister are idealized as a procreative couple; second, the idea that any child is simultaneously produced by two sibling pairs, the father and his sister, the mother and her brother; and third, that structural features, in this case, preferred matrilateral cross-cousin marriage, can have specific symbolically incestuous meanings.

The basic question which elements in the Dogon myth raise is this: Are the Dogon a special case, or does their myth make explicit certain ideas that are symbolically implied in one form or another in many descent systems? If one reflects on the stereotyped kinship roles often prescribed for parents' siblings of opposite sex in primitive cultures, it is difficult to dismiss the Dogon as unique.

II

Turning from mythology to some beliefs and customs which surround the perpetuation of the descent group: here again examples of the symbolic pairing of brothers and sisters in a quasi-incestuous manner are not far to seek. Brother and sister may together perpetuate the descent group on a symbolic level, while on a practical level marriage produces the actual descendants.

In Africa the well-known case is that of cattle-linking, in which a man obtains his wife by means of the cattle received for his sister, and she consequently comes to have a special relationship with her brother's children. The striking thing about these African cattle-linked sibling pairs is the extent to which the tie between a particular brother and sister is acknowledged as having a connection with the very existence of the brother's children, giving the father's sister special rights over them. There is a kind of double marriage, the actual one, and the symbolic one of the cattle linking. (See for instance Krige and Krige 1943: 142–46 for the Lovedu: Stayt 1931: 174, for the BaVenda, Schapera 1950: 142 for the Tswana, Holleman 1952: 66, 67, 169 for the Shona, and Kuper 1950: 102, for the Swazi.)

In Samoa, the male line of the ambilineal Manuans goes on through the good grace of each man's sister. The father's sister has the ability to make her brother or his male line barren, or can cause them to sicken (Mead 1930: 137). As the keeper of her brother's fertility, a sister becomes in a mystical sense as responsible for a man's procreation as his wife is in a biological sense.

In the Trobriands, one sees the matrilineal counterpart of the African cattle pairing. Trobriand brothers and sisters are paired off for various purposes. Not only does a particular brother supply a particular sister with food, but "This pairing off extends to other things besides *urigubu* [food]. *A sister may ask her brother to make magic designed to get her impregnated by one of the spirits of their sub-clan.* The brother who is responsible for a sister's food is the one who plays the main role of disciplinarian and tutor of her children. The other brothers are secondary in this respect. . . ." (Fathauer 1961: 250) (Italics mine).

The Trobriand preoccupation with brother-sister incest is clearly threaded throughout the descriptions of Malinowski. The origin of Trobriand love magic is based on brother-sister incest. All clans begin their mythological history with a brother and sister, the sister becoming pregnant without intercourse (Malinowski 1929: 35, 180–82). Trobriand brother-sister pairs are clearly associated with descent and figure as symbolic parents of the sister's children much as the African cattle-linking makes siblings figure as symbolic parents of the brother's children.

Among the Murngin, Warner tells us that "No sister may eat a brother's kill of kangaroo, emu, etc. until the brother's wife has had a child" (1930: 253). It is as if the sister drained her brother's sexual powers by eating his kill. The sister's actions plainly have an effect on her brother's ability to impregnate his wife.

The African, Samoan, Trobriand and Murngin instances are all cases in which the non-lineal sex has power over the fertility of the lineal sex. But sometimes the position is reversed. The patrilineal Lakher believe that if there is ill-feeling between a woman and her brother or her mother's brother, she will be unable to have children. Patently her relatives retain control over her fertility even after she marries. The ceremony which may be performed to enable her to become pregnant gives her brother or her mother's brother a major role. Either of these men places some fermented rice in the woman's mouth with a hair pin when the moon is waning, and neither of them speaks to her again until a new moon has arisen (Parry 1932: 379–80).[8]

All of these are fairly obvious cases in which brother and sister

---

[8] The Lakher also believe that if a woman's parents are dead, their spirits may be the cause of her infertility. For this last the cure is a sacrifice on the graves of the parents. Thus brothers and sisters are not by any means the *only* custodians of each other's fertility. Among the matrilineal Pende, for instance, a father is said to enable his daughter to bear children, but sometimes the anger of a mother's brother can make a woman sterile (de Sousberghe 1955: 27). Even among the Trobrianders spirit children may be the gift of a woman's mother, mother's brother, or even of her father (Malinowski 1929: 173). Among the patrilineal Nuer, a man's mother or his mother's brother can prevent him from having any male children (Evans-Pritchard 1960: 138). A Nuer son can, by violating certain taboos, render his mother barren (Evans-Pritchard 1960: 165). The curse of the mother or mother's brother among the Nuer would seem to be the counterpart of the father's sister's curse in Polynesia. Relationships of the spirits obviously can have sexual consequences. The power over fertility is often an expression of multiple structural relationships in terms of sexual symbols. Though this paper is confined to this symbolization as it pertains to brother and sister, it should be borne in mind that it can, as indicated, pertain to other relatives.

together are involved with the procreativity of one or the other of them. But the sibling link can be expressed in purely spiritual terms as well. The Mende explain the relationship with the mother's brother this way: ". . . since a brother and sister come from the same father they may be considered as one. *Therefore, all that a mother gives her child is given also by her brother, and so her brother's displeasure or pleasure is the same as its mother's.* The physical part of a person, i.e. his bones, flesh, etc. is provided by his father through the semen. . . . The child's spirit—ngafa—, however, is contributed by his mother. This explains why the blessing of the mother's people is so important to the child and why the father asks them to pray for the child when he takes it away from them. The mother is the child's 'keeper' in the same sense as a genie may have control over a human being" (Little 1951: 111) (Italics mine).

For the patrilineal Mende, then, brother and sister are triply bound. First, they are one as the bodily (i.e. descent) children of one father; second, they are one as the soul keepers of the sister's children; and third, they are descent antecedents of the brother's children. Husband and wife are actual parents, brother and sister symbolic ones. The Mende attitude is a forceful reminder of the Dogon myth.

The pairing of brothers and sisters as a symbolic couple bears on Lévi-Strauss' interpretation of totemism. Lévi-Strauss (1962) suggests that the reason why animals are suitable symbols of kin groups lies in certain resemblances between the animal world and the human world. The human world and the animal world have in common the subdivisions of their respective kinds. He stresses the fact that totemism involves the use of homologous systems to represent one another. With this general thesis I have no argument.

However, though Lévi-Strauss notes that animal species are endogamous, he does not find it logically troublesome that they are used to represent exogamous groups. Instead, he cites Bergson saying that it is not on the animality but on the duality that totemism puts its emphasis (1962: 111, 135). The material on symbolic incest and descent reviewed here suggests that this part of the Lévi-Strauss argument is superfluous. The endogamy of animal species makes animals not less, but more appropriate as emblems of descent groups. This is obviously not because of any actual endogamy in descent groups, but because descent groups are symbolically self-perpetuating. The descent element in unilineal groups is passed on from generation to generation in a self-propelling stream. To be sure, partners from other lineages are required catalysts or vehicles for the production of biological offspring, but the descent element in the offspring comes from within the lineage only. Kind reproduces kind in the animal and human kingdoms.

The beliefs examined here in which brother and sister have custody of each other's fertility, or are mutually involved in the perpetuation of the descent group, or are together connected with the body or soul of each other's children all state formal social ties in a particular symbolic idiom. Firth has said, "Kinship is fundamentally a reinterpretation in social terms of the facts of procreation and regularized sex union" (1961: 577). But if one moves from the realm of structure to the realm to symbolism, the contrary can be true. That is, relationships which are not sexual or filial in reality may be expressed in symbols having a sexual or filial content. Just as fictive kinship may be resorted to, to bind unrelated persons socially, so fictive incest and fictive parenthood can be part of the idiom of descent.

Symbolic filiation is not at all startling when it does not involve any direct mention of the incest. We are entirely accustomed to it in kinship terminology. When the father's sister is called "female father" the term implies that she partakes in her brother's paternity. Where cousins are classified with brothers and sisters they are linked in a fictitious common filiation. The extension of the incest taboo beyond the elementary family is another of the ways in which symbolic filiation may serve structural ends. Clearly descent and symbolic filiation are frequently interlocked concepts. It is not surprising then, that the brother-sister relationship which has such widespread structural importance, not only often appears as a symbol of descent, but does so in the form of a symbolic parenthood. A full recognition of this pervasive *double entendre* and its many variations can deepen our understanding of descent in kin-based societies.

6 MAGICAL HAIR

Edmund R. Leach

INTRODUCTION

THE FOLLOWING is the problem with which I am concerned in very broad general terms. Much of the work of social anthropologists involves the interpretation of symbolic behaviour. When we talk about 'social structure', we are translating into our own special jargon various bits and pieces of culturally defined behaviour which we choose to consider as 'symbols'. This is particularly obvious in the case of religious ritual; Van Gennep's generalizations on *Rites de Passage* provide a classic example, but even Frazer's rather simple-minded 'associational' theory of magic assumes that anthropologists possess some kind of golden key whereby they can blandly assert that a particular piece of stereotyped human behaviour 'stands for' or 'is a symbol of' this, that, or the other thing.

I have no wish to get involved in the philosophical morass implied in assumptions of this kind. I agree that most such interpretation has no sound logical justification. That does not deter me from attempting to interpret. Logically considered, almost the whole of psycho-analytic theory rests on the most glaring fallacies; yet somehow or other it often proves illuminating.

My intellectual difficulty is a different one. Assuming that we *can* make plausible guesses at interpreting 'symbolic behaviour', then it quickly becomes obvious that some distinction can be made between what might be called the pragmatic, or operational

Reprinted from *The Journal of the Royal Anthropological Institute* 88 (2), 1958: 147–64, by permission of the author and the Council of the Royal Anthropological Institute. This paper was the Curl Bequest Prize Essay, 1957.

content of a symbol and its communication content. This was a
point much laboured by Malinowski with regard to language.
Arguing that the linguists of his day thought of language as simply
and solely a communication device, he went to the opposite extreme and asserted that by far the most important quality of
language is that it is a pragmatic tool. It is not that words simply
say something about the state of affairs; in nine cases out of ten,
they have consequences, they alter the state of affairs (Malinowski 1932; 1935).

Now this dual quality is not confined to spoken words, it is
present in almost all kinds of symbols other than those artificial
ones which professional logicians invent with the specific intent
that they shall not be value loaded. Symbolic behaviour not only
'says' something, it also arouses emotion and consequently 'does'
something. But this poses for the anthropologist an essentially
psychological problem: Just where does the emotional content of
symbols come from, and how is it that some symbols are more
emotionally loaded than others?

In our society, if two men shake hands the behaviour has a
'meaning' which is equivalent to a statement such as: 'We two
are of the same social standing and can converse with one another
without embarrassment'. As external observers we can ascertain
this meaning by going round Europe and America and noting the
occasions when individuals shake hands and which particular
individuals do so. This technique of symbol interpretation is one
which Radcliffe-Brown (1933: 235) advocated as generally appropriate for anthropologists; it very largely dispenses with any
psychological assumptions.

In contrast, if I kiss a pretty girl on the lips the gesture has an in-
determinate 'meaning'. As before it can be part of a ritual of
greeting or farewell, but it may also have additional emotional
significance for either party individually. The external observer
can only guess at what is happening.

The main difference between these two effects of symbolic
behaviour is that the first is public and the second private. The
essence of public symbolic behaviour is that it is a means of communication; the actor and his audience share a common language,
a symbolic language. They must share a common set of conventions as to what the different elements in the language mean,
otherwise there will be a failure of communication. Broadly speak-

ing this is what we mean by Culture. When people belong to the same Culture they share between themselves various mutually understood systems of communication. Every member of such a Culture will attribute the same meaning to any particular item of culturally defined 'ritual'.

In contrast, the characteristic quality of private symbolism is its psychological power to arouse emotion and alter the state of the individual. Emotion is aroused not by any appeal to the rational faculties but by some kind of trigger action on the subconscious elements of the human personality. The extent to which our own private emotions in such circumstances are also experienced by others is something about which we can only guess.

This distinction between public and private, social and individual, is one which constantly concerns the social anthropologist. In most situations he will be well advised to leave psychological matters to psychologists and stick firmly to the public sociological facets of the case; behaviour can then be analysed in Radcliffe-Brown's frame of reference as a system of communication between structurally defined social persons. But the problem remains: Just what *is* the connection between the public and private sectors of the symbolic system?

This problem becomes especially acute in discourse between anthropologists and psycho-analysts. Analysts of diverse schools have established dogmas as to what particular kinds of symbol 'mean' when they crop up in dreams and obsessional behaviour of individual psychiatric patients. This is a matter of relevance to anthropologists because of the curious procedures that are used to validate the analysts' theories.

It is common to all schools of psycho-therapy that particular symbolic interpretations are justified by laying stress on supposed characteristics of the Unconscious. For all schools, it is common dogma that the taboos which Society imposes upon sexual and excretory behaviour result in 'repression'. As a consequence of this civilizing process the 'repressed portion of the personality' (the *id* in Freudian terminology) seeks to express its sexual and excretory wishes through the use of symbols which represent a displacement of basic genital and pre-genital interests.

Such psycho-analytical doctrines are, by their nature, incapable either of verification or disproof, but by a long established convention analysts often drag in ethnographic material to support their clinical observations. The analyst does this, it seems, so as to make his rather far-fetched interpretations seem more plausible to the lay public.

This procedure was adopted by Freud himself on a number of occasions, notably in *Totem and Taboo*. Its logical justification is provided by the now outmoded belief that 'primitive' societies are in some sense chronologically archaic. Freud (1919, chapter 1, para. 1) specifically stated that 'we can recognize in the psychic life (of primitives) a well-preserved, early stage of our own development'. By this analogy, lack of sexual inhibition in the customary conventions of a primitive society is deemed to correspond to the uninhibited behaviour of a young child in our own society. Furthermore, primitive societies are often represented as having a kind of collective personality so that the myths and rituals of primitive peoples correspond to the dreams and play of individual western children. Consistent with this, the rituals of primitive society are represented as obsessions corresponding to the obsessional behaviour of neurotics in our society. Indeed many psycho-therapists use the terms 'ritual' and 'obsessional behaviour' as synonyms. It is not merely that Freud wrote like this in 1906; eminent analysts still do so in 1956.

Given this kind of assumption, the rest follows. Primitive rituals, as displayed in the ethnographic literature, are demonstrated as containing symbolic components similar to those which crop up in the dreams and imaginings of individual psychopaths. It is then asserted that the symbols in the primitive rituals 'mean' the same thing as the same symbols 'mean' in the psycho-analyst's consulting room. This is held to 'prove' that certain types of symbolic meaning are universals for all humanity.

The logical fallacies of this argument are obvious. But the empirical fallacies are not. If an anthropologist sets out to discover what a social symbol means, considered simply as an element in a system of communication, it is very likely that he will arrive at precisely the same conclusion as that reached by the psycho-analyst by his atrocious techniques of hit or miss intuition. What is the significance of this convergence?

This is the general problem examined in this paper. So as to narrow the issue I have organized my material as a commentary on a book by a distinguished practising psycho-analyst, Dr. Charles Berg (1951). In this book the author uses anthropological materials to support conclusions of a psycho-analytic kind, much as Freud did himself. Freud's assumption that ethnographic materials have significance for psycho-analytic theory is, I believe, largely fallacious. But the converse is less clear. It may well be that psycho-analytic materials have significance for anthropological theory. This is the particular proposition which I examine.

DR. CHARLES BERG'S THESIS

Dr. Berg's thesis is briefly this. In most societies, including our own, hairdressing is a matter of ritualistic elaboration. What are the psychological mechanisms at the back of these performances? What does hair behaviour mean? Relying in the first place on clinical material he concludes that head hair is universally a symbol of the genital organs. Hair-cutting and shaving are thus to be understood as symbolic 'castration'. Once this is established, the orthodox Freudian description of *Super-Ego—Ego—Id* conflict can be neatly illustrated in terms of everyday, socially approved, attitudes regarding hair in general.

Dr. Berg further maintains that at a pre-genital level there is a common association between hair and faeces and that, in the last analysis, head hair is used as a symbol for libidinous aggressive drives of all kinds. For Dr. Berg, the apparently simple act of shaving the beard is nothing less than an attempt to control primary aggressive impulses. 'In shaving and hair-cutting we abreact our aggression by directing it against our aggressive hair' (Berg 1951: 90). Dr. Berg's total analysis is thus summed up by himself: 'We are repeating the unsolved struggle between instinct drives (genital and pre-genital) and the castrating efforts of the repressing forces, at the instigation particularly of the super-ego. The whole conflict has been displaced upwards to the socially visible hair of the head and face' (p. 94).

Seeking support for his clinical material Dr. Berg then takes note of evidence from anthropological and folklore sources. I am concerned here only with the former.

Even if we admit that anthropological materials are relevant in such a discussion, the data which Dr. Berg examines are unsatisfactory. He relies mainly on Frazer, citing ancient classical authorities of dubious ethnographic reliability. The only two modern ethnographers to be considered are Roheim, whose observations are biased by psycho-analytic presuppositions, and Malinowski, whose statements are misrepresented.

Yet if Dr. Berg had possessed a wider acquaintance with the literature, it would scarcely have induced him to change his views. There is an impressive body of ethnographic material which is quite consistent with Dr. Berg's thesis.

ETHNOGRAPHIC EVIDENCE

It is a fact that hairdressing is an extremely widespread feature of ritual behaviour, and anthropological attempts to generalize from this fact have a long history. G. A. Wilken, for example, published a paper on the place of hairdressing in mourning ceremonies as long ago as 1886. Wilken suggested that two contrasted types of ritualized hair-behaviour may be distinguished.

On the one hand the hair may be cut off and the head shaved; on the other the customary hairdressing of normal life is neglected, the hair is allowed to become dishevelled and the beard allowed to grow. Both these species of behaviour are discussed in Dr. Berg's book; he interprets the first as symbolic castration and the second as ascetic repudiation of the very existence of sex.

Wilken's own explanation of 'hair sacrifice' also presupposes that hair is a universal symbol, though not specifically a sexual one. He claims that the ritual cutting of hair is a substitute for human sacrifice on a *pars pro toto* basis, the hair being appropriate for the purpose because the head is the seat of the soul (cf. Crawley 1927, vol. I: 275).

The near agreement between Berg and Wilken on this point needs to be stressed. For Berg, the hair stands for sexuality; for Wilken the hair stands for the personality of the individual on whose head it grows. There is a precisely comparable convergence between Freud's view of symbolic association and Frazer's more simple-minded concept of homeopathic magic. What we need to consider is whether the Freudian interpretation really adds any thing to the *pars pro toto* argument.

That hair rituals may have sexual associations has been apparent to anthropologists from the beginning, but mostly they have not regarded this as a matter of crucial significance. Tylor, for example, classed ritual hair-cutting as one 'of an extensive series of practices, due to various and often obscure motives, which come under the general heading of ceremonial mutilations'. Of other such practices he mentions bloodletting and the cutting off of finger joints. He avoids reference to circumcision, but the latter rite is clearly a 'ceremonial mutilation' (Tylor 1873: 403). More recently J. H. Hutton (1928), a thoroughly orthodox ethnographer of the older school, in seeking to give meaning to Naga head-hunting practices, has laid stress on a definite, though indirect connection between hair and other more obvious phallic emblems. He maintains that the ritual taking of heads and the erection of stone and wooden phallic emblems have a common magical purpose of ensuring crop fertility, but that 'if the magical phallus be a method of ensuring fertility, it is not apparently in itself the source of fertility, for this seems to lie in the souls of the dead'. Elsewhere he argues, like Wilken, that head hair is the seat of the soul. (Hutton *in* Parry 1932: 479, note 2). Though the terminology is different, the facts cited fit well with Dr. Berg's argument. The 'soul stuff' of writers such as Hutton and Wilken is not perhaps very different from the 'libido' of the psycho-analysts.

Much of this evidence is rather antiquated, but reports from more recent fieldwork usually point in the same direction. To summarize all the evidence would require a substantial volume, but here are three widely distributed examples which show the manner in which hair rituals may acquire palpably sexual significance:

(i) Fortune (1932: 50) writing of Dobu remarks: 'The care of the hair is a reciprocal service between husband and wife. It is closely connected with intercourse. An adulterer will louse or cut the hair of the woman he has committed adultery with if he wishes to make the matter public and defy the woman's husband'.

(ii) Forde (1941, chapters 4 and 6) gives a detailed analysis of the marriage rites of the Yakö. He shows that, in this society, there is a close symbolic association between head shaving and clitoridectomy, and between hair growing and pregnancy.

(iii) Topley has recently studied a number of Chinese Buddhist monastic institutions in Singapore. In some of these, female novitiates go through a form of 'marriage' with other female members of the order and thereafter become their homosexual partners; the marriage rite consists of the spouses combing each other's hair. At a higher level of the hierarchy total sexual abstinence is required; a woman who achieves this status is known as a 'self-comber'. The sexual implications of this expression are, it seems, well known among the Singapore population (Topley 1954; also personal communication).

Such examples might be multiplied almost without limit.

Let us suppose then that the parallel is established. On the one hand Dr. Berg discovers that in the private imaginings of his individual patients there is a widespread association between head hair and libidinous energy. On the other hand there is ethnographic evidence that similar symbolism is common in the religious rituals of primitive peoples. What can we infer from this?

Firstly, does the psycho-analytic evidence provide the anthropologist with a basis for suspecting that hair symbolism has the same meanings everywhere, as distinct from particular local implications? The psycho-analyst's argument is that where a phallic significance for hair ceremonial has been demonstrated it is self-evident that this phallicism is the really fundamental principle involved, and that this fact alone accounts for the widespread use of head hair as an element in ritual. Can the anthropologist agree?

PUBLIC SYMBOLS AND PRIVATE SYMBOLS

At this point we must re-examine the distinction I made earlier between public-sociological symbols on the one hand and private-psychological symbols on the other. The distinction is simply a description of the different frames of reference in terms of which the anthropologist and the psychologist respectively examine human behaviour. The psychologist is primarily interested in the behaviour of the individual as an unique entity. Behaviour is then regarded as 'symbolic' in the sense that what is overt is deemed to be a representation of something that is covert. Both the overt behaviour and the covert 'thing' that is inferred are aspects of the same individual. Indeed, in most contexts, the psycho-analyst uses the concept of 'symbol' simply as an heuristic device for explaining his metaphysical conceptions of the nature of personality. By splitting the total personality into three inter-penetrating aspects—*Id, Ego,* and *Super-Ego*—the analyst can represent the symbol system of dreams and of private rituals as a form of communication between one level of the personality and another, but this total system of communication remains internal to the one individual. It is metaphor, not objective reality. The fact that in a clinical situation the patient communicates not only internally with himself but also externally with the analyst is an altogether exceptional case. Nevertheless, the analyst clearly likes to believe that what goes on in his consulting room somehow mirrors what is 'really happening' in the mind of his patient, so he naturally comes to regard ritualized behaviour as compulsive and obsessional; its interest, for the analyst, lies precisely in the fact that the performer cannot explain why he acts in the way he does; the 'meaning' of the behaviour is 'unconscious'.

In sharp contrast to this position, the social anthropologist ordinarily has little interest in the individual as such; his major concern is with individuals acting as members of groups. His unit of observation is not one human being in isolation but rather a 'relationship' linking one individual to another within a wider social field.

For the anthropologist, thus orientated, ritual behaviour is essentially a form of external communication between two or more individuals; it is a species of behavioural language, and, as we have seen, it is a first essential of such a language that its unit symbols should have a common meaning both for the performer and his audience. When the traffic policeman raises his hand, it is important that we should all interpret the gesture in the same way. Symbolism, so regarded, is *public* property; its immediate source is not private psychology but a cultural rule of a legal or religious type.

Thus described, the dichotomy I have made between private and public symbolism seems simple enough, but now I must proceed to qualify. I argued earlier that whereas private symbolism 'does' things—alters the emotional state of the performer, public symbolism merely 'says' things about the state of affairs. But if we look into the matter more closely we find that public symbolism is also often considered to 'do' things, that is, alter the state of affairs. Consider, for example, two closely related head rituals.

If a sovereign wears a crown at a state function, this 'says' something, it asserts that 'this is the King'. In contrast, when at a coronation, oil is poured on the sovereign's head, this 'does' something: it 'makes him a King'. In this latter case we are dealing with what is ordinarily referred to as magic; the magical act alters the situation in a mystical rather than in a material sense. Nevertheless we are still dealing with consciously orientated public behaviour. The performers know what they are about. Can the anthropologist say more than that? Can he examine the sources of magical symbols? In this instance, for example, what is there about 'pouring oil on the head' which makes the act *appropriate* for 'making' a king? Must the anthropologist simply accept the fact that 'this is the custom', or can he legitimately pick up a clue from the psycho-analyst so as to learn *why* this kind of custom makes sense?

Enquiry into the origin of the elements of a language is a legitimate academic pursuit but it has no immediate bearing upon what the elements of the language mean. Likewise we do not have to know the origin of a piece of ritual symbolism in order to understand its present meaning.

In the kind of rituals which an anthropologist ordinarily observes, the meaning of the performance, in the eyes of the assembled congregation, is seldom in doubt. Admittedly every ritual sequence has had both historical and psychological origins, but what the anthropologist can directly observe is the social context of contemporary performance. That being so, it is surely useless to enquire just *why* one set of symbolizations is employed in preference to another? Europeans wear black for mourning, Chinese wear white. In each case the special status of the mourner is indicated by the wearing of special dress. But the question of *why* one culture selects black for this purpose and another white is surely both irrelevant and unanswerable? I agree with this argument; yet I find myself unable to disagree with the psycho-analyst who starts from an entirely different set of premises.

Let us consider, for example, a particular mourning ritual in some detail. Dr. Berg (pp. 21–22), relying on Malinowski, argues thus:

> Amongst the Trobriand Islanders the essential feature of mourning is the complete shaving of the hair of the scalp. This is of interest as being in keeping with the unconscious equation: loss of the loved person = castration = removal of hair. The death of a loved person or relative is felt by the unconscious to be a castration, and this, in the custom of the Trobriand Islanders, is dramatized by the shaving of the bereaved (castrated) person's hair.

The anthropologist perceives the situation very differently. He notes, in the first place, that all those whom the Trobrianders regard as near kinsmen of the deceased take no part in the mourning procedures whatsoever. It is only the affinal kin and unrelated neighbours who go into mourning by shaving the head, and sucking the bones of the deceased, and they do so, according to Malinowski, in order to demonstrate to the deceased's kinsmen that they have not brought about the death by means of sorcery.

It must be admitted that, with a little ingenuity, this can all be squeezed into Dr. Berg's neat pattern of castration and aggression, but such an argument is distinctly artificial. For the anthropologist, the hair shaving ritual is a form of communication which serves publicly to exhibit the distinction between the kinsmen of the deceased (who do not shave) and the kinsmen of his widow (who do). The whole interest of the prolonged mourning ceremonies is seen to converge upon the person of the widow who undergoes what amounts to a kind of social death. At the end of a prolonged period of confinement, her relationship with her deceased husband's kinsmen is deemed at an end. She returns to the world of the living, grows her hair again and is allowed to remarry. The symbolism involved is social and public, not individual and private.

Malinowski does not deny that Trobriand individuals often have deep affections, but he denies categorically that the pattern of behaviour exhibited in mourning ceremonials corresponds in any necessary way to the intensity of felt emotion. Ritual behaviour, including hair ritual, is here determined by the demands of public expectation and this leaves scarcely any room at all for the play of personal inclination. But while the anthropologist feels that he understands what Trobriand mourning ritual means as a public statement, he would hesitate to explain *why* hair shaving rather than some other type of ritual behaviour should play the part it does (Malinowski 1932, chapter VI).[1]

The two arguments seem very different. Dr. Berg maintains that Trobriand mourners shave their heads as a dramatization

[1] That Trobriand head shaving implies not merely mourning but also deprivation of sexuality is plainly indicated by the obvious emasculating significance of hair removal in the orgiastic rite of *yausa* (Malinowski 1932: 231–33).

of affection for the dead. Malinowski maintains that most of those who mourn have no affection for the dead. On the contrary he asserts that they shave their heads because they are under a social obligation to do so, and that by so doing they make a public expression of certain basic facts about the social structure of the community. Those who shave their heads are precisely that broad category of affines and non-kinsmen who are suspected of hostility towards the deceased.

And yet from another point of view the two arguments are precisely the same. Dr. Berg's thesis might be reconstrued as: 'When the mourner shaves his head he is saying symbolically "I loved the deceased".' What Malinowski says is: 'All those who are suspected of hostile intentions against the deceased are required to make a symbolic gesture which says "I loved the deceased".' As regards the central point—the meaning of the symbolic act—the psycho-analyst and the anthropologist are in complete agreement. Indeed, Dr. Berg's earlier quoted remark about 'abreacting our aggression by directing it against our aggressive hair' seems to fit the situation perfectly.

That this agreement should exist seems to me very remarkable. Nevertheless the difference in standpoint must still be stressed. Dr. Berg's argument proceeds from an apparent assumption that what is 'said' in symbolic form reflects the *actual* psychological state of the actor. Malinowski's argument, on the other hand, is that the structure of the social situation requires the actor to make formal symbolic statements of a particular kind. The fact that a statement is made does not necessarily imply that the statement is true.

SYMBOLIC DISPLACEMENT IN PUBLIC RITUAL

Unless this distinction is conceded, it cannot be maintained that the ethnographic evidence lends any support to Dr. Berg's primary interpretation. Let me elaborate this point. One of Dr. Berg's illustrations to his theme is the following:

> The struggle of the early seventeenth century between Cavaliers and Roundheads is an interesting representation of the conflict between sexual libido and super-ego. The Cavaliers, who wore their hair long, indulged in women and wine and generally expressed their libidinous impulses. The Roundheads, who cut their hair short, were

Puritans—symbolically and mentally they cut off their penis—albeit they assumed substitutive and compensatory aggression.

To an anthropologist it would seem that Dr. Berg is here confusing social stereotype with individual personality. It was surely the case that there were some sexually restrained long-haired Cavaliers, as well as some licentious short-haired Roundheads? Hair behaviour was here a symbolic assertion about what was supposed to be the case rather than about what really was the case. All that the anthropologist might admit would be that, in a religious war focused on issues of puritanical ethic, it is quite appropriate that the puritan side should symbolize its position by close-cropped hair. This does not commit the anthropologist to an acceptance of Freudian theory.

Even the most sceptical anthropologist must admit that head hair is rather frequently employed as a public symbol with an explicitly sexual significance, but many would argue that this connection between hair and sexuality is accidental. They would claim too that hair, even as a sex symbol, is used in different ways.

For example, marked changes in hairdressing very commonly accompany the changes in sexual status that occur at puberty and marriage, but the pattern of change varies. Adult-hood is sometimes marked by cutting the hair off or tying it up; but sometimes it is children who wear their hair short while adults let it grow long and hang loose about the neck. I do not know of any grounds for supposing that the latter societies are more lecherously inclined than the former. The hairdressing certainly says something about the sexual status of the individual; but it cannot define his actual behaviour. It is 'common sense' that every major change in the individual's social status requires signification; change in hairdressing is employed for this purpose simply because it is obvious and easy, not because it is specifically a 'sexual' symbol.

This 'common sense' argument does not bear very close scrutiny. It is quite true that a change in hair style is, in most societies, an easy and obvious way of indicating the otherwise rather delicate matter of a change in socio-sexual status. But this is only because the genital organs themselves have been made invisible by taboo. It is only the prudery of clothing which makes haircutting a 'more obvious' symbolic act than circumcision. The 'common sense' argument thus only serves to reinforce the hypothesis that head hair is a visible symbolic displacement of the invisible genitals.

Here let me remind the reader that we are now discussing public culturally-defined rituals and not spontaneous individual actions; we are considering the possibility that where hair is used in formal ritual it is always of 'phallic' significance. This is a general proposition, and if it were invalid one would suppose that negative instances should be easy to demonstrate. But this is not the case. When the evidence is examined really carefully taking all the minor details into account, it turns out that hair symbolism is much more consistently applied than might at first appear. The 'exceptions' mostly turn out to be 'exceptions which prove the rule'. One such case is illustrated below in my discussion of Buddhist iconography; I can only advise the persistent sceptic to pursue the matter further for himself. If Dr. Berg's argument were valid there ought to be some consistent connection in Christian ritual between the wearing of beards and the tonsure on the one hand and doctrines concerning celibacy and eunuchism on the other. The history of these matters is in fact highly complex and its analysis would require a substantial essay in itself, but when fully investigated the symbolic pattern does turn out to be self-consistent and in accordance with the theory.

Taking a wider 'world view' of the evidence I must admit that I know of a small number of cases where hair is used as a ritual symbol apparently without any libidinous significance. There is a much larger range of cases where the libidinous element is present but 'several steps removed'—for example, the complex logic which makes it indecent either for a man to wear a hat in church or for a woman not to. Even so, an astonishingly high proportion of the ethnographic evidence fits the following pattern in a quite obvious way. In ritual situations:

long hair = unrestrained sexuality; short hair or partially shaved head or tightly bound hair = restricted sexuality; close shaven head = celibacy.

The equations only apply if they relate to ideal social categories rather than empirical expectations. For example, among most of the hill tribes of Burma and Assam unmarried girls wear their hair short. In some tribes the head is shaved (Hutton 1921: 27). In contrast, married women wear their hair long. The symbolic meaning does appear to be: 'Short haired women are those whose sexuality is under restraint; long haired women are those who are expected to produce children'. But the categories are status categories not behavioural categories. Although unmarried girls are expected to avoid having children, premarital sexual intercourse is perfectly normal and to some extent institutionalized. No one would think of describing the Angami Nagas as 'puritans' either in thought or deed.

PUBLIC PHALLIC SYMBOLS AND THE 'UNCONSCIOUS'

The distinction which I am here stressing between symbolization as the statement of an idea, and symbolization as description of a fact has a bearing on the psycho-analytical use of the term *unconscious*. If I understand him correctly, it is an essential part of Dr. Berg's argument that, in civilized society, the libidinal nature of hair rituals must be unconscious, although for reasons which are not clear to me, he is prepared to grant greater insight to the unsophisticated Australian aborigines. He comments thus upon an Australian ritual described by Roheim:

> The only difference between this symptom and our modern hair ritual is that in the former the symbols used (penis and incision of penis) are, as one would expect in a primitive degree of culture, certainly not far removed from their anatomical source, indeed their phallic origin is patent, whereas in our modern practice displacement and disguise are so extreme that to the average person the disguise is effective. He will not discern (without being psycho-analysed) that in dealing with hair so remote as that of his face and head he is unconsciously dealing with a phallic substitute (Berg, p. 92).

This kind of argument involves a distinction between civilized and uncivilized societies which most anthropologists find difficult to accept or even to understand. Is it really the case that the weight of modern civilization always pushes the significance of sexual symbols deep into the 'unconscious'? And if so just where does modern civilization begin? Must we still oppose the noble (uninhibited) savage and the sex-repressed product of an 'advanced' education?

Let me make my point clear. I do not want to deny all validity to the psycho-analyst's concept of repression, but I object strongly to the kind of generalization that Dr. Berg is making in this quotation. His clinical material has provided him with evidence that *some* modern neurotic patients 'repress into the unconscious' all recognition of any association between the head of the body and the head of the phallus; from this he infers that *all* ordinary members of our society do this—unless they have the benefit of psycho-analysis, and that, by contrast, all primitive savages are free of this sickness of civilization. But just where does civilization start? Were the Elizabethans primitive savages? If not, how comes it that Sir Toby Belch discussing Sir Andrew Aguecheek's hair can raise a laugh with: 'It hangs like flax on a distaff; and I hope to see a housewife take thee between her legs and spin it off' (*Twelfth Night,* Act I, Sc. 3). For that matter I doubt whether, even in a modern audience, the laughs are confined only to those who have been through a psycho-analysis!

Dr. Berg is no doubt correct in thinking that a large proportion of the puritanically educated English middle class from which he ordinarily draws his patients would repudiate any conscious association between head hair and genitalia but he is naïve if he does not realize that among other sections of the contemporary European community such association is quite explicit and conscious.

Now this seems to me an important matter. It appears to be intrinsic to psycho-analytic theory that 'phallic symbols' derive their emotion-rousing power from the fact that their meaning is 'repressed' and 'unconscious'. Yet when we meet with the use of phallic symbolism in religious rituals and in drama the meaning is usually consciously understood by the performers and consciously conveyed to the audience.

Admittedly such symbols are taboo; they arouse in the audience a sense of awe, or of embarrassment, or of obscene laughter. But the reason for the taboo is well known; these phallic symbols are 'sacred' *because* of their sexual significance, and it is taken for granted that sexual things should be taboo. A Freudian would no doubt say that since the displaced symbol is less taboo than the original genital, the 'unconscious repression' argument still holds, but to an anthropologist that argument seems thin, to say the least.

Ethnographic evidence shows plainly enough that in ritual situations everywhere displaced phallic symbolism is very common, but the phallic origin of the symbolism is not repressed. It simply is not true that a frank and uninhibited use of sex symbolism in ritual is exclusively a characteristic of ultra-primitive (i.e. unsophisticated) societies.

Let us consider some evidence from an area which has been 'civilized' for several thousand years longer than Anglo-America, the region of South India and Ceylon. In contradiction to what might be expected from the simpler forms of Freudian theory we find there that 'explicit' and 'displaced' phallic symbols are used side by side without discrimination.

HAIR RITUALS IN SOUTH INDIA AND CEYLON

As is well known, the Saivite sects of Hinduism in South India use the *linga* and the *yoni* as their principal cult objects. These do not purport to be anything other than the direct simplified representations of the male and female genital organs. No symbolic displacement is involved, though how far the average Saivite worshipper explicitly recognises the phallicism is a moot point.[2] Alongside this direct use of phallic emblems as objects of religious worship, South Indian Brahmins make an extensive use of both the anal and the genital associations of head hair to convey symbolic ritual meanings. The following is a case in point.

> Among South Indian Brahmins the rite of *simantham*[3] is performed by the husband on his wife, usually in the eighth month of pregnancy. It is of magical significance and designed to protect the child and ensure an easy delivery. The heart of the rite consists of pouring scented oil on the head of the expectant mother and parting the hair centrally from forehead to crown by means of a porcupine quill or sanctified twig (Iyer 1928–35, vol. II: 371 ff.).

Unless the symbolism were overt (parting the hair = parting the genitals in parturition), the magical performance would be quite pointless, and magic is seldom that.

[2] Archaeological specimens of *linga* from around the 2nd century A.D. are completely lifelike representations of the human phallus. According to some authorities the modern *linga*, which is greatly simplified in form is not normally recognized as a phallus by the ordinary worshipper. A considerable element of European prudery appears to be incorporated in this view (Cf. J. N. Banerjea in K. W. Morgan 1953: 61–65).

[3] This is the classical *sīmantonnayana* and is the third of the ten *samskāra* (purification rites) which a male should undergo between his conception and his marriage. In nearly all these rites the symbolic identification between the head and the genitals is extremely obvious.

Hair ritual is very prominent in many other branches of Brahmin ceremonial. In most cases the sexual association is explicit. Different sects wear their hair in different ways but the following is broadly true of all:

> *Chudakarma,* the rite of first tonsure and shaving, is a preliminary initiation rite which takes place a year or more before the formal religious induction *Upanayana* at which the sacred thread of the twice born is first assumed. The head is completely shaved except for a small tuft. The hair that remains is combed and tended with the greatest care and elaborately knotted at the end. This tonsure is preserved throughout life. The isolated tuft of hair, like the sacred thread itself, is an essential part of the dress of the male Brahmin. This peculiar style of hairdressing is ritually enforced as part of the strongly puritanical ethic which pervades Brahmin sexual behaviour. Every aspect of sex is treated as a polluting obligation. Although every male has a moral duty to raise up legitimate male descendants the virtue of sexual continence is constantly emphasized. Ultimately the highest moral action is to renounce all contaminating associations with the secular world by becoming a celibate ascetic, *sannyasin.*[4]
>
> The *sannyasin's* freedom from social obligation and his final renunciation of the sex life is symbolized by change of dress but above all by change of hair style. According to the mode of asceticism he intends to pursue a *sannyasin* either shaves off his tuft of hair or else neglects it altogether, allowing it to grow matted and lousy (Iyer, vol. II: 383; vol. I: 332–34).

Now Dr. Berg has himself commented upon this latter variety of *sannyasin* behaviour. He remarks (p. 71):

> Fakirs simply ignore altogether the very existence of their hair (cf. the ascetic tendency to ignore the existence of the genital organs). It grows into a matted lice-inhabited mass and may almost be as much a source of unremitting torment as the neglected penis itself. Apparently it is not permitted to exist as far as consciousness is concerned.

This is a very ethno-centric argument. Dr. Berg's assumption is that the *sannyasin's* behaviour is a compulsive one, welling up from some hidden springs in the individual unconscious. And no doubt if a European ascetic were to start behaving in this way it would be indicative of some complicated neurotic compulsion.

---

[4] The contradictions of Brahmanical sex behaviour have recently been brilliantly analysed by G. M. Carstairs (1957). The author does not discuss the linkage between the inculcation of moral precepts and the regulation of dress.

But in the Indian context, the *sannyasin*'s detachment from sexual interests and the fact that the matted hair is a symbol of this detachment are both conscious elements in the same religious doctrine. The correct hair behaviour—and also the correct sexual and excretory behaviour—of Indian ascetics was all laid down in the *Nāradaparivrājaka Upanishad*[5] over 2000 years ago.

In these examples changes in permitted sexual behaviour are directly linked, through education, with changes in permitted hair behaviour. For any individual brought up in such a society it is inevitable that the one shall be 'a symbol for' the other. The psycho-analyst's concept of displacement is thus largely inappropriate.

For the Brahmin the tonsured tuft 'means' sexual restraint, the shaven head 'means' celibacy and the matted head 'means' total detachment from the sexual passions because hair behaviour and sex behaviour are consciously associated from the start.

If it is true, as Dr. Berg suggests, that there is, in each one of us, an innate unconscious tendency to associate shaving and celibacy, this may account for the origin of the Brahmin custom in the remote past. But if we ask, 'Why do modern Brahmins behave in this way?', the answer is clearly, 'Because both the hair ritual and the sex customs are simultaneously a part of contemporary Hindu culture'. The association between hair and sex is not re-established anew by each individual.

I should add perhaps that the identification 'shaven head' = 'celibacy' is not peculiar to learned monks and scholars. The same equation crops up repeatedly in the ordinary social conventions of South Indian life. The rigorous celibacy imposed on a Hindu widow is notorious; one of the prime symbols of her condition is that she shaves her head. Ritual impurity (*pole*)[6] is not a concept invented by the subtle minds of anthropologists but a matter of fundamental importance in ordinary everyday life; everyone knows that impurity attaches indiscriminately both to the genital-anal region and to the head. The most typically impure things are faeces, urine, semen, menstrual blood, spittle, and hair (Srinivas 1952: 104).[7] The first requirements of a per-

[5] Source Iyer (1928–35). I have traced no European language translation to this *Upanishad*.

[6] The same word occurs in all Dravidian languages other than Telegu.

[7] Nail parings are also polluting but much less so than hair. Nail paring is commonly carried out by barbers (Srinivas 1952: 80).

son who wishes to achieve a state of purity (*madi*) is that he
must bathe and shave and avoid sexual relations (Srinivas
1952: 101–8).

Nor is this system of symbolism confined only to the Hindus.
In Buddhist Ceylon the distinction is equally explicit. Monks and
nuns are celibate and shave the head; people who lead normal
sex lives wear their hair long. And here too the hair symbol has
anal and 'pre-genital' associations in addition to its sexual meaning; note for example the Sinhalese verbal identifications:

> *thatta*—bald: *thattama*—buttocks
> *kesa* —head hair: *kesa*   —urine

CASTRATION, CIRCUMCISION AND MAGICAL SUBSTANCE

This brings my argument to a new and important stage. Writers
on Indian caste have repeatedly made the point that the 'impurity' of the barber and of the washerman is a ritual and not a
physical matter. The 'dirt' which it is the business of these specialists to handle is regarded as having some kind of potency
which sets the handlers apart as sacred persons. As Hocart
(1950: 11) has put it, 'the barber and the washerman . . .
are not so much technicians as priests of a low grade performing
rites which the high-caste priest will not touch'. So we have a
certain paradox. Head hair, while it is a part of the body is
treated with loving care, oiled and combed and dressed in the
most elaborate fashion, but as soon as it is cut off it becomes
'dirt', and is explicitly and consciously associated with the (to
us more obviously) polluting substances, faeces, urine, semen,
and sweat. Furthermore, the potency possessed by this 'dirt' has
no particular link with the person from whom the dirt is derived.
The 'dirt' is clearly magical stuff; it endows the barber and the
washerman with dangerous aggressive power, but it is not the
power of particular individuals: the *pars pro toto* explanation of
Frazerian theory fails to apply.

Before I develop this part of this discussion let me close my
debate with Dr. Berg. Evidence such as I have cited can be ex-
panded almost indefinitely. Clearly it serves to support the thesis
that head hair is widely used as a ritual symbol with genital and
anal connotations. But it seems to be a mistake to claim, as does

Dr. Berg, that this circumstance has any immediate relevance for a discussion of the *unconscious* significance of hair. This symbolism is not unconscious, it is the exact reverse. In contrast to Dr. Berg it might plausibly be argued that it is precisely because hair behaviour embraces a *widely understood* set of conscious sexual symbolizations that it plays such an important part in rituals of a *rites de passage* types which involve the formal transfer of an individual from one social-sexual status to another.

I fully accept Dr. Berg's view that when head hair becomes the focus of ritual attention this is very commonly because the head is being used as a symbol for the phallus and head hair as a symbol for semen. But Dr. Berg's supplementary opinion that the potency of this symbolism is derived from the fact that it is 'unconscious' is in no way supported by the ethnographic evidence.

But now let me return to the consideration of head hair as magical stuff, potent in itself, even when separated from its owner. Dr. Berg alleges a symbolic association between hair-cutting and castration, but does not pursue the sociological implications of this argument. Now a rite of castration, whether real or symbolic, creates two categories of persons—eunuchs and normal men, circumcised and uncircumcised, shaven and unshorn, sacred and profane. It is this aspect of the matter that has previously seemed important to social anthropologists.

In anthropological jargon the category opposition *sacred* and *profane* is given a special meaning. Roughly speaking:

sacred = abnormal, special, other-worldly, royal, taboo, sick.
profane = normal, everyday, of this world, plebeian, permitted, healthy.

In this kind of interpretation the shaven head of the monk and the matted hair of the ascetic are both equally abnormal and therefore symbols of the sacred but neither has any specifically sexual significance. Public ritual, in this mode of analysis, is interpreted as a performance which changes the social state of the performer from sacred to profane or *vice versa* (Hubert & Mauss 1898: 41). The abstract concept of *separation* is, in this analysis, intrinsic to a great deal of ritual. When an individual is 'made sacred' he has to be separated from his former profane qualities;

when he is 'made profane' again the dangerous quality of sacredness has to be removed.

Thinking in this way, anthropologists have tended to class together the ritual cleansing of body dirt, the ritual removal of head hair, tooth extraction, blood-letting, circumcision, etc. as 'rites of separation'.

Now Dr. Berg with his psycho-analytic assumptions calls such rites 'castration'. Although the latter terminology postulates an original 'cause' for the symbolization, which the anthropologists may consider 'not proven', the psycho-analytic interpretation is broadly consistent with the ethnographic facts. Can it be said to illuminate them? Before we can give an affirmative reply we must pursue the basic theory a stage further.

There is another aspect to this sacred-profane (castrated-uncastrated) dichotomy. The act of separation (castration) not only creates two categories of persons, it also creates a third entity, the thing that is ritually separated, the 'castrated genital' itself. On the psycho-analytic interpretation this castrated thing would seem to constitute an actual material piece of aggression, which is taken from the castrated person by the castrator. We ought logically to expect therefore that symbolic items of this type, objects which, in Dr. Berg's terminology, represent the castrated genital, should be felt to contain libidinous power in themselves. They should thus be magical objects par excellence—and this indeed is the case.

A great body of evidence could be adduced to show that it is precisely those types of object which are ritually separated from the individual in 'rites of separation' which are most potent in magical situations. I do not recollect any general anthropological explanation as to why this should be so, but the notion that magical power is identical with libidinal potency is at least implicit in a good deal of anthropological analysis. Cut hair is of course prominent among such magical materials.

Once again we find that this kind of symbolism is not peculiar to any one type of society. I will cite three widely different examples.

(*a*) In Sinhalese Buddhism the two most celebrated sacred objects are the tooth relic and the hair relic which are closely associated with one another. The tooth relic is in form the broken tip of an elephant's tusk. It is known as the *dhalaya* relic;[8] the word *dhalaya* has the alternative meaning of (a) a tusk, and (b) the matted hair of a religious ascetic. Hair is here a symbol of beneficial divinity.

(b) A better known case is that of the Gorgon's head with its snaky locks. This was not only phallic, as Dr. Berg himself observes—but a thing of power in itself. Even when cut off (castrated) it was still the source of deadly emanations and became the boss of Athena's shield.[9]

(c) It is in strict analogy to this that modern Borneo headhunters, having cut off the heads of their foes, proceed to use the hair to decorate their war-shields and the scabbards of their swords. Naga headhunters likewise decorate their spears and shields with human hair. The hair is evidently a powerful thing in itself.

The power in such cases is not exclusively sexual; its qualities of sacredness and taboo are those which are inherent in the notions of divinity and ritual murder. Yet it is perhaps significant that the hair used by Naga warriors is said to be provided by their sisters. Murder and incest are alike taboo (Hutton 1921: 35, note 4; Radcliffe-Brown 1939).

Hair in such a context has become divorced from the personality of any particular individual and is a protective talisman in its own right. Although this hair is without any *conscious* phallic connotation, we may note that some societies have put explicit phallic emblems to precisely the same purpose. The ithyphallic Hermes statues of the ancient Greeks were used as boundary posts because of their power to ward off evil influences.[10] In a comparable way Indian worshippers of Siva of the Lingayat sect

---

[8] *Dhalaya-dhatu* usually abbreviated to *dhalada*. There are clearly some complex esoteric implications of this association of the Lord Buddha with an elephant. It associates the Buddha rather directly with Pillaiyar-Ganesa, 'the son' of Siva, who is explicitly a phallic elephant deity and is nearly always represented as holding in his hand the broken tip of one of his tusks.

[9] For a possible analogy from Melanesia see E. R. Leach 1954: 158.

[10] These *hermae* were rectangular stone posts with heads on the top and erect phalloi on the front. The Athenian disasters in the Sicilian Expedition were widely attributed to the fact that prudes or possibly political saboteurs had mutilated many of these posts by chiselling off both the heads and the phalloi. There is an oblique reference to this event in Aristophanes' *Lysistrata*, 1. 1995. cf. Thucydides vi, 27, 1.

wear a stone *linga* on the arm or round the neck as a talisman, and so on.

Here again there is a divergence between the psycho-analytic and the anthropological viewpoints. The psycho-analyst finds the significance of the phallic emblem in the Oedipus complex of the beholder: 'it would seem to represent the parent's genitals, which must not, under threat of direct penalties, be looked at by the offspring' (Berg, p. 33). The anthropologist on the other hand regards the symbol as a material representation of an abstract idea—the fertilizing power of God. And in saying this he agrees with his informants. Devout Hindus do not deny that the *linga* represents a phallus but they insist strongly that it connotes for them the idea of deity rather than the idea of sexuality. Are we really justified in saying that this is simply a case of 'repression'?

The psycho-analyst's thesis implies a causal nexus—sacred things are sacred *because* they are secret and taboo. The anthropologist argues the other way about: Sacred objects are taboo because they are sacred—that is because they are full of dangerous potency, including sexual potency. The hidden element, the secrecy, is not, for the anthropologist, a crucial part of the pattern. Ritual phalloi are *sometimes* treated as 'secret things' (Harrison 1912: 266) but more often they are extremely public and visible.

In the anthropologist's view, ritually powerful human hair is full of magical potency not because it is hair but because of the ritual context of its source, e.g. murder, incest, mourning etc. It is the ritual situation which makes the hair 'powerful', not the hair which makes the ritual powerful (see Appendix). The distinction may be illustrated from Buddhist iconography.

HAIR IN BUDDHIST ICONOGRAPHY

The ordinary Buddhist layman wears his hair long; the celibate Buddhist priest shaves his head; statues of the Buddha himself show an individual who in dress and posture resembles the celibate priest, but the head is covered with tight curls[11] with a flame-shaped tuft (*ushnisha*) at the back. This hair, with its pubic appearance, is certainly intended to denote the Lord Buddha's

[11] The curls are normally blue in colour. This too has 'sexual' symbolic implications but I shall not discuss this aspect here.

supreme fertilizing power, but the hair derives this significance not from its shape but from the fact that it is here incongruously placed on the head of a monk-like figure. When lay figures are shown with head hair in Buddhist iconography this does not endow them with supernatural potency.

That the curly hair of the ordinary Buddha figure not only signifies potency but has this potency from its ritual context rather than from the fact of its being the hair of the Buddha is shown by two seeming exceptions to the general rule.

In the first place, in the earliest types of Buddha figure which were made at Gandhara before the present symbolic conventions were established, the carving is 'realistic' and modelled according to Greek conventions. The head is already recognized as potent but this fact is not shown in any special treatment of the hair; instead the whole head is supported by a circular halo (Luang Boribol Buribhand and Griswold 1957: 2, 8).

The second exception is that certain rather uncommon representations of the Buddha show him in a condition before he had attained enlightenment when he was seeking (mistakenly) to achieve *nirvana* through fasting. The figure is that of an extremely emaciated man, and it has normal human hair without any halo. It is the nature of the hair which shows that this is the figure of a human being and not that of 'the Enlightened One'.

And this is the conclusion of the matter. The anthropologist and the psycho-analyst are in agreement that certain types of symbol are 'phallic emblems' in a universal rather than an accidental way. The psycho-analyst assumes that the potency of these symbols is derived from something innate in every particular individual, namely sexuality as a psycho-physical motive force. The anthropologist on the other hand assumes that public ritual symbols are given potency by society and not by individuals. For society, sexuality itself is a 'symbol' rather than a first cause; it 'stands for' the creative reproductive element in the world at large.

For the psycho-analyst sex comes first. Therefore in the Hindu context, the head represents the phallus and the *linga* represents itself. The anthropologist repudiates this cause-and-effect interpretation. God (i.e. Society) comes first, and *linga* and the head alike both represent the power of God.

SUMMARY AND CONCLUSION

Let me recapitulate the main line of my argument before pointing to a conclusion. Dr. Berg on the basis of his clinical experience concluded that human hair is very commonly employed as a phallic emblem with characteristic genital, anal, and aggressive components. He has therefore interpreted the hairdressing procedures of ordinary people as private rituals of a commissive nature having libidinal impulses as their source. He has claimed that anthropological evidence supports his contention.

It is quite true that ethnography reveals an almost world-wide distribution of hairdressing rituals. These rituals are particularly prominent in mourning ceremonies but occur also in other *rites de passage* and even in rites of a less personal nature. There is substantial though not complete consistency between the hair rituals of different cultures, and it has been a common postulate among anthropologists that human hair has some universal symbolic value. Discussions of hair symbolism were fairly prominent in the early debates concerning animism and magic. The general consensus was that *hair* stands for the *total individual* or for the *soul,* or for the individual's *personal power* (*mana*). None of the early anthropologists suggested explicitly that hair might be interpreted as a genital displacement. If, however, we grant this hypothesis of genital displacement, the evidence appears to fit in well with Dr. Berg's postulate.

Public ritual behaviour asserts something about the *social* status of the actor; private ritual behaviour asserts something about the *psychological state* of the actor. We have no grounds for assuming, as does Dr. Berg, that the actors in public rituals are in a psychological condition which corresponds to the symbolism of their performance. Yet a puzzle exists. All public symbolizations start, at some point, as private symbols; what kind of interconnection exists between the two fields? It would seem that the anthropological evidence, which concerns public symbols, can have no bearing on the question of whether or not private hair symbolism is universal. On the other hand if Dr. Berg can establish his case independently this may well have significance for the anthropologist.

The latter is interested in ritual symbolism as expressing states of the social system rather than states of the individual psyche. From this anthropological point of view, *rites de passage* (e.g. birth, initiation, marriage, death) reflect the progression of the individual through set stages in the social system; these stages correspond to different degrees of maturity, different types of permitted sexual behaviour, different allocations of social power. Hairdressing is a prominent feature of such rites. Now ethnography indicates a persistent link between hair as a symbol and the phallus as a symbol and to this extent it is appropriate that hair should be prominent in rites denoting a change in social-sexual status; but the anthropologists alone have no theory which would explain why the symbolization should take the form it does.

Dr. Berg's psycho-analytic arguments do provide such an explanation. In the body of the essay I have tried to show why these psycho-analytic arguments are anthropologically inadequate but I have also indicated that they are not actually in conflict with the ethnographic evidence. The anthropologist need not accept the psycho-analyst's view, but he has no good ground for rejecting it.

Finally I have made the point that hair, as a separable part of the body, is not only a symbol of aggression but a 'thing in itself', a material piece of aggression.

Psycho-analysts are concerned with individuals and when they discuss aggression it is the aggression of individuals that is meant. The anthropologist operating at a more corporate level encounters concepts which an analyst might label 'collective aggression', that is, aggression which is not located in any particular individual, e.g. the power of God.

In public rituals, hair may sometimes be regarded as free power (aggression) as distinct from the sexuality and faecal dirt of particular individuals. Not infrequently, in a ritual context, we find that human hair is used as 'the royalty of kings' (Frazer 1915, vol. II: 180), 'the divinity of gods' (Buddhism; cf. *supra*), 'the fertility of crops' (Frazer, vol. III: 272), 'the power of sorcerers' (Mills 1937; cf. Frazer 1918, vol. II: 485, 'the *mana* of heroic warriors', e.g. the story of Samson, *Judges* 16, v. 17).

This seems to bring the argument full circle. We are back at the position adopted by Wilken, Frazer, Hutton, and others of the older anthropologists; for they too maintained that ritual hair symbolizes some kind of metaphysical abstraction—fertility, soul-stuff, personal power.

But though we are back at the beginning again I think we are led to two rather important conclusions.

The first concerns the 'function' of phallic symbolism in a pragmatic sense. I have emphasized that *conscious* phallic symbolism both direct and displaced recurs repeatedly in religious and dramatic rituals. Why? Surely the answer is that ritual makes explicit and conscious those powerful and dangerous thoughts which are *liable to become* repressed? Libidinous energy is aggressive. *Ipso facto,* if matters of libidinous import are brought into the open in the context of everyday life, there is danger to Society. But in the context of religious ritual, where everything is formalized according to set expectations, the aggressive implications of symbolic action are under control. Phallicism in ritual is thus a form of cathartic prophylaxis; it is not an expression of the repressed unconscious of the collective individual, it is a social process which serves to prevent the individual from developing sexual repressions at all.

My second conclusion concerns a more easily recognizable anthropological theme. It seems to me that our discussion has thrown new light upon the nature of magical power.

Anthropologists have held two general types of theory concerning magic; one is sociological and the other psychological.

The sociological theory is derived from Durkheim and Mauss (Hubert & Mauss 1904; 1909) and Radcliffe-Brown (1933: 264 ff.). It lays stress on the fact that magical acts are ritual acts and not spontaneous individual creations; they are products of society handed down from generation to generation. They are acts which derive their potency from the values of society as a whole, and we can only discover what these values are by observing members of the society in ritual situations.

The psychological theory is that of Frazer; it is better known and more easily understood. Frazer concerns himself not with the context but with the 'logic' of magic. His explanations are in terms of two very crude principles of association: 'first, that like produces like; and second, that things which have once been in contact with each other continue to act at a distance after physical contact has been severed' (Frazer 1915, vol. I: 52). For Frazer the essential quality of magic is that it is fallacious, and once he has demonstrated the nature of this fallacy he is satisfied. He does not consider why human beings should be prone to fallacies of this particular kind. It may be remarked that neither of these theories has really been concerned with the nature of magical potency as such.

Freud's researches into the interpretation of dreams and the association of ideas illuminate Frazer's arguments but seem scarcely to impinge on those of Durkheim. Freudian analysis explains the form of magical acts as determined by repressed wishes of an oral, anal, or sexual type. Magical power is simply a special variety of sublimated libido.

Although Freud's approach was close to Frazer's, anthropologists have paid little attention to his arguments. One reason for this neglect is that, sociologically, the explanation seems altogether specious. If magical acts are the outcome of repressed wishes, whose repressed wishes are involved? Customs, including magical customs, are taught; they are publicly acknowledged facts. That being so, what can be the relevance of talk about the repressed wishes of individuals? The magician does what society expects him to do; his own private desires provide no explanation of his actions.

While I agree that the Freudian argument is not immediately relevant to the anthropologist's problem, one implication of this paper is that the irrelevant can still illuminate!

I have been concerned throughout with the opposition between private individual (i.e. psychological) uses of symbolism and public (i.e. sociological) uses of identical symbolism. In the cases examined both the psychological and the sociological analyses lead to closely similar interpretations of the 'meaning' of particular symbols. Yet I still insist that the two arguments are *not* relevant to one another. Where it so happens that the conclusions are the same, they do not in fact support each other; where they differ they do not contradict. They are separate aspects which illuminate quite different aspects of a single general problem. Each type of analysis can give only a partial answer; each is 'correct', but only when considered within its own frame of reference.

The same argument might be put in different form. The psychoanalyst, being concerned with the inner feelings of the individual, categorizes all actions which cut away a part of the individual's body as symbolic equivalents of 'castration'. He then argues that these ritual acts have emotional force for the individual because they are in fact felt to be a repression of libidinous energy.

In contrast, the social anthropologist is concerned with the publicly acknowledged status of social persons and he notices that ritual acts in which part of the individual's body is cut off are prominent in *rites de passage,* that is to say 'rites of separation' in which the individual publicly moves from one social position to another. He might very well label all such rites 'circumcision'.

The social anthropologist's explanation of why rites of 'circumcision', so defined, should be emotionally charged comes from Durkheim. The ritual situation converts the symbol into a 'collective representation' of God and of Society. It is in the nature of rites that 'out of the commonest object, they can make the most powerful sacred being' (Durkheim 1947: 226–28).

These two arguments, the psycho-analytic and the Durkheimian, appear to be sharply contrasted, yet they are not contradictory. We can accept them both simultaneously together with a third argument, borrowed from Frazer, to the effect that magical power typically resides in objects which are detached from individuals in ritual situations—e.g. the blood, hair, nail parings, etc. of persons involved in *rites de passage.* We cannot simply merge these three arguments, but if we recognize that they all relate to 'the same thing', then we are led to conclude that magical potency, regarded as a social category, is something which inheres in 'circumcision' symbols, but that such symbolization is effective because for each individual the ritual situation is felt to signify 'castration'.

This is something more than a play on words. In merging the sociological concept of circumcision with the psycho-analyst's concept of castration we establish a bridge between the two frames of reference, and the consistency between the two modes of interpretation becomes significant. At this point, though perhaps only at this point, the psycho-analytic argument provides the anthropologist with a plausible explanation for facts which he knew already but could not fully understand.

In certain respects I must admit that the whole argument is a mere rephrasing of the obvious. Everyone takes it for granted that verbal expletives in almost any language derive their magical potency from association either with sexual and excretory function or with God. The theory propounded in this essay is that the magical power of 'body dirt' (including head hair) is of precisely the same kind. This proposition is not very novel, but the real focus of this essay is elsewhere. The question I have asked myself is: How can anthropologists justify the symbolic interpretations which they habitually make? I have not answered that question but perhaps I have illuminated some of the issues.

APPENDIX

Dr. Michael Banks has drawn my attention to the following item which appeared in the newspaper *The Hindu* on 8 January 1957. It illustrates in striking fashion a number of the themes discussed in the above paper. In particular it will be noted that the magical potency of the votive hair is not derived from the fact that it is hair or even that it is the hair of a pilgrim votary but from the ritual circumstances in which it is cut off by properly appointed temple barbers (*mirasidars*) and then offered to the God. Though the nature of the pilgrim's vows is unstated, these are likely to be concerned with sexual abstinence.

'Mr. M. Ramamurthi, Additional District Judge, Chittoor, dismissing the appeal petition filed by Mr. Kolathur Pedda Venkata Reddi and four others against the Board of Trustees of the Tirumalai-Tirupati Devasthanams on the temporary injunction passed by the District Musif, Tirupati, in favour of the latter preventing the former from shaving heads of the pilgrim-votaries who wish to offer their hair to Sri Venkateswaraswami in discharge of their vows passed the following orders.

'The Judge observed that it was not proper to decide questions of law at this stage and said that the plaintiffs (T.T.D. Board and others) did not want to prevent the appellants from carrying out their trade. There was no objection to the appellants running their shaving saloons on Tirumalai Hills and carrying on the profession of hair-cutting and hairdressing of any one who visited their saloons. There did not seem to be any objection to the appellants shaving the heads of their customers but the only thing which they were not entitled to do, according to the plaintiffs, was to shave the heads of pilgrim-votaries who wished to give their hair to the deity as offering. Therefore what the plaintiffs wanted was not an exclusive right to carry on the profession of a barber. So all that the plaintiffs wanted was, an injunction restraining the defendants from inducing the pilgrims to believe that they were offering their hair on their heads to the deity when they got their heads shaved by the appellants and other defendants.

'The Judge added that the importance of this right claimed by the plaintiffs could be appreciated when it was remembered that the Devasthanams had a share in the fees collected by the mirasidars for shaving the heads of pilgrim-votaries and the entire hair which was removed from the heads of the pilgrim-votaries was given by the mirasidar to the temple authorities. Every hair which was offered would have to be preserved and the proceeds realised by their sale would have to go to the deity. Therefore unless the hair shaved from the heads of the pilgrim-votaries found its way to the temple authorities it could not be said that the offering was made to the deity. The pilgrim-votary who allowed his hair to be shaved by a non-mirasi could not be sure of the hair being given to the temple authorities. It was true that the appellants said that they would give the hair collected by them to the temple authorities but there could be no check over it. Therefore it appeared to him that the plaintiffs had a *prima facie* case that the mirasidars were entitled exclusively to shave the heads of the pilgrim-votaries who wished to offer the hair on their heads to the deity in discharge of their vows and the temple was entitled to control shaving of the heads of pilgrim-votaries and collect the hair which was endowed to the deity.

'After dealing with the various points raised by the advocates of both sides the Judge stated that it appeared to him that the balance of convenience was in favour of issuing the injunction, and so he dismissed the appeal petition with costs.'

NOTE

The author is indebted to a personal grant-in-aid from the Behavioral Sciences Division of the Ford Foundation for facilities in the preparation of this article. Comments from various sources on draft versions of the essay are gratefully acknowledged, but particularly those from Dr. Charles Berg, M.D. (Dr. Berg died in December 1957 while this essay was being prepared for publication).

7 THE NUER CONCEPT OF SPIRIT IN ITS RELATION TO THE SOCIAL ORDER

I HAVE PUBLISHED recently a series of papers dealing with various aspects of the Nuer conception of *kwoth*, spirit. The purpose of this paper is to relate the conception to the social order, of which I have given some account in two volumes on the Nuer.

In the series of papers to which I have referred I discussed separately the various spirits of which the Nuer speak. Some of them are said to be spirits of the above: *Kwoth a nhial*, Spirit who is in the sky, whom I speak of also as God (1), *kuth dwanga*, the spirits of the air (2), and *col wic*, spirits which are the metamorphosed souls of those killed by lightning (3). The rest are said to be spirits of the below: totemic spirits (4), nature sprites (*bieli*), and fetishes (*kulangni*) (5). Each and all may, however, be referred to simply as *kwoth*, spirit.

It is evident that Nuer distinguish between their different spirits. They place them in the categories and sub-categories I have mentioned above. Some of them have proper names and other distinguishing attributes and associations. They are differentiated in genealogical and spatial representations. Nuer sacrifice to one or other particular spirit according to the circumstances. Many of the spirits are regarded as of foreign origin, the places of their origin and the times of their having been taken over by the Nuer being known. It is clear, therefore, that we are dealing with a number of different conceptions. On the other hand, it is equally clear that we are dealing with a single conception, for all the spirits are, as *kwoth*, beings of the same nature or essence. This

Reprinted from *The American Anthropologist* 55 (2), 1953: 201–14, by permission of the author and the American Anthropological Association.

problem of unity in diversity confronts not only the student of
Nuer religion but also students of many other primitive religions,
and also those of Ancient Egypt, the early Semites, Ancient
China, and the Greeks and Latins.

The great variety of meanings attached to the word *kwoth* in
different contexts and the manner in which Nuer pass, even in the
same ceremony, from one to another may bewilder us. The Nuer
themselves are not confused because the conceptual difficulties
which perplex us do not arise on the level of experience but only
when an attempt is made to analyse and systematise Nuer religious thought. The Nuer themselves do not feel the need to do
this. Indeed, I myself never experienced when living with the
Nuer and thinking in their words and categories any difficulty
commensurate with that which confronts me as I write this paper.
I do not think that the problem occurred to me then as it does
now. I moved from representation to representation, and backwards and forwards between the general and the particular much
as I suppose the Nuer do and without feeling that there was any
lack of coordination in my thoughts or that any special effort to
understand was required. It is only now that I feel confused, when
I have to translate Nuer notions into the English language and to
relate them to each other in it so that as a whole they will not only
make sense to English people but also have, as far as that is
possible, the sense they have for Nuer. This can only be done by
abstract analysis, and it is precisely when one begins to try to
make such an analysis that the difficulties arise.

It would be useless to embark on a discussion of the relation
of the conception of *kwoth* to the social structure without first
making it clear that Nuer use the word in more, and less, inclusive
senses to refer to Spirit and to a, or the, spirit, that is, either in a
general and comprehensive sense or with reference to a particular
spirit (as distinct from other spirits). When Nuer speak in the
first and undifferentiating sense they have in mind Spirit in its
oneness, in the unity of all its diverse figures, and when the word
has this general sense it can appropriately be translated "God."
When Nuer pray to, or speak of, God, though often looking to
the sky as they do so, they usually address him simply by this
general title of *Kwoth,* spirit, without the attributive "who is in
the sky." They may, however, speak more specifically of "Spirit
who is in the sky" or "our father" or "the creator of the universe,"

stressing one or other of the divine attributes, just as we may speak sometimes of "God," sometimes as "our father who art in heaven," "the creator," and so on. *Kwoth* used in a general sense and *Kwoth a nhial* are therefore interchangeable expressions denoting the same conception. On the other hand, the word *kwoth* may be used for a particular spiritual being such as an air-spirit, a totemic spirit, and so forth, without the particular spirit being indicated by name, it being understood in the context that this particular spirit is referred to. Thus they may say, for example when speaking of the lion-spirit in reference to a certain lineage "*e kwothdien,*" "it is their spirit." They also speak of a *gwan kwoth,* the owner of a spirit, and of a *yang kwoth,* a cow dedicated to a spirit, without specifying which spirit they have in mind. Those who know the circumstances will know which particular spirit is being referred to.

There is seldom difficulty, when Nuer is being spoken, in determining in which sense, the general or the particular, Nuer are using the word *kwoth* but confusion would arise were I to use in this account the Nuer word *kwoth* or the English word "spirit" without diacritical indications to cover both senses; and to maintain the distinction made by the Nuer I have used either "God" or "Spirit," whichever seemed to be the most appropriate expression in the context, in the first case and "a spirit," "the spirit," "spirits," or, more specifically, "spirits of the air," "totemic spirits," *etc.* in the second case. It will also assist us if we think of the particular spirits as figures or representations or refractions of God, or Spirit, in relation to particular activities, events, persons, and groups, for I hope to show that this is what they are among the Nuer.

The difficulty in discussing Nuer religion is that since God is *Kwoth* and each of the refractions of him is a *kwoth,* the Nuer when speaking of one of the refractions are also speaking of God, of God regarded in a particular way. When therefore they say of a spirit that "it is his spirit" or "it is their spirit" they are saying that it is God figured in relationship to a particular person or to a particular social group. In other words Spirit and a spirit are not mutually exclusive conceptions. It may help us to understand this point better if we think of Spirit as the Nuer do, as being "like the air," for, so to speak, air and *an* air are not exclusive conceptions. Thus, while we can say of any particular spirit that it is God we cannot say that God is any particular spirit, for he is all Spirit and the oneness of Spirit.

That the diverse spiritual figures of Nuer thought are to be regarded as social refractions of God will be understood better if some examples are given of the problem in action. I therefore describe, briefly and only in so far as the events directly concern the matter under discussion, what happened at a Nuer ceremony. I must preface this with an explanation. Nuer recognize three main types of responsibility for homicide: *thung,* a plain killing, often referred to as *thung muot,* homicide by the spear, because a spear is the weapon most likely to have been used; *nin diet,* a delayed killing; and *thung yika,* the death of a wife in her first childbirth, which is the responsibility of her husband. The ceremony I am about to describe concerned the second kind of homicide. When a man has been wounded and recovers but dies some months, or even years, later his death may be attributed to the wound he received and compensation for homicide exacted. A blood-feud is unlikely to break out in these circumstances, for the killing may generally be regarded as accidental and, in any case, a long period of time has elapsed between the act and its consequence; and fewer, some twenty, head of cattle are demanded than for a straight killing, though the number seems to vary in different parts of Nuerland and is probably everywhere reached by negotiation between the parties, both of whom are generally anxious to reach a settlement as soon as possible. In the ceremony I witnessed, which took place in western Nuerland, the first and final rites of an ordinary homicide were combined, the slayer being cleansed of the blood and peace between the parties being made at the same time, and it took place after only some of the cattle had been paid.

It was held because a man of the Jikul clan had wounded a man of the Lual lineage with a fishing spear some years before, and he had just died. The fact that he had been wounded by a fishing spear was important because among the western Nuer less compensation is paid for a killing by fishing spear or club than for a killing by fighting spear, for it is less likely to have been premeditated. Apart from the slayer himself, there were no Jikul present at the ceremony, which on their side was conducted by their traditional allies the Ngwol lineage and in an Ngwol village. The absence of Jikul and the holding of the ceremony in a village of a third party made it easier for the Lual to be conciliatory. After some drinking of beer, a sure sign that a settlement was certain, the people sat in the sun to watch proceedings. The heat was so intense that from time to time boys were told to place fresh cattle dung on the ground so that those delivering addresses could stand in it now and again to cool their feet. One of them interrupted his narration to ask *Kwoth* to send a shower of rain to cool him, and the downpour which put an end to the proceedings was regarded as an answer to his request. The ceremony began with the castration of the young bull to be sacrificed. An Ngwol man then drove a stake into the centre of the kraal and tethered the ox to it, and many of the men present threw ashes over its back—an act of dedication. Then lengthy invocations, taking over three hours to deliver, were spoken by a Lual man, an Ngwol man, and a leopard-skin priest of the Keunyang lineage, the dominant lineage of the area in which all these lineages have their villages. I give only the gist of what they said because most of it little concerns the question which we are considering.

Each speaker began his address by calling out his clan spearname. He delivered his address walking up and down the kraal brandishing his spear. Most of what was said was addressed to the audience, who entered into lengthy arguments with the speakers about the matter in hand, besides carrying on conversation among themselves. But in the midst of their harangues the speakers frequently addressed *Kwoth* by one or other title and explained to Spirit so addressed the circumstances which had brought the people together.

The Lual representative, who made the first speech, besides addressing *Kwoth*, Spirit, and *Kwoth a nhial*, Spirit who is in the sky, called on "*kwoth wecda, kwoth ngopna,*" "spirit of our home or community (literally, cattle-camp), spirit of our fig-tree," the fig-tree being the totem of his lineage. He began with a long account of the history of the lineage of the man responsible for the death with interminable references to past disputes, threatening that if ever the Jikul or the Ngwol fought his people again the Lual would exterminate them, to all the events which led up to the quarrel in which the dead man had been wounded, and to cattle which had been paid or promised in compensation for the homicide and the further cattle which were being demanded. Among his observations he accused the Ngwol of having buried a living ox with some beads and a spear to kill the Lual by magic, and this provoked a violent argument in which the Ngwol part of the audience retorted that the Lual had buried a dog alive in a byre to kill them (I do not know whether such practices ever really occur).

The Ngwol representative then delivered a rambling address. He often mentioned *Kwoth* in it, though not, so far as I heard, with any particular specifications. His chief point was that the Jikul were paying compensation in cattle for the dead man and that if the Lual reopened the quarrel it would be to their disadvantage, the Jikul being fully able to look after themselves if it came to fighting again. He then, from the Jikul angle, repeated the whole history of the affair, a recapitulation which stirred up involved controversy with the Lual men present. In these invocations grievances, both real and imagined, are made public because it is the rule of such gatherings that everything a man has in his heart against others must be revealed and no bitterness kept secret, and not with the purpose of complicating the issue or inflaming passions.

Finally, the leopard-skin priest, whose function is to cleanse a killer and to perform rites to prevent or terminate a blood-feud, rose and addressed the assembly. In his invocation he frequently, in addition to speaking to *Kwoth* and *Kwoth a nhial*, called on *"kwoth ringda,"* a phrase which literally means "spirit of our flesh" and which refers to the spiritual source of sacerdotal power. He told the slayer that as some of the cattle had already been paid and the remainder were about to be paid he might go abroad without fear of vengeance. He told the kinsmen of the dead man that if they started a feud their spears would miss their mark and that they would do well to take the cattle and settle the affair forever. He warned the kinsmen of the slayer not to try and hide their cattle, that is, send them secretly to the kraals of distant kinsmen and then say that they had not the wherewithal to meet their obligations. He, also, recapitulated the whole history of the quarrel, from the point of view of an impartial onlooker and arbitrator.

At the end of his address he speared the ox and those present rushed in, as is the custom on this occasion, to obtain what they could of the carcase, hacking and slicing, waving their spears, and shouting. It was a scene of great confusion. When things had quietened down the leopard-skin priest cut off some of the hair of the head of the man who had occasioned the death: "the blood which entered into his body is purged (*riem me ce wa pwonyde ba woc*), other hairs will grow (*bi miem ti okien dony*), the blood is finished (*ce riem thuk*)."

The ceremony I have described is typical in form of Nuer religious ceremonies. What I want here to draw attention to in it are the different titles mentioned in the invocations: *Kwoth*, Spirit, without further designation, *Kwoth a nhial*, Spirit who is in the sky, *kwoth wec(da)*, spirit of the home, *kwoth ngop(na)*, spirit of the fig-tree, and *kwoth ring(da)*, spirit of the flesh (the virtue of the leopard-skin priests); and there may have been others which I did not hear. Besides these titles such expressions as *gwandong*, grandfather, and *kwoth gwara,* spirit of our fathers, were used. At other ceremonies at which people of different families and lineages to those concerned in this particular ceremony have been represented I have heard references in invocations to a variety of other spirits—totemic spirits, *col wic* spirits, and spirits of the air. How are we to interpret Nuer thought about the nature of spirit as it is expressed in such ceremonies as the one I have described?

In this particular ceremony several groups were opposed to each other, and the leopard-skin priest was acting in his priestly capacity as mediator between them and to conclude a settlement by sacrifice. Each of the persons who made the invocations therefore appealed to God not only as God but also as God in his special relation to the groups they represented, and in the case of the leopard-skin priest to God in his special relation to the priestly function as well as to a particular priestly lineage. It is perhaps a poor analogy, but the circumstances may be compared to a war between European powers in which each side prays for victory to the God of its fathers, Lord of its battle line. Those engaged in the struggle do not believe that two distinct deities are being appealed to. That this is the correct interpretation is shown by a number of observations, one of the most significant being the fact that in situations in which no sectional interests are at stake but where men approach their God simply as men and in the context of their common humanity, as, for example, when furious storms are raging, in times of severe drought and famine, or when a man is seriously ill then God alone, or in certain circumstances one of his hypostases by which he is figured in relation to some particular natural phenomenon, is addressed and he is not, as it were, divided by a variety of titles along the lines of the social structure. This may also be to a large extent the case even where different social groups are involved, so long as they are not antagonistic, but have a common interest and intention. I give one such illustration.

A youth in a village where I was residing was badly wounded in the shoulder by a spear in a fight with a man of the next village. His antagonist had not intended to kill him and the people of the two villages were on good terms, so his kinsmen at once sent the spear with which the wound had been inflicted to the injured youth's home with expressions of regret and wishes for a speedy recovery. The elders of the wounded lad's home bent the point of the spear and placed it point downwards in a pot of cold water. This was done to lessen the pain of the wound, especially when it was washed, and to cool the inflammation. Next morning the wounder's village sent us a deputation, leading a goat for sacrifice. By this further indication of their regrets and of their willingness to pay compensation at once should the lad die, they anticipated a blood-feud. It was hoped in any case that the danger of death would be obviated by the sacrifice of the goat. The wound would, as the Nuer put it, "be finished with the goat."

Before the animal was sacrificed the visitors dedicated it by rubbing ashes on its back. It was then tied to a stake opposite the hut of the wounded youth's maternal grandmother and an invocation was delivered over it by a man called Lel, a leopard-skin priest and a prophet, who had been summoned from a distance to officiate, partly, I think, because his presence would give greater importance, and therefore perhaps efficacy, to the ceremony and partly because it would be a further insurance for a peaceful outcome to the incident. His address was largely taken up with reiterations that the youth would not die and with giving to God and the people a lengthy and detailed account of how the accident had occurred. He sacrificed the goat at the conclusion of his speech. Our home party then brought forward a wether and it was also dedicated with ashes. Afterwards a man of the home poured a libation of water over its tethering peg as a prelude to delivering an oration. He told the story of the accident all over again and commented on it to God in this vein: "Ah God! We call on you about this wound. There is no enmity between us (the party of the injured youth and the party of the spearer). This wound came of itself (they do not attribute it to the spearer because it was an accident and also because the youth will not die and so there will be no *thung*, debt of homicide). Throw the badness away with this ox (they call a sheep or goat "ox" or "cow" in ritual contexts). Let the wound heal. Ah, God, it is only a headache (it is not a sickness of any importance—they speak of the most ghastly wounds in this way), let it be finished, let it go right on (heal without complications). Let it be removed from the man's body. Let us be at peace." Another man of the home party also made an invocation in much the same language: "Friend (*maath*), God who is in this village, as you are very great we tell you about this wound, for you are God of our home in very truth. We tell you about the fight of this lad. Let the wound heal. Let it be ransomed (with the sheep);" and so forth. A representative of the visitors now said a few words to the same purpose and the sheep was then sacrificed. The meat of both sacrifices was eaten by the people of the home after the visiting deputation had departed; and also the carcase of a third animal, another wether which the people of the home later sacrificed after three of them had made further invocations over it in much the same vein.

In this ceremony Spirit was addressed simply as Spirit and no designated refractions were mentioned, and when on such occasions Nuer speak to, or about, Spirit without differentiating specifications they are, as I have explained, speaking to, or about, Spirit in the comprehensive conception of God the creator and the sustainer of life. This is often the case in their sacrifices, and it is the same when they pray for peace and deliverance from evil.

That emphasis is given to the refractions when a social group, acting as such and marking itself off from other groups, makes a sacrifice on behalf of itself or of one of its members in virtue of his membership of it, and that they are then to be regarded as diverse exclusive representations of God by which he is figured to the groups concerned in a special way as their patrons is evident also from other considerations. It is clear that totemic spirits of lineages are Spirit conceived of in a tutelary relationship to the lineages. The *col wic* spirits are also Spirit in a tutelary relationship to the families and lineages to which they belonged in the flesh before they were metamorphosed into spirit. Also, the spirits of the air may have a tutelary relationship to families and lines of descent, and where their attachment is more to an individual prophet he has public functions through which the spirit becomes patron of local and political communities. Totemic spirits may also, though in a rather different manner, have a secondary significance for political groups through the association of dominant lineages with tribal sections. Likewise, though to a lesser extent, nature-sprites are Spirit in a tutelary relationship to families, and even fetishes, though of a rather different complexion, are Spirit in a tutelary relationship to individuals, and sometimes to local communities to which these individuals belong. The attachment of all these spiritual figures to social groups is indicated in various ways, most noticeably in ceremonial and in payment of cattle to them at marriages.

That these spiritual conceptions lack autonomy and are rightly regarded as social refractions of God is further shown by the fact that *Kwoth,* without specific differentiation of title, can become associated with any social group or office. Thus, as we have seen, Nuer speak of the *kwoth* of a leopard-skin priest, "the spirit of the flesh." This is no particular or individual *kwoth* but is Spirit seen in relation to priestly powers and functions. An even better example is the way in which they speak of the *kwoth* of an age-set, the tutelary, nameless, spirit which protects the members of the set and avenges wrongs done to men by their age-mates. This cannot be a distinctive spirit, a spirit in its own right as it were, if only because the sets pass in turn into oblivion and are replaced by others. It is rather God thought of in relation to a particular set, just as he is also the separate, while still being the same, guardian spirit of the other sets. A parallel in our own civilization would be the way in which Madonnas of the quarters of a town are thought of by their votaries. Just as they are separate Madonnas in relation to each other and yet the same Madonna, all being pictures of the same exemplar, so the *kuth* of the Nuer age-sets are separate spiritual conceptions in relation to each other and yet all figures of the same Spirit. God is both the one and the many—one in his nature and many in his diverse social representations.

Moreover, though God is God of all men he is not only conceived of, in the various totemic and other representations we
have considered, as the special patron of descent, and sometimes
local, groups, but each family regard him, without specific differentiation of title, as having a particular relation to themselves
as a family group; and he may be spoken about in terms of a
particular household, hamlet, or village community. One hears
Nuer say in invocations, as in the one I have just recorded, "God
who is in this village," or "God who is in this home." When a
Nuer builds a byre he holds a small ceremony before the roof is
built. Beer is prepared, and before the people drink it the master
of ceremonies of the owner of the byre pours a libation of it to
God at the entrance to the byre and in the centre of it, where
the hearth and shrine will be, and asks God to give peace and
prosperity to the home, its people, and its cattle. They think
then of God looking after their home in a special way, of being
particularly attached to it so that he then becomes, as it were,
in a special sense the family's God, a household God, as well as
the God. The shrine, a forked post, is the altar of God within
the home, God of the hearth, as well as being associated with any
of his particular representations—totemic, *col wic,* air spirits, *etc.*
—in which he may stand in a tutelary relationship to the lineage
or family of the owner of the homestead, and also with the ancestral ghosts. He is spoken of in this domestic representation as
Kwoth rieka, God of the post (shrine). Further, every member of
a Nuer lineage, whether or not it has totemic or other specifically
designated spirits, will in invocations speak of *"kwoth gwara,"*
"spirit of our fathers" or in reference to the name of the ancestor
of the lineage or clan, just as the Old Testament speaks of "the
God of our fathers" or "the God of Abraham, Isaac, and Jacob."
Similarly one hears leopard-skin priests address God as *"kwoth
Geaka,"* "spirit of Gee." Gee was the first leopard-skin priest
from whom all the priests derive their powers so that the expression refers to God figured as patron of priests; though it also
has a wider, national, sense, for Gee was also the ancestor of the
most important Nuer clans.

The ambiguities which seem at first to be so puzzling a feature
of Nuer religion are, at least to some extent, resolved by considering in this way their religious ideas in relation to their social
order, for in all societies religious thought bears the impress of

the social order. Given the segmentary political and lineage structure of the Nuer it is understandable that the same complementary tendencies towards fission and fusion and the same relativity that we find in the structure are found also in the action of spirit in the social life. Just as, for example, two lineages are distinct and opposed groups in relation to one another at one level of segmentation and are a single unit at a higher level of segmentation, so spirit as conceived in relation to these segments must be divided at the lower level and undivided at the higher level. It is intelligible, therefore, that in its relation to the segmentary social order the conception of Spirit is broken up into diverse refractions, while in relation to nature and man in general the many become again the one. It is intelligible, however, only because we recognize here a logical consistency, and not because there is a necessary interdependence. There are segmentary societies in which there is no such correspondence, because they have a different kind of religion.

In the light of what has been said above it is not surprising that any number of new spirits may come into existence without disconcerting the Nuer, either being borrowed from neighbouring peoples or, in the case of certain totemic-like spirits, being derived from some unusual experience. We have good reason to believe that the spirits of the air, the fetishes, and, at any rate for the most part, the totemic spirits have recently been introduced into Nuerland, and probably the same is true for the nature sprites. I think it can be assumed—I do not see how it can have been otherwise—that there have always been different representations of *Kwoth* among the Nuer, and if this is so the old, or traditional, religion must have consisted, as far as the notion of spirit is concerned, of the conception of God and of his social refractions, the only specifically differentiated category of which were the *col wic* tutelary spirits of lineages. How then do we account for the borrowings?

They may be partly fortuitous but I would suggest that they may also in part derive from the logic of the conception of *Kwoth* in relation to recent Nuer history. During the last hundred years the Nuer have absorbed a great number of Dinka and have also been brought into closer contact, directly or indirectly, with other peoples of the southern Sudan and also with Arabs and ourselves. This provided opportunities for borrowing foreign ideas. But it may be suggested that not only was the opportunity there, but also the need. Nuer statements lead us to suppose that certain social developments were taking place at the same time. They say that the clans and lineages were being broken up by expansion, and were incorporating into their stocks Dinka lines of descent, besides assimilating politically Dinka communities,—hence the Dinka totems in Nuerland today; that prophets emerged who directed large-scale raids on the Dinka and defence against the "Turks" (the Arabs and the British)—hence the Dinka and other foreign spirits of the air; and that the peace and administration imposed on them by the government of the Anglo-Egyptian Sudan have given protection to those who wish to pursue private gain and vengeance—hence the introduction of fetishes and their spread. Ethnological evidences support what they say, and we can add that it is in accord with the logic of the Nuer conception of spirit that it should be represented by figures corresponding to these new social phenomena.

God may be thus figured in numberless ways in reference to social groups and to persons, and in relation to effects which are significant for them; and in none of them has the figure any sharply defined individuality. This is fairly easy to understand when we are dealing with refractions which are referred to simply as *kwoth* and without distinguishing title, but it may fairly be asked whether those spirits which are named can correctly be described as refractions and are not rather to be regarded as quite independent conceptions. We must distinguish here between class names and individual names. The reason why the Nuer divide the spirits into kinds, spirits of the above, spirits of the below, *col wic* spirits, *bieli,* and so forth, is that they regard them as different sorts of manifestation of Spirit and of varying degrees of importance. This is a matter I discuss later. It is rather the individual names with which we are immediately concerned.

The reason why some of the refractions have distinguishing names is, I think, mainly a matter of ownership. Spirits are sometimes owned by persons, such a person being called a *gwan kwoth,* owner of a spirit. It is unnecessary in this place to say more than that the spirit is something which he has got which others have not got and which gives him certain powers they lack. Now, no one in this sense owns God, but all the various spirits may be owned by persons and, without going into details, it may be said that the most distinctive naming of them is where individual ownership is most marked, in the cases of the spirits of the air and the fetish spirits, which have proper names and ox-names. A prophet who is inspired by Spirit has in the logic of the situation to give it a name which distinguishes it as his particular spirit from the spirits of other prophets who are his rivals for renown and influence, for the attachment here is to individuals who build up through it a personal following, and not, at least primarily, to social groups. When a spirit falls from above and enters into a man who becomes its prophet it attains its distinction by revealing through the prophet what it is called—its name; and when a person becomes possessed for the first time the immediate endeavour of his neighbours is to get the spirit to reveal its name when he is in a dissociated state. The spirit gets its name, that is, by its being owned by the person it possesses and to whom, by possessing him, it brings power and prestige. Fetishes are also owned by individuals who compete, though in a different way to prophets, for prestige and power one against another; so each fetish must have a distinguishing name. Moreover, when sickness is caused by a spirit of the air or a fetish taking temporary possession of a man, who then has this spirit, however unwillingly and transiently, it is necessary to discover its name by getting the spirit to reveal it through the lips of the sick man or of a medium, for until it is known it is likewise not known for certain what is the cause of the sickness or what steps should be taken to allay it. Thus it is through the name that ownership is established. The individuality is, in a sense, that of the person and not that of the spirit, the spirit getting its name through him.

The conclusion we have reached is that the conception of *Kwoth* has a structural dimension. At one end Spirit is thought of in relation to man and the world in general, as omnipresent God. Then it is thought of in relation to a variety of social groups and activities and to persons: to political movements connected with prophets, and in a special relation to warfare, as spirits of the air; to descent groups as *col wic* and totemic spirits; and to a variety of ritual specialists as totemic and totemic-like spirits. At the other end it is conceived of more or less in relation to individuals in a private capacity as nature sprites and fetishes. God figured as the common father and the creator is patron of all men; figured in spirits of the air he is patron of political leaders; figured in *col wic* and totemic spirits he is patron of lineages and families; and figured in nature sprites and fetishes he is patron of individuals. I give only a general indication of the main lines of social demarcation between the various types of refractions and I do not discuss exceptions and overlappings.

This impress of the social structure on Nuer religious thought is to be marked also in the natural and moral attributes of the different types of spiritual refractions. Mighty celestial phenomena and great and terrible happenings, such as plagues and famines, and the moral order which concern all men are attributed to God, while processes and events which do not have so general a range of impact tend to be attributed to whichever particular refraction or type of refraction the situation and context evoke. Likewise the refractions tend to decrease in the degree of universality, stability, and morality attributed to them the smaller the social space to which they refer. I can here give only a brief indication of this tendency, illustrated by a few examples.

God is everywhere; he is permanent and changeless in his relation to the constant elements in the natural and moral orders; he is one, and he is all-powerful, just, and compassionate. The spirits of the air are in particular persons and places, and even when their prophets are politically important persons they have a limited spread of influence; they have fallen from the clouds in recent times and their renown depends on the personal prestige of their prophets and on political circumstances, both of which are unstable factors and may be ephemeral; they are multiple, though compared with lesser spirits they are few in number; and they are unpredictable, and even capricious and ill-intentioned. The *col wic* and totemic spirits are restricted to certain lineages and families; they become tutelary spirits of these groups at certain points of time and many are sooner or later forgotten; they are numerous; and compared to the spirits of the air they are unimportant. The nature sprites and fetishes are for the most part acknowledged only by the persons who own them and their immediate kin. The fetishes certainly, and the nature sprites probably, are very recent introductions, and they enter into relationships with persons and families and are soon forgotten by their descendants. The sprites flit here and there, come into homes, and then return to the bush. The fetishes are bought and sold and pass from hand to hand, and according to the prestige of their owners their reputations wax and wane, they lose ground and are replaced by others. Both alike are potentially inexhaustible in number. Though some fetishes are feared, neither they nor the sprites are highly regarded and the fetishes are in general disapproved of. On the other hand, the lower down the scale of spirit we descend the more prominent do cultic features appear. God is approached in simple prayer and sacrifice. The spirits of the air receive more elaborate ceremonial attentions, into which enter hymns, possession, and divination. Cultic features are also prominent at the level of the *col wic* and totemic spirits. The most regular ritual attention appears to be given to the fetishes, which receive frequent offerings from their owners and in the most material form.

In relating the configuration of Nuer religious thought to the structural order of their society I am, of course, relating abstractions to one another by a method of sociological analysis. It is not suggested that the Nuer see their religion in this sort of way. Nevertheless, though they do not relate what we call the conception of spirit to what we call the social structure, the structural configuration we abstract by this process is of the same design as the symbolic configurations in which they think of their various *kuth.* The various spirits in their symbolic configurations occupy the same positions in relation to each other as they do in the structural configuration we perceive through sociological analysis.

In a typically Nuer way, they represent the inter-relationship of the spirits in a genealogical metaphor. God is the father of the greater spirits of the air, and the lesser of them are said to be children of his sons, of his lineage. The totemic spirits are often said to be children of his daughters, that is, they are not of his lineage, which is the Nuer way of placing them yet lower in the spiritual scale. The fetishes (and possibly also the nature sprites) come lowest of all in the representation of children of daughters of the air-spirit *deng.* Another way of indicating this spiritual hierarchy is in terms of descent values in their political connotation. The spirits of the air are *diel,* true or aristocratic spirits, the totemic spirits are *jang,* Dinka-like spirits, and the fetishes are *jur,* despised foreigners. A similar metaphorical evaluation in terms of genealogical and social status is made by Nuer in their classification of birds.

The inter-relationship of the spirits is represented also in the symbolism of height or space, or more accurately of the relation of sky to earth. The spirits, as we have noted, are those of the above, God being symbolized by the sky and the spirits of the air by the atmosphere, the clouds and the breezes, the lesser ones being nearer to the earth than the greater ones; and those of the below, the totemic spirits which as spirits are above and as creatures are below, the nature sprites, which may also be thought of as having a dual existence, and the very earthy fetishes, some of which speak from beneath the ground and may be described as chthonic. Implicit in this symbolic configuration is also an evaluation in terms of light and darkness, ranging from celestial brightness to subterranean darkness.

We see, and in their own way of looking at the matter the Nuer see, in this symbolic configuration, represented by positions in space, degrees of immanence. The cosmological representation of Spirit, and in particular the dichotomy between heaven and earth, the spirits of the above and those of the below, is further indicated by the mode and manner of appearances, the forms in which Spirit is manifested to humans. At one end there is pure Spirit, transcendental being which is everywhere and in nothing in particular, Spirit as it is in itself, God. God is seen only in the works of his creation and he speaks only in the language of inner spiritual experience. The spirits of the air, on the other hand, and sometimes also the *col wic* spirits, appear to men in their prophets, through whom they are known and speak. Then Spirit is manifested in totemic species, which are mostly creatures, and at the further end in things, the natural things associated with sprites and the magical substances which are the outward appearances of fetishes, which are Spirit in its lowest and most material form, Spirit which "eats" offerings and which is bought and sold. Nuer themselves draw these comparisons and it is evident from their observations that they themselves perceive that they are dealing with Spirit at different levels of thought and experience, Spirit in itself, Spirit in persons, Spirit in creatures, and Spirit in things. Moreover, I think we may conclude further that they perceive these different levels of immanence also as levels in time. This is implied in the genealogical representation of Spirit, for father must come before children and children before grandchildren; and possibly also in its spatial representation in the falling of spirits from above in a succession of descents at points in time. But it is also explicit in Nuer statements of the order in which their various spirits appeared among them. God was always there, then at various points of time the spirits of the air, the totemic spirits, and the sprites appeared on the scene, the fetishes being the most recent arrivals.

Spirit is thus conceived of by the Nuer, through their configurations of symbolic representations, as outside their social order, a transcendental being; but also as in their social order, an immanent being figured in all sorts of representations in relation to their social life and events of significance for it. Nuer go up and down the scale of these conceptions, speaking sometimes of God in a general sense as ubiquitous Spirit; sometimes in a more definite and distinctive way as Spirit who is in the sky, the creator, and the father; and sometimes in terms of one or other of his refractions.

These refractions correspond, as we have noted, with different levels of social activity, but it would be a mistake to leave the matter there, for an interpretation in terms of social structure merely shows us how the idea of Spirit takes various forms corresponding to departments of social life, and it does not enable us to understand any better the intrinsic nature of the idea itself. The varying degrees of immanence in which the conception is expressed show us that the different social levels at which Spirit is manifested are also different degrees of religious perception. Spirit is sometimes perceived, intellectually and intuitively, as one, transcendental, pure Spirit and at other times, in relation to human affairs and interests, as one or other of a great number of figures through which it is made known, in varying degrees of materialization, concretely to human intelligence. Nor is it, even with strict reference to a purely structural interpretation of the conception of Spirit in Nuer society, simply a matter of social levels, for, as we have seen, God is also experienced unrefracted at all levels, down to the individual; so that a structural interpretation explains only certain characteristics of the refractions and not the idea of Spirit in itself, which requires separate consideration. Here I have only tried to show that, and how, the conception of Spirit is broken up by the refracting surfaces of nature, of society, of culture, and of historical experience.

8 A PROBLEM OF NUER RELIGIOUS THOUGHT

E. E. Evans-Pritchard

IN A RECENT article (1953a) I discussed how the Nuer conception of Spirit is figured in different ways to different persons
and groups, producing a familiar problem of religions, that of the
one and the many. In this paper I consider the material forms in
which Spirit manifests itself or is represented, and this touches on
another familiar problem of religions, that of immanence and
transcendence. God, or Spirit in its oneness, is, properly speaking,
not figured in any material representations, nor are almost all the
spirits of the above, the spirits of the air and the *col wic* spirits,
though both God and his supraterrestrial refractions may reveal
themselves in visible forms. But the spirits of the earth, or of the
below, are represented in creatures and things. Our problem
chiefly concerns these spirits of the below. It can be simply stated
by the question: What meaning are we to attach to Nuer statements that such-and-such a thing is *Kwoth*, Spirit? The answer is
not so simple.

There are four words in the Nuer tongue which we translate, at
any rate in some of their usages, by "is": *labe*, a rare verb predi-
cating a character or quality of a person which gives him a certain
status, as *"labe kuaar"*, "he is a priest"; *te*, which predicates
something being in a place or state, usually implying a fairly
continuous condition, as *"te cieng"*, "he is in (his) village"; *a*,
which also predicates something being in a place or state, usually
indicating no more than that at the time of speech it is in that
condition, as *"jen a luak"*, "he is in the byre" or *"yen a nin"*, "he
is sleeping", and *e*, the particle which concerns us here. Father

Reprinted from *Sociologus* 4 (1), 1954: 23–41, by permission of the
author and the editor, *Sociologus*.

J. P. Crazzolara calls it the nominal copula and says that it is derived from *jen*, he, she, or it, as its plural form *ke* is derived from
ken, they; so that *e* and *ke* "are really pronouns fulfilling the functions of a copula" (Crazzolara 1933). The particle is used to tell
the listener that something belongs to a certain class or category
and hence about some quality or character it has, as *"e dit"*, "it
is a bird", *"gat Nath e car"*, "the Nuer is black", and *"Duob e
ran me goagh"*, "Duob is good man".[1] The question we are asking is what meaning or meanings it has for Nuer when they say of
something *"e Kwoth"*, "it is Spirit" (in the sense either of God or
of a divine refraction).

Nuer do not claim to see God, nor do they think that anyone
can know what he is. When they speak about his nature they
do so by adjectives which have no objective reference, such as
"great" and "good", or in metaphors taken from the world around
them: his invisibility and ubiquity by wind and air, his greatness
by the universe he has created, and his grandeur by an ox with
widespread horns. We have little difficulty in perceiving the qualities from which the metaphors derive and in recognizing their
appropriateness. They are no more than metaphors for the Nuer,
who do not say that any of these things is God, but only that he
is like (*cere*) them. They express in these poetic images as best
they can what they think must be some of the qualities of his
nature.

Nevertheless, certain things are said, or may be said, to be
God—rain, lightning, and various other natural—in the Nuer way
of speech, created—things which are of common interest. There
is here an ambiguity, or an obscurity, to be elucidated, for Nuer
are not now saying that God or Spirit is like this or that, but that
this or that is God or Spirit. Elucidation here does not, however,
present very great difficulties.

God being conceived of as in the sky those celestial phenomena which are of particular significance for Nuer, rain and light-

---

[1] There is no need to discuss the matter fully in the present paper, but it
may be well to mention that the *e* here functions as a class-inclusive particle (Duob is in the class or category of good). *"Duob ram me goagh"*
would also be translated "Duob is a good man", but the "is" here, contained
in the apposition of the Nuer sentence, is a predicate of quality (he is good).
One can also say *"Duob goaghe"*, "Duob is good", with the sense that his
state is good, with much the same meaning as that indicated by the use of
the particle *a*.

ning, are said, in a sense we have to determine, to be him. There is no noun denoting either phenomenon and they can only be spoken of by verbs indicating a function of the sky, as *"ce nhial deam"*, "the sky rained", and *"ce nhial mar"*, "the sky thundered (lightened)"*. Also pestilences, murrains, death, and indeed almost any natural phenomenon significant for men are commonly regarded by Nuer as manifestations from above, activities of divine being. Even the earthly totems are conceived of as a relationship deriving from some singular intervention of Spirit from above in human affairs. It is chiefly by these signs that Nuer have knowledge of God. It might be held, therefore, that the Nuer conception of God is a conceptualization of events which, on account of their strangeness or variability as well as on account of their potentiality for fortune or misfortune, are said to be his activities or his activities in one or other of his hypostases or refractions; and support for such a view might be found in the way Nuer sometimes speak of one or other of these effects. They may say of rain or lightning or pestilence *"e Kwoth"*, "it is God", and in storms they pray to God to come to earth gently and not in fury—to come gently, it will be noted, not to make the rain come gently.

I do not discuss this ontological question here beyond saying that were we to suppose that such phenomena are themselves regarded as God we would misunderstand and misrepresent Nuer religious thought, which is pre-eminently dualistic. It is true that for them there is no abstract duality of natural and supernatural but there is such a duality between *Kwoth*, Spirit, which is immaterial rather than supernatural, and *cak*, creation, the material world known to the senses. Rain and lightning and pestilences and murrains belong to this created world and are referred to by Nuer as *nyin Kwoth*, instruments of God.

Nevertheless, they and other effects of significance for men are *diosemia*, signs or manifestations of divine activity, and since Nuer apprehend divine activity in these signs, in God's revelation of himself to them in material forms, the signs are, in a lower medium, what they signify, so that Nuer may say of them *"e Kwoth"*, "it is God." Rain and pestilence come from God and are therefore manifestations of him, and in this sense rain and pestilence are God, in the sense that he reveals himself in their falling. But though one can say of rain or pestilence that it is God one cannot say of God that he is rain or pestilence. This would make no sense for a number of reasons. In the first place, the situation could scarcely arise, God not being an observable object, in which Nuer would require or desire to say about him that he is anything. In the second place, the word *Kwoth* does not here refer to a particular refraction of Spirit, a spirit but to Spirit in its oneness, God, and he could not be in any way identified with any one of his manifestations to the exclusion of all the others. A third, and the most cogent, reason is that rain is water which falls from the sky and pestilence is a bodily condition and they are therefore in their nature material things and not Spirit. Indeed, as a rule, rain would only be thought of in connection with Spirit, and would therefore only be said to be Spirit, when it does not fall in due season or falls too much or too violently with storm and lightning—when, that is, the rain has some special significance for human affairs. This gives us a clue to what is meant when Nuer say of something that it is God or that it is a spirit of the air, a divine hypostasis, as thunder may be said to be the spirit *wiu* or a prophet of the spirit *deng* may be said to be *deng,* especially as Nuer readily expand such statements by adding that thunder, rain and pestilence are all instruments (*nyin*) of God or that they are sent by (*jak*) God, and that the spirit *deng* has filled (*gwang*) the prophet through whom it speaks. In the statement here that something is Spirit or a spirit the particle *e,* which we translate "is", cannot therefore have the meaning of identity in a substantial sense. Indeed, it is because Spirit is conceived of in itself, as the creator and the one, and quite apart from any of its material manifestations, that these phenomena can be said to be sent by it or to be its instruments. When Nuer say of rain or lightning that it is God they are making an elliptical statement. What is understood is not that the thing in itself is Spirit but that it is what we would call a medium or manifestation of divine activity in relation to men and of significance for them. What precisely is posited by the hearer of any such elliptical statement depends on the nature of the situation by reference to which it is made. A vulture is not thought of as being in itself Spirit; it is a bird. But if it perches on the crown of a byre or hut Nuer may say *"e Kwoth"*, "it is Spirit", meaning that its doing so is a spiritual signal presaging disaster. A lion is not thought of as being in itself Spirit; it is a beast. But it may, on account of some event which brings it into a peculiar relation to man, such as being born, as Nuer think sometimes

happens, as twin to a human child, be regarded as a revelation of
Spirit for a particular family and lineage. Likewise, diseases, or
rather their symptoms, are not thought of as being in themselves
Spirit, but their appearance in individuals may be regarded as
manifestations of Spirit for those individuals. Spirit acts, and
thereby reveals itself, through these creatures. This distinction
between the nature of a thing and what it may signify in certain
persons is very evident in totemic relationships. A crocodile is
Spirit for certain persons, but it is not thought to be in its nature
Spirit, for others kill and eat it. It is because Nuer separate, and
quite explicitly when questioned about the matter, spiritual conceptions from such material things as may nevertheless be said
"to be" the conceptions, that they are able to retain the unity and
autonomy of Spirit in spite of a great diversity of accidents and
are able to speak of Spirit as it is in itself without reference to
any of its material manifestations.

So far I have been mostly speaking of the Nuer conception of
God and of those of his refractions which belong to the category
of the sky or of the above. With two possible exceptions,[2] we
cannot say that the things said "to be" these spirits are material
symbols or representations of them; or at any rate not in the same
sense as we can speak of things being symbols of those lesser
refractions of Spirit which Nuer call spirits of the earth or of the
below, in which God stands in a special relationship to lineages
and individuals—such diverse things as beasts, birds, reptiles,
trees, phosphorescent objects, and pieces of wood—for these
lesser refractions of Spirit, regarded as distinct spirits in relation
to each other, cannot, unlike the spirits of the air, easily be
thought of except in relation to the things by reference to which
they derive their individuality, and which are said to be them.

When, therefore, Nuer say that the pied crow is the spirit *buk*
or that a snake is Spirit the word *"is"* has a different sense to
what it has in the statement that rain is Spirit. The difference
does not merely lie in the fact that "Spirit" has here a more restricted connotation, being spoken of in reference to a particular

[2] The spear *wiu* may be said to stand for the spirit *wiu*. This is a rather
special case which I do not discuss here. Also, the pied crow may be said to
stand for the spirit *buk* which, if it is to be classed with the air-
spirits at all, is the most terrestrially conceived of them, sometimes almost as
everybody's totemic spirit.

and exclusive refraction—a spirit—rather than comprehensively as God or Spirit in its oneness. It lies also in the relation understood in the statement between its subject (snake or crow) and its predicate (Spirit or a spirit). The snake in itself is not divine activity whereas rain and lightning are. The story accounting for the origin of a totemic relationship may explain it as a revelation of divine activity, but once it has become an established relationship between a lineage and a natural species, the species is a representation or symbol of Spirit to the lineage. What then is here meant when it is said that the pied crow "is" *buk* or that a snake "is" Spirit, that the symbol "is" what it symbolizes? Clearly Nuer do not mean that the crow is the same as *buk,* for *buk* is also conceived of as being in rivers and also in the sky, which the pied crow certainly is not; nor that a snake is the same as some spiritual refraction for they say that the snake just crawls on the earth while the spirit it is said to be is in the sky. What then is being predicated about the crow or snake in the statement that either is Spirit or a spirit?

It will be simpler to discuss this question in the first place in relation to a totemic relationship. When a Nuer says of a creature *"e nyang"*, "it is a crocodile", he is saying that it is a crocodile and not some other creature, but when he says, to explain why a person behaves in an unusual manner towards crocodiles *"e kwothdien"*, "it (the crocodile) is their spirit", he is obviously making a different sort of statement. He is not saying what kind of creature it is, for it is understood that he is referring to the crocodile, but that what he refers to is Spirit for certain people. But he is also not saying that crocodiles are Spirit—they are not for him—but that certain people so regard them. Therefore a Nuer would not make a general statement that *"nyang e Kwoth"*, "crocodile is Spirit", but would only say, in referring to the crocodile, *"e Kwoth"*, "it is Spirit", the distinction between the two statements being that the first would mean that crocodiles are Spirit for everyone whereas the second, being made in a special context of situation, means that they are Spirit for certain persons who are being discussed, or are understood, in that context. Likewise, whilst it can be said of the crocodile that it is Spirit, it cannot be said of Spirit that it is the crocodile, or rather, if a statement is framed in this form it can only be made when the word *kwoth* has a pronominal suffix which gives it the meaning of "his spirit", "their spirit", and so forth; in other words where the statement makes it clear that what is being spoken of is Spirit conceived of in relation to particular persons only. We still have to ask, however, in what sense a crocodile is Spirit for these persons.

Since it is difficult to discuss a statement that something which can be observed, a crocodile, is something more than what it appears to be when this something more, Spirit, cannot be observed, it is helpful first to consider some examples of Nuer statements that things are something more than they appear to be when both the subject term and the predicate term refer to observable phenomena.

Nuer say of a barren woman who has taken to herself a wife who bears children to her name that she is a man. We might suppose that Nuer mean by this simply that the woman acts like a man, but they mean something rather more than that, something more like we would mean if we said that she is virtually a man. They are saying that who marries and is the pater of children is a man and that therefore the woman in relation to marriage and parenthood and with regard to social status generally is a man, and in these respects they treat her as a man. Thus, to give one example, in the division of bridewealth on the marriage of her brother's daughter she receives the cattle due to a paternal uncle and not those due to a paternal aunt. What Nuer are saying, therefore, is that she is equal to a man in social personality, that is, as a person. Physically, and regarded as an individual, she is a woman. The resemblance between such a barren woman and a man is conceptual, not perceptual, and the "is" here rests on an analogy.

When a cucumber is used as a sacrificial victim Nuer speak of it as an ox. In doing so they are asserting something rather more than that it takes the place of an ox. They do not, of course, say that cucumbers are oxen, and in speaking of a particular cucumber as an ox in a sacrificial situation they are only indicating that it may be thought of as an ox in that particular situation; and they act accordingly by performing the sacrificial rites as closely as possible to what happens when the victim is an ox. Here again, the "is" rests on qualitative analogy; and the expression is asymmetrical. A cucumber is an ox, but an ox is not a cucumber.

We may consider a final, and revealing, but rather different, example of this way of speaking, and one which is closer to the topic of this paper. The birth of twins is regarded as an intervention of Spirit in human affairs.[3] Nuer further assert of them, firstly that they are one person, and secondly that they are birds.

When they say "twins are not two persons, they are one person" they are not saying that they are one individual but that they have a single personality. It is significant that in speaking of the unity of twins they only use the word *ran,* which, like our word "person", leaves sex, age, and other distinguishing qualities of individuals undefined. They would not say that twins of the same sex were one *dhol,* boy, or one *nyal,* girl, but they do say, whether they are of the same sex or not, that they are one *ran,* person. Their single social personality is something over and above their physical duality, a duality which is evident to the senses and is indicated by the plural form used when speaking of twins and by their treatment in all respects in ordinary social life as two quite different individuals. It is only in certain ritual situations, and symbolically, that the unity of twins is expressed, particularly in ceremonies connected with marriage and death, in which the personality undergoes a change. Thus, when the senior of male twins marries, the junior acts with him in the ritual acts he has to perform; female twins ought to be married on the same day, and no mortuary ceremonies are held for twins because, for one reason, one of them cannot be cut off from the living without the other. A woman whose twin brother had died some time before said to Miss Soule, to whom I am indebted for the information, "is not his soul still living? I am alive and we are really children of God."

There is no mortuary ceremony even when the second twin dies, and I was told that twins do not attend the mortuary ceremonies held for their dead kinsfolk, nor mourn them, because a twin is a *ran nhial,* a person of the sky or of the above. He is also spoken of as *gat Kwoth,* a child of God. These dioscuric descriptions of twins are common to many peoples, but the Nuer are peculiar in holding also that they are birds. They say "a twin is not a person (*ran*), he is a bird (*dit*)", although, as we have just seen, they assert, in another sense, that twins are one person (*ran*). Here they are using the word *ran* in the sense of a human

[3] I have given a more detailed account in Evans-Pritchard 1936.

being as distinct from any other creature. The dogma is expressed in various ways. Very often a twin is given the name *Dit*, bird, *Gwong*, guineafowl, or *Ngec*, francolin.[4] All Nuer consider it shameful, at any rate for adults, to eat any sort of bird or its eggs, but were a twin to do this it would be much more than shameful. It would be *nueer*, a grave sin, for twins respect (*thek*) birds, because, they say, birds are also twins, and they avoid any sort of contact with them. The equivalence of twins and birds is expressed particularly in connection with death. When an infant twin dies people say *"ce par"*, "he has flown away", using the word denoting the flight of birds. Infant twins who die, as so often happens, are not buried, as other infants are, but are covered in a reed basket or winnowing-tray and placed in the fork of a tree, because birds rest in trees. I was told that birds which feed on carrion would not molest the bodies but would look at their dead kinsmen—twins and birds are also said to be kin, though the usage may be regarded as metaphorical—and fly away again. When I asked a Nuer whether adult twins would be buried like other people he replied "no, of course not, they are birds and their souls go up into the air." A platform, not used in the normal mode of burial, is erected in the grave and a hide placed over it. The body is laid on this hide and covered with a second hide. Earth is then carefully patted over the upper hide instead of being shovelled in quickly, as in the burial of an ordinary person.

It is understandable that Nuer draw an analogy between the multiple hatching of eggs and the dual birth of twins. The analogy is explicit, and, through an extension of it, the flesh of crocodiles and turtles is also forbidden to twins on the ground that these creatures too, like birds, lay eggs. Miss Soule once had a girl twin in her household who refused fish for the same reason—the only case of its kind known to either of us. But the analogy between multiple births in birds and men does not adequately ex-

[4] That the names, at least all those I have heard, are taken from birds lowest in the scale of Nuer reckoning requires comment, especially in view of the argument I later develop. It may be due to the Nuer habit of speaking of their relation to God—the birth of twins constitutes such a context—by comparing themselves with lowly things. On the other hand, it may be simply in keeping with the logic of the analogy. Twins belong to the class of the above but are below, just as guineafowl and francolin belong to the class of birds, which as a class is in the category of the above, but are almost earthbound.

plain why it is with birds that human twins are equated when there are many other creatures which habitually bear several young at the same time and in a manner more closely resembling human parturition. It cannot be just multiple birth which leads Nuer to say that twins are birds, for these other creatures are not respected by twins on that account. The prohibition on eating eggs is clearly secondary, and it is extended to include crocodiles and turtles—and by Miss Soule's girl fish also—not because they lay eggs but because their laying eggs makes them like birds. Moreover, it is difficult to understand why a resemblance of the kind should in any case be made so much of. The multiple hatching of chicks is doubtless a resemblance which greatly strengthens the idea of twins being birds, but it is only part of a more complex analogical representation which requires to be explained in more general terms of Nuer religious thought. A twin, on account of his peculiar manner of conception, is, though not Spirit himself, a special creation, and, therefore, manifestation, of Spirit; and when he dies his soul goes into the air, to which things associated with Spirit belong. He is a *ran nhial,* a person of the above, whereas an ordinary person is a *ran piny,* a person of the below. A bird, though also not in itself Spirit, belongs by nature to the above and is also what Nuer call, using "person" metaphorically, a *ran nhial,* a person of the above, and being such is therefore also associated with Spirit. It cannot, of course, be determined for certain whether a twin is said to be a person of the above because he is a bird or whether he is said to be a bird because he is a person of the above, but the connection in thought between twins and birds is certainly not simply derived from the multiple birth similitude but also, and in my view primarily, from both birds and twins being classed by Nuer as *gaat Kwoth,* children of God. Birds are children of God on account of their being in the air, and twins belong to the air on account of their being children of God by the manner of their birth.

It seems odd, if not absurd, to a European when he is told that a twin is a bird as though it were an obvious fact, for Nuer are not saying that a twin "is like" a bird but that "he is" a bird. There seems to be a complete contradiction in the statement, and it was precisely on statements of this kind recorded by observers of primitive peoples that Lévy-Bruhl based his theory of the prelogical mentality of these peoples, its chief characteristic being, in his view, that it permits such evident contradictions—that a thing can be what it is and at the same time something altogether different. But, in fact, no contradiction is involved in the statement, which, on the contrary, appears quite sensible, and even true, to one who presents the idea to himself in the Nuer language and within their system of religious thought. He does not then take their statements about twins any more literally than they make and understand them themselves. They are not saying that a twin has a beak, feathers, and so forth. Nor in their everyday relations with twins do Nuer speak of them as birds or act towards them as though they were birds. They treat them as what they are, men and women. But in addition to being men and women they are of a twin birth, and a twin birth is a special revelation of Spirit; and Nuer express this special character of twins in the "twins are birds" formula because twins and birds, though for different reasons, are both associated with Spirit and this makes twins, like birds, "people of the above" and "children of God", and hence a bird is a suitable symbol in which to express the special relationship in which a twin stands to God. When, therefore, Nuer say that a twin is a bird they are not speaking of either as it appears in the flesh. They are speaking of the *anima* of the twin, what they call his *tie,* a concept which includes both what we call the personality and the soul; and they are speaking of the association birds have with Spirit through their ability to enter the realm to which Spirit is likened in metaphor and where Nuer think it chiefly is, or may be. The formula does not express a dyadic relationship between twins and birds but a triadic relationship between twins, birds, and God. In respect to God twins and birds have a similar character.

It is because they do not make, or take, the statement that twins are birds in any ordinary sense that they are fully aware that in ritual relating to twins the actions are a kind of miming. This is shown in their treatment of the corpse of a twin, for, according to what they themselves say, what is a bird, the *tie* or *anima,* has gone up into the air and what is left and treated—in the case of adults platform burial being a convenient alternative to disposal in trees—as though it might be a bird is only the *ring,* the flesh. It is shown also in the convention that should one of a pair of twins die, the child who comes after them takes his place, counting as one of them in the various ceremonies twins have to perform and respecting birds as rigorously as if he were himself a twin, which he is not. The ceremonies have to be performed for the benefit of the living twin and their structure and purpose are such that there have to be two persons to perform them, so another sibling acts in the place of the dead.

This discussion of what is meant by the statement that a twin is a bird is not so far away from the subject of totemism as it might seem to be, for the stock explanation among the Nuer of a totemic relationship is that the ancestor of a lineage and a member of a natural species were born twins. The relationship of lineage to species is thereby made to derive not only from the most intimate of all possible relationships but also from a special act of divine revelation; and since the link between a lineage and its totem is the tutelary spirit of the lineage associated with the totem it is appropriate that the relationship should be thought of as having come about by an event which is a direct manifestation of Spirit.

However, an examination of the Nuer dogma that twins are birds was made not on account of totemic relationships commonly being explained in terms of twinship but because it was hoped that it would be easier to understand, in the light of any conclusions reached about what is meant by the statement that a twin is a bird, what Nuer mean when they say that some totemic creature, such as a crocodile, is Spirit. The nature of the totems and the reasons for their selection, to which some consideration was given in connection with the bird-twin expression, need not now concern us. We are inquiring only what in a totemic relationship is to be understood by "is" when it is said about some totemic creature that it is Spirit. Certainly there is here neither the sort of metaphor nor the sort of ellipsis we found in earlier statements. Nor can Nuer be understood to mean that the creature is identical with Spirit, or even with a spirit, Spirit conceived of in a particular totemic refraction. They say quite definitely themselves that it is not, and it is also evident, for the Nuer as well as for us, that a material symbol of spirit cannot, by its very nature, be that which it symbolizes. Nevertheless, though crocodiles and Spirit are quite different and unconnected ideas, when the crocodile is for a certain lineage a symbol of their special relationship to God, then in the context of that relationship symbol and what it symbolizes are fused. As in the case of the "twins are birds" formula, the relation is a triadic one, between a lineage and a natural species and God.

There are obvious and significant differences between the creature-Spirit expression and the cucumber-ox and bird-twin expressions. Cucumber, ox, man, and bird are all things which can be known by the senses but where Spirit is experienced other than in thought it is only in its effects or through material representations of it. It is, therefore, easily conceived of as being in, or behind, crocodiles. The subject and predicate terms of the statement that something is Spirit are here no longer held apart by two sets of visible properties. Consequently, while Nuer say that totemic spirits and totems are not the same they sometimes not only speak of, but also act towards, a totem as if the spirit were in it. Thus they give some meat of a sacrifice to the lion-spirit to lions, and when they sacrifice to the durra bird-spirit they address also the birds themselves and tell them that the victim is for them. Nevertheless, they make it clear in talking about their totems that what respect they show them is on account of their representing the spirits associated with them and not for their own sake.

Another difference is that whereas in the cases of the cucumber-ox and twin-bird expressions the equivalence rests on analogies which are quite obvious even to us once they are pointed out—the cucumber being treated in the ritual of sacrifice like an ox is, and twins and birds both being "children of God" and also multiple births—analogy is lacking in the creature-Spirit expression. There is no resemblance between the idea of Spirit and that of crocodile. There is nothing in the nature of crocodiles which evokes the idea of Spirit for Nuer, and even for those who respect crocodiles the idea of Spirit is evoked by these creatures because the crocodile is a representation of Spirit in relation to their lineage and not because there is anything crocodile-like about Spirit. We have passed from observation of resemblances to thought by means of symbols in the sort of way that the crocodile is used as a symbol for Spirit.

We are here faced with the same problem we have been considering earlier, but in what, in the absence of analogical guidance to help us, is a more difficult form. The difficulty is increased by Nuer symbols being taken from an environment unfamiliar to us and which, even when we familiarize ourselves with it, we experi-

ence and evaluate differently. We find it hard to think in terms of
crocodiles, snakes, and fig-trees. But a little reflection shows us
that this problem of the relation of symbol to what it symbolizes
is common to all religious thought, at least in some degree, including our own; and if we think of it in terms of our own religion
we may more easily see it in terms of theirs. We do not suppose
that any picture or image of a dove is a representation of the Holy
Spirit nor that where it is such it will have that meaning for everybody; and those for whom it has this meaning do not think that
the dove is the Holy Spirit. Nevertheless, for a Christian the dove
when used as a religious symbol has an intimate association with
what it represents—what brings to the mind with what it brings
to the mind. It seems to me that a crocodile totem is regarded in
much the same way by Nuer. They know that what they see is only
a crocodile but since it represents Spirit to some of them it is for
those people, when thought of in that way, also what it stands for.
The relationship of members of a Nuer lineage to Spirit is represented by a material symbol by which it can be thought of
concretely, and therefore as a relationship distinct from the relationships of other lineages to Spirit. There results, when what
acts as a symbol is regarded in this way, a fusion between Spirit,
as so represented, and its material representation. I fancy that
then Nuer feel that Spirit is in some way in, or behind, the creature
in which in a sense it is beholden, though when they think about
it they say that it is not, in much the same way as we may feel
that Spirit is in, or behind the material symbol of a dove, though,
if we were asked we would say it is not.

   This must, I think, be all the more so with the other spirits of
the below, the *bieli,* nature sprites, and the *kulangni,* fetishes. In
general, much of what has been said in this paper about the totemic spirits applies to these other spirits also, but there is one
important difference. In the statement "crocodile is their spirit"
both the terms of the proposition can be thought of quite separately and are indeed so presented in the statement. This is partly
because the crocodile is Spirit only for some persons and not for
others, and also because, even for those for whom it is Spirit it
also exists in its own right as a reptile and may be so regarded by
them without the idea of Spirit being involved. The reptile can
be said to be Spirit only because it is something which may represent it and is, therefore, different from it. But in the case of a

luminescence, such as a will-o'-the-wisp from rotting swamp vegetation, the appearance can scarcely be represented in thought apart from what appears in it. It does not seem to be regarded, as rain may be, as a manifestation of Spirit through a medium which can be said to be sent by, or to be an instrument of, Spirit, but as an emanation of Spirit or as Spirit itself revealed in the light, a theophany like the burning bush in Midian. Nuer speak of it sometimes as the spirit's fire, and of its fire burning. Nor is it, as a crocodile may be, regarded as a representation of Spirit which, being apart from what it represents, can be said to be what it represents. On the contrary, whilst the lights are easily kept apart in the mind from the things on which they are accustomed to appear—swamp vegetation, hippopotamuses, meteorites, and other objects—they are not themselves conceived of as other than Spirit in the form of *bieli* and under that name. They are not something that is thought to exist in its own right but can be said to be Spirit. They are in themselves Spirit, in however lowly a form. Consequently, though they have a special significance for those persons who have acquired a relationship to the *bieli* spirits, they are Spirit also for those not directly concerned with them. Rain and crocodiles are created things with which Spirit may, or may not, be associated, according to circumstances and persons, but a will-o'-the-wisp is a property of Spirit, fractionally conceived of as a spirit of a special kind, and it cannot be thought of in terms other than of Spirit.

So when a Nuer says of a light in the bush that it is Spirit the problem we have been considering has changed its form and, at least on first consideration, seems to elude, if not altogether to escape, us. For us the light is a gas arising from rotting swamp vegetation, so that the statement that it is Spirit is of the same kind as the statement that a crocodile is Spirit and whatever meaning might be attached to the one would be the same for the other. But we cannot say that they are statements of the same kind for Nuer. For them, whereas the crocodile is a thing conceived of separately from Spirit, even though in a certain sense and for certain people it may be said to be Spirit, the phosphorescence is a descent of Spirit in the form of light on to something which is not in any way said to be Spirit, such as a hippopotamus, and on which it may appear at certain times and places and not at other times and places. So we are no longer asking what sense it has for Nuer when one of them says of a thing, which is not for them in itself Spirit, that it is Spirit. We are asking what sense it has for them when one of them says of a thing which has no meaning for them other than an emanation of Spirit that it is Spirit. In the case of the crocodile what is perceived is the reptile, and in certain circumstances it may be conceived of as Spirit for certain persons. In the case of the *bieli* what is perceived may indeed be said to be just light but it can only be conceived of as Spirit for it has no other name which differentiates it from any other sort of light or fire than *bieli*. When, regarding such a light, Nuer say "it is Spirit" they are no longer saying that something is something else but are merely giving a name to what is observed; so that here "it is Spirit" belongs to the same class of statements as "it is a crocodile", and it might be held that the question we have been examining does not properly arise. Nevertheless, this is not entirely the case, as I will explain later.

What has been said of the lights of the nature *sprites* can be said also of the little bundles of wood in which the *kulangni,* the fetish spirits, have their abode, but for a different reason. A bundle of wood in which a fetish spirit has its abode is not a symbol of Spirit, as a crocodile may be. Nor is it, like the *bieli,* a visible appearance of Spirit. It is a thing where a particular spirit abides. Nevertheless, it must be difficult for a fetish-owner to regard the bundle as being just anything which serves as a lodging for the spirit. It is before the bundle that he makes his offerings and it is the bundle he points at an enemy he wishes the spirit to harm. Moreover, the bundle in itself is only significant for Nuer because it contains a spirit. The Nuer word *wal* has two senses which we may render "vegetable" and either "medicine" or "magical substance". The fetish-bundles are, of course, *wal* in the first sense. What makes them *wal* in the second sense is their occupation by spirits, and they are only meaningful objects in this second sense, because they are fashioned solely as habitations for spirits and have no significance other than is derived from this purpose and use. Hence when Nuer say of a fetish-bundle that it is Spirit they are not saying that something which also has for them a separate meaning as something in itself, which is other than Spirit, is something else, namely Spirit, but that something which has no meaning of any kind outside its being an abode and a material sign of Spirit is Spirit. So the fetish-bundles cannot easily be thought of,

as can rain or crocodile, either in terms of Spirit or in terms of
their purely material natures, but only in terms of Spirit.

But though in the case of both the lights and the bundles there
seems to be a more complete and fixed fusion between things and
Spirit than in the case of the totems, the problem of something
being something else is still present, though in a more complex,
and also a more obscure and roundabout, form. Here again, although it can be said of a light in the bush or of a fetish-bundle
that it is Spirit, the statement cannot be reversed. It cannot be
said of Spirit that it is the light or the bundle, for that would mean
to Nuer that Spirit in its oneness, as conceived of as God, is entirely the light or the bundle, which would make no sense to them.
In the statement that the light or bundle is Spirit what, therefore,
has to be understood by Spirit is a refraction of Spirit, or a spirit.
But, even so, the "is" is not one of identity, for though a phosphorescent light is a nature sprite exhibiting itself and is not conceived
of as anything else, the nature sprite may be thought of independently of the light; and though the fetish-bundle may be a
meaningless object except in relation to the fetish-spirit which
occupies it, the spirit which occupies it can be thought of independently of it. When the light is no longer visible the *biel* spirit
is none the less present for certain people as their spirit, which is
Spirit in relation to them as an idea quite apart from its sporadic
appearances as a light. A fetish-spirit takes up its abode in a
fetish-bundle of wood and it may leave it; and it also is present
for certain people as Spirit in relation to them as an idea quite
apart from its material home. In either case the spirits are thought
to come from above to earth and to be independent, as Spirit,
of any forms.

There is a further fact to be taken into consideration. When
Nuer speak of lights in the bush or of fetish-bundles as Spirit they
normally would not use the generic word for Spirit, *Kwoth*, or
even its plural and fractionary form *kuth*, spirits. They would say
of them that they were *bieli* or *kulangni*. So, whilst it is true that
bieli and *kulangni* are *kuth piny*, spirits of the below, the fact that
they alone of all the spirits are given distinctive class names and
that consequently it is possible for Nuer to explain them by saying
that they are Spirit or that they are spirits attached to certain
persons shows that though they are regarded as Spirit or spirits
they are also somehow regarded differently from the way in which

Spirit is usually regarded. So the problem here is further complicated by a third term being understood in the statement about
something that it is something else: the light is *bieli,* and the *bieli*
are Spirit; the bundle is *kulangni,* and the *kulangni* are Spirit.
This added complication may be supposed to be due to the fact
that though these spirits cannot be said to be identical with things
they are more closely bound to them than is the case with other,
and higher, spiritual conceptions; and the more Spirit is thought
to be bound to visible forms the less it is thought of as Spirit and
the more it is thought of in terms of what it is bound to. In other
words, there are gradations of the conception of Spirit from pure
unattached Spirit to Spirit associated with humans, animals, and
lifeless objects and more and more closely bound to what it is
associated with the further down the scale one goes. This scale of
Spirit, as I have explained elsewhere (1953a), is related to segmentation of the social order and is represented by Nuer by levels
of space as well as by levels and degrees of immanence. So when
Nuer say of something that it is Spirit we have to consider not
only what "is" means but also what "Spirit" means. That, however, would entail a discussion outside the scope of this paper and
is not necessary for the elucidation of the problem before us, because, though the sense of *"Kwoth"* varies with the context, the
word refers always to something of the same essence, and what is
being said, directly or indirectly, in the statements is always the
same, that something is of that essence.

We can make some contribution towards a solution of the problem in the light of this discussion. When Nuer say of something
"e Kwoth", "it is Spirit", or give it a name of which it can be
further said "that is Spirit", the "is" does not in all instances have
the same connotation. It may be an elliptical statement, signifying
that the thing referred to is a manifestation of Spirit in the sense
of God revealing himself in his instruments or in effects and
events. Or it may be a symbolical statement, signifying that what
in itself is not Spirit but represents Spirit to certain persons is for
these persons Spirit in such contexts as direct attention to the
symbolic character of an object to the exclusion of whatever other
qualities it may possess. Or it may be a statement signifying
something closer to identity of the thing spoken of with what it
is said to be, Spirit. The statements never, however, signify complete identity of anything with Spirit because Nuer think of Spirit

as something more than any one of its modes, signs, effects, representations, and so forth and also as something of a different nature to the created things which they are. They are not able to define what it is, but when it acts within the phenomenal world they say it has come from above, where it is conceived to be and from whence it is thought to descend. Consequently, Spirit in any form can be detached in the mind from the things said to be it, even if they cannot always be so easily detached from the idea of Spirit.

I cannot take the analysis further. The discussion has been, of course, from a European's point of view. He hears Nuer say of something that it is Spirit and he asks himself what they mean. The Nuer themselves do not have a philosophical vocabulary which would permit them to discuss the matter, they see no necessity to discuss it, and it soon becomes obvious to a foreign learner of their ways of thought that the relation of Spirit to things which in one way or other bring the conception to the mind is ultimately for them what we would call a mystery—in the old sense of the word of something which is revealed and intuitively, rather than intellectually, understood, not something which is hidden and unintelligible.

But if the analysis can be taken no further and is inconclusive it at least shows, if it is correct, how wide of the mark have been anthropological attempts to explain the kind of statements we have been considering. Anthropological explanations display two main errors. The first, best exemplified in the writings of Lévy-Bruhl, is that when a people say that something is something else which is quite different they are contravening the law of contradictories and substituting for it a law of their own prelogical way of thinking, that of mystical participations. I hope at least to have shown that Nuer do not assert identity between the two things. They may say that one is the other and in certain situations act towards it as though it were that other, or something like it, but they are aware, no doubt with varying degrees of awareness, and readily say, though with varying degrees of clarity and emphasis, that the two things are different. Moreover, it will have been noted that in all the seemingly equivocal statements we have considered, with perhaps one exception, the terms cannot be reversed. The exception is the statement that twins are birds, because it can also be said that birds are twins. But that is a simple statement of fact, to which we also can give assent, which does not derive logically from the statement that twins are birds but from a perception independent of that proposition; so that it does not concern our problem. Rain may be said to be God but God cannot be said to be rain; a cucumber may be called an ox but an ox cannot be called a cucumber; and a crocodile may be said to be Spirit but Spirit cannot be said to be a crocodile. Consequently, one cannot put the equal-sign between the two terms of any of these statements and therefore they are not statements of identity. I do not wish to enter into a philosophical discussion on this point, nor have I the knowledge to do so. All I wish to say is that if it is at all possible to make a statement of identity which is not purely verbal the Nuer statements we have been considering are not statements of this kind. They are statements not that something is other than it is but that in a certain sense and in particular contexts something has some extra quality which does not belong to it in its own nature; and this quality is not contrary to, or incompatible with its nature but something added to it which does not alter what it was but merely makes it something more, in respect to this quality, than it was. Consequently, no contradiction, it seems to me, is involved in the statements.

This added quality is either a conception (Spirit) or an abstraction from a concrete phenomenon (ox, bird, *etc.*) or from a social representation of it. What is prescinded and added to a cucumber is the sacrificial character of oxen and what is prescinded and added to twins is the aboveness of birds. But whether the predicate refers to a conception or to a visible object the addition makes the subject equivalent to it in respect to the quality which both now have in common in such contexts as focus the attention on that quality alone. The things referred to are not the same as each other but they are the same in that one respect, and the equivalence, denoted by the copula, is not one of substance but of quality. Consequently, we cannot speak here, as Lévy-Bruhl does, of mystical participation, or at any rate not in his sense of the words, because the two things are not thought to be really linked, by a mystical or any other bond, but only to be linked by an ideal or imaginative nexus. Therefore, what is done to birds is not thought to affect twins, and if a totem is harmed the spirit of that totem may be offended but it is not harmed by the harm done to the totemic creature.

That the relation between the thing said to be something else and that something else it is said to be is an ideal one is indeed obvious, but anthropological explanations of modes of primitive thought as wide apart as those of Tylor, Max Müller, and Lévy-Bruhl, are based on the assumption that though for us the relation is an ideal one primitive peoples mistake it for a real one; and those anthropologists who sponsor psychological explanations often make the same assumption. This is the second error. If my interpretation is correct, Nuer know very well when they say that a crocodile is Spirit that it is only Spirit in the sense that Spirit is represented to some people by that symbol just as they know very well that a cucumber is only an ox in the sense that they treat it as one in sacrifice. That they do not mistake ideal relations for real ones could be shown by many examples other than those I have given. They identify the spear used in sacrificial invocations with that of the ancestor of the clan, though they know, that what they hold in the hand is any ordinary spear, and also that the spear of the ancestor does not exist. They do not think of a man being an ox, but, as I have shown elsewhere (1953b), in the sacrificial situation they regard the ox as equivalent to the man. Nuer know that a man's herd is not really descended from that of the ancestor of his clan, but ideally it is for them the ancestor's herd when the man performs rites in which the clan as a whole is ideally present. Sickness and the sin which has brought it about are not the same for Nuer, but they speak of them as though they were the same when sacrifice is made to heal the sickness. The idea of the left hand is associated with evil, but the left hand itself is not evil. We find the same throughout the symbolism of ritual. The cutting of a gourd in two, for example, to cut a kin relationship is as much a symbolic action for Nuer as it would be for us, though they have no way of expressing this in their language. The gourd, as they know, has nothing to do with kinship, but in the rite, in entirely conscious mimicry, it is made to stand for the idea of kinship and may be said to be equivalent to it within the context of the rite which endows it with that meaning. I do not discuss these examples further here. They are merely cited as illustrations in support of the conclusions reached about the kind of statement under review.

I think that the reason why it was not readily perceived that the statements that something is something else should not be taken as matter of fact statements is that it was not recognized that they are made in relation to a third term not mentioned in them but understood. They are statements, not that A is B, but that A and B have something in common in relation to C. This is evident when we give some thought to the matter. A cucumber is equivalent to an ox in respect to God who accepts it in the place of an ox. A crocodile is equivalent to Spirit only when conceived of as a representation of God to a lineage. Consequently, though Nuer do not mistake ideal relations for real ones, an ideal equivalence is none the less true for them, because within their system of religious thought things are not just what they appear to be but as they are conceived of in relation to God.

NOTE

Other articles on Nuer religion by the same author are: "Some Features of Nuer Religion", *J. R. A. I.*, 1951: "A Note on Nuer Prayers", *Man*, 1952; "The Nuer Spirits of the Air", *Ann. Lateranensi*, in press; "The Nuer *Col Wic*", *Man*, 1949; "Nuer Totemism", *Ann. Lateranensi*, 1949; "The Nuer Conception of Spirit in its relation to the Social Order", *American Anthropologist*, 1953; "Burial and Mortuary Rites of the Nuer", *African Affairs*, 1949; "Nuer Curses and Ghostly Vengeance", *Africa*, 1949; "Two Nuer Ritual Concepts", *Man*, 1949; "Some Features and Forms of Nuer Sacrifices", *Africa*, 1951; "Nuer Spear Symbolism", *Anthrop. Quarterly*, 1953; "The Sacrificial Role of Cattle among the Nuer", *Africa*, 1953; "The Meaning of Sacrifice among the Nuer", *J. R. A. I.*, 84, 1954.

9 NYAKYUSA RITUAL AND SYMBOLISM

Monica Wilson

THE TRADITIONAL religion of the Nyakyusa people has three elements: first, there is a lively belief in the survival of the dead and in the power of senior relatives, both living and dead, over their descendants; second, there is a belief in medicines, that is, in mystical power residing in certain material substances which are used by those who have the knowledge to do so; and third, there is a belief in witchcraft, an innate power to harm others exercised by certain individuals, and in a similar power, "the breath of men," exercised by villagers to punish wrongdoers in their midst.

There are two fundamental principles of social grouping in Nyakyusa society, kinship and age (Wilson 1951), and the distinction between the ancestor cult on the one hand, and witchcraft and the breath of men on the other, coincides with these. The ancestor cult, in its domestic aspect, concerns families and lineages; and in its public aspect it concerns chiefdoms and groups of chiefdoms, for the chieftainship is hereditary, and dead chiefs are thought to have power over the countries and people they once ruled. In the villages, however, the hereditary principle does not enter; they are formed of groups of age-mates led by one of themselves, who *must* be a commoner, and may not be the son of a village headman of the previous generation. In the villages the power of dead kinsmen does not operate; but in its place there is the "breath of men" and the power of witchcraft. Power derived from medicines, on the other hand, is thought to be exercised in all types of relationship in Nyakyusa society; it is not confined either to kinship or to age relationships.

Reprinted from *The American Anthropologist* 56 (2), 1954: 228–41, by permission of the author and of the editor, *The American Anthropologist*.

The belief in the survival of the dead and the power of senior relatives is expressed in a series of elaborate rituals, one set of which is directed toward the immediate ancestors of the participants, and another set of which is directed toward the immediate ancestors of ruling chiefs, and certain distant ancestors of the chiefs' line, heroes in Nyakyusa history. The name of one of these heroes, Kyala, has been used by the missionaries to translate the word "God," but all the evidence available goes to show that Kyala was, traditionally, but one of several distant ancestors to whom regular sacrifices were made on behalf of a group of chiefdoms.

In Nyakyusa society there is little development of arts and crafts except in relation to building—they build substantial and beautiful huts and long houses—and the main form of artistic expression is in ritual. Rituals are frequent and elaborate; great numbers of people attend them and the excitement is often intense. At death, at puberty and marriage, at birth—particularly at twin birth, and in misfortune, family rituals are celebrated; and annually, before the break of the rains, as well as in times of drought, flood, pestilence, famine, or other public misfortune, sacrifices are made on behalf of chiefdoms and groups of chiefdoms to immediate royal ancestors and the more distant heroes. The greatest ritual of all is that performed at the handing over of power from one generation to another, but it occurs only once in thirty years.

This paper is concerned with the family rituals. It would have been better had it covered all the rituals of Nyakyusa society, or at least all the rituals of the ancestor cult, but that would have been impossible in one paper. It must be realized, however, that no one ritual among the Nyakyusa is fully intelligible without reference to the whole series of rituals. The principle, propounded long ago by Radcliffe-Brown, that a symbol recurring in a cycle of rituals is likely to have the same significance in each, holds good for the Nyakyusa: certain symbols of shaving, washing, eating, spreading banana leaves, scattering grain, and so forth were similarly interpreted by our informants in the different rituals of the cycle, and their full significance is apparent only when a comparison of their various uses is made. Therefore we must focus attention on the ritual cycle, rather than on particular events in it.

The analysis offered here is based on the Nyakyusa interpretation of symbols.[1] We were lucky, among the Nyakyusa, in finding people who could, and would, interpret most of the symbols occurring in the rituals, and their interpretations were in substantial agreement. It seemed, from the evidence collected, that certain symbols were understood by everyone, e.g., a variety of plantain, *itoki,* stands for a man, and the *iselya,* a sweet banana eaten ripe, stands for a woman, and this symbolism is as plain to the Nyakyusa as "breeches" and "petticoats" are to us; other symbols were understood only by some people. The most conscious of them were priests and doctors: Kasitile, a hereditary rainmaker and an elderly man, was our best informant on these matters, but there were a dozen others nearly as good. Here the interpretations must be taken on trust for there is not space to quote texts, but the texts are there and will be published.

Among the quarter million of people who are Nyakyusa- or Ngonde-speaking, or dominated by them, there are marked variations in dialect and local custom, and corresponding variations in ritual; but we found in the two groups studied in detail, the Nyakyusa proper and the Kukwe, that differing symbols expressed common ideas and sentiments, and such knowledge as we gathered of the other groups showed that, among them also, there were differences in the symbols used but a very close agreement in the ideas expressed. Local differences in the ritual idiom are taken for granted by the Nyakyusa themselves, and are related both to differences in descent and to differences in the economy of local groups. "We do this because we are Kukwe, but the Penja do it differently," and so on, and they draw direct parallels between what they do and what their neighbors do. Contrary to the commonly accepted idea that ritual is more stable than the interpretation of it, we found the same conceptions expressed in varying ritual forms. The foods used in the ritual, the symbols of separation from the dead, of the union of husband and wife—these vary from group to group; but each time there is the ritual use of the staple food, the symbolic burial and casting away of the

[1] The field material on which this was based was collected by my late husband, Godfrey Wilson, and myself, between 1934 and 1938. We were indebted to the Rockefeller Foundation and the International African Institute for research fellowships.

corpse, the elaborate purification, the symbolic marriage, and so on.

The ritual performed at death is the most elaborate of the family rituals and in it themes which recur in the others are expressed most clearly, so let us begin with it. It consists of two parts: first there is the burial, to which all relatives, and all members of the deceased's village, as well as special friends from other villages, should come; then, some days later, there is the "farewell to the dead" and ritual purification, which concern only immediate agnates and the widow or widows, if the deceased is a man, and siblings, children, grandchildren and the widower, if the deceased is a married woman (cf. Wilson 1939).

As soon as someone dies the women begin wailing, and messages are sent to agnatic kinsmen, affines, and the mother's father or brother. An autopsy is performed to discover the cause of death, and later the agent is sought by divination. The grave is dug in the swept courtyard of the homestead, close to the huts, and some hours after death the corpse is buried, wrapped in cloths and facing in the direction from which his ancestors came. A few utensils are buried in the grave and these, together with the cloths, and the cattle which are sacrificed, are believed to go with the dead to the world of the shades. (Unlike the Ila, the Nyakyusa are quite explicit on this point.) At least one cow from a man's own herd is killed at his death, and his affines—the fathers (or brothers) of his wives, and the husbands of his sisters and daughters—each bring a cow or bull to kill also. For a woman, her father and her husband each provide a cow or bull. Other relatives and friends bring cloths, or barkcloth mourning belts with which to tie up the trembling bellies of the close kinsmen of the dead, and so help to assuage their grief. Crowds of relatives and neighbors gather to wail, to dance, and to feast; the greater the feast, the larger the crowd, the longer the mourning, and the greater the prestige of the family concerned.

Everyone who comes goes to the hut where the corpse is lying, or has lain, and there greets the chief mourners and wails with them a little. The men soon move away to talk and dance, but most of the women remain tight-packed in and around the hut, wailing in unison, swaying as they sit, and weeping unrestrainedly. The men, for their part, express their passionate anger in the war dance, charging back and forth over the new-filled grave, brandishing spears, and ready to quarrel and fight at any moment. Funerals commonly did end in battles between contingents from different villages.

The dance is a form of mourning. "We dance because there is war in our hearts—a passion of grief and fear exasperates us." "A kinsman when he dances assuages his passionate grief; he goes into the house to weep and then comes out and dances the war dance; his passionate grief is made tolerable in the dance; it bound his heart and the dance assuages it." With their spears, the young men slash at the bananas surrounding the courtyard; they are added to the sacrificed cattle and the cloth to accompany the dead on his journey.

Women dance also, threading their way among the men and calling the war cry to urge them on. Gradually, on the second or third day after the death, the war dance merges into a dance of sexual display. To the Nyakyusa this is in no way incongruous; they hold that friends who come to mourn should not leave without encouraging the bereaved to turn their thoughts again to life and laughter. At Christian funerals, also, this is very noticeable; on the second or third day there is a switch from mourning hymns to joyful ones.

Death, to the pagan Nyakyusa, is something very fearful and later ritual is directed toward cleansing the close relatives from the contamination of death, separating them from the corpse, and pushing away the dead from their dreams and waking thoughts. At the same time it ensures the entry of the dead into the company of the shades of the lineage, and he is invited back to his homestead hearth.

If the deceased were a married man his heir is formally recognized, being put into a hut with the widows; then a plantain flower, representing the corpse, is buried. "We are saying to him, 'You corpse, we have finished with you, do not come here again, it is finished for ever, do not look toward us, go away'." The heir and widows, and certain other agnatic kin who are the principals in this ritual, wash in a running stream, wash again with medicine in the doorway of the deceased's hut, and then grovel to eat from the ground plantains set with pumpkin seeds. This symbolizes both the sexual act and the action of a madman, eating feces, and is the essential prophylactic against going mad. The deceased's hut has been strewn with dry banana leaves on which the mourners sleep and sit; until the actions of a madman have been mimed it is left unswept, but now the litter is cleared out and burned.

Relatives and neighbors bring gifts of millet "to greet the shade" (and he is notified of who has come), then there is a final cleansing, sweeping what dust remains in the mourning hut onto the legs of the principals, and passing a flat basket of millet, mixed with pumpkin seeds and lentils, between their legs. This is a symbol of sex intercourse, and of getting rid of the shade from their bodies, for the shade is within men as well as without, and is expelled in the sex fluids. They go again to a stream to bathe, and throw away a stem of plantains, a symbol of the corpse, into the water. Returning home, the participants run into the mourning hut and out again, one by one, as the officiant pours water mixed with powdered medicine on the thatch above the doorway and the water drips onto their bodies. This is interpreted as "bringing back the shade to the home again."

The actions of a madman are mimed a second time, then the participants are shaved, the heir kills another cow and is presented to the children of the deceased as their "father." They reply, "Thanks be, father has risen from the dead."

From some of the millet brought by friends and relatives a paste is made and offered to the shade as the food he ate. With the rest beer is brewed, and the participants drink it with *ikipiki* medicine representing the blood of the lineage. Then they shave their sprouting hair with the lees of the beer, and anoint themselves for the first time since the death. If the deceased were a married man, the formal handing over of the inheritance follows, and the widows are admonished on their duties to their new husband. The heir sits in the doorway of the mourning hut, the senior wife of the deceased hands him a billhook (such as is used for pruning bananas) and he is adjured by the relatives and neighbors present to care for the children of the deceased as if they were his own. Then he enters the hut with the women he has inherited, and must have intercourse with all of them that night. One of them knocks on the wall when he has succeeded and the officiant raises the trill of triumph and shakes a basket of seeds by the door shouting, "Ours, ours, we marvel at the thing." Until this ritual connection the heir and widows must remain continent.

Next morning the heir is formally summoned out of the hut by a man crying, "War has come," i.e., sex intercourse has begun. He sits on a stool in the doorway and there is greeted by the children of the deceased with, "Good morning, father."

Each of the inherited women goes off to her own father's homestead with the filth of intercourse on her and takes with her cooked plantains which she has smeared with her husband's semen and her own emission. These she buries in the banana grove in her father's homestead in which he prays to his shades. The heir similarly goes to his father's homestead, or that of his father's heir if he be of a junior branch of the family, and buries the plantains and semen in his father's sacred grove. Each drinks beer, mixed with medicines, with his own kinsmen. If it is a woman who has died she is replaced by a younger sister or brother's daughter, or if the family has no girl to send they offer a cow to draw water with.

This is only a very sketchy account of a complex ritual, and many of the details, which confirm the interpretation, have necessarily been omitted. There are in it nine main themes:

First, the driving away of the dead from the dreams of his close kinsmen, and measures to prevent his "brooding over them"—the word is that used of a hen brooding over chickens. A widow, in particular, must be separated from the shade of her husband before the heir, or any other man, dare have intercourse with her.

Second, the identification of the mourners with the corpse, and the separation of the shade from both. "What they do to the participants they do to the deceased. . . . If they are not cleansed he is still muddy—his fellows drive him back and say, 'You cannot come yet, you have not bathed in the river.' We throw away the corpse, the contamination of death, into the river . . . we drive the shade away off our bodies to join his fellows . . . we separate the corpse and the shade."

Third, bringing back the shade as a beneficent spirit in the home. "In the ritual we tell the shade to go away and join his fellows and then to come back with them and warm himself by the fire in our house. . . . At first the shade is in our bodies, we cast him out . . . at first it is as if we were still holding the corpse in our arms, but we throw the corpse away into the river . . . the spirit we bring back into our house."

Fourth, a miming of the actions of a madman as a prophylactic against behavior of that sort. The dead, if not separated from the living, brings madness upon them, and simulating madness is a protection against it.

Fifth, the corpse and feces are identified: "The corpse is filth, it is excrement. And so when a madman for whom they have not performed the ritual eats filth, that is the corpse; he is still holding it, they have not done the ritual for him."

Sixth, the shades are identified with semen and seeds, and their control over potency and fertility is recognized. The Nyakyusa think that they are always present in sexual intercourse, and symbols of sex intercourse are interpreted as a means of driving out the shade from the participants' bodies.

Seventh, the "food which he hoed" is symbolically given to the shade, the man who has just died, and he is urged to be satisfied: "You shade, do not think that there was little food at your ritual. . . . The food which we have eaten you have eaten . . . do not create hunger."

Eighth, the shade is acknowledged as a kinsman by eating with him food and beer mixed with *ikipiki* medicine, the symbol of kinship, before he is driven away.

Last, a dead man is formally replaced by his heir, a woman by her sister, or brother's daughter.

There is not space to describe the other rituals of the cycle even in the sketchy way in which the funeral rites have been described. It must suffice to show that the general form of the ritual is the same at death, at puberty and marriage, and at birth.

At puberty a girl is secluded in her mother's hut. Her mothers-in-law (for traditionally she was always betrothed before puberty) come formally to lay the litter on which she sits with her maids, girls a little younger than herself. There the latter spend the greater part of the day weaving mats, dancing and singing; there they entertain young men; and there they sleep. The girl washes ritually with her husband, using *ikipiki* medicine provided by his lineage as a symbol of their marriage, and eats plantains as in the death ritual. "The medicine is to create relationship. Using it means that the bride is now of my lineage." Feasts are exchanged between the two families, hers and her husband's, and after about three months she is elaborately purified and shaved, the litter is taken out and burned, she is admonished on her duties as a married woman and cries, "Put me down, mother." When her virginity has been proved, her husband brings a bull which is killed for a feast. The sacred cut (*ijammapa*) from it is buried by her father in his banana grove, and there he prays, saying: "Here is the meat. I have eaten the food of others, *come out a little,* may she bear a child at her husband's." After she has gone to her husband, she returns with plantains mixed with the sex fluids to bury in her father's grove, just as a widow does after her union with the heir.

The birth ritual is fairly elaborate at the birth of a first child, short and simple for other children, but prolonged and complex in cases of abnormal birth, that is, twin birth or breech delivery. (The same word, *ilipasa,* is used for both and the ritual is the same.) Abnormal birth is felt to be even more dangerous and terrifying than death, and a larger circle of relatives is held to be in danger than are in danger from a corpse. Affines, and mothers' relatives as well as agnates, gather for the purification. Isolation huts are built for the parents of twins, and they are formally inducted, a ritual litter being laid for them. A very large group of relatives gathers to wash with medicines and brings gifts of millet which is put to soak for beer. When that is brewed the temporary huts are burned, the parents and twins and relatives are shaved and anointed, splashed with scalding medicine, and given sausages of medicated porridge which they must eat from the ground. The parents have ritual intercourse and a mess of plantains is taken by the mother of twins to her father's grove, as by a bride or widow.

There are appreciable differences between the various rituals of the cycle: at death there is the wailing and burial; at puberty and marriage the rejoicing, the celebration of virginity; at birth an elaboration of taboos for the mother before her confinement; but here, in the space available, attention is directed to the *common content* of the rituals, the common symbolic pattern.

The framework of all the rituals is the "induction" (*ukwingesia*) with a formal laying of the litter of banana leaves in a hut into which the participant is brought to live apart from other people; the retreat or "seclusion" during which he or she lives and eats apart and is regarded as filthy, for she is "brooded over" by the shades; and the "bringing out" (*ukusosya*) when the shades are driven away and she is purified.[2] During the seclusion the participant is not only filthy but *may not* wash or shave or use cosmetics; in the death ritual she embraces the corpse, smears herself with

[2] Though the classic form of the *rite de passage* adumbrated by Van Gennep holds good, change in status is only one of several themes.

mud and ash, and mimes the actions of a madman. The madman is filthy like a corpse and so is the mourner. In the other rituals also the participant is filthy, brooded over by the shades, in danger of madness.

The symbols of purification are many: clearing and burying the litter; burning the clothes or leaves worn during the seclusion; elaborate and repeated washing and shaving; anointing the body with oil and rouge; and casting away some representation of the shade.

An element of the death ritual is the separation of the corpse and spirit, the final disposal of the corpse, and the bringing of the new shade back "to warm himself with the other shades" at the family hearth; but the distinction between the corpse which is got rid of, and the shade which is welcomed, is not maintained systematically. Repeatedly our informants spoke of the shade (*un-syuka*) being driven away from dreams and waking thought, and from men's bodies, as well as being separated from the corpse. The aim of Nyakyusa ritual is not that union with God, constantly sought in Christian ritual, but a separation, for close association with the pagan gods spells madness and death, not fullness of life. A measure of separation from the shades is a condition of fertility as well as of sanity. Intercourse cannot be fruitful until the shades of her father's lineage have "moved aside a little" from the nubile girl, the shade of a deceased husband from his widow.

All through the rituals the connection of the shades with potency and fertility is emphasized. The shades cause menstruation and sexual desire; they are present in intercourse and ejected as semen; they control conception; they control fertility in the fields. "The shade and the semen are brothers." "When they shake the millet and pumpkin seeds (after ritual connection) the seed is the semen . . . and it is the shade." The symbols of male and female, plantain and sweet banana (*itoki* and *iselya*), recur repeatedly, and the wearing of leaves of these plants is explicitly interpreted as a symbol of fertility. Intercourse between husband and wife is the culmination of the rituals of death, puberty, marriage, and abnormal birth, and is held to be essential to the health of the wife or the widow (even though she be old) as well as proof of the support of the shades for the husband or heir. A symbol of the ritual connection is offered to the shades of both lineages. Indeed the rituals of death and abnormal birth, as well as the ritual of puberty and marriage, may be interpreted as a celebration of the union of husband and wife. For the parents of twins the end of the ritual marks the resumption of married life after a break during which contact between them was felt to be dangerous; for a widow and the heir of a dead man, the end of the death ritual marks the beginning of their union. The manner in which a widow, or the mother of twins, is admonished on her proper behavior as a wife, like a girl at her first marriage, underlines the fact that the death and birth rituals are, in a sense, also marriage rituals.

The virility of a lineage is symbolized by the *ikipiki* medicine interpreted as "our blood" or "semen." With it mourners, menstruating girls, bride and groom, the newborn babies and their mothers, are treated. To provide it or use it is to acknowledge kinship: husband and wife wash with it together in acknowledgment that the wife is now "one blood" with her husband; the grandmother washes her son's child with it in acknowledgment of its legitimacy; in the death rituals the mourners eat food with it acknowledging their kinship with the shade. To belong to a lineage is to be protected, and the *ikipiki* medicine is held to protect those who are empty from those who are heavy with real semen, or other medicines.

The shade, *unsyuka*, "he who is risen from the dead," may be interpreted as the principle of life, but at the same time he is "the one beneath" (*ugwa pasi*), filthy and fearful. What men worship is life; what they fear is death, corruption; and for the Nyakyusa, as for the Christian, the two are inextricably mingled. *Imindu* means dirt, dust, rubbish, the litter of the seclusion hut, and also the shade.

I have spoken of the Nyakyusa disgust of filth (*ubunyali*) which is associated with a corpse, menstruation, childbirth, intercourse, and feces, and all these are identified in some fashion with the shade. Feces "go below to the land of the shades." "The hair of a corpse is the shade's," the hair of a girl at puberty is "the filth of her menstrual blood." In all the rituals the "filth" is buried, shaved off, burned, washed away. At the death ritual "he who is risen" is brought to "warm himself" at the family hearth, but yet he dwells in the earth and is "dirty."

The conception of impurity, uncleanness, associated with the physiological functions of coition, excretion, menstruation, and with childbirth and death is, of course, a very widespread one. The

Nyakyusa perhaps emphasize it more than their neighbors (though not more than the Jews or the Hindus) and their preoccupation with purification in the rituals is paralleled by the emphasis laid on cleanliness (*ubwifyusi*) in person, in house and courtyard, in cooking, and in disposal of excrement. Their extreme cleanliness, in contrast with their neighbors, was remarked by all the early travellers in the area and is still obvious. Houses and courtyards are swept and garnished, pots and dishes scoured, food scrupulously covered with fresh banana leaves when it is served at feasts; a good housewife is *umwifyusi,* she who is clean. Men wash daily in running water, and children are trained to take a hoe with them when they go to defecate and to bury the feces.

The horror of filth is very closely associated with the fear of madness, which is, at the same time, a fear of too close association with the dead. It is when the dead have not been driven away, but return in dreams, when the necessary separation of living and dead has not been achieved, that men go mad. Madness is most often spoken of as the penalty for neglect of the death ritual, but it is not, in theory, confined to that. "All the rituals are the same; if they are neglected men will become mad."

Besides madness, men fear sterility, debility, swollen limbs, and diarrhea "to get rid of the filth in the belly," if the rituals are neglected or taboos broken.

THE NATURE OF SYMBOLISM IN NYAKYUSA RITUAL

Symbolism is always based on an association, a feeling of likeness between things. The intrinsic quality of an object or relationship, or event, is expressed in terms of another object or action which it is felt to resemble. The images men use, the things they feel to be alike, are determined in a general way by the form of the society: the poetry of Louis MacNeice, for example, could only be that of an industrialized society, and Nyakyusa images are in terms of bananas, staple grains, smithing on a primitive forge, lineage organization, and so on. There are "cultural idioms," accepted forms of expression, which frequently recur—we talk in terms of breeches and petticoats, whereas the Nyakyusa talk in terms of plantains and sweet bananas—and these one can learn. We can understand, when it is explained, that the *ikipiki* is a symbol for the blood of a lineage, that washing under a waterfall, or lying in a stream and letting pebbles flow between fingers and toes, are symbols of purification, and so on. But though one learns the symbolism of a culture as one learns the language, and is aware that certain forms of expression are common, one cannot predict with certainty what symbols will be used in a ritual, any more than one can predict what symbols a poet will use.

The symbolism of Nyakyusa ritual, and indeed all magical symbolism, differs in this way from the symbolism of poetry: in a magical ritual things felt to be like are taken as causally connected, whereas in poetry they are just alike and that's all. In the rituals, the participants mime madness as a prophylactic against it; the pregnant woman does not linger in the doorway lest the child do likewise and delivery be protracted; the woman who is sleeping with her husband does not approach a smithy, for sex intercourse and smithing are alike and antagonistic.

This brings us to the next point: sometimes like produces like, as with the hesitation in the doorway or the "fierceness" of a pregnant woman which makes the game "fierce" if her husband goes hunting; and sometimes like things or actions are taken as antagonistic, as smithing and intercourse, seed in the belly and seed in the ground, war and "war of the mats," that is, sex intercourse. Within the field of anthropology I do not think that there are any rules, any general principles to be found, which would explain why some things are taken as sympathetic and others as antagonistic, or even why certain things are selected as like. It depends upon how the poet felt when he created his image, for the diviner or doctor who creates new ritual by modifying the old is, in this sense, a poet.

I have drawn the analogy with poetry. It is scarcely necessary to add that the same conception—purification, madness, what you will—is symbolized in many ways, and that the same symbol may represent several things to the same person.

ANALYSIS

Now we come to the deeper analysis: what do the rituals really express? The recurring symbols of Nyakyusa society have been indicated and interpreted. What ideas and attitudes underlie them?

The funeral rites are an adjustment to death through a violent expression of grief, a passionate fighting of death itself, and an assertion of life expressed in dancing, flirting, feasting on meat, deliberately attempting to push away the dead from dreams and waking thoughts, replacing the dead through the levirate or sororate,[3] and finally, seeking a scapegoat.[4] The mourners are supported by all their relatives and neighbors who must gather to weep with them and also have the obligation of cheering them before they scatter.

All the rituals, including the death ritual itself, are an assertion of the supreme importance of procreation. Reproductive power is treated as sacred, hedged about with taboos, controlled by the shades; the climax of each ritual is the meeting of husband and wife, or wives; the overt purpose health and fertility.

One manifestation of the sacredness of the reproductive cycle is that it is polluting. All the physiological functions are felt to be polluting: the shades are associated with the corpse, and with procreation, and they are filthy, unclean. Those undergoing a ritual who are "brooded upon by the shades" are also unclean, and *may not* cleanse themselves until the ritual enjoins it. Madness comes from the failure to purify oneself in the ritual, to separate from the shades. This sense of pollution, and the horror of madness with which it is linked among the Nyakyusa, is an expression of fear, and comes very close to the sense of awe; what Otto called the "Idea of the Holy." Whether or not the sense of pollution is also linked with a sense of guilt I do not know. The Freudians would assuredly interpret it in that way, but I have no evidence that the Nyakyusa feel guilty. Of their terror at death and abnormal birth, and in a lesser degree of ordinary birth and menstruation, there is no doubt. All these are felt to be polluting.

The mutual dependence of kin, living and dead, is expressed again and again. Kinsmen are "members of one another" in the sense that the death of a kinsman, or the birth of twins to a kinsman or kinswoman, affects an individual directly. Health and sanity are thought to depend upon the performance of rituals with kin; procreation and fertility of fields are controlled by dead kinsmen. The separation and linking of lineages is also expressed in the

[3] Sororate is used here to mean the replacement of a dead wife by her sister or other kinswoman, and distinguished from sororal polygyny, the marriage of two sisters simultaneously.

[4] The reactions to death postulated by Ruth Benedict as characteristic of different societies occur successively in Nyakyusa ritual. Cf. *Patterns of Culture, passim.*

conception of the *ikipiki* medicine, the "blood of the lineage," and the mess of plantains taken by a woman to bury in her father's banana grove. The differentiation of male and female, of lineages, and of local groups, is expressed in terms of crops and of cattle: what is *not* reflected in the family rituals is the age structure. It is the development of the individual rather than organized age groups which is symbolized.

All the rituals are a public and formal expression of change in status; a breaking off of an old relationship which is incompatible with the new. The dead man joins his fathers as a shade; his widow pushes him away—to separate from him is a condition of her remarriage. The maid is acknowledged as a married woman, of one blood with her husband, and the shades of her father's lineage must "move aside a little." It is the end of childhood and dependence upon her parents. The newborn infant is accepted as a member of its father's lineage; until the birth ritual is performed it is not treated as a person or acknowledged as a kinsman, and at the end of the ritual the mother, who has been separated from her husband, returns to him.

Last, there is reflected in the rituals the value set on cattle, and the dependence upon bananas and on staple grains and relishes. The dead must take cattle with them if they are to be received by the shades; sacrifices offered them are primarily of beef and millet beer, and these are offered in the banana grove.

It has been clear, since the publication of the *Andaman Islanders*,[5] that rituals both arouse and canalize emotion; they teach men to feel and teach them what to feel. The family rituals of the Nyakyusa occur when emotions are aroused anyway, at the crises of life, and they enhance and direct these emotions.

Terror at the death of their kind is common enough in animals, and it is reasonable to assume that men have an instinctive fear of a corpse, but the society may play this up or minimize it. Nyakyusa society plays it up—men tremble at death—they are expected to do so—and in the ritual they receive comfort and reassurance. They turn from death to life. I suggest that there may also be an instinctive basis for terror at birth; that the cow or bitch in labor is a terrified animal. However that may be, in Nyakyusa society the reproductive process is felt to be fearful, and most of all

[5] My debt to Radcliffe-Brown in this analysis will be obvious to all students of anthropology.

an abnormal birth. Nyakyusa Christians are quick to point out that they do not fear death, or birth, or menstruation, as the pagans do—they disregard many if not all of the traditional taboos—and that the pagans themselves fear much less than formerly; in other words, that the fear is culturally determined, or at least *enhanced*.

In all the rituals the expression of certain sentiments is compulsory, whatever the individual may feel. Nyakyusa women commented freely on the fact that certain widows were not really grieved at their husbands' deaths: "Perhaps they are just thinking about whom they will marry next," they said, "but still they must wail and smear themselves with mud and ashes." And the expression itself tends to induce the appropriate feeling. Even to an outsider the pressure of the ritual is strong: the sense of terror and grief when you are in the midst of a throng of women, close-packed, and weeping and wailing, is intense.

Radcliffe-Brown (1952: 157) has argued not only that rituals develop certain sentiments in the minds of individuals, but that a society depends for its existence on the presence of these sentiments. It can, I think, be shown that the sentiments expressed in the Nyakyusa ritual are those necessary to the continuance of the society.

In every society men must overcome death, emotionally; they must turn to life. In the death ritual the mourners are distraught, terrified. They express their grief and put it behind them; their relatives and neighbors rally round them, share their sorrow, and help them to overcome it. It is true that the ritual enhances fear, but it also overcomes it (cf. Homans 1941). It is no accident that the Nyakyusa interpret all the rituals, and especially the death ritual, as a protection against going mad, against the distintegration of the personality.

And why should the death ritual enhance fear? Why not play it down? Because in their terror people are made to realize their dependence upon their kinsmen for cooperation in performing the ritual, and the necessity for following traditional custom. All the family rituals of the Nyakyusa enhance fear and make men turn to their kinsmen and to traditional observance to relieve it. The sense of awe (which is linked with the idea of pollution) expresses dependence upon the gods, the ancestors, and so upon kinsmen. In short, fear makes for the solidarity of the kinship group, and for cultural continuity. It is also apparent that fear of supernatural sanctions helps to maintain order in Nyakyusa society. The fear of the gods makes men "walk humbly and do justly." And in so far as the rituals nourish the sense of awe, they strengthen the force of supernatural sanctions.

The public acknowledgment of change in status, of new responsibilities (expressed very pointedly in the admonition), impresses on individuals their changing obligations within the kinship group. The rituals are a symbolic weaning from childhood, from a former marriage, or from deceased parents, and compel acceptance of a new position.

Societies depend not only on sentiments of mutual dependence among their members, but also on their physical survival—on the will for reproduction among them. Certain groups seem to lose this, though we know little of the reasons why they do so. The Nyakyusa rituals express the supreme importance of procreation and regulate it. Procreation outside marriage is mystically dangerous, pregnancies are deliberately spaced, and the reproductive life of women limited by certain taboos. Thus conception is confined to the times when the chances for the child's survival are best, and the care of children in a family is ensured.

The word *ritual* has been used all through this paper and no reference has been made to ceremonial. I make a distinction between the two (Wilson 1939), using ritual to mean a primarily religious action, that is, an action directed to secure the blessing of some mystical power or powers. The action may be a negative, i.e., an avoidance or taboo, as well as a positive one. Symbols and concepts are employed in rituals, but are subordinated to practical ends. Ceremonial, on the other hand, is an elaborate conventional form for the expression of feeling, not confined to religious occasions; any emotional situation, whether religious or secular, may be clothed in ceremony, and a ceremony is not enforced by mystical sanctions, only by conventional ones. In short, a ceremony is an appropriate and elaborate form for the expression of feeling, but a ritual is action believed to be efficacious. A ritual is often embedded in ceremonial which is not held to be necessary to the efficacy of the ritual but which is felt to be appropriate. Both ritual and ceremonial have a function in rousing and canalizing emotion, but ritual, by relating its symbols to some supposed transcendental reality, affects people more deeply than a ceremony, which some will describe as "mere play-acting."

Finally, I hold that rituals reveal values at the deepest level. There is much woolly talk of values and of how to study them, of how to achieve system and objectivity in the observation of them. Surely men express in ritual what moves them most, and since the form of expression is conventionalized and obligatory, it is the values of the group which are revealed. I see in the study of rituals the key to an understanding of the essential constitution of human societies.

10 SYMBOLIC VALUES AND THE
INTEGRATION OF SOCIETY AMONG
THE MAPUCHE OF CHILE

Louis C. Faron

INTRODUCTION

THE MAPUCHE are best known to anthropologists by the generic term "Araucanian," under which are subsumed the now extinct Picunche, the heavily acculturated Huilliche, and the Mapuche, the "people of the land." The Mapuche live on more than 2,000 small reservations in southern Central Chile, where they engage in field agriculture and raise cattle, horses, sheep, and other animals. Their population is estimated at 200,000, and they occupy an area roughly the size of Delaware. After resisting White soldiers and settlers for approximately three hundred years, they were finally defeated in the Rebellion of 1880–82 and placed on reservations. Their society underwent numerous important structural changes, and cultural modifications took place as well, as a result of the reservation system (see Faron 1956, 1961a, 1961c); but they have survived as one of the largest functioning indigenous societies in the New World. In this paper I would like to analyze a most significant aspect of the cultural and social ambient of the contemporary Mapuche, one which has considerable implications for any consideration of social stability or change.

Following Durkheim, Radcliffe-Brown wrote long ago that "it is in ancestor-worship that we can most easily discover and demonstrate the social function of a religious cult" (1952: 163). Since the propitiation of ancestral spirits is central to the scheme of Mapuche morality (see Faron 1961b), it could possibly be argued that concern with ancestral spirits in some way conditions most aspects of Mapuche social life. However, this line of inquiry might

Reprinted from *The American Anthropologist* 64 (6), 1962: 1151–64, by permission of the author and the American Anthropological Association.

easily bog down in a morass of tortuous evaluations and judgments, as does Durkheim's classification of phenomena into sacred and profane categories, and, in any case, would not seem to result in the creation of a total impression of the relationship between Mapuche ideational and social systems. But it may be possible to discover a more fundamental principle than ancestor propitiation in Mapuche society, in which the total structure of symbolic values may be related to the social order. This is the line of inquiry pursued here.

In Durkheim's treatment of the sacred and profane, one encounters a consideration of what are clearly moral values of society. It is according to these values that the sacred and profane categories are defined. But one is confronted with much a priori reasoning and tortuous argument to the end of establishing all phenomena in categories of either sacred or profane dimensions. The pervasive notion of dualism among the Mapuche, at least at first glance, would seem to lend itself to orthodox Durkheimian classification. A sacred-profane dichotomy certainly exists in Mapuche thought. But by no means all Mapuche values, even paired as they are in sets of complementary opposites, are amenable to dichotomization in Durkheim's terms. Thus, the sacred-profane classification is not fully applicable to the Mapuche system of values or, at least, does not encompass it. This, it might be said, is well enough—interpretative difficulties serving to indicate the empirical limits of analysis in the framework of a sacred-profane dichotomization of the Mapuche world view. But this actually leaves very much to be desired, because the limits of analysis seem to be reached or approached at the outset.

From a number of examples of this kind of difficulty which suggest themselves, I select the possible classification of shamans as sacred and sorcerers as profane. With respect to the Mapuche, this is a pointless classification, since both shamans and sorcerers have a numinous quality, and since even sorcerers, clearly evil on most occasions and in most contexts, at times have the important role of operating on the positive side of the moral universe when called upon to exact vengeance. Durkheimian thinking would probably deny this interpretation, but the alternative route it suggests is, I feel, unattractive and dangerous. It would take one entirely outside the limits of Mapuche thinking, the relationship between the conceptual model and its empirical foundation becoming most tenuous. Sacred phenomena are viewed as good by the Mapuche, but not all good is sacred. Sacred-profane and good-evil concepts actually cut across one another when unadulterated Durkheimian reasoning is brought to bear on them.

The value of any anthropological concept is measured by its usefulness in understanding and ordering social and cultural phenomena. Since these phenomena are social and cultural and do not exist in a vacuum, they must be ordered in correspondence to the manner in which they are viewed by the people themselves. This is not to say that the Mapuche need visualize a total structural order, but that their partial, piecemeal, and seemingly orderless views be consistent with whatever conceptual order is imposed upon their social and cultural system by the anthropologist. I take my cue, therefore, from the Mapuche themselves.

The interpretative difficulties of the sacred-profane approach are resolvable once it is recognized that the underlying motif of Mapuche thought it not a comprehensive good-evil or sacred-profane set of references but, rather, a dualistic world view into which good-evil, sacred-profane, and other antithetical categories are subsumable as relative and partial expressions of the total order of society. Numerous sets of value symbols are amenable to arrangement consistent with Mapuche notions of this dualistic ordering of the universe and, of especial interest here, the structure of symbolic values may be related significantly to the ordering of social institutions.

THE CONCEPTS OF "HANDEDNESS" AND COMPLEMENTARY DUALISM

The most comprehensive theoretical framework for this kind of analysis has been suggested by Robert Hertz, a student of Durkheim, and more recently has been refined and applied to great advantage by Rodney Needham[1] in the analysis of Southeast Asian, Indonesian, and African material. Hertz dealt with the phenomenon of complementary opposition in his essay, "The Pre-eminence of the Right Hand: A Study of Religious Polarity" (1960), and noted that in many if not all societies "honors, desig-

---

[1] I express my thanks to Rodney Needham for introducing me to the Hertzian scheme and for giving the manuscript of this paper a critical reading.

nations, prerogatives" were accorded to the *right* hand, whereas the *left* hand held an ancillary if not despised position. Enlarging on this theme, Needham writes:

> The symbolic opposition of right and left and a dualistic categorization of phenomena are so common as to seem natural proclivities of the human mind. What is to be noted here is the particular way in which these notions are symbolically related to the divisions of . . . [a particular] society . . . (1958: 97).

The theoretical interest which underlies this kind of analysis is phrased by Needham as follows:

> . . . to determine through a consideration of symbolic usages whether or not there are more abstract structural principles underlying both social relations . . . and other aspects of . . . culture which are not obviously connected with them (1958: 89).

The result may provide a "total structural analysis."

Whether it does or not would seem to depend on the type of descent system and the structural relations surrounding marriage. Needham suggests that the relationship between value system and social structure is most complete and significant in societies organized around systems of prescriptive alliance and that "marriage preferences . . . have no structural entailments in the total social system comparable to those of a prescriptive system . . ." (1958: 75). The Mapuche have a system of strongly preferential matrilateral alliance. It is my contention that the symbolic and social order of the Mapuche are related in a most significant manner and that they, therefore, may be viewed as representations of a single conceptual scheme—one in which the dualism noted in the ideational construct of complementary opposition is reflected in a dualistic ordering of social institutions. I feel also that these notions of dualism are revealed in the system of *preferred* matrilateral marriage.

If the phenomenon of complementary dualism in association with a right-left polarity of symbolic values is to be used as an analytic tool, it must be able to satisfy certain requirements. For one thing, it must comprise a symbolic arrangement of sets of socially significant polarities. That is, the polar opposites must be logical constructs which together form some sort of conceptual unit. If this much is satisfied, a cultural analysis of the value system is possible. But more than this is needed for the sort of interpretation attempted here. These conceptual units must in turn have some significant relationship to the institutions of society as conceived by the people themselves. In the case of the Mapuche, this relationship is most clearly seen in the area of ritual belief and action where there exists an association of numerous ideas and values with right and left hands, which enable a Hertzian type of analysis to be made. Handedness serves to symbolize the polarity in thought, values, and their social correlates. By analogy, this dualism is discoverable outside the immediate ritual sphere.

The general problem at hand is that of relating seemingly disparate ethnographic data to one another so that they make sense taken singly or together. Now, in Mapuche society, as in many others, it is apparent that the system of kinship and marriage largely dominates the field of social relationships (see Faron 1961a, 1961b, 1962); that the nature of the marital bond, therefore, is a significant factor in social interaction. Mapuche marry kin in a strongly preferential system which is matrilateral and which involves sets of relatively stable wife-giving and wife-receiving, patrilineal descent groups. It is clear that this system entails prohibitions which constitute moral rules. There is also a further connection between marriage-linked lineages (reservation groups) and ritual congregationalism which, over and above a number of obvious concordances between marriage and other social institutions, is expressive of a unified system of morality (see Faron 1961c, Chaps. 8, 9). In order to make more than a series of piecemeal functional statements of the relationship between Mapuche morality and its expression in various social institutions an integrating concept, such as complementary dualism, is needed.

Mapuche social relationships are in fact shot through with notions of complementary opposition. Many of these are clearly discernible, some as sacred-profane, good-evil, superior-inferior, and so forth—all in analogic or explicit association with a right-left dichotomy. Where the preeminence of the right hand exists as a concept of symbolic importance in society, we may expect to find notions of superior, good, health, and so forth, associated with the right. The logic of dualistic reasoning places complementary notions of inferior, sickness, and so on, with the left. Even in the absence of unmistakable (i.e., verbalized) association with handedness, an ordering of other values may be obtained by analogy with reference to right and left. Indeed, a Hertzian analysis is possible even in the absence of specific mention of handedness (cf. Needham 1960a: 115).

SYMBOLISM AND SOCIAL STRUCTURE IN MAPUCHELAND

Perhaps the clearest association between phenomena which belong on the right and those which belong on the left is seen in the symbolic attachments of good and evil in the Mapuche scheme of religious morality. Some of the most obvious of these are tabulated below and then discussed for exemplification.

TABLE 1. MAPUCHE SYMBOLIC ATTACHMENTS TO RIGHT AND LEFT HAND

Left	*Right*
evil	good
death	life
night	day
sickness	health
wekufe (evil spirits)	ancestral spirits
sorcerer	shaman
underworld (*reñu*)	afterworld (*wenumapu*)
kai kai	*tren tren*
poverty	abundance
hunger	fullness

In Araucanian, *kuk* means "hand," *wele* means "left," and *man* means "right." *Welekuk* and *mankuk,* or simply wele and man, with kuk understood, signify respectively "left hand" and "right hand." There is an unmistakable and literal connection between left and evil, and right and good. For example, *piukeman* (*piuke:* heart) is an expression equivalent to *kume piuke* (*kume:* good) and means "pure in heart," "free from evil." *Wesa* (evil) and *wele* (left) are also used interchangeably. *Welenkin,* for example, refers to leftness and means a heart palpitation which forebodes evil or misfortune. Similarly, *welethungun* (left talk) means to speak evil (especially of one's self in contemplation of suicide). An "evil-headed" or "crazy" person (possessed of evil forces) is alternately called *wesa lonko* (*lonko:* head) or *wele lonko.* In a small number of other words, there is also this literal connection between handedness and qualities of good and evil, but permissible improvisations actually would extend the number of such words infinitely. For the most part, however, the association is analogical in a conceptual scheme in which phenomena associated with evil are linked to the left "half" of the universe and those associated with good linked with the right. The right hand column in Table 1 contains obviously good phenomena and the left their complementary opposites, as these entries are paired by the Mapuche. They constitute a partial expression of the over-all dualistic order of the Mapuche universe.

There are other clear-cut right-left associations from which analogies may be drawn. When, for example, ancestral spirits appear as Hawks of the Sun, in answer to a ritual summons or in a dream, they may make peculiarly significant gyrations to indicate the propitiousness of some act or plan or the effectiveness of ritual supplication. Whatever the motivation, if they circle to the right it is taken as a good omen, as an indication that events will go well, that prayers have been or will be answered. If they circle to the left, prayers will not be answered, evil is foreshadowed.[2] Some human error, some sin, is indicated. Perhaps a sorcerer remained undiscovered at a funeral or fertility rite. If so, further propitiation is called for, the stigma of impurity or ritual imperfection lingering until a compensatory ritual is held. The Mapuche do not, however, erect insurmountable barriers to their own well-being. Bad omens or visions of evil usually occur before or during, rather than after, the staging of some ceremony, their mitigation providing one of the motives for holding the ceremony, or prolonging and perfecting it.

A similar association of right and left with good and evil occurs when anyone is startled by a bird's song near at hand. If the bird is to one's right, it signifies the presence of an ancestral spirit and presages good fortune. If on the left, it is taken to represent the embodiment of evil and to presage evil. When one dreams of taking a left fork in the road, instead of a right turn, this is also interpreted as an evil omen. Stories of moral import are geared to this left-right theme, insofar as persons who turn right enjoy riches, huge quantities of food served in banquet style, and general good fortune. Those who take the left turn suffer poverty, hunger, and

---

[2] While the historical sources do not contain detailed enough data useful to the kind of interpretation attempted here, one repeatedly reads that shamans used to forecast the outcome of military and other ventures according to the flight of birds. Could these have been Hawks of the Sun? Could their flight have constituted the right-left gyrations alluded to above?

general misfortune. Not until the steps are retraced (similar to the repetition of ritual prayer) and the right fork gained do persons throw off the aura of evil and come to enjoy the blessing of good fortune.

The ritual priest (*ñillatufe*) cuts off the right ear of the sacrificial sheep and holds it aloft in his right hand, while offering prayer to ancestors and the pantheon of Mapuche gods. The blood of the sheep is placed in a special wooden bowl to the right of the main altar, the sacred leaves of which are periodically aspersed with it during the *ñillatun* fertility rite. Likewise, the sheep's heart is cut out and held aloft in the right hand of the ñillatufe, who passes it to his chiefly assistants lined up along his right (and the right of the altar), who, as the ñillatufe, bite into it, hold it up in their right hands, and offer ancestral prayer. By the time the heart has stopped twitching, it is placed in the crotch of the main altar. The right ear of a sheep is also severed in the *konchotun* ritual, a sort of blood brotherhood, which may occur during ñillatun, in which the two participants swear lifelong friendship and mutual obligation on the sheep's blood.

There seems to be a clear enough association between good phenomena and the right hand, so that ancestral spirits, shamans, *tren tren* (the magic mountain), day, and life itself may be placed on the right and, their complementary opposites, *wekufe,* sorcerers, *kai kai* (usually an evil serpent or sea bird), night, and the death in which forces of evil deal, on the left. In these instances there is always some association between rightness and leftness and, respectively, good and evil. Many other sets of symbolic values may also be ordered with reference to a right-left dichotomy.

While all the above-mentioned entries would seem to serve well as a clear-cut ordering of symbolic values associated with good and evil, there are other pairs of opposites which, while linked in Mapuche thinking, are not clearly good or evil, either to the Western "mind" or to the Mapuche themselves. Yet they are classifiable as either right or left hand symbols by analogy to the previous list, and by their relatively superior or inferior qualities, as these are verbalized by the Mapuche. Most of these entries have special significance for ritual occasions and, in this context, are commonly verbalized with regard to right-left associations (Table 2).

This list concerns mostly natural elements and directions, as these are ordered into a dualistic scheme. There are earth, land, sacred soil, known and unknown land; sky, "heaven," and celestial bodies; colors. West, north, winter, cold, below, blue, sin, outside, are all in some way connected to death and, therefore, analogically related to the evil forces which cause it and the leftness which symbolizes it. East, south, summer, warm, land, above, yellow, white, expiation, altar, and ceremonial field are

TABLE 2.   OTHER MAPUCHE RIGHT-LEFT ASSOCIATIONS

Left	*Right*
west	east
north	south
winter	summer
cold	warm
moon	sun
(water)	blood
speech	ritual language
ocean	land
below	above
blue	yellow
black	white
layman	priest
sin	expiation (ritual)
(outside)	ceremonial field

associated with good and the right hand. In some cases the association is direct and literal but, in all cases, these sets of opposing yet complementary values are analogically connected with right and left. Sun, blood, ritual speech, and priest are all associated positively with ancestral spirits and the gods. East is the orientation for all ritual action and, ideally, the entrance to Mapuche houses should face east. West is associated with death, as is the ocean which ancestral spirits must cross before arriving safely in the afterworld. The ocean is the spirit's final barrier in its journey to *nomelafken* (*lafken:* ocean; *nome:* other side) or as it is sometimes rendered *wenumapu* (*wenu:* above; *mapu:* land). The north is the origin of cold, harsh winter rains, starvation, and general hardship. It is also the place of origin of the Inca and the Spaniards, the collective *winka*. Moon is placed in opposition to sun and in the left-hand column because of its connection with female menses. Below and above are literally inferior and superior categories which serve to qualify the characteristics of many phenomena, and they are analogically compatible with evil and good, left and right. *Minche* (below) *mapu* (land) refers to the grave, similar to the way in which *reñu* (underworld) refers to the subterranean region inhabited by witches and all forces of evil. Minche connotes as well defeat in either physical or supernatural combat. Wenu (above) is clearly associated with sun, the haven of ancestral spirits, the domain of the gods, and so forth, and is placed on the right by analogy to good connotations. Black and blue (not always differentiated) are associated with rain and/or death. Black and dark blue banners symbolize rain in the ñillatun agricultural fertility rite; white banners and sky-blue banners with yellow figures symbolize sun and good weather. The funeral wake (*kurikawin:* black assemblage) and mourning in general are symbolized by black. The cold, rainy, death-dealing month of August may be called *kurikuyen* (black month or black moon). Certain relatives of the affinal category may be called *kuripapai* (black women), and so on.

The following sets of complementary opposites involve, for the most part, categories of inferior (left) and superior (right) statuses, although, with respect to winka (outsider) and incest, we are again confronted with notions of evil. I have grouped the following categorical sets separately into Table 3 in order to present them as the final step in demonstrating that the same dualistic principle inheres in the ordering of social phenomena as that which has been shown to characterize the complementary opposition of symbolic values. Many "problems" of interpretation are cleared up or at least placed in new perspective by applying this conceptual scheme to Mapuche values and their social correlates. The left-hand column contains inferior categories relative to the right-hand column.

TABLE 3.   MAPUCHE INFERIOR-SUPERIOR AND LEFT-RIGHT HAND ASSOCIATIONS

Left	*Right*
woman/child	man
kona	*lonko*
junior	senior
subordinate lineage	dominant lineage
gift-receiver	gift-giver
wife-receiver	wife-giver
incest	marriage (with MBD)
winka	Mapuche
reservation	ritual congregation

There is a differential evaluation of the sexes in Mapuche society which is consistent with a left-right (woman-man) dualistic set of symbols. There are many indications of male superiority and association with the right, as well as with good and the sacred. Ancestral spirits, for example, are dealt with as though they all were male (elders and chiefs: *lonko*), and these have a close working relationship with the sons of the gods. Female ancestors are soon dropped from the roster of propitiated ancestral spirits and are eventually subsumed into the general ancestral category, *kuifiche*. It is the male of the god-set who is propitiated and supplicated first; then prayers are directed to his wife, who is propitiated only once or at least much less often than her divine husband. None of this seems incongruent with a patrilineal, patrilocal, and patripotestal society.

There are other indications of male dominance and a clear association between females and inferiority, if not evil. But there is a relativity of symbolism involved here which should not be overlooked. Women, for example, are barred from participation in the council of elders (males) which discusses procedural plans for ñillatun and which offers private (i.e., among themselves as representatives of their respective lineages) prayers to ancestral spirits during the preparatory phase of fertility ceremonies. Women are clearly associated with sorcery and are considered the most able sorcerers by virtue of being females, and, by analogy, may be placed on the black, cold, death-ridden side of the conceptual universe.

An interesting matter of the relativity of these sets of values enters at this point. It is that male shamans are not considered fully masculine by the Mapuche. Some are suspected of being homosexual. All or most dress in women's clothing (cf. Needham 1960b: 26–27) during their performance. Others are blind, crippled, or mentally unstable. All of these characteristics are non-masculine in Mapuche eyes and, furthermore, are associated with the occult part of the universe of which sorcery is a part. But this is not to say that shamans are viewed as aligned with the forces of evil. For the Mapuche, shaman-sorcerer comprises a logical set of complementary forces symbolizing, respectively, good and evil, with right and left associations. It is inconsistent with Mapuche thought to include males in shamanistic roles, even *thungulmachin* (the shaman's male helper) having occult powers which are not wholly masculine. Therefore, male practitioners are attributed female characteristics. The shaman is not the logical opposite of the ritual priest (ñillatufe) in Mapuche thinking, even though shamans sometimes complement the activities of the ñillatufe in ñillatum. The ñillatufe has quite a different relationship to the supernatural than the shaman; he does not enter the spirit world, but is tied to it formally by virtue of birth into a particular patrilineal descent group and in the line of succession of chiefs. He is, therefore, at the same time political, lineal, and spiritual leader of the dominant lineage of his natal reservation, the group which is most clearly responsible for the staging of ñillatun, caring for invited participants and honored guests, and bearing heaviest responsibility of a moral nature for the successful enactment of the ceremony. The shaman has a quite different role.

The kona-lonko dichotomy also points up the relativity of these sets of complementary categories. Lonko (chiefs and other elders) are clearly in a socially superior position with respect to their male kinsmen. Formerly, they exacted tribute from them and others in their following and, even today, receive obligatory prestations on certain ritual occasions. They are also accorded the privilege of attending work parties in which they appear as titular heads, doing little or no work themselves. The lonko who is also ñillatufe receives abundant quantities of food, not as payment for his services to the congregation (as is the case with the shaman), nor as a gift, but rather as his due levy—with the understanding that this food will be distributed for ritual purposes.

Kona and lonko are related as junior and senior, but the junior-senior dichotomy is expressed in a number of other ways as well. The use of kinship terms expresses the superiority of the senior members of Mapuche society (uncles, fathers, grandfathers) to whom respect is accorded by all others. The same kinship idiom is extended to groups of relatives in the marriage alliance system. Males of the wife-giving unit are called *weku* (maternal "uncle"), which is a respectful designation, whereas males of the wife-receiving group are called ñillan ("the one who has purchased"), at best a designation of inferior social status.

Titiev mentioned that there was a feeling of "latent hostility" with respect to ñillan, and that this "person" is considered as a "potential traitor" (1951: 48). I would say that these facts might be interpreted to greater advantage as indicating that certain wife-receiving groups or segments of any large wife-receiving group are placed in a relatively suspect social position in which more than mere social inferiority is implied. These are the wife-receiving groups which have not maintained sustained marriage ties in the matrilateral system, or those just initiating such alliance, and which, because of that, might be suspected of actually practicing homicidal sorcery. It is members of such receiving groups who *must* put in an appearance at funeral ceremonies of the lineage who formerly provided them with wives or else bear the brunt of general suspicion and possible retaliation. It is their failure to meet the former obligations of ritual participation which lays suspicion upon them, just as the fulfilment of such obligation has the opposite effect with respect to units which maintained sustained and multiple intermarriages over several generations. In their obligation to bury in-married women in the same ground as lineal ancestors is symbolized a dualistic separation of the two descent groups and the commitment of the socially inferior group to sustain the responsibility and cost which burial entails.

With respect to the subordinate lineage-dominant lineage set, little more need be said. The subordinate lineages are localized on the reservation by sufferance of the dominant one. Members of subordinate lineages look to the dominant one for political and ritual leadership (on well-functioning reservations) and, in any case, are forced to trace descent back to the time of the original chief in order to validate certain of their reservation rights. The greater rights of the dominant lineage have worked their effect on both the size and the composition of dominant and subordinate lineages throughout Mapucheland, and it will be easily understood that it is from the subordinate lineages that most young people emigrate to the cities and farms of Chile and Argentina, being accorded fewer real opportunities than members of dominant lineages to gain a living on their natal reservation. In some cases, when feelings run high, members of these subordinated lineages are called by the opprobrious name winka, usually reserved for Whites.

The superiority of gift-givers to gift-receivers is not absolute, although in any particular situation gift-receivers are in an inferior position, momentarily at least. With respect to ceremonies such as *trafkin* and konchotun, in which gift-giving is important, the persons involved alternate periodically (yearly) as giver and receiver. But the recipient at any phase of the cycle is under moral obligation to return the gift at the next juncture, placing himself in an inferior position until the completion of the next phase of the cycle; symbolizing a mutual though cyclically asymmetrical obligation. Since a gift must be reciprocated, the receiver is in a position of formal obligation to the giver. When the return is made the other party becomes recipient in turn; and so on.

When gifts are placed in the coffin, a practice called *rokiñ,* the obligations of the living to the dead are expressed, but the proper bestowal of rokiñ binds the departed spirit to watch over the living. The relative, and shifting, inferiority-superiority of gift-receivers and gift-givers is an integral part of the network of marriage alliances.

Let us turn to a brief consideration of wife-giving and wife-receiving. Titiev's assertion that there is equal exchange of marriage wealth (1951: 101) is wholly inconsistent with Mapuche values and their social correlates. The inferiority of the group which pays bride-price is symbolized in a number of ways (see Faron 1961c; 1962). Rather than being equal, there is a great, symbolically significant, and obligatory imbalance in goods transferred at the occasion of marriage, consistent with the relative inferiority of the wife-receiving group.

There is no direct exchange of women between Mapuche lineages, the system being one of generalized exchange, strong preference accounting for the vast majority of marriages being contracted with matrilaterally linked groups (see Faron 1961c). On the face of it, this is a triadic structure in which are involved one's own lineage, one's wife-giving lineage, and the wife-receiving group into which one's lineage sisters marry. This relationship is symbolized in the kinship terminology, in which wife-receivers are designated as ñillan ("the one who has purchased") and wife-givers as weku (maternal "uncle"). One's own lineage consists of brothers, fathers, etc. The terms used for one's own lineage members are potentially extensible to all Mapuche who do not fall into a marriage-linked category which, more than a sentimental attachment to fellow Mapuche, expresses the structural boundaries of the marriage system. But the necessarily triadic structure involved in this kind of exchange system reduces to dyadic component relationships with respect to any marriage-linked units, affinals always standing in either the ñillan or the weku category, as wife-receiver and wife-giver, with respect to each other.

Now for the problem of why the Mapuche insist that marriage with mother's brother's daughter is the ideal union, one which they say was law (*admapu*) a generation or so ago. As I have indicated elsewhere (Faron 1961a,c), genealogies do not show that marriage with a real mother's brother's daughter takes place with significant frequency; that it is in fact a rare occurrence. Since all marriageable women are called by the same term, *ñuke*, men marry, in the absence of exact genealogical knowledge, classificatory mother's brother's daughters in a generalized system of exchange. Therefore, the anthropologist's acceptance of this statement as literal truth is unfortunate (cf. Titiev 1951: 38 et passim). But what does the Mapuche expression of this ideal marriage form mean? Elsewhere (Faron 1962) I have suggested that this is a cultural device for expressing a relationship of great importance in the most intimate familial terms possible, the implication being that this is a mechanism for achieving or expressing solidary relationships. This is only a partial explanation of what such expression might mean to the Mapuche. A fuller explanation now suggests itself; one which relates to the notion of incest and which is understandable in terms of the dualistic ordering of the social system. It is simply that the cultural ideal of mother's brother's daughter marriage symbolizes complete observance of the matrilateral rule (admapu) by which marriage is not only preferred between two stable, intermarrying lineages but is proscribed between males and the groups into which their lineage sisters, daughters, and granddaughters marry. Mother's brother's daughter marriage is a shorthand or symbolic expression of both lineage exogamy and matrilateral preference, in complementary opposition to incest, which would result from its infraction.

I have already indicated the general sense of the concept winka, a term reserved especially for non-Mapuche, although sometimes used in anger or fear with respect to nonrelated or out-group Mapuche. For the Mapuche, all the indigenous peoples of the world are Mapuche; all colonizers winka. Their questions about "Mapuche" in the United States or in other countries call

Figure 1. Geographic Orientations of the Mapuche.

this to the anthropologist's attention. There seems to be a fairly clear-cut dichotomy here.

Related to the concept of outsider or stranger, however, is the notion of geographical divisions in Mapucheland itself, that is, among Mapuche. The word Mapuche means "people of the land," and all Indians classified as Araucanian call themselves Mapuche, standing as each does in the center of his own little world. Mapuche residing to the north are referred to as Picunche (*picun:* north), to the south, Huilliche (*huilli:* south), to the east, Puenche, and to the west, along the coast, Lafkenche (*lafken:* ocean). Some writers have taken these geographico-directional classifications to mean that fixed political and ethnic divisions existed among the pre-reservation Mapuche. There seems no good evidence in the literature in support of this conclusion. Rather, these are clearly relative terms by which all Mapuche are able to orient themselves and sort out blocks of other Mapuche if necessary. Non-Mapuche are never classified in these terms— are never called *che* (people)—remaining an undifferentiated totality, winka. This, then, is the wide-angle view: there are Mapuche on the one hand and winka on the other. There are also regional or geographical orientations among the Mapuche themselves. And within the ritual congregation there are other important classifications made: one's lineage mates, one's wife-receivers (ñillan), and one's wife-givers (weku). Figure 1 depicts this conceptualization of structural categories in Mapucheland.

The correspondence between region and ritual congregation is great, if not always complete. The reservations are alien political and economic constructs of Chilean derivation to which the Mapuche have made accommodations. The region, however, is the seat of ritual responsibility, the locus in which matrilateral marriage alliances form their tightest web for any person or group, the stage on which the drama of life and death is enacted (see Faron, 1961c, Chaps. 8, 9). The region as ritual congregation has moral unity, offers protection against the most malevolent forces of evil, is the center of ritual sacrifice to ancestral spirits. It is the center of the Mapuche world. Its dimensions are unknown to the outsider; it is apart and sacred to its membership. It is fundamental to the continuity of Mapuche religious morality.

11 MORALITY AND THE CONCEPT
OF THE PERSON AMONG THE
GAHUKU-GAMA

K. E. Read

INTRODUCTION

THIS PAPER is primarily an essay in comparative ethics, being
an attempt to compare the traditional ethical categories of
Western European culture with those of the Gahuku-Gama, a
people of the Eastern Highlands of New Guinea.[1] I am more
concerned with interpretation than description, for, as I understand it, ethics deals with the theory of value rather than with
value judgments as matters of historical or anthropological record.[2] In other words, in order to understand the moral life in a
particular culture it is inadequate to restrict investigation to the
elucidation of moral rules, or to an empirical examination of
the reasons why they are obeyed. The moral judgments of the
Gahuku-Gama are also important to the extent that they manifest a specific ethical orientation, a particular ontological conception of man and of human relationships which may be compared
and contrasted with the traditional ethical emphasis of our own
culture.

The comparison of different moral systems may be undertaken
from several points of view. We may be content with a simple

Reprinted from *Oceania* 25 (4), 1955: 233–82, by permission of the
author and the editor, *Oceania*. The author has permitted the omission of
certain parts of the original paper.

[1] My field work among the Gahuku-Gama was carried out during 1950–
52, when I was a Research Fellow of the Research School of Pacific
Studies, the Australian National University. Some preliminary information
on the Gahuku-Gama is contained in my papers (1952 and 1954).

I would like to express my gratitude to Dr. Phyllis Kaberry and Mr.
James McAuley, both of whom have read the present paper and have given
me valuable assistance.

[2] I use the term value in the ethical sense of the "right" and the "good."

listing of the forms of behaviour which are considered right and wrong, or we may adopt a socio-functional type of enquiry in which moral values are examined in relation to different social structures and different forms of social organization.[3] A third possibility—not neglected in the past, though somewhat unfashionable in more recent years—could be the attempt to analyse and to compare the categories of thought which constitute a people's ethics, the conceptual framework of their moral life, the mode or orientation of different moral systems. This is the kind of enquiry which I intend to pursue. I am aware that it involves me in a number of theoretical and methodological problems and that the validity of such an approach has been the subject of controversy. Thus, the intellectualistic or philosophical interpretation of native behaviour has been consistently criticized by those anthropologists who conceive of their discipline as a positive natural science on the model of modern physics. I do not intend to enter this argument. The conflicting points of view have been summarized recently by Bidney and I need only state that his conclusions are an adequate statement of my own position.[4] This means that although the Gahuku-Gama do not explain their value judgments in terms of the concepts which I shall employ, their moral behaviour and their beliefs nevertheless imply a specific ethical outlook; they are the expression of a particular ethical pattern which is amenable to logical and systematic explanation.

But while my paper is concerned with an ethical problem, certain questions which engage the attention of some moral philosophers are excluded from the investigation: for example, the theory of good or of obligation as such, the manner in which values are apprehended or espoused, and the processes whereby moral perplexities are resolved. This is not because the Gahuku-Gama have no moral problems. They are, from time to time,

---

[3] Cf. the general treatment of morality by Raymond Firth (1951).

[4] Cf. David Bidney (1953: 156–82). Raymond Firth apparently excludes my particular interest from the purview of anthropological enquiry. He states, for example, that in studying morality the anthropologist "is not concerned directly with questions of ethics—the abstract, philosophical examination of the bases of right and wrong in general (and) the assumptions on which such notions are founded" (1951: 183–84). Cf. also a statement of this point of view by L. P. Mair (1934: 256–57) and G. Parrinder's reply (1951: 11). Placide Tempels makes the same point (1949: 23 ff.).

clearly faced with situations which necessitate a choice from among a number of alternatives, though I think that their possible choices as well as the probable conflicts are more limited than in our own culture. But granting the values espoused and recognized by the Gahuku-Gama, it is assumed that the resolution of moral perplexities takes place in accordance with universal principles.[5] To affirm otherwise would be tantamount to admitting biopsychological differences, whereas the primary assumption is that "moral man" is "moral man" the world over, endowed with identical capacities and consisting of certain moral and intellectual minima. Differences in intellectual endowment do not, therefore, account for the ethical pattern of Gahuku-Gama culture, though it is obvious that the New Guinea native is intellectually less sophisticated than ourselves. The point of departure, I suggest, lies in the Gahuku-Gama concept of the person, using this term in its ethical sense. This is the principal theme of my paper.

THE GAHUKU-GAMA

The congeries of tribes which I call the Gahuku-Gama are situated in the valley of the Asaro River in the Eastern Highlands of New Guinea. They are broadly uniform in culture and language but, like the majority of the groups of Melanesia, have no centralized authority. Power is distributed laterally through each tribe and its component segments, and there are no persons or body of persons vested with an over-all political control. At the same time, language and culture, certain critical relationships, attitudes and activities enable us to identify the tribes as a whole and to distinguish them from those surrounding them.

The Gahuku-Gama are agriculturalists, cultivating sweet potatoes as their staple crop. They live in villages which are sited on ridges and which give a commanding view of the surrounding country. These settlements may contain as few as twenty or as many as fifty houses arranged in a straight line in front of a cleared area of land (*gapo* or *numuni apa*). Strictly speaking, the houses are women's dwellings, for until recently—and in many groups the rule is still observed—husbands did not sleep with their wives. Each village had one or more men's houses, situated

[5] I use the terms "espoused" and "recognized" values as defined by Eliseo Vivas (1950: 217–18).

either in the settlement or at some distance from it. The social structure follows a segmentary pattern and is based on principles of kinship and on a balanced opposition between solitary local groups which effectively controls the use of force and takes the place of centralized political machinery.

The smallest permanent group is the four generation patrilineage. This is not named, but its members tend to form the nucleus of a residential group and possess certain critical rights to land which serve to distingish them from other similarly constituted groups. For most purposes, however, the identity of the patrilineage merges into that of a larger patrilineal group which I shall call the sub-clan. This group also is not named, but it is readily distinguished by a descriptive phrase (*ha'makoko dzuha none*) which may be translated as "the people of one root." Members of the sub-clan consider themselves to be true blood relatives, all descended from a common named male ancestor. The sub-clan, however, is not a true lineage, for although its members conceive of it as a genealogically structured unit they are normally unable to trace true genealogical connections with all those who belong to it. There are a number of reasons for this. Firstly, while it is necessary—because of land rights and property inheritance—for members of the true patrilineage to remember exact genealogies, exact relationship is less important for members of the sub-clan than the tradition of common descent and the remembering of the common ancestor. At the fourth generation or higher, therefore, there is a tendency to recall the names of only sufficient individuals to explain a connection between the component true patrilineages. In other words, there is a continual telescoping of the genealogical framework so that at any point in time the sub-clan appears to have a depth of, at the most, five generations.

The sub-clan is a corporate group. Its male members normally reside together in the same settlement. They possess common rights to land; they participate in a wide range of corporate activities and they have a common symbol of their unity in the sacred *nama* flutes which are associated with the major ritual.

The sub-clan is again a segment of a larger named patrilineal local clan. Members of the clan believe that they are descended from a common ancestor but are unable to name him. They nevertheless believe themselves to be related. Kinship terms used within the patrilineage and sub-clan are extended to members of the clan and clans are mostly exogamous. They are also corporate groups. Their members possess common rights to land; they participate as a group in the major ritual and are required to support one another in disputes with members of other clans. Members of the clan may live in the same village or in a number of contiguous settlements within the clan's common territory.

Several local patri-clans are linked to form a named tribe. Members of the tribe refer to themselves as "one people" and claim to be of common origin, though they cannot point to any common ancestor. Clans within the tribe are contiguously situated. The boundaries of the tribal territory are known and the whole area is generally referred to by the name of the tribe. Members of the tribe have certain common rights within this territory, the most important being the right to graze pigs on any unoccupied or vacant land. Tribal unity is expressed in certain ritual obligations at initiation and in the great pig festivals, and in some instances there is a preference for in-group marriage. Finally, and most importantly, warfare is excluded within the tribe, all disputes being capable of amicable settlement. Because of this "normal" expectation of internal peace, the tribe may be identified as the largest politically effective group.

Segmentation within some tribes shows dualistic features. The smaller tribes comprise two named patrilineal local clans which are usually exogamous. The two largest tribes are also subdivided into three named sub-tribes and, with one exception, these sub-tribes each comprise two named clans which, again, are usually exogamous. Marriage is permitted, and may be preferred, with the clans of other sub-tribes of the same tribe, but it is not a closed clan system. The remaining tribes are without this subdivision into major sub-tribal segments, comprising only a number of linked local clans. These tribes differ from the simple two-clan tribe in that they comprise four, six and, in one doubtful instance, seven named clans. Clans in the multi-clan tribe are normally grouped into a number of linked pairs. Thus, a four-clan tribe usually consists of two exogamous pairs of clans while a six-clan tribe may have three such pairs. The tendency towards a dual organization is most marked in those tribes where we find that the linkages between clans results in two exogamous clans opposing two other exogamous clans. Marriage between these pairs is not, however, enjoined, though in particular circumstances it may be preferred, and although this preference is sometimes accompanied by reciprocal ritual duties, there is not a clearly defined or recognized moiety division.

There is one further grouping which occurs only between pairs of tribes and which therefore follows a strictly dualistic pattern. Any two tribes which are linked in this way also acknowledge an inclusive name which is a compound formed from the names of the major associated groups (e.g., the linked tribes Gahuku and Gehamo acknowledge the common name Gehamo-Gahukuve). The association is permanent and is conceived of as traditional. It involves obligations of hospitality as well as collaboration in certain ritual, and it is also accompanied by a preference for in-group marriage. Linked tribes, finally, do not make war on one another though they resort to feuds. Warfare is described by a special word (*rova*) which distinguishes it from feuding (*hina*). In warfare the aim is the complete destruction of an enemy and his means of livelihood, and each single tribe is opposed to other tribes which are regarded as traditional enemies and, consequently, as being permanently "at war" with one another. Feuds, on the other hand, arise out of some specific dispute. They are fought only for redress and are expected to be concluded amicably, either by payment of compensation or by ceremonial reconciliation. In other words, they represent only a temporary disturbance of friendly relations, and the importance of the linkage between tribes is the fact that it provides for a larger, though less cohesive socio-political association.

As the most characteristic and frequently recurring inter-tribal activity, warfare indicates a marked cultural emphasis on physical aggression. Enemy tribes, in many instances, are no more than fifteen minutes walk apart, and in the continually fluctuating fortunes of war each group has suffered an astonishing number of vicissitudes. The vanquished and the dispossessed were compelled to seek refuge with their friends and allies, and from time to time during its more recent history each tribe has been scattered and dispersed over a wide area. But conquered groups never ceased hoping for revenge, and they aimed to achieve it by forming alliances with their stronger neighbours. Not infrequently, these alliances resulted in one group suddenly attacking the people who had given it refuge, for, except in the relationships between linked tribes, political expediency outweighed all other considerations.

Physical aggression, however, is not confined to inter-group hostility; it is the warp of the cultural pattern and is manifest alike in many day-to-day situations as well as many institutional contexts. Both men and women are volatile, prone to quarrelling and quick to take offence at a suspected slight or injury. They are jealous of their reputations, and an undercurrent of tension, even latent animosity, accompanies many inter-personal relationships. Dominance and submission, rivalry and coercion are constantly recurring themes, and although the people are not lacking in the gentler virtues, there is an unmistakeable aggressive tone to life. The majority of social rewards go to the physically strong and self-assertive, to the proud and the flamboyant, to the extroverted warrior and orator who demands, and usually obtains, the submission of his fellows. As a result, we find that people are markedly aware of themselves as individuals. They possess a strong feeling for or awareness of what I shall later refer to as the idiosyncratic "me," and the majority of social situations reveal a high degree of ego involvement. These statements are supported by the results of a projective test administered to a sample of twenty-five men and twenty-five women. The test is one of three devised by Professor S. F. Nadel to be used experimentally by his students in New Guinea, and while it is not, by itself, an adequate basis for generalized assessments of personality or dominant cultural attitudes, the results corroborate my remarks concerning the aggressive bias of Gahuku-Gama culture and the tendency to describe and to assess each situation in terms of the subject's own involvement. But leaving these matters aside, it is time to indicate the more important characteristics of Gahuku-Gama morality.

MORAL BEHAVIOUR

Morality is an aspect of evaluation. All social life, as Nadel has pointed out, may be said to implicate or to involve the idea of value, in that being aimful it expresses preferences, ideas of worth, of what is desirable or undesirable (Nadel 1953: 265–73). Clearly, however, the concept of value in this generic sense covers many forms of conduct which are not equivalent; worth, desirability or undesirability possess differences of degree as well as referring to different qualities in things. Conduct which is moral is conduct which involves the notions of duty and the ideal, of obligation and intrinsic desirability. It is conduct judged in terms of such qualities as good and bad, right and wrong—goodness and rightness being here conceived in an absolute sense; indeed, it is the absolute nature of the good which gives to moral values their particular requiredness. Although all social behaviour is not invested with a moral quality, moral values tend to pervade the greater part of social life, forming a relatively autonomous system whose influence is sought and felt by most individuals and institutions. From the sociological point of view, moral norms are, above all, directives for action. Possessing requiredness, they lead to conformity, ensuring, for example, that in specific situations certain choices are normally made and that behaviour is thus channelled in certain directions. In other words, moral values are one of the principal regulative mechanisms of culture. Indeed, in small scale, undifferentiated societies which rely to a large extent on self-regulation—where, for example, there are few *sui generis* legal institutions—the social order may be seen to depend quite largely on the requiredness of moral values which are simply held (Nadel 1953). It follows that in these societies there is usually a close consistency between the norms which constitute the moral system and the social structure.

To be effective, it is obvious that moral values must be internalized and generally accepted by the majority of those who constitute the group. It is equally obvious that they must be capable of generalized expression, for moral judgments are the criticism of conduct in terms of generally accepted notions of the good. Such judgments, as Firth has said, are notable for the ease with which they tend to be uttered: "they cost so little" (Firth 1951: 184). But we do them an injustice if, for this reason, we regard them simply as the expression of states of emotion. They possess, too, an intellectual component which, though present in varying degrees, bears on the nature of the good and of obligation as these are conceived by a particular people. Thus, a majority of our own moral judgments imply the Christian ethic of personal freedom and responsibility, the transcendent and objective nature of the good and our common obligations in a moral universe. By way of contrast, the moral judgments of other peoples may be couched in terms of practicality; they may eschew the speculative and abstract and they may stress the immediate claims of inter-personal relationships. The assertion of right and wrong is in each case not only emotionally but also ideologically founded. The good is not simply what people feel to be right but also what they think or believe to be right, and we may thus regard their moral judgments as the expression of a particular ethic, as involving, among other things, some conception of human nature, of man's relationship to man and of the obligations which devolve on him through certain presupposed conditions of existence.

Among the Gahuku-Gama, people do not normally appeal to abstract principles but rather emphasize the practical consequences of moral deviation. Instead of saying it is "good" or "right" to help others, they state quite simply that "if you don't help others, others won't help you." Indeed, in a possible majority of instances, the practical consequences of disregarding moral norms is fairly readily apparent, if not as obviously direct as in this particular illustration. Thus, disrespect for elders, lack of regard for age mates, failure to support fellow clansmen, incest or breaking the rules of clan exogamy all involve practical penalties, not explicitly stated in each case but undoubtedly understood by the individuals who assert that the norms concerned are right. Sociologically, in fact, the right must frequently be regarded as the cognitive counterpart of what Nadel refers to as an instrumental nexus, the extent, that is, to which a norm or activity is the focal centre of a series of activities which may be impeded if it is impeded by variation (Nadel 1953: 267). At the same time, this is not quite the same thing as saying that Gahuku-Gama ethics are avowedly utilitarian, for although in most instances the right is that course which can be proved pragmatically to offer the most satisfaction, or to result in the least dislocation, the agent also conceives it to be right intrinsically. He is in varying degrees aware of the pragmatic effects, but rightness is itself an aspect of his awareness, being, as it were, an irreducible value which he attaches to certain things in certain situations. In short, moral norms are not merely instrumental imperatives. They possess an ontological element, and I shall try to show that for the Gahuku-Gama this is bound up with a particular conception of man which does not allow for any clearly recognized distinction between the individual and the status which he occupies. This is the theme I wish to develop now, and I shall approach it by way of a description of Gahuku-Gama morality. I cannot, however, attempt a complete account of all the occasions and events which are made the subject of moral judgments and shall confine myself to those which seem to me to be most critical.

As an introduction to the subject, a few additional remarks on the general form of Gahuku-Gama moral assertions may be appropriate. They frequently express moral statements as universals on the pattern of "help others so they will help you," or "give food to those who visit you so they will think well of you." But the practical rider may be omitted, and the moral directive then takes the simple form of "it is good to obey your elders"; "it is bad for brothers to quarrel"; "it is right for a man to fence his wife's garden"; "it is good to think of your sister and her children"; "it is bad to slander your fellow clansman," or "it is good to be friendly with your age mates." We may note, however, that people do not assert that "it is wrong to kill," or that "it is right to love everyone," while of the other universal commands of Christianity a large number are conspicuously absent. The Gahuku-Gama, for example, do not say that one should practice forbearance in all circumstances; indeed, their injunctions against adultery, against lying, thieving and slander should not be accepted as applying to all the situations in which the individual may find himself. There is nothing unusual in this. It is simply another way of saying that we are dealing with a tribal morality as distinct from the universal morality of Christian teaching. In other words, Gahuku-Gama assertions of what is right or wrong, good or bad, are not intended to apply to all men; they are stated from the position of a particular collectivity outside of which the moral norm ceases to have any meaning. Thus, the manner in which people behave who are outside the tribal system of inter-group and inter-personal relationships is virtually a matter of indifference. More than this, the individual does not regard himself as being bound to them by any moral obligation: it is justifiable to kill them, to steal from them and to seduce their women.

There is a more important point, namely, that within the group itself there is what might be called a "distributive" recognition of moral obligation. For, while the moral assertions are clearly the expression of values acknowledged by all members of the group, the individual is not bound to all his fellows in like degree. As a moral agent his responsibilities vary considerably according to the positioning of other individuals within the system of inter-personal and inter-group relationships. Any particular moral norm may therefore have a more or less relevance or required-ness according to the individuals involved in a specific situation. In other words, it is not simply that the applicability of a certain norm may be temporarily affected by particular circumstances. The distributive character of Gahuku-Gama morality lies rather in the fact that each agent recognizes that his moral obligations to others are differentially apportioned.

We may express this in an alternative way. From the standpoint of the group at large the Gahuku-Gama recognize common moral obligations. Certain values are acknowledged, recognized and es-poused by all members of the group: they are held in common. Obligations may also be said to be common in a second sense, when a relationship between any two or more individuals entails reciprocal moral duties which are identical or complementary. Thus, we may speak of the common obligations of husband and wife, of brothers, age mates, of parents and children, of members of linked clans and so on. But there is a sense in which we cannot use the term, as implying, that is, that every individual recognizes an identical moral responsibility towards all other individuals. The Christian ethic, on the other hand, requires us to do just this. It is our responsibility to regard every individual in the same moral terms; all make the same moral demands of us. We may argue, of course, that the historical forms of Western European morality have also been distributive. The ideal, nevertheless, has achieved expression in many of our most cherished institutions, and the Western conception of individuality, of personal integrity and obligation, as well as many of our grounds for social and political criticism, are quite clearly derived from it. The contrast is, therefore, significant, and fundamentally ethical, being con-cerned with different ontological conceptions of man and of hu-man relationships and with the nature of moral obligation. The distributive morality of the Gahuku-Gama explicitly recognizes significant differences in the individual's moral obligations and responsibilities to other people, and while these differences are closely related to a particular social structure, they imply, too, an ethical outlook which in itself is of considerable importance. Thus, to return to my original phrasing of the question, this distributive character involves what is from the Western point of view a basic failure to distinguish an ethical category of the person. It is a failure to separate the individual from the social context and, ethically speaking, to grant him an intrinsic moral value apart from that which attaches to him as the occupant of a particular status. I will be citing other evidence to support this view, but for the moment we need to examine more closely the distributive nature of the moral system.

The morality of kinship provides an obvious starting point, for not only is the pattern of each individual's daily life, from birth to death, quite largely determined by kinship, but it is also that subject on which the anthropologist may justifiably claim to speak with most authority. Disregarding the treatment given to it by earlier historical and evolutionary schools, the study of kinship by anthropologists in this century has taken two principal directions: some have been primarily concerned with a socio-functional analysis while others have been mainly interested in the study of kinship structure. For some time, too, these different approaches tended to keep apart, the formal and essentially static structural analysis becoming for some the principal aim and sole end of social anthropology. More reasonable counsels— which, indeed, appear to be gathering the greater following— stress, however, that the two are inter-dependent and that structure is not a reality *sui generis* to which all activities contribute. It is argued, rather, that structure appears only within the context of specific aims, interests and activities, and that it is from these that it derives its meaning and significance. As we might expect, those who have adopted the socio-functional approach have been more ready to give explicit recognition to the moral character of kinship relationships.[6] Yet on the whole they have taken this quality as given and have concerned themselves primarily with analysing the relationship between kinship and other aspects of social organization. This is not said in disparagement, for in a sense we can take this nature for granted. Firth, for example, has remarked that "the transmutation of biological relations into so-

[6] Meyer Fortes (1949) is a notable exception among studies of kinship structure. To Fortes, the essence of the Tale kinship system is "its function as the primary mechanism through which the basic moral axioms of a society of the type represented by the Tallensi are translated into the concrete give and take of social life" (p. 346).

cial relations is intelligible for the ordinary member of society only in terms of appeal to customary notions of what is right," and for kinship to be the effective organizing principle it is, it must be firmly grounded in the moral order (Firth 1951: 210). Thus, in the analysis of economic or political organization we do not need to give separate consideration to the moral aspect of kinship relationships. The fact that such relationships channel behaviour, that they determine the choices made, implies that they are felt to be right.

It is hardly worth saying that different patterns of behaviour, different social rights and obligations are enjoined between an individual and his different categories of kinsmen. What is of more importance, however, is that these differences also possess a moral quality. Thus, we may speak of the reciprocal moral duties of elder and younger brothers, and we may compare the ideal in this instance with the kind of behaviour enjoined between kinsmen who are age mates. A younger brother, for example, is expected to be mindful at all times of his elder brother's superior status. He is required to show the latter respect, to accept his criticism, to heed his wishes and to obey his commands. There are moral duties on the side of the elder brother too, for he has to see that his younger brother does not want. The latter looks to him for assistance in obtaining a wife, for pigs with which to start his household and for a fair share of their father's property. From the younger brother's point of view, however, the moral quality of the relationship is primarily one of constraint, of obedience and the acceptance of discipline. It contrasts, therefore, with the moral relationship between kinsmen who are the same age. Here, the ideals of friendship and equality are stressed. Mutual help, frankness, a comradeship which is expressed in sharing one another's secrets and in freely asking and giving—all these add their measure to the moral quality of the age-mate relationship. The comparison could be carried further, to take in, one by one, all the categories of kin which a man recognizes. The moral quality of the individual's relationship with his mother's brother is, for example, quite different from the moral quality of the ties he has with his father's brothers, different again from those which he recognizes with his wife's parents and her brothers, and different again from his responsibilities towards his sister's husband. Finally, we could extend the examination to the various groups of which a man is a member, contrasting his moral rights and responsibilities towards members of his sub-clan with those towards members of his clan and these with his obligations towards members of other clans of the same tribe.

These characteristics are sufficiently commonplace to stand without elaboration. Indeed, it could be said that our own moral system possesses many comparable features. Thus, we might point to the different moral obligations of a father to his children, of an employer to his employees, of the members of a club or other association to one another, in fact of any of the thousand and one socially recognized relationships between two or more individuals. Closer examination suggests, however, that the diversity in our moral obligations is more apparent than real, for we recognize that there is—or at least that there should be—a certain common measure of ethical content in all our relationships. Ideally, we may say that certain duties are felt to be independent of status. There are minimum responsibilities which apply to all the circumstances in which the individual finds himself, and there are actions and attitudes which are considered wrong in all situations.

Ultimately, this common measure of rights and responsibilities depends on the intrinsic ethical value which we attach to the individual. We recognize, that is, that all men, in virtue of this intrinsic worth, have a valid claim to be treated as moral equals; they make identical demands which, as moral agents, we are required to respect. Needless to say, moral reality shows varying degrees of approximation to or departure from the ideal, but we cannot, for that reason, deny that the ideal has any influence. Many, if not all, of the social reforms of the past one and a half centuries could be viewed as attempts to correct conditions in which practice has seemed to obscure or to depart too far from it. Similarly, many feel bound at times to criticize and to oppose political movements which show a calculated or cynical disregard for the moral rights of the individual. In other words, while our moral system possesses some distributive features, I suggest that these also embody certain common principles. Ideally, in our moral relationships we operate, as it were, from a fixed ethical perspective, the perspective of the person and his moral claim, regardless of social ties or status, to a certain minimum consideration. That this claim is frequently couched in different terms does not alter the issue; nor is it affected materially by the fact that the ideal has seldom, if ever, received complete expression. The essential point is that we acknowledge that all men, in virtue of their nature as such, make certain basic and invariant moral demands of us.

It is in the absence of any comparable conception of obligation that the distributive character of Gahuku-Gama morality is most clearly revealed. Contrasted with our own fixed ethical perspective, that of the Gahuku-Gama is continually changing. Men, in other words, are not conceived to be equals in a moral sense: their value does not reside in themselves as individuals or persons; it is dependent, rather, on the position they occupy within a system of inter-personal and inter-group relationships. Moral obligation, therefore, is distributive in the sense that it is also dependent on and varies with this social positioning of individuals. This does not mean simply that certain relationships obviously involve or charge the individual with differential duties. In our own society, for example, a father has specific duties towards his own children which he is not called upon to assume in respect of others. In like manner among the Gahuku-Gama the parent-child relationship involves specific obligations which we would not expect to find between, say, a man and the children of his wife's brothers. I refer, however, to a fundamental difference between the two systems, the distributive character of Gahuku-Gama morality issuing from the fact that there is no common measure of ethical content which should serve as a guide for the moral agent in whatever situations he finds himself.

Stated as sharply as possible, moral obligations are primarily contingent on the social positioning of individuals. They are not derived from, neither do they refer to anything which is intrinsic to the nature of the agent himself or to the nature of other human beings as such. Thus, in a way which is quite different from our own traditional point of view, the differential duties associated with status are the principal constituents of moral obligation, and this is therefore seen to change or vary according to the individuals or groups involved. The result may be described as a continual narrowing or contraction of the moral judgment, due to the fact that the right, in any given instance, has basically a social connotation. This, of course, is also true of ourselves, for our moral norms refer to what we consider to be the appropriate form for human relationships. But rightness is nevertheless an independent and invariable quality which transcends any given social context, whereas with the Gahuku-Gama it is the social context itself which largely determines the moral character of a particular action. It is not, then, simply that we can observe a distributive apportionment of duties at the descriptive level, but rather that this distributive element is the expression of basic ethical principles.

Evidence is not lacking to support this interpretation. Thus, from the Western point of view, it is significant that in the situations which normally arise moral judgments are not phrased in terms of what is appropriate or inappropriate in the relationships of men considered simply as human beings. This does not mean that the Gahuku-Gama have no conception of behaviour which is becoming or, conversely, unbecoming to men as such. They say, for example, that "men are not dogs," quite clearly meaning to imply that there is a certain minimum of behaviour which is considered appropriate to human beings.[7] Indeed, any culturally standardized pattern of behaviour could be said to possess this particular "rightness." From the individual's point of view, there are therefore minimum standards which can be said to apply to him as a human being. The important point is that these basic or generic conceptions of rightness and wrongness are not universalized: the Gahuku-Gama do not go on to argue or to assert that because man *is* a human being—because, that is, of some inherent quality which distinguishes him from other animals—there are invariable standards which he must apply in his relationships with all other human beings.

This is a difficult distinction to make, but it is necessary for us to be quite clear what it involves. From the individual's standpoint, there are minimum standards which are appropriate to him as a man, in the sense that if his behaviour deviates too far from the norms concerned he will be acting in a manner contrary to that which is recognized as the way in which men should behave. Even

---

[7] Sexual behaviour is a case in point, though even here disapproval is rarely expressed in terms of a particular practice being contrary to human nature. Thus, the attitude towards masturbation is not that it is intrinsically wrong, but rather that it is unnecessary. Homosexuality, too, is foolish rather than immoral. People denied any knowledge of it, but they were not morally affronted by the idea, taking the more practical view that it would be silly, as well as undignified, to indulge in it.

at this level it is probably closer to the facts to say that if he acts in a particular way, his behaviour will be contrary to that which is appropriate for a man of the Gahuku-Gama. For although he may be charged with "unmanly" conduct, identical behaviour on the part of other peoples is not necessarily stigmatized. Confronted, for example, with a description of customs which are aberrant from the Gahuku-Gama point of view, people do not say that they are wrong; they do not pronounce on their moral quality but rather adopt the attitude that the customs concerned are curious possibilities, neither intrinsically right nor wrong, which they themselves would not consider correct.

This attitude is not unusual, and its sociological implications are fairly obvious. I have brought it in merely to illustrate, at one extreme, the Gahuku-Gama failure to universalize a concept of human nature and moral obligation, which they nevertheless possess. Unlike ourselves, in other words, human nature as such does not necessarily establish a moral bond between individuals, nor does it provide a standard against which all actions can be judged and either approved or disapproved. We are confronted instead with what I have referred to as a continually changing moral perspective. The moral judgment operates, as it were, at a number of different levels. At one level, certain things are approved for men as men. At other levels the rightness or wrongness of an action varies according to the status of those who are involved. Homicide provides us with an obvious example. Stated briefly: it is wrong for an individual to kill a member of his own tribe, but it is commendable to kill members of opposed tribes, always provided that they are not related to him. Thus a man is expected to avoid his maternal kinsmen in battle though other members of his own clan have no such moral obligation towards these individuals. Within the tribe, too, homicide is regarded with varying degrees of moral reprehension, according to whether the individuals involved are, for example, members of the same sub-clan, of different sub-clans of the same clan, or of different clans. Our own attitude towards parricide or fratricide may be cited as comparable, but there is this difference. The Christian attitude towards homicide is indissolubly linked with the intrinsic personal value of the individual and our traditional teaching emphasizes that it is the taking of innocent human life as such that is wrong. With us, the individual life has, in other words, an absolute value which is greater than and quite sharply distinguished from a value which is conferred by a specific social tie or by membership of a particular social group. With the Gahuku-Gama, however, it is clear that the value of an individual life is primarily dependent on these social criteria. Thus, the reaction to homicide emphasizes the moral nature of the social bonds between individuals and groups of individuals rather than the inviolability of human life itself.

Considered as they bear upon the theory of primitive law, these remarks have a familiar ring. I refer to what Nadel has called the "social range" of offences (Nadel 1947: 501–4). Thus, he has pointed out that among the Nuba the evaluation of a crime such as homicide, and the sanctions which it provokes, varies according to whether it occurs "within the clan or outside it, in or outside the political unit." Homicide within the Nuba kinship group or clan is an unpunishable offence, in the sense that it does not provoke forceful retaliation by the members of the clan or its segments. Between clans, however, punishment is exacted in the form of blood feud and revenge. The sociological explanation for the unpunishable nature of intra-clan homicide is seen to lie in the principle of self-help on which the law is based. Homicide within the clan affects a group which is so closely knit that although its unity has been violated by the act, it would be violated in even greater measure by retaliation. Punishment is therefore left to supernatural agencies or it is excluded altogether. There is a comparable situation among the Gahuku-Gama and, since Gahuku-Gama law is also founded on self-help, the same sociological explanation may be advanced to account for the absence of forceful retaliation following homicide within the sub-clan. But, as Nadel has also stressed, the failure to take retaliatory action implies a moral attitude wherein this particular act is regarded with such abhorrence that it is unthinkable, beyond the realm of human sanction. Indeed, Nadel prefers to speak of the "sin" of intra-clan homicide as compared with the crime of homicide between clans. My own point is that human life is given a variable value, depending on the social positioning of different individuals. It is unthinkable to kill in certain contexts, wrong in others, right in others, and a matter of indifference in others. In each case, the moral nature of particular social bonds is the important factor rather than anything intrinsic to man as such. To sum up: morality is primarily contextual. The moral judgment does not operate from the fixed perspective of universal obligation for the moral assessment of behaviour varies in different social contexts, according, that is, to the different values placed on different individuals in different contexts.

I regard this failure to universalize a concept of moral obligation—and to grant an invariant ethical value to the individual—as the most important characteristic of the moral system. I have referred in passing to homicide as a case in point, but lest this should be thought a special or exceptional instance, it could be shown that the vast majority of moral norms are similarly restrictive or distributive. A few examples must suffice to clarify this position.

Christian teaching holds that man, as person, has a moral duty to himself and to others to tell the truth. To lie is to act in a manner which is contrary to his true nature, a denial of the transcendant value which he embodies. To the Gahuku-Gama, on the other hand, the value of truth is not absolute, nor is it related to intrinsic human nature. The prudent individual is truthful, because "lying makes people angry; it causes trouble," and most people wish to retain the good opinion of those with whom they are in close daily association. But there are circumstances in which deceit is not considered wrong. Thus, men have frequently asked me to hide their personal possessions in my house and to take charge of their cash for them, so that they may plead poverty if their affinal kin demand any of the ceremonial payments to which they are entitled. Nor does anyone expect an individual to admit his guilt if he is charged with some offence by a member of another clan. Similarly, the truth is not expected from members of other groups if, in the event of some claim or quarrel, there is the possibility of gaining a greater advantage by concealing it. To lie and to be deceitful may be regarded as bad, but almost in the same breath people joke about the manner in which they have either misled others or have escaped the consequences of some of their actions. An examination of all these occasions shows that the moral evaluation is primarily contextual, dependent, that is, on the nature of specific social ties rather than on the recognition of a moral absolute.

Turning to the morality of property-holding, we find a similar situation. Firth has pointed out the difficulty of making a sharp distinction between borrowing and stealing in many primitive communities, instancing the fact that theft involves more than taking an article without having obtained the prior permission of its owner (Firth 1951: 196). Kinship ties, he says, "may give a moral umbrella to the abstraction of the article," and he concludes that "the classification and the moral evaluation of the act depend in part on the moral evaluation of the ties between the participants." This is a neat expression of the situation among the Gahuku-Gama. Theft, or converting another's property to one's own use, is considered wrong, but kinsmen—in virtue of the moral quality of the social ties between them—are permitted a large measure of freedom with one another's goods. Generally speaking, a man is not expected to be angry if a kinsman appropriates something belonging to him provided the latter tells him what he has done, and even if the owner is not notified he seldom regards the act as theft. He is angry. He chides his kinsman for omitting to inform him of the action, but he does not feel as injured as if it had been a member of another clan or someone to whom he was not related. Moreover, theft is regarded as more or less reprehensible according to whether it involves members of the same clan, of different clans of the same tribe, of friendly clans of different tribes, or of groups without any recognized social ties. In the past, for example, pig stealing was considered a legitimate way of scoring off a rival group; and even between friendly clans or between different clans of the same tribe, a good deal is condoned provided it is not found out. The Gahuku-Gama remark quite casually that "everyone steals," and they have no compunction about keeping some item of property which they come by accidentally, even if there is no doubt as to the rightful owner's identity. In short, the moral nature of specific social ties is primarily responsible for defining the limits within which the appropriation of the property of another is right or wrong. Respect for property, like the virtue of truth, is not a moral absolute.

Finally, we may turn to the attitude towards adultery. Here again the moral evaluation of adultery depends primarily on the moral evaluation of the ties between the parties concerned.[8] Adultery within the sub-clan and the clan is strongly condemned,

[8] H. Ian Hogbin draws attention to this fact in his paper (1938). The situations which he describes for Wogeo are in most respects similar to those which arise among the Gahuku-Gama.

for the anger and the enmity which it creates are contrary to the moral ideal that the members of these groups should assist and support each other. People will even deny that it occurs, and though they recognize that a man who has been wronged in this way has cause to show anger, and to seek redress for the injury, they invariably express resentment for the informant whose tattling has been responsible for bringing the matter into the open. Action has to be taken if the offence is brought to the wronged husband's notice and he, in turn, makes a public issue of it; but the general attitude is that it would have been better for all concerned if the offence had passed unnoticed. At the opposite extreme, adultery with women of different tribes is regarded lightly, as hardly worthy, in fact, of moral censure. It is necessary to conceal it, but men boast a good deal about their own affairs and they will quite proudly display the scars left on their thighs by the arrows of irate husbands. They are less ready to admit adultery with women of different clans of the same tribe, but here too one receives the impression that if a man can get away with it, no great moral blame attaches to him. Moral disapproval is more pronounced than in the previous instance, but it is far less emphatic than in cases of adultery within the clan or sub-clan. In other words, moral evaluation is again contextual. Adultery is not wrong universally and intrinsically, that is in the sense of being contrary to man's moral constitution. The wrongness of the act depends on the evaluation of the social ties between the individuals involved.

We are brought back, then, to the ground on which a moral obligation is felt to rest. With our own traditional teaching, I have tried to show that this ground is ultimately the person, and since all men, irrespective of status, are also persons, they are bound by a common measure of obligation. The source of moral authority, moreover, is seen to lie outside the system of social relationships which bind men to one another as members of society. Moral duty is never simply synonymous with social duty, for the moral agent is required to look beyond the form of particular relationships and the differential rights which they involve, and to measure these against the invariable and inherent value which he and all other men possess. It will be clear by now that the Gahuku-Gama conception of obligation is based on a fundamentally different view of human beings. We will look in vain, for example, for any comparable concept that men, as men, are bound to one another by a moral tie which is wider than, and subsumes, the ties that link them socially. In short, my examination has tended to show that men are not primarily persons, in the moral sense, but social individuals. The analysis, however, is not complete, for we have yet to see what ideas of man's nature are held by the Gahuku-Gama and what ethical consequences, if any, they involve.

HUMAN NATURE AND THE BASIS OF OBLIGATION

To the Gahuku-Gama, the human individual is a complex biological, physiological and psychic whole. Though their knowledge of these several aspects of man's nature is understandably limited, they nevertheless regard them as being inter-dependent. Anatomically, man consists of a number of articulated parts which together make up his body. He also consists of certain internal organs having specific functions and amongst which the heart, liver, stomach and viscera are the most important.[9] In addition, he is constituted by a psychic factor. But though he can be thus analysed, with considerable detail, into a number of components, the individual, the living personality, is more than the sum of these various parts. The biological, physiological and psychic aspects of his nature cannot be clearly separated. They exist in the closest inter-dependence, being, as it were, fused together to form the human personality. To an extent which it is perhaps difficult for us to appreciate or understand, the various parts of the body, limbs, eyes, nose, hair, the internal organs and bodily excretions are essential constituents of the human personality, incorporating and expressing the whole in each of their several functions. It follows that an injury to any part of the body is also comparable to damage to the personality of the individual sustaining the injury. Similarly, the loss of any of the bodily substances through excretion is, in a rather obscure sense, the loss of something which is an essential part or element of the whole, a loss to the per-

---

[9] The Gahuku-Gama do not ascribe any importance to the brain, nor have they any conception of its function. Cognitive processes are associated with the organ of hearing. To "know" or to "think" is to "hear" (*gelenove*); "I don't know" or "I don't understand" is "I do not hear" or "I have not heard" (*gelemuve*).

sonality itself. This idea clearly underlies most of the customary forms of greeting, ways of expressing obligation and appreciation. The most common form for each of these situations is the verbal expression "let me eat your excreta,"[10] or variations such as "your urine," "your semen," etc., accompanied either by a gesture of the up-turned, open hand to the mouth or by grasping the buttocks or genitals of the individual concerned. It is, of course, possible to interpret this as a conventionalized expression of submission, particularly when it is contrasted with the imperative form "eat my excreta!" one of the gravest of insults. There is no doubt that a token submission is intended, but in order to understand the full meaning of the phrase it is also necessary to grasp the more obscure relationship between the physiological functions of the human organism and the individual personality itself. The expression is then seen to be a statement which also conveys a sympathetic recognition of the individuality of the person concerned. This, I suggest, is what is implied in the following explanation given to me by one informant. "A man," he remarked, "walks about. He excretes. His fæces leave him, fall to the ground. I am sorry for him, sorry to see him there (i.e., on the ground). I tell him I am sorry." This idea is not, perhaps, very different from the common assumption, underlying most forms of contagious magic, of a sympathetic identity between objects which have been in contact with one another. It would be a mistake, however, to regard the two ideas as equivalent, for while it is true that this sympathetic relationship between objects is felt to exist, the Gahuku-Gama go a good deal further than this in regarding the various parts and functions of the human organism as inseparable elements of a man's individuality, and therefore as expressive of his personality. For corroborative evidence, we may turn to other customary usages.

The word "skin" (*gupe*) is used in a wide variety of contexts to convey information and to express ideas about others.[11] A man may be said to have a "good" or a "bad" skin, the word in this sense referring to his moral character. To incur an obligation to others (as, for example, the obligation to return in kind the valuables contributed to a bride-price) is rendered as "having a

[10] I.e. *ase roko ve*, or *serokove*, contractions of *ase roko nonuve*, lit. "fæces making I eat."

[11] *Gupe* refers to "flesh" as well as "epidermis."

debt on one's skin." Similarly, the discharging of an obligation, the act of making gifts, of giving compensation or returning the services of others not only "loosens" the debt on one's own skin but also "makes good the skin" of those to whom one is obliged. Doubt as to a person's motives, or lack of personal knowledge of his character is commonly expressed by the phrase "I do not know (or have not seen) his skin." The word is used, too, to express socio-cultural similarities and differences. Thus the members of a particular descent group may refer to themselves as "one skin," or they may employ the same phrasing to denote that other groups possess a similar culture (i.e., "their skin is one kind with us"). By way of contrast, members of other descent groups are said to be "another skin," and cultural differences are explained by saying "their skin is another kind." Finally, the word is used in expressing personal sorrow or loss at the death or absence of a particular individual and, in the latter case, of joy at his return (e.g., "I will not see his skin again," or "I hold (or see) your skin; my belly is good").

While it is easy enough to find parallels to these usages amongst ourselves, it would be an over-simplification to regard them merely as metaphorical expressions. They denote a specific concept of individuality, an outlook or ideology which does not recognize any sharp distinction between the physical and psychic constituents of man's nature. Indeed, whereas we ourselves tend to take man's natural physical character for granted, and whereas we tend to think of him as an individual mainly by reference to his temperamental qualities, the Gahuku-Gama place a much greater stress on the former. They insist on regarding the individual as a psycho-physical whole and, to them, man's physical nature embodies his specific identity—constitutes him individual —as much as the diacritical qualities of temperament. Something of this outlook may possibly be seen in the marked physical demonstrativeness which characterizes most inter-personal relationships, as in the continual caressing of arms and thighs in greeting or in expressing sympathy, sorrow and affection for another. On approaching a group of people, a man (or woman) walks slowly round the company, halting at each individual to caress his thighs, his shoulders, his arms or his calves, or he kneels down and encircling the other's waist with his arms, holds him in a full embrace. In greeting an older woman, a man may also lift her breasts, exclaiming sympathetically on the fact that they are no longer firm. The customary verbal expression which accompanies these gestures is *moka'ne*. Its literal meaning is obscure, but according to context it indicates pleasure, sympathy, affection and gratitude.

This outlook also appears in the customary standing embrace in which members of either sex press their bodies together, and also in a strongly developed sense of man's physical dignity. It can be seen, too, in the common practice of self-mutilation and in a fairly extensive range of other usages. Thus, to take a single example, a man (or woman) who cuts his hair is bound to recompense his relatives and age-mates. Men and women normally wear their hair in long ringlets reaching to their shoulders. If they seek employment in European households, leave their villages to work on coastal plantations, or if they receive Christian baptism, they are required to cut it short. Nowadays, an increasing number of both the young and the old also cut their hair simply to demonstrate that they are sophisticated men-of-the-world. When a man cuts his hair for any reason, his relatives and age-mates go into mourning, plastering their bodies with clay and ashes and perhaps even cutting off a finger. He is required to "make their skin good" by killing at least one pig and giving them valuables. Each time my own hair was cut my adoptive relatives and age-mates put on the signs of mourning.

Finally, the emphasis on the physical aspect of man's nature is revealed quite clearly in many of the ceremonies associated with the growth and development of children. One of these, known as *agoka hukukave* (lit. "his nose they cut"), is performed at least once, and occasionally more frequently, during the period before a boy's initiation or a girl's first menstruation. It is designed to draw attention to the child's physical development and, on the child's behalf, to recognize and to recompense all those who have had an interest in its welfare. The ceremony includes a feast and a distribution of valuables in which the maternal kin are the principal recipients. Normally, the child's father decides when to hold the feast, but if he shows reluctance or tardiness his hand may be forced by his wife's kinsfolk, who express to him their desire to honour their sister's child. They point out that the child is growing up, and they inform the father that they are anxious to "make its skin good," to bring gifts of food and to paint and decorate the child's body. Their request can only be refused at the risk of being accused of insufficient interest in the child's welfare and the father is therefore compelled to make the necessary arrangements. At the ceremony, the child is painted and decorated and solemnly escorted down the length of the village to the assembled company, men and women uttering shrill cries of appreciation. The child is shown the gifts which its father intends to make on its behalf and it is told that "these are for those who honour your skin, who have affection for your skin and make it good."

The term *agoka hukukave* is used for a variety of ceremonies concerned with physical conditions and development. For example, it refers to the ceremonial welcome given to initiates when, after their seclusion in the men's house, they are met in the village by crowds of men and women who break bamboos of cooked food against their legs. The ceremony I have described above may be performed several times by a wealthy father. It is obviously an occasion which serves the purpose of instructing the child in kinship obligations, and it also draws attention to the rights of maternal kin in respect of sister's children. At the same time, it expresses the Gahuku-Gama's marked interest in the body and in the physical aspect of man's nature. Apart from the formal usages already detailed, this interest is also evident in a life-long desire for close physical contact with other people. Arms are continually reaching out to encircle children and to press them hard against an adult's body; open lips are continually seeking the baby's mouth, its genitals or its buttocks. Men and women sit and walk with their arms round one another's shoulders, and lying side by side, the girl's arm pillowed on the boy's forearm, the courting couple rub their lips and chins together until the skin breaks and bleeds. In other ways too—ways which soon become so familiar that an observer ceases to notice them—we can see this preoccupation with the body. It is reflected, for example, in the attention lavished on the skin, in the long periods which people spend de-lousing each other, in their delight in bodily ornamentation and decoration, in titivation and in the ceremonial application of unguents—pig's grease and other substances—to the hair, the limbs and other parts of the body. Indeed, this fixed interest in the physical aspect of man's nature and the continual attempt to make physical contact—to touch, to hold or to caress and to pass remarks about another's physical attributes—is one of the most noticeable elements in inter-personal relationships.

The Gahuku-Gama believe, however, that in addition to the body the human individual is also constituted by a psychic factor, *meni*,[12] which is the essential principle of human nature, the whole "self" or personality. If we use the term in its most comprehensive sense, we may call this psychic element the soul, for *meni* is the basis of conscious and continuous individual existence. At the same time, we need not expect to find an exact equivalence between the *meni* and the Christian concept of the soul. *Meni* is rather the breath-soul, the principle of life which animates the physical organism, and at death it simply ceases to exist.[13]

There is thus an initial difference between the Gahuku-Gama and the Christian concepts, for the former does not entail or include any belief in a personal survival. No one knows, or indeed speculates what happens to the *meni* at death; the life principle simply "departs," ceases to be, and with its departure the individual himself ceases to have any existence, in the sense of any real personality. What does remain, if anything remains, is neither soul nor body but rather a "shade," something which lacks any positive characteristics and which has no fixed place of abode. Death means, therefore, an almost complete oblivion and certainly the extinction of any positive individuality. There is no belief in an after-world, nor any reassurance that the personality persists in some different form. The dead simply pass from the world of the living; thereafter they are beyond the reach of human knowledge and there is virtually no further personal contact between them and their descendants. A man who has married the widow of an age-mate may, perhaps believe that some illness has been caused by the disapproving shade of the deceased husband and, characteristically, he then performs a rite to "send the dead away." But this is an exceptional situation and, in general, the dead are not believed to retain any personal interest in the living. They cannot revisit their descendants. They neither punish nor approve and therefore are neither to be feared nor placated. Thus,

---

[12] 1st, 2nd and 3rd persons possessive: *nemeni, gemeni, ameni.*

[13] The word *gika* (*ni-gika, gi-gika, a-gika*), that is, "neck," is used interchangeably with *meni.* Thus, one may say *ameni ramana* or *agika ramana*, meaning, in both cases, "his soul good (it is)." Of the two terms, *gika* is possibly used more frequently, the simplest explanation being that the neck, from which the breath issues, is the organ most closely associated with the breath-soul. It is, as it were, the seat of the animating principle.

although the fundamental religious belief of the Gahuku-Gama may be characterized as a belief in an unnamed ancestral power, this power itself is impersonal and is more readily inferred or felt than expressed or described in words. It is not formulated in any dogma, and the living state that they have no knowledge of its source or the manner in which it operates.[14]

The relation of the soul to the body in the Gahuku-Gama concept of personality thus involves the rejection of dualism. What we are faced with is not a dichotomy of soul and body but a psycho-physical unity in which the parts are mutually dependent. *Meni,* the breath-soul, is the animating principle and, in a sense, the personality, the "self"; but it depends on the body and separated from the body it loses all positive characteristics. Similarly, the body is conceived to be an integral part of the whole, the personality, whose consciousness is diffused throughout it, and differentiated into the local consciousness of its particular members. Thus, the various parts of the body have each their ethical and psychic qualities. The limbs, the skin, the internal organs, the hair, the nose and bodily excretions are "members of the whole," and, as such, they both contribute to and partake of the nature of the whole. Once we grasp this, innumerable usages and figures of speech appear in a new light. We can, for example, more readily appreciate the concern and sympathy which even the smallest cut or injury to the body evokes, and self-mutilation, deliberate injury to one's own body, assumes a new significance if viewed in relation to this concept of psycho-physical unity.

It is in this light that we must also view the physical indignities which are heaped on certain offenders, e.g., the fairly common practice of stripping an adulteress and beating or throwing dirt

---

[14] I take this opportunity to correct certain statements which I made in an earlier paper (1952: 9). I stated that: "The spirits of the recently dead are felt to concern themselves in certain situations which confront their living descendants. They are thought to punish those who transgress accepted norms of conduct with illnesses and other misfortunes. Their favour must then be sought by means of prayer and sacrifice." Subsequent field work made it clear that the spirits of the recently dead are not generally concerned with the conduct of the living. They neither bestow favours on nor punish their descendants and they cannot be regarded as arbiters of moral conduct. I have referred to one possible exception, when a disapproving "shade" may be held responsible for the illness of a man who has married his age-mate's widow, but even here there is no question of moral disapproval, for there is no rule against such marriages. The situation reflects, however, the latent jealousy and hostility between age-mates.

on her genitals. Wronged or suspicious husbands are also known to punish a wife by thrusting a stick into her vagina. This form of retaliation may evoke criticism, but the woman's sympathisers are moved to express their disapproval not so much because of the peculiar viciousness of the attack but rather because it is directed against this particular part of the body. In short, they see it as an unwarranted indignity to this particular organ. "Does he think so little of her vagina that he does this to it?" they ask. "His thought is not straight in this. The vagina holds his penis. Why should he treat it thus?"

Similarly, it is easier to appreciate everyday expressions in which parts of the body are used to indicate or describe an aspect of character or type of behaviour. Thus, determination, wilfulness or recalcitrance in another is usually expressed by saying "his nose is strong," or again it is customary to indicate a state of uncertainty, suspicion or furtiveness by remarking that the individual concerned "conceals his nose." People will also claim to be able to tell if a person is not telling the truth by looking at his nose, or they will sum up his character by saying "I know his nose; he is of such and such a type." Finally, the injunction that a wife must not touch her husband's nose or his hair gives formal recognition to the physical aspect of his personality, to that indivisible whole which is his specific and unique identity. Word for word, there is almost a literal correspondence between the ideas expressed by St. Paul (I Corinthians XII, 12 ff.) and the manner in which the Gahuku-Gama regard the parts of the body. They would, for example, readily understand and wholeheartedly concur with the statements in verse 26: "And whether one member (of the body) suffer, all members suffer with it; or one member be honoured, all the members rejoice with it."

The essential unity of the personality and the rejection of any dichotomy of soul and body is also emphasized in Christian teaching. St. Thomas, for example, maintains that soul and body are related as form to matter. Indeed, man is the centre of contact between these two great realms and in his nature he unites them in mutual dependence. By this, the Christian does not mean that the soul depends on the body for its ultimate existence or that it dies in the physical dissolution of death. He understands, however, that the relationship between soul and body is intrinsic, not temporary or artificial, and that the body itself is therefore integral to human nature, at least in so far as its powers belong to and are finally gathered up in the life of the soul. The Gahuku-Gama concept of man's nature is in broad agreement with this position but, if it is possible, they apparently affirm that there is an even closer and more intimate connection between the physical and psychic elements of human personality. In this, their ideas are closer to those of the Old Testament than the New Testament; they think of the dead as "shades in Sheol" rather than as the "souls" of Christian teaching. But at this point all similarity ceases, for the Old Testament also affirms—and the New Testament makes it a principal article of faith—that there is one aspect of his nature that relates man to God and makes him accessible to God. Christian teaching, in other words, introduces and emphasizes the theistic idea that both soul and body are of Divine creation. Furthermore, the fact that they are so closely interrelated in present experience suggests that God has brought them into existence together: they are complementary expressions, on different planes, of the one entire personality. Thus, the Christian believes that man's first duty in all things is towards the Divine Creator. God is man's origin and his end, the reason for his existence, and to be faithful to the Divine Source, man is bound to ascertain God's will for him and to do what God requires. It is from this that a Christian derives his strong sense of sin, of actions which are contrary to his true nature and therefore an offence to the Divine Creator. In contrast, it is very doubtful if the Gahuku-Gama ever experience sin as the Christian understands it. A man may feel "shame," a temporary embarrassment, even remorse or self-pity, but he certainly does not live with the knowledge of sin as the Christian does. "Shame" is rendered by *nogoza helekave*. *Nogoza* (*nogoza, gogoza, agoza*) is also used for the juice of fruits and other substances, e.g., *muli agoza,* lemon juice. The verb *helekave* (3rd person singular, near present tense) means "to die" or interchangeably with *nivisekave,* to "desire," or "want," e.g., *nenetakum gumu helekave* or *nenetakumu givisive* (or *givisekave*), "what do you want (desire, like)?" Finally, *nivisekave* also means "to be ill." Thus, *givisekave,* "you are ill." It is apparent that the phrase *nogoza helekave* refers to an affective state and that the use of *nogoza* in this context points to a physically based conception of feelings and emotions. Indeed, the seat of the emotions is located in the stomach and we may infer

that the affective state of embarrassment is conceived of as a
"disturbance" or "change" in the "juices" of the individual undergoing the experience.

A word or two on conscience may also be appropriate to this
context. Hogbin has suggested that for most of the Busama "the
notion of conscience has little meaning," and that apart from a
small handful of converts who have "really absorbed" Christian
teaching, "goodness is dependent on expediency" (Hogbin,
1947: 283–87). We would not expect to find that the Gahuku-
Gama—or, for that matter, the Busama—had formulated a notion
equivalent to the Christian concept of conscience, embodying,
that is, the particular theistic views of right and wrong associated
with Christianity. The Concise Oxford Dictionary, however, defines conscience simply as the "moral sense of right and wrong,"
and unless we are prepared to argue and to demonstrate that a
particular people have no generally accepted ideas of what should
be done in certain situations, we cannot exclude the operation
of "conscience."

In any case, the Gahuku-Gama is a stranger to contrition in the
Christian sense and a stranger to that particular affective and
cognitive state which the Christian calls the "sense of sin." In
short, man is accountable only to his fellows and morality is
purely secular. There is a general belief in an impersonal ancestral power which lies behind the continuing order, but man is not
responsible to it, and though he depends on it he cannot offend
it. He can deny it or cut himself off from it, for example by destroying the sacred *nama* flutes and discontinuing the practices
associated with them, but this is not a sin or an offence which
has any spiritual consequences, for at the worst it can only mean
that he has gambled his shield against the vagaries and uncer-
tainties of nature.

Further, the ancestral power is not interested in Gahuku-
Gama moral life. It is not concerned with questions of ethics,
and none of the people's supernatural beliefs possess any ethical
content. Contrasted with the Christian viewpoint, the ground and
source of moral obligation lies wholly within the social medium
itself; it is "internalized," located within and deriving its requiredness from the system of inter-personal and inter-group relationships.

I found it extremely difficult—I would almost say impossible—

to observe anything one could describe as a distinctively religious fervour, awe or reverence at any of the ceremonies I witnessed. Even the sacred flutes are treated with a casualness which contradicts their importance as a symbol and channel of access to the ancestral power, and though there is great excitement and evident emotion at particular gatherings, it is the tension and excitement of the crowd, its stimulus the food, the finery, the personal human contacts and secular ambitions to impress, to show to one's best advantage. This accords with the well-known Durkheimian analysis of primitive religious experience, and I have already stated my general agreement with Durkheim's position (Read 1952). There is, however, this difficulty. If we adopt Durkheim's conception of a "sacralized" society we could, in contradiction of the statements I have made above, argue that all moral rules therefore possess a quasi-religious or supernatural sanction. There is nevertheless a distinct difference between the kind of moral obligation to which we can point under these circumstances and that which is explicitly recognized in Christian teaching. The source of the one remains essentially internal while the other is external to the social medium.

As with the concept and awareness of sin, so also the higher consciousness of person—of such immediate significance to the Christian—is foreign to the Gahuku-Gama. A highly developed feeling and regard for the "lower" psycho-physical self, the idiosyncratic "me" is clearly evident in a wide range of characteristic behaviour. It finds expression, for example, in the art of oratory, in the stance and gestures of the speaker, his wide-flung arms, the way he beats his breast, and in the content of his speech, his boasting, his continual and vigorous references to himself, his importance and his abilities. (The style of oratory has a marked affinity with that of the Homeric heroes and Beowulf; e.g. the boasting of Beowulf in the Hall of Hrothgar when he tells of his exploits against Breca.) The desire to dominate, to stand out from one's fellows, to receive their submission and their adulation, are among the most pronounced characteristics of Gahuku-Gama inter-personal and inter-group behaviour. The brilliantly decorated dancer aims to be the centre of attraction. Pigs and valuables seldom change hands without exaggerated references to their donor's industry, his reputation and his greatness; the warrior seems tireless in recounting his exploits and the average individual readily flares with anger at a deliberate or suspected slight or injury to his self-esteem.

The theme of dominance and submission is strikingly illustrated by the following practice. After a dance, a man may go to the house of one of the performers. He sits down outside until someone enquires the reason of his visit, whereupon he replies that the performance of the man concerned has "killed" him (*helekave*). He then greets the performer with a stylized shout and the latter is compelled to make him a gift of valuables. This is the highest compliment that can be paid to a dancer, the performer accepting it as an acknowledgment that he has surpassed everyone else and that his accomplishments have seriously unsettled or emotionally disturbed his visitor. But ceremonial occasions, both great and small, bring the most opportunity for formally giving vent to the qualities of aggression and self-assertion. The customary way of receiving guests is for the hosts to rush towards them as they enter the village, to surround them and leap up and down, brandishing weapons, shouting and crying out such phrases as "Now you eat pig! I have killed my largest pig, the pig I have reared and fed! Now look and see where is the home of pigs; say who it is who has a name for pigs!" There are innumerable other instances, for most festive or formal gatherings contain an element of competition, and in consequence, the majority of them provide an opportunity for boasting and display.

A sense of self-importance is also imparted to children from their earliest age. Continually passed from hand to hand, kissed and caressed, they are always a centre of adult attention. Lovingly decorated and indulged, their infant and childish attempts at self-expression and display are consciously encouraged and their behaviour is a never-failing source of amusement and parental pride. In the ceremonies associated with their growth and development, they are greeted with praise and shouts of appreciation, and the solemn small boy or girl, befeathered, oiled and hung with ornaments, walking through a throng of leaping, shouting men, accept it all, the honour and the excitement, as though it were his just due. For boys, the climax of this adult interest comes at the conclusion of their novitiate, when they leave the men's house and are ceremonially conducted back to the village. During their seclusion, their elders have been busy collecting every kind of finery and decoration for them, plaiting new arm and ankle bands, dyeing bark cloth and making their new clothes. All this is placed on them in the men's house and at dawn, in a ferment of excitement, they come outside to the waiting throng of women. Their hair piled high in a chignon wrapped in bark cloth, painted and weighed down with plumes and the vast frames which are attached to their shoulders, they are greeted with tears and shouts and they stand motionless and speechless while in the surrounding throng an old woman cries and holds her hands to her belly, arms reach out to touch and caress them and appraising eyes and excited voices consider some final embellishment for their beauty. Then, when the sun has risen, they enter the village in a long procession and for the remainder of a highly emotional day of dancing and feasting they are the centre of attraction.

To sum up: Modesty is not a virtue; the respected and successful are those who are most loud in their own praise and most positive in their expressions of self-importance. Pride is something to be worn like a banner, and though he may be loved, considered good and shown some esteem, the unassuming and retiring person is never a major influence in the life of the community, for unwillingness to wrangle and to boast is tantamount to an admission that one is a nonentity.

Together with this strongly developed sense of self, the Gahuku-Gama also give full recognition to the idiosyncrasies of others, noting the manner in which they characteristically behave, their foibles and their typical reactions. There can be little doubt that they conceive of their fellows as distinct personalities, some humorous, others stern and unrelenting, some easy-going and to be treated with familiarity, some wise, some foolish and each endowed with a specific quality or qualities which set him off from others, which make him the individual he is. But this sense of idiosyncratic self does not necessarily involve the higher consciousness of person. The latter is an awareness of the self and of others which goes beyond this experience and this recognition of the idiosyncratic me. Difficult as it is to express concisely, its essential quality may be described as the consciousness of an identical nature in all men. In other words, the diacritical qualities of temperament which constitute our "normal" knowledge of others have no significance, no meaning at the level of awareness which is personal consciousness. The consciousness of person surmounts these differences, is independent of them and similarly, it is independent of the pattern of social relationships, roles and status. In short, to "know" the person we must conceive of all men in the same way; we must be aware of a common basis in the individuality of ourselves and others, and we must view this common factor as essentially apart from or above the social medium in which men live. We may argue, of course, that our "normal" knowledge of ourselves and others is not of this nature, but at the same time we can deny the concept of the person only at the risk of denying the foundation of our concept of natural justice and many other of our distinctive and most cherished ideas.

One result of this consciousness of person is the Christian sense of living for and in the sight of the eternal. Regarding temporal existence as a sojourn, the Christian looks to death to open the way to a realization of his true nature. On the other hand, for the Gahuku-Gama death means the virtual end of the personality. Beyond life there is no reality and, in consequence, his thought, his motives and his actions are more firmly grounded in the present. Eternity does not come within his perspective. He has little knowledge of the past. His genealogies are shallow; his history is almost exclusively confined to events within living memory and he has few myths or legends. His future, too, is unknown. The reality of life is thus like a light which illumines a space between two areas of darkness. Man lives out his whole existence within a time perspective of four generations.

It is clear, then, that neither in their beliefs nor in their behaviour is there any evidence that the Gahuku-Gama regard themselves or their fellows in a manner which is comparable to our own traditional view, as creatures who are endowed with a unique, objective and intrinsic value and an individuality which is distinct from the status they occupy, the roles they play and the system of relationships in which they live. Committed to a purely psycho-physical conception of man's nature and strongly aware of his idiosyncratic identity, the Gahuku-Gama, at the same time, tends to regard himself and others principally as figures in a social pattern. But he does not regard his fellows as featureless entities, figures devoid of individual character and motivation, lacking the ability to choose and continually moving in response to some external and impersonal compulsion. This

view of primitive man has been fashionable and it has been said
that the closely knit fabric of primitive society hinders the development of personality and independent character. Primitive
conduct is "best understood in the light of what is regarded as
crowd psychology. In a typical crowd the public opinion exercised
by the individual members on each other, and, reactively, on
themselves is not properly their own, since it does not proceed
from a critical and intelligent self . . . Each man looks outwards,
taking his cue from his neighbours in their mass (and) his conduct is merely the expression of a mobbishly caused and received
impression."[15] In the whole history of mankind there has probably never been a society which fits this analysis and, certainly,
nothing I have said and nothing I know about the Gahuku-Gama
supports it. We cannot conclude that the intelligence of the
Gahuku-Gama is different from our own; we cannot deny him
standards, and the ability to choose rationally between alternatives; nor can we take from him the faculty of reflection and regard his judgments merely in terms of sense perception. Yet in
the more subtle sense of Durkheim we may, I think, conclude
that his outlook is fundamentally sociocentric. His community
life is lived on a relatively small scale; the majority of his relationships are personal and direct and the bonds of kinship and of
local contiguity constitute the framework of his social system.
These characteristics of simple societies are sufficiently well
known to stand without further elaboration, and while they do
not preclude the existence and expression of what we regard as
the fundamental human qualities, they are nevertheless consistent with a socially orientated outlook and conception of one's
fellow man. To the Gahuku-Gama, the palpable differences between people, the idiosyncratic variations in their natures, are
like a shimmer which overlies their social identity. They are not
unaware of these variations; they do not ignore them; but they
do not distinguish, as clearly as we are accustomed to, between
the individual and the status which he occupies. They tend, in
other words, to categorize, to see men largely in terms of their
position in a system of social rights and obligations.

Let me emphasize again that this particular outlook does not
reduce one's fellow men to a featureless and uniform grey; nor

[15] Marett (1911). I cite this paper merely as a relatively concise statement
of a particular point of view.

is it incompatible with a desire to stand out from the crowd and to shine in the eyes of others. It is, however, a view which penetrates beneath the surface diversity of character and temperament and which fixes the individual in relationship to the social pattern. People may, and in fact do, move out of position and thereby, in a somewhat paradoxical sense, they lose or forfeit their identity. Conversely, the more outstanding a man is the more he is held in, and the more pronounced his own esteem the more closely he identifies himself with his status. Individual identity and social identity are two sides of the same coin. We ourselves are accustomed to distinguish between them, and we recognize that although man lives and moves within a social medium he is nevertheless an entity who stands essentially apart from and above it, a view, it may be added, which is extensively reflected in our literature. By way of contrast, the outlook of the Gahuku-Gama implies a rejection of this dualism. There is no real dichotomy between man and society, no essential separation of the individual from the social pattern.

Of course it does not follow that idiosyncratic differences are unimportant. Age-mates, for example, are expected to be the closest of friends, but although the formalities of friendship are generally maintained with all of them, it is clear that men have a greater affection for and feel a closer bond with some than others. People are probably very well aware of this, but it is only to an outsider, such as the anthropologist, that they can express their personal preferences. The same could be said for most other relationships, but even when we have made every allowance for the manner in which differences in temperament and character may modify a formal bond, the fact remains that, to his fellows, status—his position in the system of social rights and obligations—is a basic and inseparable constituent of each man's identity. Indeed, it is possible to conclude that for most purposes and in most situations social identity is more important than idiosyncratic individuality.

(Dr. Phyllis Kaberry has drawn my attention to the fact that among the Abelam of the Sepik River, people may choose, on the basis of idiosyncratic affinity, to live and work with men who are not related to them, and that the kinship system is then "manipulated" to fit these individuals. I did not come across anything of a comparable nature among the Gahuku-Gama [if, that is, we exclude a small number of men living matrilocally in a predominantly patrilocal community, or some other men who preferred to associate themselves with age-mates rather than with members of their own patrilineage or sub-clan]; but I should point out that I am not denying the individual all freedom to choose from among his fellows or to distribute his affections. Indeed, the fact that the system is manipulated to "fit" these cases may be cited in support of my thesis.)

Individual idiosyncrasies, however, are not without significance in determining the way one regards one's fellows, but whether a man is characterized as good or bad, dominant or ineffectual, generous or selfish, he is, at the same time, a member of one's own clan or patrilineage, kin of one's wife or mother, an age-mate, member of the tribe or sub-tribe, relative or stranger, known friend or potential enemy. It follows, too, that the Gahuku-Gama is not free, as we are relatively free, to choose from among his fellows on the basis of idiosyncratic affinity those with whom he will associate. His attitudes towards others and his possible relationships with them are defined by his own and their position in the social pattern, so that while he may feel more strongly attracted to one age-mate rather than another, and while he may choose to make this man his special friend and confidant—and to live and work with him—he can exercise his preference only within a particular category of people. The nature of his ties with others precludes him from regarding them as potentially capable of the same affective bond.

This outlook is reflected in a general difficulty to appreciate or understand friendship between Europeans. People, for example, were puzzled by my own friendship with certain of my European neighbours. They could not fully appreciate a relationship which was based solely on a mutual regard for one another and which sprang from an affinity of ideas and interests, and in order to account for it they invariably postulated some specific social tie between us: we were age-mates, clansmen or "one-kind," a phrase which is used for members of the same tribe. In short, the Gahuku-Gama do not enter into casual friendships on the European pattern. A form of bond friendship exists. It involves reciprocal obligations of hospitality and some minor kinds of economic assistance between individuals of different tribes, but, significantly enough, the Gahuku-Gama do not use the pidjin

English term for friend (*pren*) to designate this relationship. *Pren* is only used reciprocally by age-mates, who are members of the same tribe.

Stated as concisely as possible, we may say that the Gahuku-Gama regards his fellows primarily as social individuals. People are viewed largely in terms of status, or, to put it a little differently, the individual and his social role are not clearly separable.

To his fellows, the social role is an intrinsic constituent of each man's identity and, as such, it contributes an essential element to their awareness of him; it becomes, as it were, an inseparable component of his individuality. The ethical consequences of this outlook have been indicated already: it results in what I have called a narrowing or contraction of the moral judgment. By this I mean two things: firstly, that the moral rules of the Gahuku-Gama are not universals in the sense that they are not conceived as deriving from or referring to something which is inherent to man's nature; man is not bound by a duty to himself or others which is greater than or cannot be contained in his social relationships; and secondly, I mean that not only the individual's moral obligations but also his judgments of others are to a large extent dependent on the presence or absence of a particular social bond.[16] In looking at his fellows, the Gahuku-Gama sees them primarily as people to whom he is differentially bound by a particular tie or social relationship.

The tendency to see people in terms of social ties is clearly evident in many of the responses given in projective tests. It is also a matter of everyday experience and observation. I recall, on one occasion, accompanying a party of men to a festival at a settlement which was three hours' walk from the village where I was living. As we were returning home I noticed that a youth of about fourteen years of age was walking behind one of my com-

---

[16] Radin draws attention to a similar moral emphasis among the Winnebago. The Winnebago, he remarks, are enjoined to love everybody but not to love them all equally. They would regard the Christian ideal as not only impossible but also untrue, leading, in practice, to manifest insincerity, for according to the Winnebago, it is the "manner in which, in your relations to other members of the tribe, you *distribute* this emotion" that is worthy of approbation (Radin 1927: 73). It may be added that in this passage—as in others where he makes use of the comparison—Radin shows a misunderstanding of basic Christian teaching, for the Christian does not regard love as an emotion, but as an inclination of the will, so that one can "love"—will the good—of another person whom one does not "like."

panions. The two of them exchanged an occasional word but did not seem to be paying much attention to one another. Suddenly, however, the older man called out to me excitedly, and on turning round I found him standing with his arms around the boy's shoulders. He explained to me that in the course of some casual enquiries he had made the discovery that the youth was a very distant maternal kinsman. Thereafter, he showed the greatest solicitude for his companion, and when we left the boy at his own village he embraced him several times. Later, he expressed his astonishment at the meeting by remarking that he had not known that he had any relatives at the boy's village. "I do not go there," he said. "I walk by other roads. But now," he added, "I will go there if I come this way. My maternal kinsmen will know me and take care of me."

Men are similarly constituted. Moreover, they possess a dignity which sets them above other animals. It cannot be said, however, that the Gahuku-Gama consider this sense of human dignity to have any far-reaching moral implications. Human beings, as such, possess intrinsic value, but it is not, as in Western teaching, an incommensurable worth which stands above all other values and which defines the moral duty of the individual to himself and to his fellows. Where the moral life is concerned, the value which each man possesses as a human being is relatively insignificant, for one's moral responsibilities and duties vary substantially according to the positioning of other individuals within the social structure. Although, in other words, the Gahuku-Gama recognize the claim of all men to a common humanity, they do not consider that this involves them in identical moral duties. Ethically speaking, men are not *primarily* human beings but individuals to whom one is related by social ties which carry different moral implications, and it is therefore possible to grant an individual humanity yet not be bound to him by any moral obligations.

CONCLUSION

In this enquiry, I have not attempted to give a complete account of Gahuku-Gama morality. I have, for example, made few references to the specific values which are acknowledged by these people, because my aim has been interpretation rather than description, and my examination has been directed towards the clarification of what I believe to be a more fundamental problem. In short, I have been concerned with ethics rather than with morals, with the attempt to arrive at some understanding of the nature of Gahuku-Gama morality, its principles and general characteristics, its basic assumptions concerning man and their bearing on moral obligation. Not the least of my aims has also been to compare the ethical outlook of the Gahuku-Gama with that of Western European culture, as exemplified in the traditional teaching of Christianity. This implies, of course, that different ethical systems may be compared and evaluated objectively, that moral diversity is not proof of ethical relativity. I am aware, however, that some authorities who agree with me on this point may nevertheless find cause to criticize the terms employed in my comparison, that I may, in fact, be held guilty of an initial over-simplification in speaking of "the" morality of Western European culture or of Christianity.[17] Such strictures carry no great weight in dealing with a small-scale, relatively homogeneous group such as the Gahuku-Gama, but it is common knowledge that in our own society there are differences of opinion on quite fundamental moral issues between the various groups professing Christianity, and between these and other non-Christian members of the community. At the same time, I suggest that there is a central core of Christian teaching which is traditional, in the sense that it possesses historical continuity, and which is widely accepted. Diversity and differences within the framework of Christian teaching—no less than the variations presented by different moral systems—should not, in fact, be permitted to obscure a common element; and in respect of that which is common we may reasonably speak of "the" Christian ethic, of a Christian conception of man, of the good and of obligation.

Beginning, therefore, with the concept of the person—as being both basic and traditional to Christian and thus to Western European teaching, I have attempted to elicit from it certain ethical characteristics and, in turn, to compare these with the assump-

---

[17] Cf. Morris Ginsberg (1953: 3): "It is a gross oversimplification to speak of 'the' morality of the Greeks, 'the' morality of the Romans or the Egyptians, or of 'the' Christian or 'the' American way of life, as is often done in studies of comparative ethics."

tions and outlook of the Gahuku-Gama. In a more comprehensive study, additional criteria may have been introduced.[18] Yet if we regard my enquiry as being concerned with a single theme, I suggest that it has also served to focus attention on certain major variations. What I have in mind is not the simple fact that the Gahuku-Gama permit or approve some things which we condemn, but that their ethical system also reveals more fundamental or deep-seated differences, that certain of its characteristics point to genuine differences in moral perception and moral consciousness.

Once again, I am not referring simply to differences in the moral attitude towards specific acts, though these, too, may be compared and objectively evaluated. In this sense, there are not only differences of moral perception between different cultures but there may also be changes in moral perception within a particular culture at different points in time. Theologians would agree, for example, that Christian ethics do not constitute a closed system in which there is no provision for the development of a deeper moral insight into the nature of acts and their consequences. Fundamentally, however, in this case the ethical contrast centres on a differing concept of man, of moral obligation and responsibility. Thus, from the moral standpoint of our own culture, man is conceived to be a unique centre of individuality, the embodiment—as person—of an absolute value which sets him in some measure over and above the world in which he lives. The ground and source of moral obligation is, as it were, externalized, not only in the sense that it is a spiritual principle which confers on man his incommensurable worth, but in the sense, too, that the moral standard is conceived to be autonomous: there is an explicit distinction between the good and the right and that which is simply desirable in a human or social sense. In short, the moral duties of the person are greater than any of the duties which the individual possesses as a member of society. His moral responsibilities, both to himself and to others, transcend the given social context, are conceived to be independent of the social ties which link him to his fellows. To the Gahuku-Gama, on the other hand, man is primarily a social individual, a member of this or that particular social group, some-

[18] E.g. the criteria suggested by Ginsberg (1953: 14–15).

one who occupies a particular position in a system of social rights and obligations. Moral responsibilities devolve on him as such, rather than by virtue of any qualities which are intrinsic to his psycho-physical nature. The moral agent is the individual in his various social capacities. His responsibilities are not conceived as being constitutionally determined, nor have they any explicit extrasocial reference; they are dependent on the presence or absence of particular social bonds. Thus, it is not to human beings as such that men are morally bound, but to human beings as members of a particular collectivity.

This involves a further basic difference in perception. From the standpoint of Christian ethics, men are moral equals. As persons, their value is constant and is independent of status. They possess identical rights and are charged with identical responsibilities. Precisely because of this, they are also bound to one another by a common measure of obligation. But it is not so with the Gahuku-Gama; indeed, the contrast between the two systems is most sharp at this point. Thus, the ground of obligation is not conceived to lie in human nature as such, either, that is, in the nature of the agent himself or in the nature of other men as men; it resides, rather, in the nature of the ties which link them socially to one another. In short, the moral judgment does not operate from any basis of universal obligation. There is no explicit recognition of the moral as a category *sui generis,* as constituting a distinct order of nature and action which possesses its own intrinsic requiredness and which involves man in a common measure of responsibility. By this I do not mean that morality is a matter of expediency, but rather that there is no explicit separation of moral categories from the social context: the moral order and the social order are not differentiated conceptually. This means that it is the evaluation which is placed on different social ties which is primarily responsible for determining the nature and extent of moral obligation, and therefore the rightness or wrongness of a particular action. These qualities are variable absolutes—if I may use such a contradiction in terms —for the moral judgment is largely of a contextual character. It operates with a continually changing perspective, the moral differentia being the variable value which men possess as members of a particular group or as individuals who occupy a particular status.

Whereas I have spoken of the failure of the Gahuku-Gama to distinguish an ethical category of the person—their failure, that is, to grant the individual an intrinsic moral value and thus to recognize that men are bound to one another by a common measure of obligation—Ginsberg refers to "the range of persons to whom moral rules are held to be applicable," and he uses this as one of his criteria for ethical evaluation (1953: 119). While not equivalent, these two ideas have more in common than the difference in terminology might at first suggest. Ginsberg makes it quite clear, for example, that his "range of persons" is not to be understood in a merely quantitative sense. He also has in mind qualitative differences in moral consciousness which are associated with differing conceptions "of the human person himself." He therefore disagrees with those (like Boas) who assert that there have been no fundamental changes in moral ideas, who hold that all that has happened is that the same basic duties have been gradually extended to larger groups. This position, Ginsberg remarks, "hardly does justice to the history of moral universalism and especially of the ideas of equality and the intrinsic value of the individual as such."

There is one final point. One of the most noticeable characteristics of the Gahuku-Gama is their unconcern with and their unwillingness to judge actions or situations in which they are not personally involved. Moral offences and breaches of rule which do not affect them either as individuals or as members of a particular group stand, as it were, outside the range within which the moral judgment operates. Such acts may be discussed; indeed, people are always prepared to ask questions about them and to listen to those who are able to supply them with details. They may shake their heads and murmur sympathetically, but their attitude is one of puzzlement rather than condemnation. Pressed for an evaluation, their usual reply is a neutral "I don't know" (*gelemuve*), and it is exceedingly difficult to ascertain whether the act is regarded as right or wrong. Persistent enquiries sometimes produce a tacit acknowledgment that "it is not right to do this," but the informant normally adds "I don't know what they think," and thus virtually evades the issue. In most cases, a judgment one way or the other is simply not made, and the investigator—having suffered a good deal of initial frustration —soon learns not to expect one. Nor are the Gahuku-Gama alone among New Guinea peoples in showing this unwillingness to judge. Dr. J. B. Watson of Washington University has told me that he has also come across it among the Agarabe of the Eastern Highlands. Dr. K. O. L. Burridge of the University of Malaya has mentioned a similar attitude among the Tangu of Madand District, and I have heard it referred to by Miss Chowning, from the University of Pennsylvania, among the Nakanai of New Britain.

It does not follow from this that the Gahuku-Gama are devoid of moral sensibility or, even less, that they are unable to judge; but a fundamental difference in moral perception is, I think, involved. The failure to judge or, at least, the neutral attitude towards actions and situations in which the individual is not himself involved is, for example, consistent with the contextual character of the moral system. It is understandable, moreover, if we accept the proposition that the Gahuku-Gama do not distinguish their moral categories with the precision to which we are accustomed. What I mean is that we seem to be confronted with a basic difference in conceptualization, in the extent, that is, to which ideas of the right and the good are formulated systematically, and in the degree to which the moral is conceived to constitute an autonomous order. In this sense, there is a marked disparity between the degree of abstraction achieved by our own traditional system and that of the Gahuku-Gama. The latter has no body of explicit principles, no formal code of ethics, in the sense of a more or less coherently stated and inter-connected system of moral concepts: it has nothing to offer which is comparable to the integrated concepts of the person, of a natural moral law and a universal moral order. Abstract ideas of the good, of the basis of right and wrong, do not interest the Gahuku-Gama. Their moral rules are, for the most part, unsystematized—judgments which refer to specific situations rather than to any explicit ideology of right and wrong as such. In short, the moral indifference to which I have referred does not imply the absence of a moral sense or of anything which we can recognize as an objective standard. But compared with our own system, it does indicate a difference in the degree to which the principles underlying right behaviour are abstracted from the social context and related to a generalized concept of the good and of obligation.

12 ANIMALS IN LELE
RELIGIOUS THOUGHT

Mary Douglas

L ELE RELIGIOUS life is organized by a number of cult groups. For a long time they seemed to me to be a collection of quite heterogeneous cults, uncoordinated except for a certain overlap in membership. In one of them, the Diviners' group, entry is by initiation only, though the candidate is supposed to give evidence of a dream summons. In another, the Twin Parents, there is no initiation. Parents of twins have no choice but to pay the fees and become Twin Diviners. In another, the Begetters, candidates must have begotten a child, pay fees and undergo initiation. Members of this group, who have begotten children of both sexes, are qualified for entrance into another group, which makes a cult of the pangolin[1] (*manis tricuspis*). Lastly there are Diviners of God (*Bangang banjambi*) who are supposed to acquire their power not by initiation, but by direct communication with supernatural beings, the spirits. The primary objects of all these cults[2] are fertility and good hunting.

The Pangolin cult is the only one in which an animal is the cult object. In the other cults parts of certain animals are reserved to initiates: the head and stomach of the bush pig to Diviners, the chest and young of all animals to the Begetters. Or parts of animals or whole animals may be prohibited to them as a condition of their calling: Twin Parents must not eat the back of any

Reprinted from *Africa* 27 (1), 1957: 46–58, by permission of the author and the International African Institute.

[1] The pangolin is a scaly ant-eater.
[2] The Begetters are an exception, their initiation being mainly a *rite de passage*. They give indirect support to the other fertility cults by honouring virility and penalizing impotence.

animal; so many animals are prohibited to the Diviners of God that they practise an almost vegetarian austerity.

Regarding these practices the Lele offer very little explanation of the symbolism involved. The different animals are associated traditionally with the different cults. The symbolism of the bush pig is relatively explicit. It is the Diviners' animal, they will say, because it frequents the marshy sources of streams where the spirits abide, and because it produces the largest litters in the animal world. In very few other instances is the symbolism so clearly recognized. In most cases one would be justified in assuming that no symbolism whatever is involved, and that the prohibitions concerning different animals are observed simply as diacritical badges of cult membership.

If this be the correct interpretation of the different observances, one must equally accept the view that there is no single system of thought integrating the various fertility cults. At first I felt obliged to adopt this point of view. Believing the Lele culture to be highly eclectic and capable of assimilating into itself any number of cults of neighbouring tribes, I concluded that the connexion between the various cults was probably only an historical one, and that in the absence of historical or ethnographic data from surrounding areas, it was impossible to take the problem any further.

Although I could never get a direct answer that satisfied me as to why the pangolin should be the object of a fertility cult, I kept receiving odd scraps of disconnected information about it and about other animals in different religious and secular contexts. Gradually I was able to relate these ideas within a broad framework of assumptions about animals and humans. These assumptions are so fundamental to Lele thought that one could almost describe them as unformulated categories through which they unconsciously organize their experience. They could never emerge in reply to direct questions because it was impossible for Lele to suppose that the questioner might take his standpoint on another set of assumptions. Only when I was able to appreciate the kind of implicit connexions they made between one set of facts and another, did a framework of metaphysical ideas emerge. Within this it was not difficult to understand the central role of the pangolin, and the significance of other animals in Lele religion. The different cult groups no longer seemed to be disconnected and overlapping, but appeared rather as complementary developments of the same basic theme.

The Lele have a clear concept of order in their universe which is based on a few simple categories. The first is the distinction between humans and animals.[3] Humans are mannerly. They observe polite conventions in their dealings with each other and hide themselves when performing their natural functions. Animals satisfy their natural appetites uncontrolled. They are regarded as the 'brute beasts which have no understanding' of the Anglican marriage service. This governing distinction between men and animals testifies to the superiority of mankind. It gives men a kind of moral licence to hunt and kill wild animals without shame or pity.

A subsidiary characteristic of animals is held to be their immense fecundity. In this, animals have the advantage of humans. They give birth to two, three, six or seven of their young at a time. Barrenness in humans is attributed to sorcery: barrenness in animals is not normally envisaged in Lele ideas about them. The set incantation in fertility rites refers to the fecundity of the animals in the forest, and asks why humans should not be so prolific.

The third defining characteristic of animals is their acceptance of their own sphere in the natural order. Most animals run away from the hunter and shun all human contact. Sometimes there are individual animals which, contrary to the habit of their kind, disregard the boundary between humans and themselves. Such a deviation from characteristically animal behaviour shows them to be not entirely animal, but partly human.[4] Two sets of beliefs

---

[3] See my article (1955), in which I give in detail the various situations of cooking, eating, washing, quarrelling, &c., in which these categories become evident.

[4] Domestic animals and vermin are major exceptions. Before the recent introduction of goats, pigs, and ducks, the only domestic animals which the Lele kept were dogs and chickens. There is a fable which describes how the first ancestors of these, a jackal and a partridge, came to throw in their lot with man, and how both dogs and poultry are continually begged by their forest-kin to leave the villages of humans. Conventional attitudes to both of these in a number of situations are consistent with the notion that a domestic animal is essentially an anomaly. For rats, which infest the huts

account for the fact that some wild animals occasionally attack humans, loiter near villages, even enter them and steal chickens and goats: sorcery and metempsychosis. I do not propose to describe them here.

Apart from these individual deviants, there are whole deviant species. Breeding habits, sleeping, watering, and feeding habits give the Lele categories in which there is consistency among the secondary characteristics, so that different species can be recognized. Carnivorous[5] animals have fur and claws as distinct from vegetarian animals, such as the antelopes with their smooth hides and hoofs. Egg-laying creatures tend to fly with wings. Mammals are four-footed and walk or climb, and so on. But some species defy classification by the usual means. There are four-footed animals which lay eggs, and mammals which fly like birds, land animals which live in the water, aquatic animals which live on the land.

AVOIDANCES IN CONNEXION WITH ANIMALS

These problems in animal taxonomy struck me first when I inquired into the food prohibitions observed by women. Some animals they avoid simply because they are anomalous, no ritual sanction being involved. For example, there is a 'flying squirrel', the scaly tail, which women avoid, because they are not sure what it is, bird or animal.[6] I have described elsewhere (Douglas 1955) their self-imposed prohibitions on foods which they consider disgusting apart from any religious symbolism. Here I am concerned with the provisions made in Lele religion for regulating human contact with animals. Restrictions on the contact of women with one species or another is the most usual ritual rule.

A wide diversity of animals are classed as 'spirit animals'

---

of humans, Lele feel nothing but disgust. In conformity with their attitude to other anomalous animals, they never eat dog, domestic rats, or mice, and women extend the avoidance to a number of other rats and to all poultry.

[5] For brevity's sake I use here some terms of our own categorization. Lele use no one word to render 'carnivorous' exactly, but they indicate carnivorous animals by the term *hutapok*—animals with skins, or 'furry animals'. I do not know any Lele term for 'oviparous' or 'mammalian', but it is clear that the manner of reproduction provides criteria for classification as surely for the Lele as for our zoologists, for their descriptions never fail to mention an animal's breeding habits.

[6] Significantly, its zoological name is *anomalurus Beecroftii.*

(*hut a ngehe*). I could not clarify in what sense these creatures are spirits. In some contexts they are spoken of as if they were spirits or manifestations of spirits. In others they are animals closely associated with spirits. They can be divided according to the restrictions which are imposed on women's contact with them.

Women may never touch the Nile monitor (*varanus niloticus*) or the small pangolin (*manis tricuspis*). Concerning the pangolin I shall say more below. The Nile monitor is a large aquatic lizard. The Lele describe it as a cousin of the crocodile, but without scales; like a snake with little legs; a lizard, but bigger, swifter, and more vicious than any lizard. Like the crocodile, it is a large, potentially dangerous amphibian.

Women may touch, but never eat, the tortoise and the yellow baboon (*papio cynocephalus kindae*). The tortoise is a curious beast. Its shell distinguishes it from other reptiles but, as a four-footed creature, it is anomalous in that it lays eggs. The baboon is interesting in several ways. Unlike other monkeys it is reputed not to be afraid of men, but will stand up to a hunter, strike him, talk, and throw sticks at him. When the troop of baboons goes off from the grass-land to the water, the females pick up their young in their arms, and those which are childless hitch a stone or stick into the crook of their arms, pretending that they too have babies. They go to the water, not merely to drink, but to wash. Moreover, they shelter in deep erosion gullies which are associated by the Lele with spirits who are thought to dig them for their own inscrutable purposes. Some of these gullies are very deep and become rushing torrents in the rains. As one of the ordeals of initiation, diviners have to climb down into one of these gullies and carry back mud from the bottom. Baboons, then, are unlike other animals in that they will stand up to a man, they experience barrenness, they wash, and they undergo one of the ordeals of initiation.

There is one animal which women never eat unless they are pregnant. It is the giant rat (*cricetomys dissimilis proparator*) which has a white tail and burrows underground. It is associated with the ghosts of the dead, perhaps because of the holes in the ground. The ghosts of the dead are often referred to as *bina hin,* the people down below. The habit of sleeping in a hole also seems to be associated with the spirits. Several of the spirit animals which women have to avoid are characterized as sleeping in holes, but I am not confident about this category, as there are other burrowing animals which are not classed as spirit animals. The porcupine (*hystrix galatea*) and the giant pangolin (*manis gigantea*) are spirit animals which women may not eat if they are pregnant. The ant-bear (*orycteropus afer*), which digs holes to escape from its pursuers, may be eaten by women except during the four months immediately following a certain fertility rite.

Water creatures are all associated with spirits and pregnant women must avoid them. The wild bush pig (*potamochaerus koiropotamus*), as I have already said, is a spirit animal because it frequents the streams and breeds prolifically. Pregnant women avoid it. There are two antelopes associated with spirits, which women must avoid during pregnancy. One is the water-chevrotain (*hyemoschus aquaticus*) which hides itself by sinking down into the water until only its nostrils appear above the surface. The other is *cephalophus grimmi,* whose idiosyncrasy is to sleep in daylight with its eyes wide open, so soundly asleep that a hunter can grab it by the leg. This habit associates it with the spirits, who are supposed to be active at night and asleep in the day. The little antelope is thought to be a servant of the spirits, resting in the day from its labours of the night.

So far as I know, this is the complete list of the animals whose contact with women is normally restricted. There are local variations. In the north crocodiles may be eaten by pregnant women; in the far south women's post-natal food includes squirrels and birds, i.e. animals of above (*hutadiku*) as opposed to ground animals (*hutahin*). In reply to my queries, Lele would merely reiterate the characteristics of the animal in question, as if its oddity would be instantly appreciated by me and would provide sufficient answer to my question.

No doubt the first essential procedure for understanding one's environment is to introduce order into apparent chaos by classifying. But, under any very simple scheme of classification, certain creatures seem to be anomalous. Their irregular behaviour is not merely puzzling but even offensive to the dignity of human reason. We find this attitude in our own spontaneous reaction to 'monstrosities' of all kinds. Paul Claudel (in *Le Soulier de Satin,* Troisième Journée, Scène II) understood it well, in depicting the disgust of a seventeenth-century grammarian confronted with a female whale suckling her young in mid-Atlantic:

> Vous trouvez ça convenable? C'est simplement révoltant! J'appelle ça de la bouffonnerie! Et pense que la nature est toute remplie de ces choses absurdes, révoltantes, exagérées! Nul bon sens! Nul sentiment de la proportion, de la mesure et de l'honnêteté! On ne sait où mettre les yeux!

The Lele do not turn away their eyes in disgust, but they react to 'unnatural behaviour' in animals in somewhat the same way as did the author of Deuteronomy—by prescribing avoidance.

> Every beast that divideth the hoof into two parts, and cheweth the cud, you shall eat. But of them that chew the cud, but divide not the hoof, you shall not eat, such as the camel, the hare and the rock-badger . . . these shall you eat of all that abide in the waters, all that have fins and scales you shall eat. Such as are without fins and scales, you shall not eat. (Deut. xiv. 7; Lev. xi. 4–5.)

The baboon, the scaly tail, the tortoise, and other animal anomalies are to the Lele as the camel, the hare and the rock-badger to the ancient Hebrews.

THE PANGOLIN

The pangolin is described by the Lele in terms in which there is no mistaking its anomalous character. They say: 'In our forest there is an animal with the body and tail of a fish, covered in scales. It has four little legs and it climbs in the trees.' If I had not by chance identified it at once as the scaly ant-eater, but had thought of it always as a scaly fish-like monster that ought to abide in the waters, but creeps on the land, its symbolic role would not have eluded me for so long.

Anomalous characteristics, like the scaly tail, would set the pangolin apart but would not explain its association with fertility. The fertility of humans is thought to be controlled by the spirits inhabiting the deepest, dampest parts of the forest. The symbolic connexion of water with fertility and with the spirits who control human fertility, is fairly explicit for the Lele. All aquatic things —fishes, water-animals, and water-plants, as well as amphibians— are associated with the spirits and with fertility. Creatures which have the same outward characteristics as aquatics, but live on the land (the pangolin), or which are essentially land animals but

frequent the water (the water chevrotain), are also associated with
the spirits. In this context the pangolin's association with fertility
becomes clear.

According to the Lele, the pangolin is anomalous in other
ways. Unlike other animals, it does not shun men but offers itself
patiently to the hunter. If you see a pangolin in the forest, you come
up quietly behind it and smack it sharply on the back. It falls off
the branch and, instead of scuttling away as other animals would
do, it curls into a tightly armoured ball. You wait quietly until it
eventually uncurls and pokes its head out, then you strike it dead.
Furthermore, the pangolin reproduces itself after the human rather
than the fish or lizard pattern, as one might expect from its appearance. Lele say that, like humans, it gives birth to one child at a
time. This in itself is sufficiently unusual to mark the pangolin out
from the rest of the animal creation and cause it to be treated as a
special kind of link between humans and animals.

In this respect the pangolin would seem to stand towards humans as parents of twins stand towards animals. Parents of twins
and triplets are, of course, regarded as anomalous humans who
produce their young in the manner of animals.

For a human to be classed with animals in any other connexion
—because, for instance, of unmannerly behaviour—is reprehensible.
But to vie with animals in fertility is good. Men do not beget by
their own efforts alone, but because the spirits in the forest consent. The parents of twins are considered to have been specially
honoured by the spirits. They are treated as diviners and are exempt from the initiation which ordinary men must undergo if
they wish to acquire magic powers. Twin children are spoken of
as spirits and their parents as Twin Diviners (*Bangang
bamayeh*). They pay an entrance fee into their own cult group, and
learn 'twin-magic' for fertility and good hunting.

The most striking proof of the high ritual status enjoyed by
parents of twins is that the usual ritual disabilities of women are
disregarded in the case of a woman who has borne twins. She at-
tends the conferences on twin-magic on exactly the same footing
as the men, performs the rites with them, and at her death is supposed to be buried with all the other diviners. This is quite out of
character with the normally subordinate position of women in
Lele ritual. Parents of twins are regarded as having been selected
by the spirits for a special role, mediating between humans and

animals and spirits. Pangolins perform a corresponding role in the animal sphere.

HUMANS, ANIMALS, AND SPIRITS

Lele religion is based on certain assumptions about the interrelation of humans, animals, and spirits. Each has a defined sphere, but there is interaction between them. The whole is regarded as a single system. A major disorder in the human sphere is presumed to disturb the relations which ought to exist between all the parts. Major disorders in the other spheres are not expected to occur.

Animals live their lives, each behaving according to its kind. Their sphere does not impinge on the human sphere. No animal will molest a human, enter a human habitation, or steal chickens and goats, unless made to do so by sorcery. Nor will an animal become a victim to a hunter unless the spirits are willing. For their part, humans cannot expect to intervene in animal affairs, even to sight or pursue, still less to kill an animal, unless their relations with the spirits are harmonious. The approval of the spirits is assured if human relations with each other are peaceful and if ritual is correctly performed. The goodwill of the spirits notwithstanding, the hunter's success may be spoilt by sorcery.

The hunt is the point at which the three spheres touch. Its significance far surpasses its primary object—the supply of meat. The whole range of human aspirations—for food, fertility, health, and longevity—is controlled by the spirits and may be thwarted by sorcery. If the hunt fails, the Lele fear that their other enterprises also are in danger. Not only do they feel angry at a wasted day and meatless fare, but they feel anxious for the recovery of the sick, for the efficacy of their medicines, for their whole future prosperity.

In the delicate balance between humans, animals, and spirits, certain humans and certain animals occupy key positions of influence. Among humans, the Begetters' Group honours those who have been blessed with a child. At their initiation rites ribald songs mock the sterile. The Pangolin cult honours those who have been blessed with children of both sexes; the Twin cult honours those who have been blessed with multiple births. The qualification for membership of any of these cults is not something which a man can achieve by his own efforts. He must have been chosen by the spirits for his role as mediator between the human and the supernatural. In theory, the candidates for the Diviners' Group are also believed to have been made aware of their vocation in a dream or by spirit-possession, though in practice men are known to fake this qualification. Once initiated these men have access to magical powers which can be used on behalf of their fellows.

In the animal world certain creatures mediate between animals and humans. Among these the pangolin is pre-eminent. It has the character of a denatured fish: a fish-like creature which lives on dry land, which bears its young after the manner of humans, and which does not run away from humans. In order to see the full significance of its fish-like scales, one should know more of the symbolic role of fish for the Lele.

Fishes belong so completely to the watery element that they cannot survive out of it. Bringing fish out of the water and the forest into the village is an act surrounded with precautionary ritual. Women abstain from sexual intercourse before going fishing. Fish and fishing gear, and certain water-plants, cannot be brought into the village on the day they are taken from the water unless ritual is performed. The woman who is carrying the fish sends a child ahead to fetch a live firebrand with which she touches the fish. The other things are left for one night in the grass-land before being taken into the village.

I might interpret this behaviour by saying that they wish to avoid any confusion of the dry and the watery elements, but this would not be a translation of any Lele explanation. If asked why they do it, they reply: 'To prevent an outbreak of coughing and illness', or, 'Otherwise the furry animals (*hutapok*) will get in and steal our chickens, and coughing will break out among our children.' But these are merely elliptical references to the communion between spirit, animal, and human spheres. The furry animals which steal chickens and cause illness are not ordinary carnivorous animals, but sorcerers' familiars, whose access to the sphere of living humans is made more difficult if the proper distinctions between human and animal, day and night, water and land,[7] are correctly observed.

In accordance with the symbolism relating fishes with fertility and with spirits, pregnant women and novices for initiation must

[7] I have given an outline of the most important of these distinctions as they appear in ritual, in Douglas (1954).

totally avoid eating fish. Certain fishes are more specially associated with spirits than others, and diviners are supposed to avoid eating them. Fishes do nothing to bridge the gap between human society and the creatures of the forest. Unprepared contact with them is potentially dangerous and is hedged with ritual. People in a marginal ritual condition avoid them altogether. But pangolins, part fish, part animal, friendly to humans, are apt for a mediatory role. This, I suggest, is the context of the underlying assumptions by means of which the Lele cult of pangolins is intelligible to themselves. This is why killing and eating pangolins, with proper ritual observances, are believed to bring animals in droves to the hunter's arrows and babies to women.

PANGOLIN RITUAL

In a village of forty men and fifty women, all the adult male pagans save one were Begetters, sixteen were initiated Diviners, three men and their wives were Twin Parents, four men were Pangolin initiates. I was present and able to record the results of a number of hunts in the dry season of 1953.

All the villages to the north, and many to the south of my village had adopted a new anti-sorcery cult, Kabengabenga, which was sweeping across the whole Kasai district. It promised hunting success, health, and long life to its initiates by threatening automatic death to anyone who attempted sorcery after initiation. Men and women in Kabengabenga villages brought pressure to bear on their kinsmen in other villages to follow their example and rid themselves of sorcery, and those who hesitated were accused by the initiates of culpable neglect if any of their kinsmen fell ill or died. Deaths in Kabengabenga villages were attributed to the boomerang action of the cult magic, so that anyone who died was held to be convicted of attempted sorcery. The mission and the Administration had taken strong action to stop the spread of the Kabengabenga cult, and in our own village the young Christians threatened to run away if the village were initiated.

Tension was running high in the village. Hunting failures, personal or communal, were attributed to sorcery; so also was sickness. Scarcely a night passed without someone shouting warnings to unnamed sorcerers to desist, to leave the sick to recover, to leave the hunter in peace to kill his quarry. They were begged to consider the reputation of the village in the eyes of other villages. One old man declared: 'The villages to the north and the villages to the south have taken Kabengabenga. They are all watching us. They used to say: "The men of Lubello kill quantities of game, without taking Kabengabenga." Now we go out hunting, and we come back empty-handed. That is a disgrace. They watch us and say we have sorcerers in our midst.'

Alternative explanations for misfortunes were offered. The senior Pangolin man said that after a strange woman had entered the village recently, it was discovered that she had borne twins; no twin-rites had been performed to prevent her entry from spoiling the village; the twin-parents should now perform rites and send the village on a hunt that would make good the breach of the twin-ritual.

On 6 August the twin-parents duly consulted together. A twin-parent is supposed to be an 'owner' of the village (*muna bola*) in the sense that his or her anger would render hunting fruitless unless a rite of blessing were performed. One of them, therefore, drew attention to her ulcerated leg, and protested that, in spite of the callous disregard of others in the village, she held no grudge against them for their neglect. If she had been heard to complain, it was in pain, not in anger. She performed the ritual of blessing. Instructions were given for a hunt for the next day.

7 August The hunt was moderately successful; although four duikers escaped, two small 'blue duikers', one water chevrotain, and one young bay duiker were killed. The success was attributed to the performance of the twin-ritual.

There was no more communal hunting until 12 August. Individual hunters complained of their lack of success, and considered the village to be 'bad'. The senior official diviner of the village, the *ilumbi*, was informally approached and asked to take up his magic for the next hunt. It required some courage and tact to ask him to do this, as he was widely thought to be the sorcerer responsible for the bad condition of the village. On the eve of the hunt, he ordered those who had quarrelled to pay fines, and announced that he would do magic. Before the hunt one of the Pangolin men spoke a blessing, in case his grief at the obstinate and rude behaviour of the young Christians should spoil the hunt. They drew three covers, saw little game, killed only one adult and one young 'blue duiker'—a quite negligible bag. The *ilumbi* felt discredited. He announced that the animals which he had seen by divination had been escaping behind the hunters; next time he would do different magic.

13 August In the dawn an old man got up and harangued the sorcerers, asking what they ate if they didn't like animal meat? Dogs? People? What? He warned them that he did not consent to the illness of children in the village.

During the day it transpired that the twin-ritual was still outstanding. The village had been tricked into believing that the successful hunt on 7 August had been the result of twin-rituals whereas, in fact, the junior *ilumbi,* himself a twin-parent, had persuaded the others to let him try a 'spirit magic' which had been highly successful a month earlier. Everyone was angry at the deception. The senior Pangolin man, who had originally diagnosed that a breach of twin-ritual had 'spoilt the village', declared that if only the twin-parents had been frank, the diviners themselves would have stepped in to perform the necessary twin-rites. Twins (*mayehe*) and spirits (*mingehe*) are all the same, he said, and initiated diviners do not need to beget twins in order to do twin-rites. Angriest of all was the senior *ilumbi,* hurt in his pride of magic, who now saw the reason for the failure of the hunt he had arranged on 12 August. More serious than being made to look a fool, he had looked like a sorcerer chasing away the game. In the next village the *ilumbi* had been hounded out for failure to produce game, and in the old days he would have been made to take the poison ordeal. He was obliged to dissemble his anger, as the village could be 'spoilt' by the ill will of any of its ritual officers.

In the next week men refused to go on a communal hunt as the village seemed obviously 'bad', i.e. infected with sorcery. Individual hunters had some success: a duiker was caught in a trap, a man chanced on a wild sow just after she had farrowed and easily shot her and killed her young; and a large harnessed bush-buck was shot. In spite of these successes, there was an atmosphere of frustration and acrimony in the village.

On 24 and 27 August the women went on two long fishing expeditions. While they were away there was little food, and work in the village just ticked over till their return. On 28th two pangolins were killed. When the women came back the atmosphere in the village had changed overnight to one of general rejoicing. The village evidently was felt to be vindicated in the eyes of its

Kabengabenga critics. A neighbouring village asked to be allowed
to send a candidate for initiation into the Pangolin cult. Among
the ritual specialists annoyance about the overdue twin-rite still
rankled, but the Pangolin rites had to take precedence now.

The junior Pangolin man announced on behalf of the initiates
that the village was 'tied' (*kanda*), that is, that sexual intercourse
was banned until after the eating of the pangolin and the shedding
of animal blood in the hunt that should follow the feast. Etiquette
appropriate to the presence of a chief in the village was to be observed. He used the words: '*Kum ma wa:* The master is dead. Let
no one fight.' *Kum* can be translated as master or chief. Unfortunately a quarrel between children dancing broke out, adults took
sides, and blows were struck. A fine had to be paid to the Pangolin group for this breach of ritual peace.

29 August   A meeting was called. The village was in a ferment
because a man had been caught seducing the wife of the senior
Pangolin man. The latter refused to carry on with the Pangolin
initiation and feast.

30 August   There was a spate of early-morning speeches. The
senior Pangolin man was reproached for turning household affairs
into village affairs, and for making the village suffer for his private
wrong. Someone pointed out that if the pangolins were left to
rot, the people of the next village, who wanted their candidate
vested with Pangolin power, would think we had refused to eat the
pangolin to spite them. All those who had quarrelled were roundly
taken to task in public speeches. All were convinced that to go
hunting while the senior Pangolin man was feeling angry would
be useless.

31 August   Village opinion, originally sympathetic to the senior Pangolin man, now turned against him. He was insisting that
full adultery damages should be paid before he proceeded with
the Pangolin rites. There was anxiety lest the pangolins should go
bad; they had already been dead five days. If they were to go bad
without being eaten with proper ritual, the whole village would
go 'hard' and suffer for a long time, until Pangolin magic had been
done again. Repeated injunctions were made to keep the peace
until the pangolin hunt. Two more cases of fighting occurred.

2 September   Fines for fighting were all paid up, and the major
part of the adultery damages had been given. Ritual was performed
to make the way clear for hunting the next day. The two *ilumbi*,

the four Pangolin men, and the twin-parents met and agreed to do two rites: twin-ritual and Pangolin ritual, for the hunt.

3 September Before the hunt, two twin-parents aired their grievances; one on account of her ulcerated leg, which she felt no one took trouble to diagnose and cure; the other complained that her husband had abandoned her for a new young wife. Her husband's colleagues replied for him that it was nonsense to suppose that a man would leave a woman through whom he had attained three of God's callings or vocations (*mapok manjambi*). He was, through her, an initiate of the Begetters, of Twins and of the Pangolin. She was reminded of the danger to the village if a woman who was in these three senses one of its 'owners' were allowed to nurse her anger.

The hunt that followed this concerted ritual effort was a failure. Seven animals in all were seen, but only two small duikers were killed. There was great anger and agreement that the village was bad. However, blood had been shed and the Pangolin feast could proceed. After the Pangolin rites had been performed, people assured each other, we should all see great quantities of game being brought back. The pangolin would draw animals to the village. The next day was fixed for the feast.

That very afternoon a third pangolin was killed. There was great satisfaction. 'Just as we were saying "Tomorrow we shall eat pangolin, and invest new members" . . . behold, another pangolin comes into the village!' They spoke as if the pangolin had died voluntarily, as if it had elected to be the object of Pangolin ritual and to offer itself for the feast of initiates; as if it had honoured this village by choosing it.

At night the junior Pangolin man announced that no one was to fight, above all no one was to fight secretly. 'If you must fight, do it openly and pay up. He who fights tonight, let him be rich. The fine will be twenty raffia cloths.'

5 September The Pangolin feast and initiation rite were eventually held. I was unfortunately unable to see the rites. I was told that emphasis was laid on the chiefship of the pangolin. We call him *kum,* they said, because he makes women conceive. They expressed shame and embarrassment at having eaten a *kum.* No one is allowed to see the pangolins being roasted over the fire. The tongues, necks, ribs, and stomachs were not eaten, but buried under a palm-tree whose wine thenceforth becomes the sole prerogative of the Begetters. Apparently the new initiate was made to eat some of the flesh of the first two pangolins which were in process of decay; the more rotten parts, together with the scales and bones, were given to the dogs. The senior initiates ate the flesh of the more recently killed animal. All were confident that the hunt on the following day would be successful.

6 September The hunt went off in good heart, twenty men and eight dogs. It was an abject failure. Powerful sorcery was evidently at work, since all ritual had been duly performed. People discussed the possible significance of a leopard that had been heard to bark in the precincts of the village that night, and of leopard tracks that had been seen on the way to the hunt. The leopard is one of the forms which the *ilumbi* is supposed to be able to take, and the *ilumbi* was suspected of having gone ahead of the hunters in leopard's guise, and scared off the game. The *ilumbi* himself, realizing that suspicions of sorcery were again directed at him, suggested that he would gladly go with the rest of the village to take Kabengabenga magic, if only the Christians did not hold such strong objections. He evidently saw it as a means of clearing his own name. In his youth he had twice taken the poison ordeal and confounded his accusers. He also suggested to me privately that he might leave the village and live elsewhere, as his enemies had never forgiven him for the disputes over women in which he had been embroiled.

In the meanwhile, the village was still 'tied': the ban on sexual intercourse had not been lifted since 28 August, and could not be until blood had been shed in a hunt following the feast of Pangolin initiates.

9 September A hunt took place in which one small duiker was killed. The ritual requirement was fulfilled, and the ban on sexual intercourse was lifted, but from every other point of view it was felt to have been a failure.

ACCURACY OF LELE OBSERVATION OF ANIMALS

Writing strictly from the point of view of religious symbolism it is not relevant to ask how accurate is Lele observation of animal behaviour. A symbol based on mistaken information can be fully effective as a symbol, so long as the fable in question is well known. The dove, it would seem, can be one of the most relentlessly savage of birds.[8] The pelican does not nourish its young from its own living flesh. Yet the one bird has provided a symbol of peace, and the other of maternal devotion, for centuries.

However, it would be interesting to know whether the symbolism described above is based on fables or not. I must confess that I was able only with great difficulty to identify most of the animals. Many of the rarer ones I never saw alive or dead and in any case should not have been able to recognize them at sight. I was fortunate in securing the kind collaboration of Monsieur A. J. Jobaert, Warden of the Muene Ditu Game Reserve, who knew the Kasai and several of the local languages well. By sending him the native names in two local languages, together with a description, I obtained translations into French, Latin, and English, and these names were checked again by Mr. R. B. Freeman, the Reader in Taxonomy at University College, London. My remarks are based on identification obtained in this roundabout and unreliable way. The point I thought it most important to check was whether the Lele are right in considering the breeding habits of pangolins anomalous: first, do pangolins give birth to their young one at a time? Second, how unusual is this among the smaller mammals? In pursuing this inquiry I was interested to find how little scientifically tested knowledge there is concerning the manner of reproduction of mammals, common and uncommon. Such information as is available serves to justify the Lele in both these views (see Asdell 1946: 184).

One interesting point that I am still unable to elucidate is the principle on which the Lele discriminate between the small pangolin (*manis tricuspis*) which they call *luwawa,* and the giant pangolin (*manis gigantea*) which they call *yolabondu,* making a major cult of the first but not of the second. Zoologists may be able to give information about the distribution and habits of the two species which may throw light on the question. It may require an historical solution, since Pangolin cults are found in other parts of the Congo (Biebuyck 1953).

[8] Lorenz, *King Solomon's Ring.*

13 THEMES IN THE SYMBOLISM
OF NDEMBU HUNTING RITUAL

Victor W. Turner

FOR THE NDEMBU tribe of Northern Rhodesia[1] the hunt is more than a food quest; it is a religious activity. It is preceded and followed by the performance of rites and is believed to be beset with perils of an ultra-human order. I have discussed the social importance of hunting among the Ndembu in a number of previous publications,[2] and will therefore confine myself to repeating that this importance does not derive from the objective contribution to the food supply made by the chase. It arises partly from the high ritual status of the hunter and partly from the fact that for the Ndembu hunting epitomizes masculinity in a society jurally dominated by the principle of matrilineal descent. In agricultural production (mainly the cultivation of cassava, finger millet and maize), and in the preparation of food, women's work has major importance, though men today are increasingly drawn into the cultivation of crops for cash while hunting declines with the shooting out of game.

Ndembu recognize two main branches of hunting: (1) *Wubinda,* which includes every recognized technique for killing animals and birds—firearms, bows and arrows, spears, snares, traps, pitfalls, nets, the use of bird-lime, etc.; (2) *Wuyanga,* the skilled use of guns. Although women and children snare small animals and birds, this activity is not described as *Wubinda;* this term is reserved for the killing or catching of bigger game. Forest

Reprinted from *Anthropology Quarterly* vol. 35, April 1962: 37–57 by permission of the author and the editor, *Anthropology Quarterly.*

[1] I am indebted to the Center for Advanced Study in the Behavioral Sciences for providing me with the opportunity to write up this material.
[2] See V. W. Turner 1953, 1957, 1961a.

game is hunted all year round, except at the height of the rainy season, but animals are hunted on the plains which stretch around the upper reaches of rivers—most of the Ndembu territory in Mwinilunga District in northwestern Northern Rhodesia lies on the Congo-Zambezi watershed and is therefore an area of river sources—mainly when the grass has grown long enough to give the hunter adequate cover.

During the period of my field research guns were by no means plentiful among the Ndembu. According to the 1951 District Report (kindly made available to me by Mr. R. C. Dening, the then District Commissioner), 68 breechloading guns and 1154 muzzle-loading guns had been registered at District Headquarters. These figures refer to the whole of Mwinilunga District, which includes not only 18,346 Ndembu, but also 13,107 Kosa people. The total tax-paying population of adult males was recorded as 10,542. The ratio of approximately one gun to nine adult males is probably not wildly incorrect. Quite a high proportion of the guns are ancient flintlocks, used as currency in the nineteenth century slave trade, and are inefficient and dangerous to use. Thus few men can hope to possess guns, and of these fewer still become really proficient hunters.

To the two main branches of hunting correspond two cults, also called *Wubinda* and *Wuyang'a,* and the latter has many of the characteristics not merely of a profession but even of a vocation. The gun-hunter (*chiyang'a*) is often a solitary adept who spends much of his time alone or accompanied by a single apprentice—who is also a candidate for admission to the cult—in the wild bush with all its visible and invisible dangers. He is assisted by the guardian spirit of a deceased hunter-kinsman and by magical charms, he performs rites to propitiate the spirits of hunter-dead before he ventures into the bush, and he is believed to encounter there the inimical powers of witches, sorcerers, ghosts, were-lions and persecuting ancestors.

A *chiyang'a* is also a *chibinda* (a hunter with bows and traps), but not every *chibinda* is a *chiyang'a*. *Wubinda* is the older cult and is said to have come with the forbears of the Ndembu when they migrated from the kingdom of Mwantiyanvwa, the great Lunda chief in Katanga, more than two centuries ago. *Wuyang'a* is believed to have been introduced, along with the first muzzle-loading guns, by Ovimbundu traders who came regularly from

Kasanji and Bihe in Western Angola to purchase slaves and bees-wax in the mid-nineteenth century. But it shares many features of its symbolism with *Wubinda* on which it must have been speedily grafted.

RITUAL OF AFFLICTION

Wubinda belongs to a category of Ndembu ritual which I have called 'ritual of affliction.'[3] The rites belonging to this category are performed to propitiate or exorcise ancestor spirits which are believed to bring misfortune, illness or reproductive disorders. The victims are their living kin. The alleged motives for afflicting vary, but it is commonly said that the victim has neglected to make offerings to the spirit at its shrine or has forgotten the spirit 'in his heart.' Affliction is conceived to be a sharp rebuke for such negligence. In almost every case I have been able to observe of illness or misfortune treated by ritual of affliction there has been an additional factor of social disturbance. The victim has here been afflicted as a representative of a quarrel-ridden social group (a village, matrilineal descent group or extended family), even if he or she is not held to be personally blameworthy. I have heard it suggested that such affliction is "good" (-*wahi*) because the ritual to remove it "brings to light" (*ku-solola*) and so dispels the quarrels (*madombu*) and grudges (*yitela*) in the group.

There are various modes of affliction. Women, for example, are afflicted by ancestor spirits (*akishi*, singular *mukishi*) with a number of clearly defined reproductive troubles, each kind corresponding with a named mode of affliction. For example, an ancestress "coming out in (the mode of) *Nkula*" (as Ndembu put it) afflicts her kinswoman (nearly always in the matrilineal line) with menstrual disorders. The rites to propitiate such spirit-manifestations might be termed "gynaecological" rites. Hunters, too, are afflicted with different kinds of bad luck in the chase by dead hunter kinsmen (patrilateral as well as matrilineal).

To each mode of manifestation there corresponds a curative rite which bears its name. Thus "*Nkula*" is performed to cure a patient "caught" by the "*Nkula*" manifestation. *Nkula* cult-members are recruited from those who have been its former patients. The

[3] Turner 1957: 292–303.

patient is thus also a *candidate* for admission to the cult association, while the *doctor* is simultaneously an *adept*. Such associations of adepts cut across corporate groups with a kinship or local basis and across one another. They are called into transient being and action by a diviner's verdict. The divination séance itself may be regarded as a phase in a social process which (1) begins with a person's illness, reproductive trouble or misfortune at hunting; (2) continues into informal or formal discussion in the local community as to what is to be done; (3) representatives of the community are sent to a diviner; (4) there is a séance terminated by the diviner's diagnosis of the nature, cause and agency of affliction and his recommendation that a certain type of rite should be performed; (5) the next phase is the actual performance of that rite.

WUBINDA—GENERIC HUNTSMANSHIP

The cult of *Wubinda* is an assemblage of five rites called respectively: (1) *Mukala;* (2) *Chitampakasa;* (3) *Kalombu;* (4) *Mundeli;.* (5) *Ntambu.* Each of these names denotes a specific manifestation of a hunter-ancestor, and much of the symbolism of the propitiatory rite is expressive of the attributes of that manifestation. Thus the senior adept in the *Mukala* rite makes whistling noises and at one stage wears strips of hide, each with a ridge of fur, because the *Mukala* manifestation is thought to whistle game away from the hunter and to wear these *"mazang'a,"* part of the garb of hunters in bygone times. *Mukala* may be performed for a young man who has just started to hunt seriously, though spirits may manifest themselves in this mode, so Ndembu think, to established hunters as well. But the other modes of affliction only affect experienced hunters who have already been accorded cult-names.

WUYANG'A—THE GUN-HUNTERS' CULT

The cult of *Wuyang'a* differs from *Wubinda* in that it consists of a graded series of four rites, each of which indicates the attainment of a certain degree both of proficiency in killing animals and of esoteric knowledge of the cult mysteries. These grades of initiation into *Wuyang'a* are: (1) *Kuwelesha,* "causing to be washed"—in this case with pounded leaf-medicine (*nsompu*). Here the novice or apprentice in "huntsmanship" (as *Wuyang'a* might be termed), having enjoyed a measure of success in shooting animals with an inherited or borrowed gun, is deemed worthy of being washed with a decoction of bark-scrapings and leaves taken from a number of tree species, each of which is thought to impart some aspect of "huntsmanship" to the would-be hunter; (2) If the young hunter has demonstrated his prowess he undergoes *Kusukula,* "Initiation (into huntsmanship)." At the end of this rite he takes a special hunter-name from a collection of names reserved for initiated hunters; (3) *Kutelekesha,* "Causing to cook (meat)." This is both a celebration of the hunter's skill and success over a long period and a feast in honor of his guardian ancestor spirit who has provided him—and through him his dependents and fellow villagers—with a regular supply of meat. In the course of this rite much meat is given by its sponsor to hunter-adepts and to the general public; (4) *Mwima,* "Ripeness" (from *kwima,* "to bear fruit"). This is the *dernier cri* in praise and self-praise for a gun-hunter. Only the greatest hunters are bold enough to hold *Mwima* which is a sign that a man has "finished huntsmanship." Incidentally, the term *mwima* is also applied to the forked branch shrine planted in honor of a hunter's spirit. We shall shortly discuss this structure in detail, but it is worth mentioning in passing that the "fruit" borne by it are trophies of the chase, the heads and entrails of antelope and other game. In all this an important analogy is made by Ndembu between what they consider is woman's dominant role, the bearing of children, and man's, which is the bringing home of carcasses from the hunt. In hunters' and women's rites of affliction the same symbols stand respectively for a multiplicity of kills and a multiplicity of children. Women do not possess a *mwima,* and indeed their reproductive powers are endangered by close contact with "the things of huntsmanship," but the values associated with *mwima* are those which assert a parallel between the many kills desired for a male hunter and the many new lives desired for a mother.

HUNTING RITES

Since space is limited I can do little more in this paper than indicate a few of the main themes running through the symbolism of

Wubinda and *Wuyang'a* and of the mortuary rites of professional hunters. In a previous article[4] I discussed the semantic structure and properties of some of the principal symbols found in Ndembu ritual and there distinguished between three "levels" or "fields" of meaning possessed by such symbols. I pointed out that many ritual symbols are *multivocal* or *polysemous,* i.e., they stand for many objects, activities and relationships—there is not a one-to-one relationship between symbol and referent but a one-to-many relationship. Each major symbol has a "fan" or "spectrum" of referents (denotata and connotata), which tend to be interlinked by what is usually a simple mode of association, its very simplicity enabling it to interconnect a wide variety of referents. Some of the symbols we shall shortly consider have this polysemous character. I shall consider them firstly on the level of their *exegetical meaning,* secondly of their *operational meaning,* and thirdly of their *positional meaning.* The first level, briefly, represents the interpretations of my Ndembu informants—in this case of hunter-adepts—the second results from equating a symbol's meaning with its *use,* by noting what Ndembu do with it, and not only what they say about it, while the third level of meaning consists in examining a symbol's relationship to others belonging to the same complex or *gestalt* of symbols. I hope to show that this set of methodological tools has its uses in exposing to view the deeper layers of a society's system of values.

Simply because each ritual symbol is so dense with significance, the task of presenting, classifying and analysing the referents of even a few interrelated symbols is necessarily a long one. For ritual, in one important aspect, is *quintessential* custom; what is distributed through many fields and situations of secular life is condensed into a few symbolic actions and objects. For every kind of hunting rite, itself an epitome of a whole sector of Ndembu culture, a quintessential feature is the *temporary shrine* erected to the hunter-ancestor, who is either afflicting his living kinsman with bad luck or has already been propitiated and is regarded as the source of his good fortune in killing game. This shrine typically has three main components, and may be associated with further symbolic units according to the specific rite that is performed. These three components are: (1) a forked branch known as

---

4 Turner 1961b.

chishing'a, muchanka, or, as we have seen, in the case of a supreme hunter, *mwima;* (2) a small piece of termitary earth trimmed into a block of rectangular shape and laid at the base of the forked branch, which is firmly planted in the ground, facing the ritual assembly or "congregation"; (3) a braid of grass, of the *kaswamang'wadyi* species, which grows to a considerable height on the plains.

THE EXEGETICAL MEANING OF CHISHING'A

Each of these components is a complete system of meaning, and may be analysed at the three levels of interpretation discussed earlier. Let us, then, consider the forked branch at the level of indigenous exegesis. In explaining what a symbolic object stands for, Ndembu normally look to two of its characteristics, its name and its natural properties, as the *fons et origo* of interpretation. Let us then consider the name *chishing'a,* commonly applied to these shrines. My informants are in general agreement that the term is derived from the reflexive form of the verb *ku-shing'a* or *ku-shing'ana,* "to curse," i.e., *kudishing'a,* which means "to curse one another." This may well be an instance of fictitious etymologizing[5] but fictitious etymology, like *homonymy,* (i.e., increasing the senses possessed by a word by adding to them those of a word of the same form but different derivation), is a device whereby the semantic wealth of a word or symbol may be augmented. Whether this is the case or not, my informants are also in agreement in stating that "meat (*mbiji*) is a cause of quarrels (*madombu*), and in quarrels people curse one another"—with implications of the use of sorcery.

"Meat is a cause of quarrels" in two basic situations. In the first place, hunters often conceal from their fellow-villagers that they have made a kill, pleading dolefully that they have had no luck. Meanwhile, they have divided the meat secretly among the members of their elementary family and personal friends, instead of in customarily specified joints among the members of their village matrilineage. If this is later discovered grudges (*yitela*) will develop, leading to the invocation of ghosts to kill the hunter, if the situation is not remedied. Such an invocation is known as

[5] For others, see Turner 1961b: 57, etc.

ku-shing'ana, a "curse." In the second place, even when the meat is distributed in public, villagers tend to quarrel about the amount given to them; e.g., a classificatory mother's brother will demand an equal share with a full mother's brother. Thus jealousy (of the hunter's prowess), envy over the distribution of meat, hatred of the hunter by those who have been cheated, and quarrelling between individuals and factions over amounts (quite a bunch of deadly sins, not to mention greed!) are regularly associated with the hunter's role. One informant told me, "a hunter eats good meat while others starve, and they say that he ought to find bad luck because he does not give them meat." Another said that "hunting is sorcery (*wuloji*), for hunters have snake-familiars (*malomba*) which kill their relatives to increase their (the hunters') power." For each tuft of the victim's hair the hunter is said to acquire the power (*ng'ovu*) to kill an animal. But far from feeling shame on account of their bad reputation, hunters, like big businessmen, seem often to rejoice in being known as "hard guys" and in song and invocation to hunter spirits refer to themselves by terms normally considered opprobrious, such as "adulterers who sleep with ten women a day" and "great thieves." They take pride in the envy directed against them for they say that only those who are successful are envied. To be "cursed" is part of what they term their "pride" or "dignity" or "self-praise of huntsmanship" (*kudilemesha* or *kudivumbika kwaWuyang'a*). Yet there is ambivalence in Ndembu society's attitude towards the hunter for he is, when all is said and done, the provider of the most prized food of all.

There was no agreement about the meaning of the word *muchanka.* One informant said that it was "an old word for the way animals move when a hunter is chasing them." *Mwima,* as we have seen, means "ripeness" or "bearing fruit," and this may refer to the skulls of buck and other trophies "borne" by the forked branch.

The name *chishing'a,* then, is heavily charged with the irony of huntsmanship. The meaning of the hunter as provider of blessings is expressed by language of quite opposite tendency. Let us now consider the natural properties of the forked branch. These provide further sources of meaning. They may be subdivided into two aspects: (1) the species of trees used for the *chishing'a;* (2) the shape of the *chishing'a.*

Trees, bushes and herbs play the important part in Ndembu ritual that they play in the ritual of other forest Bantu. Each species is thought to have its own virtues, both for treating illness and in religious rites. But there is a crucial distinction to be made between these two major uses. When trees are used in the empirical treatment of illness, usually in the form of pounded leaves, scrapings of bark and sliced roots mixed with hot or cold water, emphasis is laid on their directly physical effects on the senses. Thus in the treatment of pyorrhea, "medicine" (*yitumbu*) made from the sliced roots of various trees is heated and the patient is made to rinse his mouth with it. The aim of the treatment is "to remove pain so that the bad teeth will fall out by themselves." Among the ingredients are the roots of the *mwalu* tree, which is used "because it is bitter and can kill the disease" (*musong'u*—a "disease" has certain animal and human characteristics, it can "move," "curl up," "think," "go away," "die"). *Musosu* is used because it is rather "sweet" and deadens pain. *Kambanji-banji* is "hot" (*yeya*) and drives off the disease. *Kapepi* is used "because it sets the teeth on edge by its bitterness (*wukawu*), so that the bad ones drop out."

Now the same term, *yitumbu,* is applied to pounded vegetable medicines used as potions and lotions in religious rites. But the nature of the association-chains in these rites is quite different. Here certain selected natural properties of the tree are regularly connected with values, moral qualities, principles of social organization and with religious beliefs. I have many statements from informants which actually identify the *yitumbu* used in a rite of affliction with the mode of affliction in which an ancestor spirit has "emerged." Thus the leaves of trees which secrete red gum or have red wood or roots are used in the "medicine" with which a woman patient is washed in the *Nkula* rite. An ancestress who "comes out in *Nkula*," as Ndembu say, afflicts her victim with menorrhagia and other periodic disorders, involving the loss of blood which, so the people think, should cohere round the implanted "seed of life" (*kabubu kawumi*) to form an infant. The patient is exposed to a hot fire so that fragments of leaves should adhere to her when the medicine has dried. These fragments are said to be a "symbol" (*chinjikijilu*) of the spirit (*mukishi*) "in Nkula." The "red" properties of this mode of affliction are here represented by the green leaves of trees which are ritually standardized as "red" (*-chinana*). "Redness" is a complex concept in Ndembu ritual, and in *Nkula* alone it stands for (1) menstrual blood; (2) maternal blood, "that is clear and good and shown at parturition,"; (3) the principle of matriliny itself—a matrilineage is called *ivumu*, "a womb"; (4) the *Nkula* cult; (5) the historical continuity of the Ndembu with the great Lunda empire, whose foundress, Luweji Ankonde, suffered from menorrhagia and was cured by the first *Nkula* rite. In the hunting cults, "redness" has a further "fan" of referents, associated mainly with the shedding of the blood of animals. But the forked branch shrine though it is frequently splashed with offerings of blood is not a red symbol but, in terms of its color symbolism, a white one. It is made from five species of trees. These are not used interchangeably, but the kind of rite determines the kind of shrine-tree. The same species also provide ingredients for hunting "medicines," of the ritual type we have just been discussing. Whether these species are used for medicines or shrines their referents remain the same.

The five[6] species are:

1 *Musoli*   Vangueriopsis lanciflora
2 *Museng'u*   Ochna sp.
3 *Kapwipu*   Swartzia madagascariensis
4 *Kapepi*   Hymenocardia mollis
5 *Mubula*   Uapaca sp.

MUSOLI

Musoli is employed as "medicine" in rites to restore female fertility as well as in hunting rites. This tree has edible yellow fruit, much appreciated by duiker and other woodland buck during the early rains. Snares are set beneath *musoli* trees to trap these animals. Ndembu say that the name *musoli,* derived from *ku-solola,* "to make visible" or "reveal," is connected with the capacity of the tree to draw forth animals from their hiding places in the bush, and make them "visible" to hunters. This is a "natural" capacity of the tree, as we would say, but Ndembu see in it something more. It is for them a particular instance of a power underlying all life,

---

[6] Some informants have told me that the *kabalabala* tree is also made into a *chishing'a,* but I have no detailed information on this point.

the power of "making visible." Thus *musoli* medicine is given to a barren woman so that she will "make children visible" (*ku-solola anyana*), and to a hunter "to make animals visible" (*ku-solola anyama*) for him. *Musoli* has the further sense in the hunting rites of "producing to view a large gathering of people" (*ku-solola luntu lweneni* or *chipompelu cheneni*). The reasoning behind this is that just as the many fruits of the *musoli* bring out of hiding many animals, so will its ritual use bring many people to praise the hunter who has sponsored the rite, and who (it is implied) has killed many animals. The *Musoli* tree, therefore, represents the prowess of the hunter at his profession and the fame (*mpuhu*) it confers on him.

MUSENG'U

The Ndembu derive the name of this species from *ku-seng'uka,* "to multiply." The tree bears a great number of tiny black edible fruits, and informants connect this prolificity with its name. It is also connected with the term *ku-seng'ula,* "to bless"—in practice by blowing "medicine" in the ears. Like *musoli, museng'u* is used in both hunting and "gynaecological" rites; in the former it represents "a multiplicity of kills," in the latter "a multiplicity of offspring."

KAPWIPU

This tree is also known as *mutete,* and it is from this ritual usage that Ndembu normally commence its exegesis. *Mutete* itself is the first word of a phrase *mutete manyangi wuta wachashi,* literally, "the one who cuts huntsmanship" (i.e., "cuts up and distributes meat"), "the empty gun" or "the gun that misses its aim." In explanation of this phrase an informant told me: "A hunter was in the habit of killing many animals, but then he missed his aim once or twice. Others told him to hold his gun correctly, for the shaking of his mind caused him to miss. They played a hunting drum (i.e., performed *Wuyang'a* or *Wubinda* rites) for him and instructed him to shoot properly. After this, he never missed. So he praised himself thus: 'At first I killed animals, later I failed to do so, then after missing I killed again.' "

The *mutete* tree, then, epitomizes the whole process of *Wu-*

binda, i.e., hunting as a set of rites of affliction. Good luck depends on the favor of hunter ancestors, and they will withdraw their assistance from you, sometimes to punish you for distributing meat unfairly, sometimes because a ritually impure person such as a woman or an uncircumcised boy has eaten the sacred portions of meat (head, lungs, entrails), called *yijila* ("tabooed things"), reserved for the hunter. But this withdrawal, and even active persecution, is something other than merely punitive. For the Ndembu have the notion that affliction is also a sign of election. The afflicting ancestor spirit wishes to become "your spirit" (*mukishi weyi*), in other words your guardian or patron spirit. First, however, you must do something for him; you must perform rites for him, both private and public, and demonstrate that you have "not forgotten him in your liver" (the seat of the emotions in Ndembu belief), by making offerings either on his grave, if it can be found, or on a *chishing'a* specially planted to him. The identity of the hunter-spirit is established by divination, as also is the mode in which he is manifesting his displeasure. At the public phase of the rite, it is considered pleasing to the spirit to mention his name often in invocations and praises. This is considered a form of *ku-solola,* of "revelation." If the spirit has been placated he will "help you to kill many animals," and so contribute to your eventual fame as a great *"Mwima"* hunter. The motto of the Ndembu might well be "you must suffer to succeed." It is this theme that is so signally represented by the *kapwipu* or *mutete* tree. In this case it is the "name only" (*ijina hohu*) that determines the chain of associations, not the properties of the species. But we shall see that *kapwipu* shares certain physical properties with the other species mentioned which make it suitable for use as a *"chishing'a."*

KAPEPI AND MUBULA

I must discuss these species briefly owing to shortage of space, and say that *kapepi* is connected with terms meaning "wind" and "breath," and stands for the desired invisibility and ubiquity of the hunter, while *mubula,* another fruit-tree, is etymologically connected with *ku-bula,* "to make fire by steel, flint and dry-moss tinder" as hunters do in the bush—it also refers to the firing of their flintlocks.

THE SHAPE OF CHISHING'A

A *chishing'a* is a branch forked in one or more places, stripped of all its leaves and bark. The species I have mentioned are said to be termite-resistant and to have a "strong wood," representing the "strength" (*wukolu*) of huntsmanship. It has been said to me repeatedly by Ndembu hunters that string cannot be made out of the bark of any of the trees used for these shrines. "If they were string-trees, they would tie up (*ku-kasila*) the huntsmanship of the candidate." In just the same way string-bearing trees may not be used in gynaecological ritual for fear of "tying up" the fertility of the patients.

The prongs of the extremities of the branches are sharpened by the knives of hunter-adepts. This is to represent the "sharpness" or "keenness" (*ku-wambuka*) of huntsmanship. As informants said: "*Wubinda wawambuka nang'ovu*"—"huntsmanship is sharp with power." The causative form of *wambuka, wambwisha,* means "to whet a knife," and it is as though the hunters were trying to "whet" the candidate's huntsmanship. Forked-branch shrines are common throughout Africa, and they are by no means always associated with hunting cults. But what is interesting in the present context is that Ndembu ascribe to such shrines senses which do express the values of their hunting culture. One of the marks of a viable ritual symbol may be said to be its capacity to move from society to society without marked change in form but with many changes in meaning. Though referents are lost in transference, new referents are readily acquired. Certain symbols arouse an almost universal response, much as music does. This is a problem that would repay investigation in terms of a detailed comparative study.

The whiteness of the exposed wood in each species of *chishing'a* is also held to be significant by Ndembu informants. Whiteness (*wutooka*) in Ndembu ritual has many connotations. These include: strength, health, good luck, ritual purity, authority, good will between the ancestors and the living, the clear and known as opposed to the obscure and unknown, life, power, breast milk, seminal fluid, the whiteness of cassava meal and roots. In the context of hunting ritual the qualities of health, strength, toughness, luck at the hunt, virility and a state of *bon rapport* with the ancestors, tend to receive special stress among the "white" senses.

THE OPERATIONAL MEANING OF CHISHING'A

The way a symbolic object is *used*, I have suggested, forms an important part of its *meaning*. Before we can fully appreciate what the *chishing'a* "means" to Ndembu, therefore, we must enquire how it is collected, set up and thereafter utilized. A *chishing'a* may be cut: (1) by a solitary hunter; (2) by a hunter and the "great hunter" who is training him, known as his "mother of huntsmanship" (*mama daWuyang'a*)—for among the matrilineal Ndembu the term "mother" refers to one who nourishes with knowledge as well as with milk and is used metaphorically of male authority figures and teachers—and (3) by a group of hunter-adepts. When the latter collect a *chishing'a,* one hunter lays his axe to the root while the others seize hold of the branches and bear down on them while they sing the melancholy, nostalgic songs of their cult. A hunter-adept explained this as follows: "the hunters pull down the tree together to prevent it falling by itself—if it fell of its own accord the huntsmanship would be lost." Here again we find "huntsmanship" (*Wuyang'a* or *Wubinda*) being regarded almost as though it had physical properties, like a fluid that may be spilt, or a charge of electricity that may be carelessly expended.

The operational level of meaning is the level on which we may observe most clearly the sociological concomitants of ritual symbolism, for we observe not only *what* is done with the symbol but *who* does it. Here the unity and exclusiveness of the hunters' cult association is clearly portrayed. This is further exemplified in the setting up of the *chishing'a* in some kinds of rites. For example, in *mwima,* the celebration of a great hunter's prowess, the hunters excavate a hole with their gun butts, then lift up the *chishing'a* collectively by means of their gun barrels, place it in the hole and tamp it in firmly all together with their hands.

This *chishing'a,* and indeed the *ayishing'a* (the plural form) of all *Wuyang'a* rites, is planted in the hunter's village near the shrine trees planted to his matrilineal ancestors. But for many of the rites of *Wubinda,* the generic cult, the *ayishing'a* are inserted in large termite hills in the bush. *Ayishing'a* are also inserted in hunter's graves located at the fork of two paths leading from the village. It is of these *ayishing'a* that Ndembu say: "*Chishing'a* is the first place to which a hunter brings meat when he has made a kill. It is a *mutulelewa*, a place where meat is put. The whole carcase is put there before the hunter takes it to village to be eaten." The sacred portions of the animal, mentioned above, are placed on the *chishing'a*, as an offering to the hunter-ancestor. In the *Mukala* rite, for example, when a hunter has made a kill he washes the *chishing'a* with blood, impales pieces of *yijila* on the prongs and expresses his gratitude to the patron-spirit who has manifested himself in the form of *Mukala*, a mischievous entity which drives and whistles the game away from the hunter until propitiated. When the hunter, on learning from a diviner that he is being afflicted by an ancestor in the form of *Mukala*, first sets up a *chishing'a*, he chooses one of *musoli* wood, plants it and invokes the spirit-manifestation as follows: "You, my kinsman who have already died, if you are the one who has come out in *Mukala*, now listen to me. Tomorrow, when I go into the bush to look for animals, you must cause me to see them quickly. I must kill animals by gun or trap." He then puts some powdered white clay (*mpemba* or *mpeza*) in his mouth, and draws a line with the moistened clay from the *chishing'a* towards himself, places some on his temples, down the center of his brow, spits some on his shoulders, and draws a line of white upwards from his navel. "He puts it on his temples, beside his eyes," an informant said, "to see everything perfectly clearly (i.e., to spot animals in hiding or at a distance), on his brow that his face should be white or lucky, on his shoulders because he carries his gun and meat on them, and on his stomach, that there might be food in it." Then the hunter spits white powder on the *chishing'a*.

The hunt that follows may be regarded not merely as a utilitarian food quest but as in some sort a rite of sacrifice. But it is not strictly comparable to the sacrifice of pastoral peoples, who give to the Deity or the ancestors a valuable animal as a token of their homage, penitence and atonement. For the hunter has no animal to offer. The animal must first be given to him by the hunter-spirit, and this is already a sign of partial reconciliation, of the spirit's provisional approval of the hunter's worthy intention. Nevertheless, until the hunter has made his offering of the blood and *yijila* at the *chishing'a* shrine he has not fully demonstrated his intention to propitiate and revere his ancestor. It is as though the spirit, in giving him an animal, were putting his expression of good will to the test. Moreover, there is an element of gift-exchange, of transaction, about the relationship between spirit and hunter that contrasts with the attitudes of submission and adoration found in fully-developed sacrifice to a deity.

Among the Ndembu the ancestors do not represent or embody the moral order so much as continue after death to interact with their living kin, in terms of their human likes and dislikes. In most ritual contexts, not remote ancestors but the spirits of the comparatively recently dead are involved, and these spirits are believed to afflict the living not only in punishment for wrong-doing but also because they themselves still harbor ill-will against them on account of quarrels they took part in when they were alive. For the Ndembu, the moral order is felt to transcend both the living and their deceased kin, to be in fact something axiomatic in terms of which both the living and the spirits of their ancestors must seek to become reconciled.[7] The mutual bargaining that for Ndembu characterizes the dealings of dead with living has a severely practical aspect. If the dead use their powers of invisibility and panic-making to drive animals towards the hunter, he will feed them with blood and cause their names to be remembered among men. For the dead depend on the living—to be sustained by food, offerings and memories—and the living depend on the dead—for strength, health, fertility, fame and good fortune. The moral order that decrees piety to the dead and compassion for the living is felt to be higher than both and in some obscure way to be connected with the High God *Nzambi* or *Shakapang'a*. But *Nzambi* is not directly worshipped; "He is so far away," the people say.

THE POSITIONAL MEANING OF CHISHING'A

A major—one might even call it *nuclear*—symbol like *chishing'a* is nearly always found in regular association with other symbols which, like adjectives in language, qualify or extend its meaning. I have mentioned earlier that a hunter's shrine typically consists of a *chishing'a,* together with a small piece of termites' nest and a

[7] I hope to demonstrate this in a book on Ndembu ritual I am at the moment writing—*The Forest of Symbols.*

braid of *kaswamang'wadyi* grass. Small termitaries, known as *mafwamfwa* (singular, *ifwamfwa*), domed or finger-shaped, are a familiar feature of the Ndembu woodlands and plain margins. In circumcision and funerary rites they have an explicitly phallic significance. The swarming life within them is pointed out as a sign of "procreation" (*lusemu*). But in hunting rites, the *ifwamfwa* is usually shaped into a cube and is either placed just in front of the *chishing'a*, or the branch is inserted in a hole in it (e.g. at *Kusukula*). Such a cube is called *katala kamukishi*, "the little hut of the ancestor spirit." The spirit is thought to visit its "hut" during and after the rite. The small termitary also represents in hunting rites the large termite hills (*tuwumbu*, singular *kawumbu*), sometimes fifteen feet or so in height, which stud the Mwinilunga bush. Informants say: "A termite hill is a favored site for hunter-spirits, who like to live on high places and, like lions, climb up them to see if there is game about." It was also pointed out to me that hunters hide themselves behind termitaries, large and small, when they stalk their quarry. Finally, in some *Wuyang'a* rites (such as *Mwima*) the termitaries are called *yimbumba*, a term which represents a dome-shaped cover of molded moistened earth raised on graves. The same term is applied to small termitaries placed in a ring round a dead hunter's head, which is allowed to appear above the surface of his grave. Hunters are buried, sitting upright, "like alert lions," and an opening is made in the ring of termitaries, "so that they may see clearly." Thus the symbolism of the termitary includes in its exegetical meaning references to burial practices peculiar to hunters, to the hunter's stealthy pursuit of game, to his vigilance, to his leonine traits (indeed the very name of the rite *Ntambu* signifies "the lion") and to the feeling that his proper "home" is in the bush (represented by the termitary "hut") rather than in the village. Besides these senses there are overtones of "fertility" and "virility" from other rites in which termitaries represent these qualities.

The braid (*chibaba*) of *kaswamang'wadyi* grass is placed underneath the first fork (*mpanda*) of the *chishing'a*. Its name is derived from *ku-swama*, "to hide," and *ng'wadyi*, "the bare-throated francolin." At *Kutelekesha*, in the course of invoking hunter-ancestors, the hunters say: "Today this grass is *kaswamang'wadyi* where all the animals and birds in the bush conceal themselves. If an animal is hidden in the grass, may we hunters be quick to see it, that we may shoot and kill it and be well pleased. May we carry it back and eat its meat. Do not hide it from us. It must appear, you must reveal it quickly" (*muyisololi swayiswayi*). The familiar theme of "making visible" (*ku-solola*) is again exemplified. Ndembu believe that the use of this grass in ritual will make the hunter invisible to the game he stalks.

The twist of grass divides the *chishing'a* into two sections. This division has meaning for the Ndembu. Below the grass, ancestor spirits come "to drink blood." On the forks, trophies of the chase are hung. "The hunter must resemble the ancestor spirits," I was told, "the animals will not see him on account of the grass." The prongs of the divided branch may be said to represent the hunter's power to kill animals, power which he obtains from the ancestors by feeding them with blood. The spirits are believed to "emerge" (*kw-idikila*) from the earth in which they have been buried, into their "grave-hut," and ultimately into the *chishing'a* itself.

Features of the topography which have importance for hunters are thus represented in combination: *chishing'a* = forest; *ifwamfwa* = termitaries; and *kaswamang'wadyi* = grass plains. Here we have the familiar ritual principle of association by *pars pro toto*. When we consider these three symbols together we must also note the important division between the visible animals and the invisible spirits, whose property of invisibility is desired by the hunter so that he may approach and kill the game. These conjunctions and divisions are aspects of the positional meaning of *chishing'a*.

THE SEMANTIC MORPHOLOGY OF CHISHING'A

Although the *chishing'a* forked branch shrine is an important element of Ndembu hunting ritual, there are hundreds of other symbols in the system, some of which are full or partial expressions of the same basic themes, while others represent different themes. Each of the *Wubinda* rites, for example, has its own ritual "plot" and idiosyncratic character. But *chishing'a* may fairly be said to typify the hunting symbol, since it is found in every hunting rite.

Starkly simple in outward form, a mere forked stick bare of bark, it is, as we have seen, rich in meaning. Let me try to express this semantic wealth diagrammatically, so as to bring out the semantic structure of this symbol.

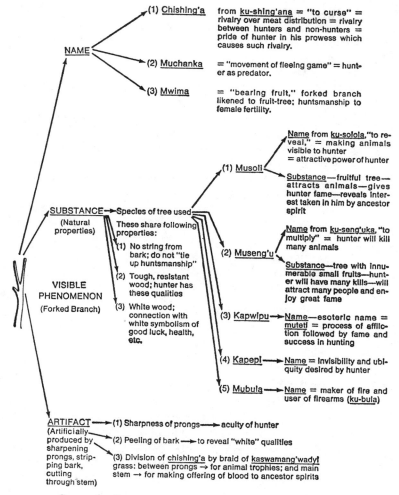

NAME

(1) Chishing'a — from ku-shing'ana = "to curse" = rivalry over meat distribution = rivalry between hunters and non-hunters = pride of hunter in his prowess which causes such rivalry.

(2) Muchanka — = "movement of fleeing game" = hunter as predator.

(3) Mwima — = "bearing fruit," forked branch likened to fruit-tree; huntsmanship to female fertility.

SUBSTANCE
(Natural properties) → Species of tree used

These share following properties:
(1) No string from bark; do not "tie up huntsmanship"
(2) Tough, resistant wood; hunter has these qualities
(3) White wood; connection with white symbolism of good luck, health, etc.

(1) Musoli — Name from ku-solola, "to reveal," = making animals visible to hunter = attractive power of hunter

Substance—fruitful tree—attracts animals—gives hunter fame—reveals interest taken in him by ancestor spirit

(2) Museng'u — Name from ku-seng'uka, "to multiply" = hunter will kill many animals

Substance—tree with innumerable small fruits—hunter will have many kills—will attract many people and enjoy great fame

(3) Kapwipu → Name—esoteric name = muteti = process of affliction followed by fame and success in hunting

(4) Kapepi → Name = invisibility and ubiquity desired by hunter

(5) Mubula → Name = maker of fire and user of firearms (ku-bula)

VISIBLE PHENOMENON
(Forked Branch)

ARTIFACT
(Artificially produced by sharpening prongs, stripping bark, cutting through stem)

(1) Sharpness of prongs → acuity of hunter
(2) Peeling of bark → to reveal "white" qualities
(3) Division of chishing'a by braid of kaswamang'wadyi grass: between prongs → for animal trophies; and main stem → for making offering of blood to ancestor spirits

Semantic Structure of the Forked Branch Symbol.

The following may be said to comprise part of the "meaning" of a *chishing'a*:

1   *Social Relationships*

   a   Between hunters and non-hunters
   b   Between hunter's elementary family and matrilineal kin
   c   Between full and classificatory matrikin of hunter

d   Between hunter and "his" hunter ancestor-spirit (most frequently the mother's brother or father)
e   Between hunter and his instructor in "huntsmanship"
f   Between fellow members of the hunters' cults

2   *Values*

a   Toughness of mind and body
b   Efficiency in providing meat
c   Piety towards the hunter ancestors
d   Making known or visible what is unknown and hidden
e   Fertility (multiplicity, fruitfulness)
f   Hunters' skill in concealing themselves from animals
g   Fairness in meat distribution
h   The sacredness of age and sex distinctions (taboos against eating of *yijila* by women and uncircumcised boys)
i   Suffering that good may come of it
j   Acuity of hunter's responses
k   Skill in the use of weapons

3   *Topographical Features*

a   Forest
b   Plains
c   Termite hills and nests
d   Burial sites

All these referents[8], merely at the level of Ndembu exegesis, are possessed by a piece of stick, a bit of grass and a fragment of termitary. This but a single example of the mighty synthesizing and focusing capacity of ritual symbolism. It might almost be said that the greater the symbol, the simpler its form. For a simple form is capable of supplying associative links of a very generalized character; it displays a feature or features which it shares, literally or analogically, with a wide variety of phenomena and ideas. Thus the whiteness of *mpemba* clay recalls the whiteness of milk and of cassava meal and, more than these, such abstract ideas as *freedom from* impurity, goodness "without spot," etc.

[8] And others—implicit in those aspects of the symbolism which connect it with such sectors of the ritual system as life-crisis ritual, gynaecological ritual, veneration of village ancestors, anti-witchcraft ritual, divination procedures, etc.

Finally, it must be stressed that the *chishing'a* is regarded by Ndembu not as an object of cognition, a mere set of referents to known phenomena, so much as a unitary power, conflating all the powers inherent in the activities, objects, relationships and ideas it represents. What Ndembu see in a *chishing'a*, made visible for them in its furcate, ambivalent and awe-inspiring nakedness, is the slaughterous power of *Wubinda* itself.

14 BLOOD, THUNDER, AND MOCKERY OF ANIMALS

Rodney Needham[1]

To the memory of C. G. Jung

THIS PAPER ATTEMPTS, in a preliminary and limited fashion, the investigation of problems posed by a practice common to the Semang of Malaya and the Penan of Borneo.

I

Maxwell reported nearly a century ago that thunder is greatly dreaded by "the wild tribes" of Perak. "When it thunders the women cut their legs with knives till the blood flows, and then catching the drops in a piece of bamboo, they cast them aloft towards the sky to propitiate the angry deities" (1879: 48). This custom has since been firmly ascribed to the Negritos (Semang,

Reprinted from *Sociologus* 14 (2), 1964: 136–49, by permission of the author and the editor, *Sociologus*.

[1] The research on which this article is based was conducted among the Penan in 1951–52 with the aid of a Senior Studentship awarded under the auspices of the University of Oxford by H.M. Treasury ('Scarborough') Committee for Studentships in Foreign Languages and Cultures, for which I express my gratitude. Apart from an unpublished doctoral thesis, "The Social Organisation of the Penan" (1953), there exists no general account of the Penan.

I revisited the Penan in June–September, 1958, with a Research Fellowship generously awarded by the Cultural Relations Programme of S.E.A.T.O., but at that time the issue discussed here had not struck me, and I did not take it up again among the Penan. I was re-reading Evans on the Negritos of Malaya, and only when I came to the passages on blood and thunder did it occur to me that I had some notes on similar matters among the Penan. Hence the partial and inconclusive character of the investigation made here.

Pangan), and has acquired a fair prominence in the ethnographic literature on Malaya.

Skeat and Blagden write that "during a storm of thunder and lightning" the Semang draw a few drops of blood from the shin-bone with a knife, mix it with a little water in a bamboo receptacle, and throw the mixture up to the sky, shouting "Stop!" (Skeat and Blagden, 1906, vol. II: 204). A woman was the only person actually seen to perform this rite.

Schébesta makes extensive references to it. In the first incident described it is a woman who stabs her shin with a "splinter of bamboo" during a violent and prolonged thunder-storm: she wipes the blood into a bamboo filled with water, sprinkles a little on the ground, and then throws it into the air, first towards the direction of the thunder and then to "every quarter of the heavens", shouting "Go! Go!" (1929: 87–88). In another place he writes that at the sound of thunder "every adult" conscious of misdoing will snatch up his knife and perform the blood-sacrifice (p. 192), implying that men as well as women do so. The thunder is a sign of the displeasure of Karei, the god of the Semang, at certain transgressions known as *lawaid karei;* these include playing noisily and roughly, lewd language, adultery, playing with animals, burning a leech, mocking a monkey, killing hornets and certain birds, sleeping too close to one's child of the opposite sex, incest, disrespectful address to relatives, open demonstration of joy at a reunion, drawing water with a rusty black pot or a burnt bamboo, looking at oneself in a mirror in the open air, and murder (Schebesta, 1929: 96, 97, 109, 189, 190, 191–92). The aim of the sacrifice is said to be "expiation" (p. 221); when Karei receives the blood, he anoints his chest with it (p. 192). If it were not given, the consequences would be terrible; Karei would tear trees up by the roots, floods would burst out of the ground, and everybody would be washed away (p. 192). The *hala,* or shaman, however, does not practise this blood-sacrifice (p. 258).

According to Evans, Karei makes thunder and punishes for sins, but his wrath can be averted by a blood-offering (1937: 152). Animals are men who did not perform this rite (p. 161). The blood is drawn from the outer side of the right shin; a little is poured on to the earth and the rest is thrown up towards the sky (p. 171); one informant said that it was thrown with the left hand (p. 172). The photographs (facing pp. 180 and 184) show a woman drawing blood, apparently with a bamboo, and casting it aloft with her right hand. The shaman (*halak*) is a "very child of the divinity" and does not offer blood-sacrifice when others do (pp. 207–8).

Williams-Hunt says that the blood is taken with a sharp bamboo, caught in a leaf, and then thrown into the sky; heavy thunder-storms are punishment by Karei for "sin" (1952: 75).

To judge by Hastings' *Encyclopaedia of Religion and Ethics* and Frazer's *The Golden Bough,* with their great range of reported custom, and by general reading and enquiries, this rite is singular to the Negritos. It is, however, practised by at least one group of Penan in middle Borneo.

II

At Long Buang, on the left bank of the middle Apoh River, a tributary of the Tutoh, which itself flows into the Baram, there is a small longhouse inhabited by a group of settled Eastern Penan. The Penan are traditionally, and for the most part still are in fact, forest nomads subsisting on wild sago and game, but a few groups such as this have settled. The Penan of Long Buang, however, still spend long periods away in the forest, hunting and working sago, using their house as a base, and they are in relatively frequent communication with various groups of related nomads. It is in this group at least that a blood-offering, taken from the leg, is made to a god at the onset of thunder.

I observed it in 1951 (when I had been only about five months among the Penan), during a sudden and very noisy thunderstorm. When the thunder began to crack, two youths, Lingai and my namesake Lidem, with whom I had been in lively and jocular conversation, immediately took their knives, distended the joint of the right middle toe, and tapped lightly with the tip of the blade until blood came; then they scraped off the blood with the edge, held it in the rain dripping from the eaves, and flicked the mixture of blood and water out of the house. As I recollect, the blood was definitely not thrown downwards, and it could not have been cast directly up into the sky, given the overhang of the roof, but was shaken outwards with an underhand motion.

This rite is called *menyat apun,* to beg pardon, or *menyat kesian,* to beg pity or favour. (*Apun* is clearly related to the Malay *ampun,* pardon; *kesian,* to the Malay *kasehan,* pity, kindness, compassion.) The blood-offering was followed immediately by the action of *motong bok,* to burn the hair of the head. This consisted in seizing a strand of hair from the fringe hanging over the forehead, singeing it with a glowing brand from the fire, and throwing the wood out into the rain. This rite does not absolutely require an invocation but may be accompanied by the following words, uttered very rapidly and in a monotone:

> *Iteu, bok na' ngan ko, Baléi Liwen.*
> *Maneu tong tilo, tong bono.*
> *Bé' pu'un amé ngeliwen ka'au,*
> *keja'au laka mutan, keja'au laka tevengan,*
> *é'é pelike'*
> *tong gien, tong gaten.*
> *Bé' irah pu'un salu' wang ko ngan belalang, latéi, semuhei.*
> *Ma'o la keh liwen la'a.*

This may be translated:

> Here is hair (of the head) that we give to you, Baléi Liwen.
> Apply it to the genitals.
> We are not laughing at you,
> as big as the *laka mutan,* as big as the *laka tevengan,*
> folding up quickly at the stimulation (tickling).
> We are not laughing at your *belalang,* at the earth-worm, at the
>   *semuhei*-snake.
> Let there be no more [thunder].

Bono is said to have no everyday meaning; it is *ha' baléi,* spirit-language, and is used here simply to "balance" (cf. Elshout, 1923: 122) *tilo,* genitals. *Ngeliwen* is the only word to occasion any real concern about the meaning of the invocation. It was explained to me as laughing (*mala'*), or joking, talking playfully (*ha' seminga'*); but among the Western Penan the word means to take fur from monkeys and other non-terrestrial animals, burn it, and throw it aloft, as a concluding part of the funeral ceremony. The Eastern and Western dialects of Penan differ considerably, and there is no necessity that a word in one shall mean the same in the other, but it would be more satisfactory all the same to be surer about the real Eastern Penan sense. The word looks as though it might be compounded of the verbal prefix *nge-,* and *liwen,* the name of the god Baléi Liwen, and thus mean something like to invoke that god; grammatically, it is rather more probable that it may be formed from a word *keliwen*, but I have no such word in my vocabularies.[2] The word *ja'au*, in *keja'au*, may have the meaning here, as in other contexts, of "respected". The *laka mutan* is a creeper which I have not seen; it is viscous and like a sundew, perhaps *Drosera indica* (Ridley, 1922, vol. I: 687–88) or some such plant, for it is said to catch and devour insects. *Laka tevengan* is said to have no meaning, but to balance *laka mutan;* *gien*, similarly, balances *gaten*, to itch or feel an irritation. *Wang* balances *belalang*, which is described as a small furless animal (not be found in Banks, 1949), about six inches long, living underground. The *latéi* was described to me as a small snake, but I later discovered that among the Western Penan at any rate it is an earth-worm; it is not an omen-animal. The *semuhei* is an omen-snake; probably, if the Penan name is related to the Kenyah word rendered as *semoi* by Haddon (1901: 384), *Doliophis bivirgatus (flaviceps)*.

As the invocation makes plain, the blood and hair are offered to the god Baléi Liwen. His body is of stone, and it is with this that he makes thunder. He is not, however, a spiritual personification of thunder, in which case his name would be Baléi Nekedo, but a god whose attribute is thunder. The only explanations of the custom that I recorded are that he does not like to see people enjoying themselves, and therefore emits thunder; and that he will not permit people to mock the creatures named in the invocation. If he is really angry he fells trees and casts thunder-bolts. The blood-offering will usually appease him if made by only one or two people, but if the thunder continues and everybody then offers blood or burns hair it will surely stop. I do not know whether any category of person is exempt from this ritual duty.

III

I much regret that I did not pursue any more detailed or useful enquiries into this practice among the Penan; I never observed it again among Eastern Penan, and the Western Penan do not make this blood-offering. It should prove helpful, nevertheless, to examine its elements in relation to other Penan usages and be-

[2] A descriptive vocabulary of Penan is in an advanced stage of preparation and will be published in due course.

liefs. We shall confine ourselves for the most part to evidence also recorded among the Penan Buang.

There is, so far as I am aware, no other occasion on which one's blood is offered to a spirit. The only times at which a man will let his own blood are at the contraction of a blood-pact (Needham, 1954), when the exchange of blood is presided over by the bamboo-spirit (Baléi Bolo among the Eastern Penan, Baléi Lēpek among the Western Penan), who is represented by the bamboo knife with which the incisions are made (the name of the pact itself means "to incise"); and at the piercing of the glans penis for the insertion of the penis-pin,[3] or of the ear for the insertion of a leopard fang or an ear-ring, which are not rituals and are not accompanied by an invocation or witnessed by any spirit. Tattooing, which punctures the skin and causes slight bleeding, is not practised by the Eastern Penan. The Penan, indeed, are very much concerned about any shedding of human blood, particularly of an untoward kind, and they make a great fuss when someone is cut and there is any considerable effusion of blood.[4] Scars, correspondingly, are regarded with a mixture of intent if covert interest and disquiet. Penan were obviously and intensely curious, for example, about a rather extensive scar on my leg, but nobody ever asked me what caused it or even alluded to it in any way; yet when one day I asked a man what had caused a severe gash in his forearm (in fact, the tusk of a charging boar, a common source of injury), they instantly and eagerly seized advantage of my indiscretion to put the same question to me. Their reaction was one of demonstrative horror at the contemplation of the scar (as if they had never seen it before), and of great relief at being able to talk openly about the gravity of the wound and the loss of blood.

Another incident concerning human blood is of special interest here. I was travelling with Penan in the area at the headwaters of

---

[3] An ethnographic and historical comparative monograph on this device has been in preparation for some years, and is intended to be published when the press of other concerns abates.

[4] Cf. "The Kenyah is . . . very afraid of blood, which is the reason that haematemesis is regarded as an especially severe illness, and that persons who die from bloody injuries are also treated as bad corpses", i.e. they are thought to die bad deaths condemning them to become malicious ghosts (Elshout, 1923: 128). The vomiting of blood (haematemesis) is a dreaded divine punishment, e.g. for breaking a blood-pact, in the eyes of both the Penan (Needham, 1954) and their cultural congeners the Kenyah.

the Paong river, on the western slopes of Mount Kalulong. There are countless leeches in these high rain forests, and within minutes of starting a march one can have scores of them on one's body. This area was particularly thick with them, and at the end of the day we sat around the fire removing them from our feet and legs. The Penan did so mainly by running the edges of their knives down their legs and then flicking the squirming mass of leeches from the blade backwards into the surrounding forest; leeches in the groin or other crevices were picked out by a firm pressure between the thumb and forefinger and were similarly flung into the vegetation, from which the nearer ones would begin a new progress back towards us. No attempt was made to kill or injure them, though there is no express prohibition on doing so, e.g. by cutting them in two.[5] After a considerable time at this tedious and rather exasperating task, I plucked a particularly large and swollen leech from between my toes, and, on impulse, cast it with some satisfaction into the fire. At once there was a vehement expostulation from one of my companions, telling me not to do so. Another man placatingly suggested that it did not really matter so much,[6] but the former nevertheless snapped "I don't like it" (*yeng akeu kēlu*), and continued a muttered grumble for a little while. It is particularly to be deplored that I did not, as seems so obvious now, try to get to the bottom of this incident,[7] for here too we have an intriguing parallel to a Semang idea. We have already seen above that among them it is a "sin against Karei" to burn a leech (Schebesta, 1929: 189); and according to Skeat and Blagden, among the Semang again, "if forest leeches . . . are prycked from the person and burnt in the fire outside the shelter, tigers will be sure to scent the burning of the blood and will hasten to the spot" (1906, vol. II: 223).[8] From

[5] I recount these details because the leeches were plump with human blood, as was obvious from the stained blades where they had been cut, and our concern here is with the behaviour of the Penan with regard to this fact.

[6] Perhaps because it was I who did it, and not a Penan.

[7] I can only plead that I was too weary, almost exhausted, by long and fast marching in this steep country, to do so at the time; and I must suppose that I forgot to bring it up later. Certainly, I had quite forgotten the Semang report, and, especially since I behaved myself afterwards, this was the only such event that I observed.

[8] The Behrang Senoi, also in Malaya, believe that to burn a leech entails being struck by lightning and destroyed by the storm; and the Ulu Kampar

the precision of the description, viz. that the leech is picked from the body and that the tiger smells the burning blood, it seems clear that the defining factor is the presence of human blood in the creature, not the nature of the leech as such.[9]

Menstrual blood, not surprisingly, is believed by the Penan to be dangerous to men, and there is a strict prohibition (*kilin ja'au*) on incurring any contact with it; to do so would cause fever and ill fortune (*saa' urip*).

Blood, though not human blood, is sometimes offered to the spirits in other circumstances than at thunder. If a man commits adultery, he has to give his wife, who is believed to suffer sickness because of the wrong done to her, a jungle-knife, a cooking-pan, and a hen.[10] The knife is to cut the throat of the hen, the blood of which is drained into the pan and then thrown into the forest, where the spirits (*baléi*) drink it and will then no longer afflict the wife.

Hen-sacrifice is also practised in consulting the thunder-oracle. Baléi Liwen, the thunder-god, can be asked about the future during a thunder-storm, e.g. about whether a man's sick wife will live or die. The hen is sacrificed (*peliwa*) and the god is questioned: if the woman is to die the thunder continues, if she is to live it ceases. If, as will typically be the case, the Penan are in the forest and have no hen, the feathers of a hen can be used instead; and it is of special interest that the feathers, symbolising blood, are dipped in rain-water and then thrown into the air.

Beliefs about rain and wind in general, i.e. not thunder-storms,

---

Sakai similarly believe that "to pull a jungle leech off the body and burn it in the fire" will cause a disastrous storm (Evans, 1923: 199, 201). It is to be noted that these peoples are not Malays, and that although they are not Negrito either they speak, as do the Negritos, languages which are closely related to Mon-Khmer.

[9] The leech may nevertheless have a special significance in Borneo, for among the Bahau of the Apo Kayan it is used as an art-motif in company with such important representations as the *naga,* the lizard, the dog, and masculine and feminine genitalia, and is freely used on sword-scabbards (Nieuwenhuis, 1900, vol. II: 362, 365; cf. Plate CV, Fig. 1, No. 6).

[10] The Penan do not customarily keep hens in the forest, and do not eat them or their eggs, but they can obtain them (delaying the ceremony, if necessary) from their Kenyah and other trading-partners when they take their forest products down to the longhouses. Pfeffer reports of one group of "Punan", actually Western Penan, living west of the Bahau, that they made no blood-sacrifices but took a cock with them wherever they went in the forest and plucked feathers from it to place as offerings in the usual cleft stick (Pfeffer, 1963: 130).

are not particularly revealing, but they nevertheless have some significance. A charm (*sihap*), made of stone, wild rubber, or anything that certain spirits (*ungap*) direct, is used to subdue or reduce a storm or high winds (*matang kepu, magen kepu*); and if a light brisk shower of rain falls through the sunlight, this means that spirits are descending to look at men's doings. There is thus a spiritual aspect to these aerial phenomena as well as to thunder.[11]

The related, and ritually equivalent, ceremony of burning the hair at the crash of thunder has not such suggestive parallels as we have established for blood. The hair of the head (*bok*) is the seat of one of the three "souls" (*sahé*) which the Penan Buang recognise. Clippings of it, taken from the right (not the left) side of the head of certain relatives, are ritually deposited near the grave after a funeral, and a fire is made nearby; the shade (*ada*) of the hair is employed by the deceased as cane in making a shelter in the afterworld, and that of the fire becomes the hearth-fire. As for the burning brand, this is also used in seeking an omen (*amen*); it is thrown to the right after dark, and if a spirit (*ungap dau merem*, in this case) replies from the forest, in one of the numerous voices that it may assume, the question is answered.

This brief survey of certain other usages does not yield an elucidation of the blood-sacrifice to the thunder-god, but it does suggest a collocation of mystical ideas which, taken together, provide a background to the rite. Blood is clearly an important symbol, not efficacious in itself, by the possession of some inherent virtue or power, but because it establishes a relationship with the spiritual world. It is evidently valued partly for itself, however, by Baléi Liwen, who applies the (blood or) hair to his genitals, and by the spirits who consume it, and it is accordingly offered as a prestation to them. This, presumably, is the prime reason that it is forbidden to burn an engorged leech in a fire, for one thereby not only misapplies but destroys what is proper to the spirits or to the blood-pact which they assure. Thunder is also a means of communication, from the spiritual world to men; it is a message, either of adjuration or of forewarning, and the latter can itself be elicited from the thunder-god only by means of other spiritual

---

[11] Cf. Zeus descending on Danaë in a shower of gold, this being interpretable as a thunder-shower falling upon the earth.

agents. Hair, which is singled out (unlike blood) by the belief that
it has a "soul", is also a prestation to the spiritual world, both to
gods and to spirits of the deceased. Finally, fire too effects communication between spirits of various kinds, not only the thunder-
god, and mankind. But all this adds up to no more than the
wholly expectable conclusion that the offering of blood or hair,
and the ritual employment of fire, are not isolated or singular
acts but form part of a body of general conceptions about the
relations between the spiritual world and this.

IV

The comparative issue may best be posed by the following table
of parallels between the Semang and the Penan customs:

	Semang	*Penan*
1	blood taken from the leg	blood taken from the leg (foot)
2	mixed with water	mixed with water
3	thrown upwards	thrown outwards/up-wards
4	offered to thunder-god	offered to thunder-god
5	to expiate transgression	to beg pardon
6	mockery of animals	mockery of animals
7	blood applied to god's body (chest)	hair/blood applied to god's body (genitals)
8	god uproots trees if unap-peased	god uproots trees if unap-peased
9	prohibition on burning leech/blood	prohibition on burning leech/blood.

By the common conditions of their forest life, the Semang and
the Penan exhibit certain general similarities in their social forms
(size of group, paucity of formal institutions, segmentary association, range of social contacts, etc.), but in every other respect
there is the extremest difference between them. The Semang are
Negritos, speaking a Mon-Khmer language, and are entirely distinct on both counts from their Malay neighbours. The Penan
are mongoloid in physique, speak a Malayo-Polynesian tongue,

and are culturally almost identical with their settled neighbours such as the Kenyah. The Semang and the Penan do not share a common Indonesian tradition, and in any case the rite is not performed by the Malays or other related peoples, but to judge by the literature is performed in Malaya only by the Negritos. There is just no connexion, historical or cultural, between the two peoples. Whatever can the reason be, then, for such a striking parallelism of rite and belief? If, as cultural anthropologists, we have any specific competence at all, we surely ought to be able to say something about this quite remarkable concordance.

Blood is an archetypal symbol, variously employed but universally attributed with a special significance; hair has attracted a similar symbolic attention (cf. Wilken, 1912); and fire has a mystical importance comparable to that of blood. The general prominence of these elements in the situation can therefore be readily appreciated.

Thunder, both in Malaya[12] and in Borneo, is an appalling natural phenomenon, seeming to crack and reverberate menacingly on the very surface of the forest canopy and shaking the guts of the human beings cowering underneath. Falling trees, brought down by storms, are a grave danger to the Penan, and I have reports of at least two families almost obliterated by trees falling on shelters and crushing the occupants.[13] (If merely heard toppling heavily in the far distance, the long tearing sound of their descent muffled by the forest, they are an inauspicious omen.) It is therefore little to be wondered at that the Semang and the Penan[14] should both assign a special place to thunder in their religious beliefs, and that both peoples should say that their god uproots trees in his anger.

The matter of mockery of animals might be thought of less consequence, in one respect, since what is of first importance is the common rite, performed similarly in expiation or propitia-

[12] Perhaps it should be made explicit that this is no mere supposition. I have not only marched through Malayan forest as an infantryman, but have in fact travelled in Negrito territory, on the slopes of Gunong Tahan, in search of a group of Negritos (Needham, 1960b: 67–68).

[13] M. Pfeffer was himself very nearly killed in this way, the tree landing only a few yards from his shelter (Pfeffer, 1963: 233).

[14] Not to speak of other peoples, living in far less hazardous circumstances, throughout the world (see the *Encyclopaedia of Religion and Ethics*, Index, s. v. "Thunder").

tion, and what the particular transgressions related to the rite
may be is secondary, but the prohibition on this odd offence
among both Semang and Penan is nonetheless intriguing. The
best example of this idea elsewhere that comes to mind is the
concept of *djeadjea* held by the Ngaju in southeastern Borneo, a
people of very different cultural tradition and historical connexions from the Penan. *Djeadjea* are words or deeds which offend
the gods and which are punished, significantly, with death by
lightning or by petrifaction in a storm; they include incest, calling
people or animals by inappropriate names or saying things about
them which are contrary to their true natures (e.g. that a louse
dances or that a rat sings), and burying an animal alive while
declaring that one is burying a human being (Hardeland, 1859:
25, s. v. *badjea*). The word is related to *hadjadjea,* which actually
means "to mock" (*verspotten*). Schärer characterises "mockery
of animals dedicated to the godhead", together with incest and
adultery, as a "severe offence", entailing calamity for the individual and his whole community. The thunder-god, Nyaro, is
angry and darkens the sky, and a great storm breaks. The village,
it is believed, used to be washed away and all its inhabitants
turned into stone in the river. Even today, floods or droughts ruin
fields and crops, and the transgressor himself dies "like a tall
tree in the forest cracked by the storm" (Schärer, 1963: 99).

The parallels of concept and imagery seen here between
Semang, Penan, and Ngaju are indeed striking. Their effect is
scarcely diminished by the consideration that the Penan and the
Ngaju live in Borneo, for these peoples are widely separated by
some of the most accidented terrain in this vast island, and they
are culturally very distinct from each other. Among both of them,
nevertheless, connected with mockery of animals, we find thunder, stone, flood, and falling trees, an impressive concatenation
of symbols and mystical ideas to be expressed by such separate
peoples.[15] The central concept among each, however, and one

[15] Other examples are reported by Evans from the Dusun of north
Borneo, a people culturally very distinct again from either the Penan or
the Ngaju. The Dusun are much afraid of thunder-storms, which they
ascribe to certain spirits; dressing up a monkey, dog, or any other animal,
brings on a "punishment storm". The people of one village are related to
have dressed up a frog and a green lizard, and to have made them dance;
for this, they and their village were turned into a boulder. Thunder, lightning, and floods are brought by a "punishment animal", the *mondau* (a

probably to be traced among the Semang also, is the social value
of order and the total disapprobation directed at any confusion
of categories.[16] This is a structural feature of other mystical
ideologies also, far removed from this part of the earth, and has
to do with general characteristics of human thought. Our attention reverts, therefore, to the congruence of imagery among
Semang, Penan, and Ngaju, and the high interest of this remains.
It might somehow be possible to infer elucidatory connexions,
however tenuous, between the Penan and the Ngaju, but it seems
quite out of the question plausibly to conceive any concurrence in
the pasts of the Ngaju and the Semang which could account for
the symbolic complex, prominent among them both, of thunder-
stone-tree-incest-mockery of animals.

The further appearance of stone, however, in these mystical
contexts (it will be remembered that the body of Baléi Liwen is
of stone, and the thunder-bolts that he casts are believed to be of
stone) brings us to the most general issue raised by such ideas.
Stone has an ancient and secure place in the symbolisms of mankind, to the extent that we may claim that it has an efficacy, a
power over the mind, sufficient to accord it also (together with,
e.g. blood, fire, water, tree) the character of an archetypal symbol. When we find these symbols associated, therefore, we are
not confronted with a special problem, for by their very essence
this concomitance is what we should expect or at very least be
perfectly prepared to encounter. Yet this generality itself conflicts
with everything that we have been accustomed to think about an
irreducible opposition between nature and culture; for here we
seem to have what we may call "natural symbols", whereas it is
precisely the defining characteristic of culture, in complete contrast to nature, that it is symbolic.

What is meant here by the word "natural" is that certain things
in nature seem to exert an effect on the human mind, conducing

---

mythical tiger-like creature), which hates people to "torture or burn jungle
leeches"; one reason for this "thunder tabu" is that leeches become an-
noyed by the smell of their burnt companions and attack the *mondau*, which
is thus provoked to punish their persecutors. One Dusun man explained
that "jungle leeches that are sucking, or have sucked, our blood must not
be burnt in the fire or with a cigarette end, because if we do this we are
burning our own blood" (Evans, 1953: 26, 145–47).

[16] This topic will be found elaborated at some length, with regard to the
whole South Borneo grouping of cultures, in a forthcoming monograph on
Ngaju symbolic categories.

to symbolic forms of the most general, and even universal, kind.
They seem, namely, to make a primordial impress on the unconscious mind of man as a natural species, producing an affective
response which is as natural to the organism (to its distinctive
brain) as the motor language of bees or the phototropism of
marigolds is natural in other realms of life. This response, when
translated (however variously) into language or ritual, constitutes a universal symbolism.[17] Now if we accept that the universal is the criterion of nature, and that the rule (including the
rules of communication governing any symbolism) is that of culture, then we have in such symbols further examples of the kind
of conceptual "scandal" which Lévi-Strauss has pointed to in the
case of incest (1949: 9). On the one hand, that is, certain symbols seem as natural to mankind as are, for instance, the rules of
logic which it everywhere recognises, while on the other hand
symbols are regarded as by definition exclusively cultural. It is in
this context, it might be concluded, that the Semang and the
Penan usages have to do with what has been called "the central
problem of anthropology, viz., the passage from nature to culture" (Lévi-Strauss, 1962a: 99); and this, indeed, is exactly what
is made clear to us by the Semang belief that animals are men
who did not make the blood-sacrifice. But the opposition nature/
culture is as aptly to be established within man as between him
and the rest of creation, and the present investigation, to the
converse of the customs with which it deals, may rather be taken
as a minor and laconic contribution to the task of "reintegrating
culture with nature" (Lévi-Strauss, 1962b: 327).

We may be persuaded to conclude that such considerations,
combined with the natural circumstances of life for the peoples

---

[17] Cf. Bosch: ". . . The appearance of tree-conceptions with various
peoples on earth has been greatly influenced by the tendencies of human
genius, universally alike. . . . The intricacy of Indian tree-symbolism in
the later stages of its development should not blind us to the fact that the
original idea was simple and natural. . . ." (1960: 248). See also Needham, 1960a: 31.

Lévy-Bruhl refers to such creatures as the eagle, lion, tiger, and crocodile
as "natural" symbols of power, not arbitrarily chosen but offering themselves as direct representations of the force which they embody. He wishes,
however, to make a distinction between a Western view of them, according
to which they are the expressions of an abstractly conceived quality, and
that of primitives, who are held to sense their inherent quality and to feel
a "participation" (1938: 174).

concerned, provide us with some understanding of the grounds for the practice of blood-sacrifice to a thunder-god in Malaya and in Borneo; but if the symbolic values involved are in fact so general, and the effect of thunder so palpable, why is it only the Semang and the Penan who make such an offering—and why, in any case, is the blood taken from the leg? Or, to stretch out this cryptic matter to a new extent, what did Hamlet mean when he charged it to Ophelia, as an offence in women, that they did "nick-name God's creatures"?

15 HYENA AND RABBIT:
A KAGURU REPRESENTATION OF
MATRILINEAL RELATIONS

Thomas O. Beidelman

I

THIS PAPER has two purposes: (1) to present a text in Chikaguru, a Bantu language spoken by the Kaguru of East Africa: this language has not been properly described by linguists and no extensive text in it has yet appeared; (2) to present a tale (the text) which serves as an interesting illustration of certain problems in Kaguru society.[1]

In the first part of this paper, I present this tale in a free English translation with a few notes in explanation of certain details in the story.

In the second part I discuss the significance of this tale as a means by which one may gain insight into certain important problems in one African matrilineal society.

Two appendixes at the end of this paper present the original Kaguru text and an attempt at a literal translation, together with a list and a very brief discussion of the published material dealing with the Kaguru language.

II

The Tale of Hyena and Rabbit

Once there was a great famine in the land. Rabbit and his uncle[2] Hyena got together in order to discuss how they could manage

Reprinted from *Africa* 31 (1), 1961: 61–74, by permission of the author and the International African Institute. The author has permitted the omission of a text in Chikaguru.

[1] This study is based on field work carried out in northern Kilosa District, Tanganyika, during 1957–58 under a Ford Foundation grant administered by the University of Illinois.
[2] Mother's brother.

until the famine ended at the coming harvest. When they met, Rabbit said to his uncle Hyena, 'Uncle, this is a great famine. What do you think we should do until things get better? Let us sell[3] our mothers. If we keep them, there will be too many of us to get enough to eat.'

Hyena said, 'I think it is better if we kill our mothers. Then we can peddle their flesh in order to get wealth for buying food for our households.'

Rabbit grudgingly agreed to this suggestion. He said to Hyena, 'This is good advice. When shall we kill them? My mother is far away. Shall we start with yours?'

Hyena agreed. He said, 'Whichever one is present, that one we shall kill.'

So they went to Hyena's place, and when they got there, they caught the old woman, the mother of Hyena. Here and there she rushed, crying in vain until she was stabbed. The flayed meat was put in a basket and the two started off to peddle the meat until it was all sold. Then Rabbit began to feel upset and could not bear to kill his mother on account of the famine. So he lay low for many days. The time for Rabbit to kill his mother came and he was very upset. For this reason he hit upon the idea of going hunting and by good fortune he killed a bushbuck in a trap. He was able to flay this in a hurry and then took it to Hyena's. He said, 'Uncle, are you there?'

Hyena replied, 'I am here, sir![4] Why?'

Rabbit said, 'The old woman is ready. The meat is here.'

Hyena answered, 'Hee! Hee! Hee! That is what you've been putting off doing. Now our famine is ended.'

They passed around with their meat until they had none left.

[3] Sell her into domestic slavery. In the past elder Kaguru sometimes secured wealth or paid heavy fines by selling the junior members of their matrilineage. These persons were usually redeemed later by payments by their matrilineage. Such persons were usually sold to other Kaguru and were not sent out of their local area. However, sometimes buyers of such persons sold them to third parties such as Arab slavers. Domestic slaves furnished labour for their masters. Slave women were the most desired. While the children of free women belonged to the matrilineages of their mothers, the children of slave women were entirely subject to their fathers and were quasi-members of their fathers' matrilineages.

[4] The term *mugosi* is translated as 'sir'. It is a form of polite address used to males (kin and non-kin) who are held in high respect. Hyena evidently expects that Rabbit has arrived to fulfil his obligations. See the next footnote.

But the famine continued in the land. They didn't have anything to eat.

Every evening Rabbit went off to the place where he had hidden his mother so that Hyena should not know that she was still alive. That was where Rabbit was eating. But Hyena was really hit by hunger. To whom could he go to eat? He didn't have any mother left.

One day Hyena asked, 'You, Uncle,[5] where are you eating? Why aren't you getting thin the way I am?'

Rabbit said, 'I have no place to eat. I am like this no matter how bad a famine there may be.'

Many more days passed and Hyena became unconscious. After a few more days he died. Then Rabbit went to the cave where he had hidden his mother. He called out, 'Old woman, Hyena is no more. He is dead. You are free!' Then Rabbit stayed peacefully with his mother for many happy years.

III

The Kaguru are sedentary Bantu cultivators living in east-central Tanganyika and are organized into approximately 100 matrilineal clans which are each composed of many matrilineages. Before colonial rule and the introduction of a hierarchy of chiefs, the Kaguru had no centralized political system. The cluster of settlements in each series of valleys or ridges formed its own politically autonomous group. Local groups tended to be built up upon the matrilineages of the clan which had gained dominance in an area. The need to maintain fairly large groups for self-protection from the raids of neighbours kept Kaguru settlements far larger than they are today and encouraged far more lineal solidarity than at present. In this period local matrilineages and their affinal connexions constituted the largest stable social and political groups. The details of Kaguru clan and village organization are not

---

[5] Among the Kaguru, mother's brother (*bulai* or *kolodyo*) and sister's son (*mwihwa*) terms are sometimes used in reverse of their normal order. A mother's brother is a person who aids a sister's son, but such aid is reciprocal. When such terms are used in reverse order, a sister's son is reminded of his duties to repay the kindness and care of his mother's brother. In this case, Hyena is reminding his well-fed sister's son that food should be shared, since Hyena gave Rabbit a share when he (Hyena) had some.

directly relevant to the problems of this paper.[6] The problems presented here concern the different relations between men and women within Kaguru matrilineages. They derive from certain features common to matrilineal systems, viz. the relations between men who hold authority and women who serve to link such men with one another.

In the tale of Rabbit and Hyena the four characters are all members of one matrilineage. They are: two males, Rabbit and his mother's brother, Hyena; and two females, the mothers of Rabbit and of Hyena:

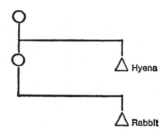

The tale describes relations between these four persons during a time of extreme difficulty. The Kaguru face constant problems in their social and physical environment. In the past they suffered not only from raids for women and livestock but also from famine. Today most of their difficulties are confined to raising resources for marriage, fines, education, medical expenses, and litigation. The problem of serious famine is only an extreme and traditional example of the many difficulties which beset all Kaguru and which encourage members of a Kaguru matrilineage to support one another. While such difficulties usually encourage co-operation and solidarity between the members of a matrilineage, if these difficulties are very serious they may sometimes formally separate certain matrilineal kin who are already potentially divided in their loyalties. It is often through such disputes that new matrilineages are formed.

The four individuals in this tale comprise a short-hand model of a Kaguru matrilineage. Each represents an entire category of persons.[7] Let us first consider the two males. Hyena is Rabbit's

[6] For a description of Kaguru social organization, see Beidelman (1963).
[7] Rabbit represents all junior males within a matrilineage, i.e. (in a lineage diagram) all males of ego's generation. Hyena represents all senior

mother's brother (*bulai* or *kolodyo*[8]) and Rabbit owes him obedience and respect. Rabbit's disobedience to Hyena rests upon the assumption that Hyena does not deserve such authority and respect if he is found to be motivated merely by selfish reasons. If such authority is severely abused, a man may refuse to obey his mother's brother and may sever kinship ties with him.

The authority and power of men within a matrilineage depend upon reciprocation of aid and support between men and their sisters' sons. In their earlier years sisters' sons may depend upon mothers' brothers for economic and political aid and may have few resources of their own. But as these young men mature and establish their own households, they are able to repay the benefits they received from their seniors. The power of such lineage leaders and the solidarity and continuity of a matrilineage depend upon this. In the tale, this reciprocity may be seen in the Kaguru practice of reversed usage of kinship terms on occasions in which a senior male desires repayment and aid from a junior, e.g. a man calls his sister's son 'mother's brother', to remind him of his obligations.

Kaguru relations of authority within the matrilineage involve almost exclusively persons of the same generation or of proximate generations. Within generations men have authority over their sisters, and elder siblings have authority over their juniors; between generations men have authority over the children of their sisters.

---

adult males within a matrilineage, i.e. all males within ego's mother's generation.

The tale presents the members of a matrilineage in a social vacuum. The positions of fathers and affines are ignored. Wealth, political power, and other factors also determine men's power and the number of kin whom they can control, but these factors also are neglected.

The affines of Hyena and Rabbit are not mentioned in this tale. I suggest that this is because Kaguru consciously think of the tale as an illustration of only one problem: the conflict of loyalties within a matrilineage.

There is a potential conflict between women's obligations to their brothers and to their husbands. Kaguru women sometimes obtain advantages by playing off these two groups of males against each other. Although the tale neglects this aspect, in real life Rabbit's mother would probably seek support and protection from her husband against any unjust demands from her brother.

[8] Kaguru informants insisted that *bulai* and *kolodyo* may be used interchangeably. The word *kolodyo* derives from *lukolo* (root), a Kaguru term for a clan or a matrilineage. *Kolodyo* means 'head of a *lukolo*'. The term *bulai* is the term more frequently used in address.

Now let us consider the two females. These are Hyena's mother and her daughter, Rabbit's mother. These two females link the two males within the matrilineage. The names of these women are not given in the tale. Kaguru usually refer to women by teknonyms. Women owe their social positions to their relations to men. When they are young, they are spoken of as the daughters of their fathers; after they bear sons, they are spoken of as the mothers of their children, especially their sons. A woman with no children does not reach full social maturity.

The roles of Kaguru women as intermediaries depend in Kaguru eyes upon their exclusion from formal authority. Because of this exclusion, Kaguru describe women as 'disinterested and unbiased', having at heart the best interests of all the men and women born into their matrilineage. Women may have strong feelings concerning their various relatives, but ideally they should not be concerned with power in the way that men are. Instead, they should be concerned with the solidarity of the entire group and with maintaining goodwill and co-operation between the various persons whom they link.

Kaguru women sometimes serve as mediators in disputes. Although they possess no formal authority, they may be appealed to as moral authorities and go-betweens for men. Their security and influence derive from this intermediary and supposedly neutral position between persons with formal authority. Let me give three examples of this: (1) A man may fail to obtain the co-operation he demands from his sister's son. He may appeal to his sister to urge her son to obey him. If she is reluctant to do this, her brother may appeal to their mother to persuade his sister in this. (2) A youth may require aid for his education or for paying a fine. He may ask his mother to urge her brother to help him. If this woman fails she may appeal to her mother, who may ask the man to grant his sister's pleas. (3) In the past, women often served as custodians of wealth. Several men within a matrilineage may disagree as to how to divide such wealth. If they are siblings by one mother, they may deposit the wealth with her or perhaps with one of their sisters. In this way, it is available to all men if they need it, but none of them has exclusive control over it. This refers not only to wealth from inheritance but also to wealth obtained from brideprice.

Kaguru men are linked by women through women's dual roles as mothers and as sisters. Such a system works so long as women feel equally the demands and obligations entailed by both these roles, i.e. the demands of both their children and their brothers. However, it is quite clear that in certain severe disputes a woman may be called upon to choose between two men, i.e. between her son and her brother or her mother's brother. Kaguru invariably assign primacy to the mother–child relationship, and in any dispute in which such a choice is demanded women support their children and reject their brothers or mothers' brothers.

Here are two such situations:

1 Shortly after Yohanna's daughter, Margareti, was married, she became pregnant by her secret lover. This was her cousin, Yohanna's sister's son, Musa. Her husband returned Margareti to her father, Yohanna, and demanded that Yohanna return the brideprice. Yohanna refused, insisting that this was a matter between the husband and the offending youth. Yohanna said, 'I only gave you a wife; I am not responsible for who sleeps with her.' Musa's father

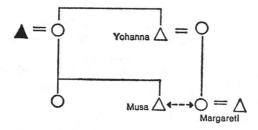

had died and therefore the youth insisted that his uncle Yohanna was responsible for him. The youth's mother, Yohanna's sister, supported this. They both demanded that Yohanna refund the brideprice. Yohanna insisted that Musa should himself repay the money since he was the trouble-maker. Yohanna's sister angrily left her brother's settlement, even though they had previously been quite close. (Their parents were dead.) The sister said she was going to seek witchcraft against Yohanna and later became renowned for her powers in exorcizing spirit-possessed women. When she died, Yohanna attended her funeral but many bitter words were exchanged between him and her sons. Later, when Yohanna became ill and died, his sons blamed the witchcraft of Yohanna's sister's children. They said that these children had inherited witchcraft from their mother (see Beidelman 1963).

2 Madikuli and her son Musegu lived in the village of her brother, Chadibwa. Musegu was caught having sexual intercourse

with Chadibwa's wife. Adultery is an offence meriting a fine, but adultery with a mother's brother's wife was traditionally a very serious offence sometimes punished by death. Today government law treats this as any other type of adultery and it is settled by a fine. Musegu paid a very large fine, but Chadibwa said that he did not want the youth in his village any longer. Musegu went to his mother

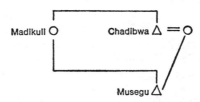

(his father is dead) and asked her to intercede for him. Chadibwa told Madikuli that if she stood by her son, he would know that she had supported the youth's adultery. He told her that she must throw her son out. Madikuli refused and continued to defend her son. Chadibwa tried to drive his sister and her son from his village. The Kaguru court urged Chadibwa to allow the two to remain. Chadibwa adamantly refused and the woman and her son left.

In our tale two males within a matrilineage meet to decide how to cope with a difficult situation. Rabbit suggests that they pawn the women of their matrilineage in order to obtain resources. This was a fairly common practice in the past. Such women could be retrieved later by the payment of certain fees. Men within a lineage obtain wealth and other advantages in brideprice, fines, and alliances by the manipulation of women. Selling women into slavery is an extreme example of such manipulation.

Hyena rejects the idea of pawning the women and suggests that they be killed. But this would dispose of the women irretrievably, and with this the matrilineage would be doomed to extinction.[9] The junior male, Rabbit, accepts this decision, but the tale implies that this is due to Rabbit being an obedient sister's son: the text states that Rabbit grudgingly (*nheifo-nheifo*) agreed. Although Rabbit is more properly called *Sungula* (the word for rabbit), in this and the following situations he is referred to as *Chibuga*. *Chibuga* means 'a small creature' and this term is used whenever Rabbit commits an act which is wrong but which is

---

[9] In the tale there are only two women within the matrilineage. If Rabbit had a sister, the problem of extinction would not be raised.

done at the order of his mother's brother, Hyena. The name *Chibuga* emphasizes Rabbit's junior status as a sister's son and Rabbit's obligation to submit to his senior, Hyena. Thus the onus for the crime falls solely upon Hyena.

Kaguru males are expected to obey their mothers' brothers even though some of their duties may appear odious, for such duties are said to be for the good of the entire matrilineage. However, the suggestion to kill these females is clearly not for the good of the matrilineage, since it involves the annihilation of its generative half. The act which Hyena tells Rabbit to do is in direct conflict with Rabbit's obligations to his own mother. This is also the case with Hyena, but in the tale Hyena appears utterly aberrant and quite pleased to commit such a heinous crime.

Within a Kaguru matrilineage there is a conflict between the chain of authority of males and these males' obligations and sentiments towards females. Both are necessary for the working of the Kaguru system, but Hyena has chosen to give priority to his own aims. He includes Rabbit in his plan and therefore sets the males against the females within the matrilineage. Hyena uses the females of his matrilineage in a way not only harmful to them individually but harmful to the lineage as well.

The conduct of Hyena and of Rabbit is sharply contrasted in the tale. Hyena kills his own mother. This is the most wicked act which Kaguru can imagine. But Hyena also tries to persuade Rabbit to commit a similar crime. Rabbit's intended victim is Hyena's sister. In a sense Hyena is therefore trebly guilty. His offences are matricide, intended sororicide, and evil influence on his nephew. By a ruse Rabbit avoids killing his own mother, but does not prevent Hyena from killing his (Hyena's) mother, Rabbit's maternal grandmother.

It may be asked why Rabbit agrees to the death of his maternal grandmother. Kaguru do not conceive of authority or great respect towards alternate generations. Authority, both jural and moral, is vested chiefly in the first ascending generation. Kin of alternate generations are equivalent and their relations are essentially informal, non-authoritarian, and at times even of a highly jocular character. The respect for and protection of Hyena's mother are essentially the responsibility of Hyena and it is Hyena's abnegation of this responsibility upon which the entire plot depends. Even though Rabbit may have aided Hyena, this was done by Rabbit in his role as *Chibuga* (small creature), the junior member following his mother's brother.[10]

However, Rabbit has a far more important reason for acceding to this crime. In a sense Rabbit may even secretly desire his maternal grandmother's death. So long as this old woman lives, there are very strong sanctions for solidarity between all her lineal descendants and Hyena remains in relatively secure power. Upon her death the process of lineage segmentation may begin and Rabbit may hope to assume some power himself, even while Hyena still lives.

Let us suppose that Hyena's mother has several daughters besides Rabbit's mother.[11] The descendants of these various females form potential lineage segments united under one common living ancestress, Hyena's mother. Hyena has jural authority over these persons and uses the mediative influence of his mother and sisters to exert his power. When Hyena's mother dies, there is no longer a living link between these various groups. She may still be appealed to as a dead spirit, but this is far from being as effective as she was in life. Hyena remains the titular head of the group, but he will have more difficulty than before in exerting his power. Males in each lineage segment are always attempting to exert their own interests. A mother of one of these males sees herself occupying a position analogous to that of Hyena's mother and she may encourage her son in his claims for independence.

Rabbit gains by Hyena's crime so that one might say that he has proved to be even craftier than Hyena. Kaguru freely admit that a man may look forward to the death of his mother's brother since he wishes to assume power himself. In this tale the crime of Hyena (we shall see that he is a witch) makes his death not only convenient to Rabbit but morally right as well.

Kaguru speak of the struggle for power between men within a matrilineage, but they seem to avoid discussing the fact not only that men gain power from the deaths of mothers' brothers whom they replace but that they gain by the deaths of certain females

[10] Rabbit can place responsibility for Hyena's mother's death upon Hyena. Rabbit cannot easily do this with his own mother. The Kaguru insist that obligations to one's own mother outweigh all other social obligations.

[11] In the tale no such sisters appear. Nor are we told that Rabbit has sisters. However, one may presume that so long as Rabbit's mother lives it is possible she may bear such offspring. In Rabbit's eyes perhaps the greatest value of his mother is that she may provide him with sisters.

as well. In fact, it would seem that the deaths of these females are even more important prerequisites to obtaining power or independence than are the deaths of males. The death of an elderly female linking many descendants constitutes the structural weakness which may lead to segmentation.

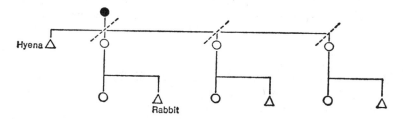

Once this murder has been accomplished, the entire moral and structural situation within the matrilineage vastly alters. Rabbit need obey or aid Hyena no longer since Hyena has shown himself to be a wicked relative. With the death of Hyena's mother, the senior female linking Rabbit's mother and Hyena is gone, and Hyena's control over Rabbit's mother and thus over Rabbit has decreased. In the tale Hyena presents the murders of his own mother and of Rabbit's mother as inextricably linked. An antisocial act against one female involves the other, and if Hyena becomes motherless while Rabbit does not, Rabbit's position within the matrilineage is strengthened at Hyena's expense.

In all the cases I encountered in which Kaguru siblings severed social relations by disowning each other, by accusation of witchcraft, or by grave insult, the mother uniting such siblings was dead. This does not mean that such siblings automatically break their relations when their mother dies. But there is a greater likelihood than before that future quarrels may become irreconcilable.

After the murder of his grandmother, Rabbit neglects his responsibilities to Hyena. Not only does Rabbit avoid the evil act which Hyena has urged, but he does not help starving Hyena when he is asked to do so. Hyena asks why Rabbit is still fat and apparently not suffering from starvation. He addresses Rabbit not as 'sister's child' (*mwihwa*) but as 'mother's brother' (*bulai*). Rabbit offers no assistance and Hyena dies.

The fates of Hyena and Rabbit affirm the Kaguru social and

moral order. Hyena has no mother to care for him and he has
forfeited the aid of his sister's child by his crime. He therefore
starves to death. Rabbit has protected his mother and her care
enables him to survive the peril of the famine. When I asked
Kaguru if this tale had a moral, they replied that the moral was
obvious: You may have many mother's brothers but you have
only one mother and her well-being is essential to your own.

IV

A final set of motifs remain to be explained. These are: (1) the
use of these particular animals, Rabbit and Hyena, to illustrate
this tale; (2) the extreme violence of Hyena's behaviour, viz.
murdering his mother rather than merely pawning her, and selling her flesh, presumably for cannibalistic purposes.

These motifs are explicable in terms of Kaguru beliefs in witchcraft which are inextricably associated with Kaguru concepts of
anti-social behaviour (Beidelman 1963).

Kaguru tend to interpret most anti-social behaviour, especially
the failure to meet obligations towards kin, as witchcraft. A person of any age or sex may be a witch. While some witches have
medicine for their power, really dangerous ones are considered
inherently evil and able to work much of their harm by sheer ill
will. A witch is said to work at night, to delight in injuring others,
to devour human beings, and to travel through the air clinging to
the belly of a hyena. Witches tend to have moral and physical
attributes which are the reverse of those desirable in normal
human beings. The most terrible of all witchcraft acts are associated with the suspected murder of lineal relatives and/or incestuous relations with such kin. Kaguru say that all real witches
are incestuous and cannibalistic, and that these habits show how
inhuman witches really are.

It may be possible to interpret certain portions of this tale in a
Freudian manner in order to find indications of incest. I am not
competent to carry out such analysis, but I offer one example of
such sexual symbolization. Hyena stabbing his mother may be
interpreted as symbolic sexual intercourse with her. The Kaguru
themselves clearly recognize such symbols and incorporate them
into their songs and jokes. One of the best known initiation songs
taught to boys and girls goes: Youngster, don't go outside early

or you will meet a rhinoceros with a horn; it will be stabbing and cutting and they (*sic*) will be showing their parts (of the body) which are red. Young Kaguru are taught that the real meaning of this riddle-song is: A young person should not leave his or her bachelor-hut too early and enter a parent's hut or he will surprise his parents having sexual intercourse (a forbidden sight).

The characters of Rabbit and Hyena are sharply contrasted in Kaguru belief. A rabbit is usually seen as a somewhat playful, clever, and sympathetic creature—although Kaguru also enjoy eating rabbits. On the other hand, a hyena is considered to be the epitome of all that is objectionable and unclean. The hyena is a sly creature, but Kaguru also say that a hyena is not so sly as he thinks he is, for a hyena is often bettered at his own game. In addition to being a 'duped trickster', the hyena is invariably associated with witchcraft and thus with all that is anti-social and immoral in Kaguru life. It is quite clear that these two sets of characteristics fit the two protagonists in the tale.

The existence of two different species of animals within one matrilineage is analogous to the potential existence of two different types of Kaguru within one matrilineage. There are moral Kaguru and there are anti-social, immoral Kaguru, i.e. witches. The witch is quite alien to normal Kaguru, even though they may all be of the same matrilineage. Some of the most vehement accusations of witchcraft occur between members of the same matrilineage. Although Kaguru believe that witchcraft is inherited matrilineally, they admit that not all members of a matrilineage need be witches because one member is: sometimes this characteristic fails to be transmitted 'in the blood'.[12] A witch's inhuman tastes for human flesh and for incest mark such a person as a species apart.

Hyena shows himself to be the epitome of a Kaguru witch, i.e. an extremely anti-social and socially unmanageable person. Murdering his mother and peddling her flesh may be interpreted as extreme examples of what any anti-social and uncooperative behaviour is considered to be. Kaguru sometimes describe selfish, witch-like behaviour as 'devouring and murdering others'.[13]

[12] Kaguru say that they are related to their mothers by blood, to their fathers by bone and the solid parts of the body.

[13] As I have shown in my paper on Kaguru witchcraft, an economically or politically powerful person is often unmanageable by his subordinates

In the past a Kaguru suspected of witchcraft was killed if he or she was found guilty by ordeal. Today suspects cannot be dealt with so easily, although witchcraft accusations and suspicions are still very prevalent. At best, a Kaguru may practise counter-witchcraft or he may avoid a suspected witch. The fate of Hyena is therefore an idealization which may give comfort to some Kaguru: Hyena's witchcraft leads to his own destruction. Most Kaguru regret that the witches whom they suspect are about them are never punished.

V

Conclusion

In the tale of Rabbit and Hyena a social problem of great concern to the Kaguru is presented in simple and relatively innocuous form. The problem is that of conflict and division within a matrilineage, the most important social unit in Kaguru society. It is therefore not surprising that Kaguru consider the offenders in such cases to be witches, i.e. the most wicked and inhuman persons they can imagine. Ideally such persons' anti-social behaviour should lead to their own destruction—even though in life it seems to many Kaguru that such acts go unpunished.

These conflicts are inevitable. But it is important that, when they do occur, (1) the persons considered guilty of causing such conflicts should be punished, and (2) when loyalties conflict, the proper choice between them should be made.

The Kaguru are keenly aware of the conflict between the interests of male authority and its potentially selfish abuse, and of the obligations of children towards their mothers. The interests of men are seen as ultimately divisive outside the context of the women who link them with one another. A dead man may be replaced in his authority by another, often by his sister's son. A man has no lineal offspring, but a woman has and her death leaves an irreparable gap in the position of mediator between the potential lineage segments formed by her offspring. Furthermore,

---

and he is frequently suspected of witchcraft because of this. Among the Kaguru it is often the affluent and the powerful who can afford to act in an anti-social manner. Therefore we should not be surprised to find that in this tale the witch-like person is Hyena, the superior person within the matrilineage.

each woman's death represents the loss of a genitrix for her lineage and thus a threat to its perpetuation. Men have no such importance. If choice between allegiance to men and to women must be made (and Kaguru insist that such situations are to be avoided if at all possible), Kaguru invariably endorse the obligations to a mother, without whom the matrilineal system has no meaning.

16 THE ANTHROPOLOGY
OF TIME-RECKONING

David F. Pocock

THIS PAPER IS less of a completed argument than a report on work in progress, work which resulted from dissatisfaction with a certain statement of my own advanced several years ago. I had, in a brief paper to the Royal Anthropological Institute, described the manner in which two castes in Gujerat had changed their status; one of them, the Patidar, had undergone this change rapidly and within the living memory of many. I concluded the paper with the observation that although the Patidar were aware that some of their customs had changed and that they had in the course of a few generations risen above those who were now their inferiors, they did not in general allow this experience of mutability to extend to their Brahmans. Their Brahmans were of course pure by heredity and raised above the effects of history. And yet at the same time, sometimes in the course of a ceremony which depended for its efficacy upon the unquestioned status of the Brahman, they showed themselves capable of throwing that very status in doubt by suggesting that these were Brahmans of recent growth, pseudo-Brahmans. Equally the peasants would admit the claim made by the local Untouchables that once they had been kings in Gujerat who had fallen to their present condition as a result of some failure in kingly virtue, or sin (Pocock 1955: final paragraph).

Now it is evident from all that we know about the caste system that status is not dependent upon achievement. The Brahman is not elected or promoted, he is what he is because he and his ancestors have always been what they are. And the Untouchables

Reprinted from *Contributions to Indian Sociology* 7, 1964: 18–29, by permission of the author and the editor, *Contributions to Indian Sociology*.

likewise. In this scheme of things history can have no place and
so long as the people themselves are unconscious of any change,
all is well. In such a circumstance we may know what we call the
history of a people and compare it with the collective representations of those people but we are not faced with the problem that
emerges when the people know that they have changed and continue, nevertheless, to live in a world whose values depend upon
immutability. Here we have a choice: Either we credit these people with an immense capacity for self-deception, an ability to live
in permanent contradiction with their experience, or we must
re-examine the assumptions in the light of which these facts constitute a problem.

One way of dismissing the whole subject would be to say that
the phenomenon of contradiction is in a sense a pathological one
resulting from the gradual decline of caste values and the rapid
rise of the Patidar under the British. Against this I simply advance
caution. These facts are not irrelevant but I prefer to look first
and find whether it is possible to take a general sociological view
of the matter, both outside and inside India, a view which the
particular facts of Patidar history can then supplement.

At the outset two terms have to be distinguished, they are time-
reckoning and duration. These I shall distinguish by reference to
the work of two authors, Nilsson and Van Gennep. For the
present it is sufficient to note that as anthropologists we are concerned with the way in which people reckon time and not with
any enquiry into the nature of time itself.

Nilsson's work *Time-Reckoning* is the essential starting point
for enquiries of this nature and the initial criticism which has to
be made does not damage his major contribution. He announces
his formal position as follows:

> In the matter of the indications and reckoning of time we have
> not to do with a number of conceptions which may be supposed to
> be as various and numerous as we please. At the basis lies an ac-
> curately determined and limited number of phenomena, which are
> the same for all peoples all over the globe, and can be combined
> only in a certain quite small number of ways. These phenomena
> fall into two main groups: 1) the phenomena of the heavens—sun,
> moon, stars; 2) the phases of nature, the variations of the climate
> and plant and animal life—and these latter are of course dependent
> upon the sun (Lund 1920: 2–3).

In other words Nilsson is saying that time-reckoning resides, in some sense, in these natural phenomena, and the fully developed and rational systems of time-reckoning in the modern world develop as man understands the motions of these natural phenomena more and more.[1] He says, for example, "the units of time-reckoning are given by the motions of the heavenly bodies" but he adds "and the more intimately these enter into the life of man, the more important do they become." And this latter statement gives us our sole concern as anthropologists, because it is by no means inevitable that a given society should find the movement of the heavenly bodies useful in ordering its affairs. Much of the evidence which Nilsson used shows how selective different peoples are in relation to natural phenomena in this regard.

Nilsson's major contribution is that systems of time-reckoning are not necessarily continuous. In his language time-reckoning is preceded by time indications. By continuous time-reckoning Nilsson means the mathematical calendar systems with which we are familiar, in which units of time (seconds, minutes, days, etc.) accumulate and add up to the next larger unit. Discontinuous time indications are exemplified from all over the world and are characterized by reference to events. Thus: six moons, three harvests and so on. The moons or harvests are not units and are not interconnected by other units with which they are considered to be equal. What is counted is the event. This aoristic method Nilsson calls *punktuell* since the calculation is based upon a *punktum*—a particular point. Before going on it might be pointed out that Nilsson is incorrect in supposing that the use of time indications is limited to primitive society, as will be recognised by anyone who recalls how often our continuous time-reckoning lets us down when we are trying to locate an event in the past and how often we are obliged to have recourse to some other event which occurred before, after or simultaneously with the event we are trying to place.[2]

[1] The same error is implied by Leach in an essay which briefly joins my argument but rapidly diverges from it. E. R. Leach "Two Essays Concerning the Symbolic Representation of Time" in Leach 1961.

[2] While re-typing this paper I overheard in a public-house an argument concerning the time of arrival of a newcomer to the district. This was conducted fruitlessly in terms of number of years until the landlady recalled what she had been wearing at the time, which she remembered because it was on the occasion of Her present Majesty's wedding. Once this was fixed the date was then easily arrived at.

It might seem that these time indications are simply synec-
dochical and poetic ways of "telling time." But the *punktuell* or
"eventual" character comes out when we look at the primitive
evidence. Professor Evans-Pritchard states categorically of the
Nuer that although they are aware of the natural rhythms of the
universe they do not use them as points of reference:

> . . . the concept of seasons is derived from social activities rather
> than from the climatic changes which determine them (Evans-
> Pritchard 1940: 95).

Again, the Nuer division of the year into two "halves" is not
abstract time-reckoning:

> The words *tot* and *mai* are not pure units of time-reckoning but
> stand for the cluster of social activities *characteristic* of the height
> of the drought and height of the rains . . . (Evans-Pritchard 1940:
> 99, my italics).

This author notes of the divisions of the Nuer day that it is the
activities that determine the time indications so that

> . . . there are as many points of reference between [our] 4 and
> 6 a.m. as there are for the rest of the day (Evans-Pritchard 1940:
> 101).

That is the period which sees the greatest social activity centering
upon the cattle.

An important difference between continuous time-reckoning
and the time indications which Nilsson does not bring out relates
to the kind of activity. It does not need to be argued at length
that the more diverse are the activities of a number of people or
groups, the more abstract and systematic must be the time-
reckoning if any form of co-ordination is desired or effected. The
larger co-ordination subsumes the less. This is true of political
activity as much as of economic activity. Two men who go out
separately to fish in the morning can arrange to meet again when
the fish are no longer rising. This event will bring them together
at roughly the same time. If one has gone to hunt and another to
fish, some other indication than their activities must be found,
such as the position of the sun. In political organization the
activity (or, in the case of the Nuer, the coming into being) of
a political group overrules the activities of the smaller groups,
and with the activities the time indications to which they relate.

In Europe, for example, the Christian, Jewish and university years are subsumed in the national and continental calendars.[3] In more primitive societies the time of the chief or king's court overrules the time of villages. Among the Nuer we can see from the set of concentric hemispheres by which Professor Evans-Pritchard represents their political consciousness that these are not only socio-spatial categories as the author calls them but also temporal ones (Evans-Pritchard 1940: 114). The time indications of the homestead give way progressively to those of the tribe just as finally the time-reckoning of the Nuer is subsumed in that of the European world which is at once the most systematic and abstract in the series. The important aspect of this progressive subsumption is that what are opposed at any point in the series are not two distinct conceptions of time but a time indication on the one hand and a number of individual people or groups on the other whose previous activities are in that context seen as having mere duration. If I am alone I am not the creature of my society's system of time-reckoning. My life and my activity endure and it is only through interaction with others that I am subject to time. The man who is fishing carries on until he stops, sleeps until he wakes, eats and then goes on fishing. These activities are not meaningful in terms of time except insofar as other people are concerned. Similarly, at a moment of co-ordination in social life what is meaningful is the synthesis in relation to which the elements, whether individual people or groups, are meaningless. As a temporary conclusion we can suggest that the relation of the individual person or the individual group to the larger whole is intimately related to the relation between time-reckoning and mere duration.

It is at this stage that Van Gennep's classical work *Les Rites de Passage* (1909) takes on a new relevance. And this relevance seems to lie exactly where Marcel Mauss, in his review of the book, failed to see it. His acid comments in the *Année Sociologique* may be remembered:

> M. Van Gennep can see nothing but separations, margins and aggregations . . . It is obvious that all rites imply movement. Since there is nothing in the world but the sacred and the profane any

[3] The different calendars do not add up, nor except in the eyes of an observer "cut across each other". From the point of view of any one the others do not exist.

positive act is either the consecration of a profane individual or the desacralization of a sacred person. If one acts ritually it is to change something. At this degree of generality, the thesis becomes a truism (*Année Sociologique* 11: 200–2).

I trust not to have done Mauss an injustice if I say that he appears to have ignored Van Gennep's emphasis upon what he calls "le pivotement de la notion de sacré" in which we recognise that relativity of the relation between the sacred and the profane that has become commonplace in our own time (Van Gennep 1909: 16–17; 1960: 12–13). The rather substantialist division of the world into sacred and profane that Mauss seems to take for granted vanishes and, indeed, it could be argued that *Les Rites de Passage* is a book as much about the inflection of the sacred and the profane in primitive society as it is a book about certain kinds of rite. Here Van Gennep has something to say of the greatest relevance to this discussion. It is usually accepted that the importance of the book lies in its description of the biological individual passing through an almost hierarchical series of rites. It is, I think, significant that in English anthropology at least, the term has come to be used almost exclusively in describing initiation rites at puberty when both the biological and hierarchical aspect are most to the front. Now Van Gennep is careful at the outset to emancipate himself from the narrow consideration of groups and relations between groups. For him society is, properly speaking, composed of societies, or better, particular conditions.[4] Thus we are able to relate the condition of being married, which implies no necessary group affiliation, to the condition of being a member of an age-set, which does. In a word the discussion is not about the life history of individual people or individual groups as they move, but about the reaction of society to such individuals. If distinctions of age are important, or if distinctions of occupation are important, or distinctions between sacred acts and profane ones—if all these distinctions mark the centres of value for a society, then it is quite obvious that these are precisely the areas in which individual preference, natural sympathy and biological development, summarily the fact of difference, must be subordinated to principles upon which that society places

---

[4] See French edition, p. 1, 4. The English translators speak of social groupings and subgroups where Van Gennep has written "society" and "categories."

value. Difference, whether in the individual person or group, is experienced, biological duration for example cannot be ignored, but through rites these differences are subsumed. The notorious unevenness of biological development, the vagaries of human wills constitute a threat to the valued order. We can imagine what would happen to the distinction between pre-puberty and manhood in a given society if it were left to the biological process to produce men. On the contrary society does not change precisely to the extent that it is able to cope with the effects of duration by denying them any individuality and consequently any historicity. Following the schema of the *rites de passage,* the individual person or group is cut off, isolated and then restored. But in this restoration individual distinctions and differences are translated into social ones. Van Gennep is then talking not about particular rites and finally not only about the inflection of the sacred and the profane in particular societies. He is talking about the nature of society as a complex of meaning maintaining itself against forces that would devalue it, render it meaningless. Forces which are nevertheless conditions of its existence.

This play of society against the corroding effects of duration can be observed in a field apparently quite distinct from that of time-reckoning, the field of primitive law.[5] Dr. P. Howell, writing of Nuer law (1954), speaks of their concepts of right and wrong —*cuong* and *dueer. Cuong* means upright in the moral and in the material sense. A post is *cuong* if it stands upright in the ground. A man of good behaviour is *cuong* also. *Cuong* is used in the sense of right when, in a dispute, one says that a man has *cuong* on his side, or he has more *cuong,* more right, than another. *Dueer* is the opposite of *cuong*. It means to miss the mark in hunting and also to be at fault in moral matters. Now, although Professor Evans-Pritchard has told that "strictly speaking the Nuer have no law" we may nevertheless observe from Howell's account of arbitration among the Nuer the same relation of society to the individual event—in this case a dispute—as we found in our discussion of Van Gennep. For the Nuer, *cuong* and *dueer* cannot be used or defined abstractly—there is no one primary meaning to which the other meanings are secondary. The anthropologist may define them by accumulating what they have meant at dif-

[5] Cf. the discussion of Gluckman's material in Pocock 1961: 106–8.

ferent times but his is the outsider's view. For the Nuer, if a man takes another's life (not during war) his act cannot be immediately classified as *dueer*. Whether he had *cuong* on his side or how much right he had, this can only be ascertained by consideration of the particular moment in the life of the society in which he acted. The effect of this we may observe when we see what happens after the introduction of legal tribunals among the Nuer. The English notions of justice initially demanded consistency and it seemed only just that some law of precedent should be established. Thus if on one occasion a man was fined ten cattle for stealing another's wife, then if another man did the same thing he also should be fined ten cattle. This was contrary to Nuer notions of right, for they could not see that the superficial similarity of the two acts made them of equal moral value, for the two men were not the same nor were the two women, and all the parties stood in different relations to different people (Howell 1954: 23–24). For the Nuer, each case should be considered as an unique event, but always in the light of the notions of *cuong* and *dueer* which are eternal and unaffected by time. The difference between the Nuer and the English in this matter is the difference between their reactions to the unique. The Nuer recognise it in the event but deny it historicity or value, it happens and it is over. The English on the other hand value it and give it determining power over subsequent events. For the Nuer the absolute resides in the terms *cuong* and *dueer;* for the English it has come to reside in the event. It is interesting to note in this connection how, in English law, the notion of equity has evolved to correct the rigidity of the law, so that equity is to the law what among the Nuer the circumstances of a particular event are to the unchanging principles of right and wrong.[6]

Provisionally we come to a sociological use of the term individual, whether person, group or event, by relating it to the term duration, which is after all a succession of meaningless individuals in this sense. The use of the term *individual* here to refer to the human experience of particularity and uniqueness should not be confused with the normal sense of (valued) Individual as it is used in everyday English. Here the recognition of the individual is simply the recognition of the effects of duration and it is duration

[6] Cf. R. Lingat 14: "The dharma, through its atemporal nature, is immune to the changes of the ages."

and not the individual which is put in opposition to the social.[7]

To return to India: it is I suppose by now a commonplace that traditional Indian society sets little value upon history. Nevertheless it is, I think, interesting to consider what happens in that society to the experience of duration, that experience of the particular which is, however denied or devalued, a part of the human experience. At the outset everything points to the annihilation of the particular and of duration. We have the well known cycles of time repeating themselves *ad infinitum*. The *mahayuga* follow each other. Each is divided into four *yuga,* each one of which is shorter than those that preceded it and each is marked by a progressive moral and physical deterioration. According to some Puranas, Vishnu takes his tenth incarnation at the end of each Mahayuga (*kalki avatāra*), overthrows the mlecchas, heretics and Shudra kings who will by then be dominant and then inaugurates another *mahayuga* beginning with its golden age, the *kṛta* age.

It is of course the last *yuga,* the Kaliyuga (the age of Kalyavan —death and time itself) which is the best known. Although shorter than the preceding ages it endures for 432,000 years, of which only 5,049 have elapsed. In fact this Kaliyuga is the time in which men live. The Hindu as we know and have known him is a creature of the Kaliyuga; according to Kane, the idea that man lives in an age of degeneration evolves simultaneously in Hindu thought with the whole cyclical theory of time-reckoning (Kane 1946, vol. 3: ch. 34). The characteristics of the Kaliyuga taken by themselves are almost a parody, certainly a dramatic statement, of the effects of duration ungoverned by concepts of time and human lives ungoverned by society. There is a progressive decay of all that gives meaning to Hindu life, a deliquescence of all value. But, of course, this experience is not seen as an isolated and rectilinear process. It is given meaning and value by its place within a whole system of time-reckoning. The horror of duration and the human experience that things fall short of the ideal are

---

[7] I am grateful to L. Dumont for a lengthy correspondence on this point which revolves around the question of terminology. Both here and in my *Social Anthropology* the intention is to use the term "individual" as a fact of experience which is only opposed to society as the meaningless, or non-conceptual to the conceptual and meaningful. I am aware that it is open to misinterpretation and no doubt some alternative term must be found which will distinguish the individual in this sense from the valued and conceptualized individual of Western theology and philosophy.

made tolerable by being made understandable. The Kaliyuga is the night that follows the day, and morning will come—even though that morning will belong to somebody else.

The theory of *kalivarjya* plays an important part in the justificatory role of the *mahayuga* scheme. The drinking of *soma* and alcoholic liquors, the practice of offering cows in sacrifice, the right of Brahmans to steal in times of need are condemned not as eternally wrong but simply because unsuited to people living in a corrupted age. Thus not only are departures from the current ideals justified but changes in social practice can be recognised and justified by reference to the condition of the time. The changes which duration inevitably brings about are recognised, but they are recognised only to be subordinated in a wider and changeless scheme. In short the Kaliyuga is not homogeneous with the other *yuga*, it is opposed to them, and the radical difference is that it is the age of time which is actually lived.

Parallel to this and at another level we may consider the great theory of successive births which is a counterpart of the caste hierarchy. Here apparently the individual is lost in a succession of births and can be said to achieve *satya*, true being, only by rebirths through the hierarchy of things and men. Nevertheless, and I think my experience is not unique, I was struck by the indifference of the greater part of the peasantry in Gujerat to this belief which they still formally accepted. Quite apart from those who were recognised bhagats, everyone placed over against the idea of rebirth a faith in devotion itself, in *bhakti*. Sectarian allegiances are strong in this part of Gujerat it is true, and we do not need to argue for a connection between sect and *bhakti*. But what is the effect of this double belief? Certainly reincarnation is intimately associated with the dignity of the Brahman to the extent that both rest upon a basic notion of hierarchy. But it is evident that for the people themselves their sectarian adherence or, if they do not formally belong to a sect, their private *bhakti* constitutes the religious reality. Thus at the highest levels of the Patidar caste where many belong to the relatively modern Swaminarayan sect, the Brahman is reduced to a village functionary, no less essential than the barber but no more so. I would go so far as to say that the Brahman tends to become profane. Even at lower levels of the Patidar caste there is ambiguity: a man says that he believes in, accepts the existence of this god or that when he is speaking in the context of Brahmanic practice, but he speaks of adoration or worship when he refers to his Bhagvan.[8]

We have come close once more to the problem with which the paper started. But it has almost ceased to be a problem, for we have moved away from a sociology of harmonies and the resolution of contradictions to a sociology that operates in terms of contradictions and disengages the structure which is founded on them. We have on the one hand an *experience* of change and duration set against a *system* of values that appears to deny it. On the other we have a belief in the individual's capacity to achieve salvation set against the formal negation of the individual contained in the doctrine of transmigration. And I have said that the peasants I studied affectively stress the former, i.e. *bhakti*. There is a parallel here but I believe we can go still further.

Let us return to the theory of the cycles of time. The progression of the cycle from freshness to decay, from dawn to sad evening is inexorable. The gods themselves are no less subject to it. Nevertheless we find the element of intervention even here. We have the belief growing in strength from the Middle Ages onwards that Vishnu plays with the cycles of time. His avatars come increasingly to be considered as interventions on the behalf of society or some virtuous individual. He is believed to break through the progressive decay, arrest its course and even reverse it. This is a remarkable contradiction and one of which our texts seem to be aware for we find some attempt at a reconciliation. The final avatar of Vishnu, Kalki, is to intervene in that he punishes the wrongs of that time but, because his intervention coincides with the last moments of the Kaliyuga, the righteousness which he restores is in fact the inauguration of a new *Kṛta* age. So also Krishna in the Gita: "Oh son of Kunti, at the end of each *kalpa* all natures become one with me and again as each *kalpa* begins I send them forth from me again."[9]

In the relation of the two theories, the avatar theory and the *kalpa* theory, we have then another parallel. But this time there is an important link. For although Shiva has been associated with

---

[8] The distinction is between *mānavū*—to affirm the existence of, and *bhajavū*—to worship, revere, adore.

[9] *Bhagavadgītā*, IX. 7.

bhakti (notably, I suppose, in the Shvetāshvatara Upanishad) the pre-eminent object of *bhakti* in later years is Krishna as avatar of Vishnu. And how appropriate this is we see when we consider that just as *bhakti* is opposed to, cuts through, the inevitable succession of rebirths, so Vishnu cuts through the inevitable succession of the yuga.

To conclude: our problem was how we could reconcile the experience which the Patidar have of change with their adherence to a set of values which denies change. We examined this relation of mobility to fixity in terms of the relation of the social to the individual or particular and the relation of the repetitive eternal to the unique event. It seemed possible to equate the two instances of particularity under the term duration, a fact of experience, as opposed to time-reckoning which is social and conceptual. We observed in some societies how the effects of duration are played upon and devalued. We saw nevertheless that the fact remains as a challenge to that total, meaningful complex which we call the social. In Indian theories of time-reckoning we found a highly complicated recognition of the opposition, a parallel to that which exists between the order of castes and the doctrine of *bhakti*. The "problem" among the Patidar is then only a version of a pan-Indian pattern. When that is established it is profitable to go on and consider what is distinctive about the particular balance which the Patidar strike between the opposed notions. We can observe a greater emphasis among them upon *bhakti*, upon history and the individual but we should be mistaken, were we to imagine that this must be an exclusive emphasis, a choice between what seem to us to be contradictory notions.

17 CONCEPTS OF TIME AMONG THE TIV OF NIGERIA

Paul Bohannan

THE TIME NOTIONS held by the Tiv of central Nigeria[1] are of importance in analyzing all aspects of Tiv society and culture, but are basic to political structure, to the study of quasi-historical myths and legends, especially those of migration, to mystical beliefs, and to studies of social change among them. The present article deals with (I) the main Tiv words relevant to "time," (II) the ways Tiv indicate time and lapse of time over short periods, (III) the ways they indicate time and lapse of time over long periods, including periods which exceed the lifetime of a single person; it ends (IV) with some implications of the fact that Tiv indicate but do not measure time.

I

All the Tiv words which might be translated "time" can be better and more accurately translated into English another way. There are several adverbs and adjectives expressing long and short duration: for example, the word *cha* means "far" and is used of space, of time, and of kinship. However, such words are not dependent on time indication or reckoning for their primary meanings.

Reprinted from *The Southwestern Journal of Anthropology* 9 (3), 1953: 251–62, by permission of the author and the editor, *The Southwestern Journal of Anthropology*.

[1] Field work was carried out among the Tiv from July 1949 to July 1950, from June 1951 to January 1952, and from June 1952 to January 1953. I wish to thank the Social Science Research Council and the Wenner-Gren Foundation for financial support, the Colonial Social Science Research Council and the Government of Nigeria for supplementary travel grants.

There are at least three nouns (*shighen, dzum, icin*)[2] which mean "occasion." However, slight differences are apparent in their contexts of usage: only *icin* can be counted: one time, two times, etc., are *icin i môm, acin a har,* etc. Only *shighen* can be used in the sense of "Now is the time" (*shighen kuma er*). Although *dzum* applies to longer intervals from the referent action than the other two, all three of these words are used for "at that time."

All are used primarily in clauses which would be, in English, "when" clauses: "When he came" (*dzum u a ve . . .*) etc. It should be stressed that these "when" words remain nouns in such contexts. I believe that the adverbial notion "when" is missing in Tiv (though its place is adequately catered for by the "occasion" words). It is the "occasion" words which introduce an event with which another event is to be correlated.

II

Time Indication by Natural Phenomena

When it is necessary to place an incident in time, as it often is, Tiv do so by referring it to a natural or a social activity or condition, using solar, lunar, seasonal, agricultural, meterorological or other events. Tiv ritual is not associated with a calendar, and for this reason ritual events are not usable as time indicators as they are in many societies.

Among Tiv, time is indicated by a direct association of two events. "He came the day I left" is an association of two events to indicate time; "I was married in the year we were fighting the so-and-so" is another; "We will leave when the sun is there" (pointing to a position in the sky) is yet another.

Tiv use the same word for sun (*iyange*) and for the period between sunrise and sunrise. Though there are other words to describe other aspects of the sun—*ou,* for example, means "the sun" when one is discussing the heat of the sun—there is no other

[2] I have used the regular orthography, devised by the Dutch Reform Church Mission, used by literate Tiv. The consonant written *gh* is a velar fricative, voiced in all except the final position; *c* is English *ch;* other consonants have approximately their English value; ô is the open o, British "hot" or American "taught"; all other vowels have approximately Italian values.

word for the period of a day and a succeeding night. Thus, a day is a "sun."

The most common method of time indication during the day is to point to the position in the sky which the sun will occupy at the time under consideration. There are, however, several parts of the day which have names, which may be used with or without the pointing gesture. There are words for dawn[3] and for early morning[4] and for late morning.[5] There is a word (*tetan*) for indicating the heat of the day, when the sun is more or less directly overhead. This word, as antonym to night (*tugh*), also means "daylight" and by extension, "not connected with witchcraft," because witches operate at night. *Ikiye* is the period from about 4:30 to sunset.

Tiv are much less specific about time during the night. The time between dusk and about 10 o'clock is called "sitting together" (*teman imôngo*). After that follows "the middle of the night" (*helatô tugh*), which overlaps with the "time of the first sleep" (*icin i mnya môm*); "the time of the second sleep" (*acin a mnya ahar*) is about 3 AM or a bit later. The pre-dawn breeze (*kiishi*) gives its name to the period just before dawn.

Months can be counted and referred to by the Tiv word *uwer* which applies both to the moon and to the period between one new moon and the next. "The moon comes out" (*uwel u due*) means both the time between the new moon and full moon, and also the new moon itself. However, if Tiv point to the sky with the words, "When the moon comes out here" (*uwel u duwe hen*), they are referring to the date of the lunar month when the moon will be in that position at dusk. "The dark of the moon" (*uwel u ime*) is a time of quiet nights; people are most likely to catch cold or to be bewitched at this time of month, Tiv say.

Though administrators, missionaries, and literate Tiv translate the English word "month" by the Tiv word "moon" (*uwer*), and

---

[3] *Sev*, usually used in the full idea "dawn is breaking" (*sev mbu aven*), which also means, in narrative, "the next day."

[4] *Pepe*. If the word is repeated *pepepepe* (sometimes accompanied by a gesture with the fingers indicating smallness) it means "very early in the morning" and includes dawn. The more times the word is repeated, the earlier the time referred to.

[5] *Nomyange*–male sun. This is occasionally divided into "little male sun" and "big male sun"–centering about 9 o'clock and 11 o'clock respectively. "*Mtan*"–"the shining" may also be used with "big" and "small" to indicate the same times.

use transliterations of the English month names, Tiv themselves
have no lunar month names.

Moons are sometimes counted by pregnant women to determine their stage of pregnancy. According to them, the period of
human gestation for a male child is nine moons and for a female
child eight moons. Some women make marks on their hut walls
to indicate the passage of the moons. The marks seldom tally
with the event: that they do not do so is put down to human error—either the woman made two marks one month, or forgot one
or more months. The discrepancy does not affect the belief.

Tiv refer to years by counting "dry seasons" (*inyom*). There
are two distinct seasons in Tivland: the dry season lasting from
November to April, and the wet season extending from May to
October. The wet season as a whole is called *fam*, which is also
the more specific name for two periods within it, but wet seasons
are not counted for the purpose of enumerating years.

Both the wet and dry seasons are subdivided for purposes of
reference. In April, during the cyclones which precede the return of the rains, there is a period of varying length which Tiv
call "stripes of dry and wet season" (*karegh u nyom, karegh u
fam*). The comparable period which precedes the dry season is
called the same thing, with the order reversed (stripes of wet and
dry season). These seasons also have other names: that before
the wet season is sometimes called "the heat of the body" (*icen
iyologh*) while that before the dry season is sometimes called
"the approach (lit. enlightening) of the dry season" (*wanger
nyom*).

The wet season (*fam*) is itself divided into five "seasons":
"new rain" (*wulahe*) in May, "planting (guinea corn)"
(*tswagher*)[6] in June and early July, the *fam* itself in July, sometimes running into early August. At this time of year there is
often a break in the rains called the "little dry" by the British—
Tiv call it "mid-*fam*" (*atôatô fam*), after which the "*fam* returns"
(*fam hide*) during September and the first part of October (the
wettest time of the year).

The dry season is divided by different harmattans, the dust-
bearing northerly wind from the desert. The first appearance of

---

[6] Both the operation and the time of year are called *kpilin ivor* in
northwestern Tivland.

the harmattan haze and wind, about the first of December, is called "the harmattan which dries the okra" (*hil u kelen atur*). The next is the "harmattan of the broken calabash" (*hir u abebejôndugh*) and the third and longest, from early February stretching well into March, is the "grand harmattan" (*hil u vesen*). Since the harmattan winds and dust do come and go, but are not divided neatly into three every year, there is always disagreement about the "correct" term for the current harmattan. Furthermore, the order of names varies in different areas, and some people will list by name as many as five or six various harmattans.

Though seasons are not sharply defined, each does have its climatological peculiarity. *Tswagher,* for example, is a time of cloudy and turbulent skies, but there is little rain. So long as this sort of weather is to be found, and the millet is not yet ripe, it is said to be *tswagher.* As soon as the millet is harvested, and the cloudy weather has given way to rains, it is *fam.* If one of these conditions has occurred but not the other, it may be either *tswagher* or *fam.* It does not really matter to Tiv where one ends and the next begins; no social or ritual events depend upon it.

Tiv make no correlations between these seasons and "moons" —I have asked specifically and exhaustively about this point.

Agricultural activities are used to designate portions of the year; although they are, of course, roughly correlated with seasons, they are to Tiv more precise than seasons. "The time for clearing fields" means September-October in the south, December in the northwest and in the east: the differences are due to ecological conditions. "The time for planting millet" is about April in all areas.

Tiv "seasons" are determined as much by agricultural activities as by climatological changes. Instead of saying, "We cut the guinea corn when the first harmattan comes," as we would do in English, Tiv just as often say, "The first harmattan comes when we cut the guinea corn." This reversibility is indicative of the fact that neither event is considered primary or basic to the other. Instead of an implied causal relationship, there is mere association of two events.

Besides agricultural activities, the cycle of crop rotations and fallow periods—covering four or five years—are occasionally used as time indicators for slightly longer periods. "That happened just before we cleared the field now in beniseed" indicates a period approximately two and a half years ago (in the south—the time varies, of course, with the different farming practices in different areas).

Time Indication by Social Phenomena

Tiv, particularly those in the central and southern areas, recognize a five-day cycle of days, each day of which is named after a market. Europeans in the area call this period a "market week," though Tiv do not have any word for the five-day period except the word "market" (*kasóa,* from Hausa, *kásua*).

Most Tiv markets are held every five days.[7] These markets are named for their founder or for the present-day market master (*tor kasoa*) or for the name of the lineage in whose territory they are located, or sometimes for streams or hills nearby. Many markets have two, or even three, names. These markets, in turn, give their names to the days on which they are held. Tiv have no names for the days of the five-day cycle other than the names of particular markets.[8] Since each market is held every five days, the day names form a repeating series of five. People generally refer to the days by the names of those markets which are nearest to their homes, and therefore most frequented. This habit gives rise to changes in day names within relatively short distances. A day name will, of course, be understood in many adjacent areas where it is not used. An example will illustrate this point:

MARKETS IN DIFFERENT AREAS

Day	E. MbaDuku	Iyon	S. Ute	Vande Ikya
1	Atsar	Atsar	Atsar	Ingwa
2	Iyon	Iyon	Pev	Sharwan
3	Aichwa	Dar	Aichwa	Agbo
4	Chukwan	Ajio	Ako	Wankar
5	Angur	Adikpo	Adikpo	Gbako

[7] Some few are held every ten days. Protestant missions have established Saturday markets in areas immediately under their influence, and in the northeast, at least, other markets have been put into the seven-day cycle, which runs concurrently with a five-day cycle.

[8] Udam, to the south of Tiv, have day names which are sometimes applied to markets.

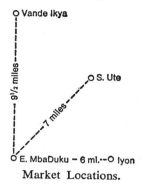

Market Locations.

"The day of Iyon market" (*iyange Iyon*) is used in the area of Iyon itself, and some six miles to the west, in MbaDuku; at no greater distance to the northwest, however, the same day is called "the day of Pev market" although everyone in that area knows that Iyon and Pev markets are held on the same day and has no difficulty if a stranger uses the other term. The same day, at Vande Ikya, is called "the day of Sharwan market" or "Sharwan day." People of this area know both the other nearby markets held on that day, but use their names only when travelling in the area where they are in general use. If one were to continue north another few miles, people would be hazy as to exactly which day Iyon market is held. It is considered polite, when travelling in Tivland, to use the day names in current use in the locality where the traveller finds himself. If he does not know the customary day name, he will use another, often adding that he does not know if that is correct local usage; the local people will then set him right. Several times I have been reprimanded in Iyon for using the day names of the Eastern MbaDuku market cycle; they are perfectly well understood, but people say, "You are here now; you must call the days as we do."

The range within which the name of a market is commonly used as a day name is roughly proportional to the size of the market. Atsar and Adikpo markets are both very large ones, with the result that people from large areas attend them, and days take their names from these markets over a larger area than, say, Angur or Pev markets, both of which are quite small.

Tiv not only make appointments and time references within

the terms of these market cycles, they count them as well. "I have been here three markets" means that the local market has been held three times since the speaker's arrival—from eleven to fifteen days.

All Tiv know that Europeans use a seven-day week. Their translations for day names are "day of beginning work" (*iyange i hiin tom*) for Monday, "second day of work" (*tom yange a har*), etc. Saturday is usually *Saadi,* and weeks are sometimes counted by counting Saturdays. Sunday (*Lahadi*) is however the more usual day to be counted for "weeks," because it is of somewhat greater importance for most Tiv. Tiv say that in the past they did not have a day of rest, but since the Europeans first showed them the custom, it is widely observed.[9] Sunday is important nowadays, having been introduced as the European day of rest, and become associated with beer drinking. The best Tiv beer takes seven days to brew, and though beer may of course be set and drunk on any day, both operations are commonly done on Sunday. In the northwest, where there are very few markets, the days of the seven-day week are often called by the names of processes in the brewing week, the "day for drinking" (*iyange i vihin*) generally being Sunday. The "day for drinking" may, however, change with every new batch of beer.

Weeks are counted by some Tiv by counting "worships" (*adua*). This is the Hausa word for Muslim prayer which has been adopted by Christian missionaries for church services. The word is today generally known, and is used to indicate both Christian church services and the week.

There are several points of special importance in the material so far presented. Tiv refer to time by direct association of two events, one of which is likely to be, but need not be, of a meteorological or social nature, and a part of a cycle or a repeated series. Moreover, Tiv indicate lapse of time either by indicating the span of time commensurate with the period between two natural or social events in a well-known series, or—more commonly—by counting repetitive natural or social events.

Suns, moons, and dry seasons—days, months, and years—as

⁹ Tiv had almost undoubtedly heard of a day of rest before European penetration—their southern neighbors, the Udam, have one day of their five-day market week in which they do no work; Hausa observe Friday, the Muslim sabbath, in a rough and ready sort of way.

well as markets and weeks: in each case reference is to a recurrent natural or social phenomenon which can be counted. That this is a matter of *counting* is of special importance.

Although there are various named periods during the day, and various named seasons during the year, there is no word which means a subdivision of a day, and there is no word for "season." There is no notion of periods of the day which can be counted: nothing of which you can say that there are four or five between dawn and dusk. Likewise, it is impossible to say that there are four or five "seasons" or "sub-seasons" during the wet season, for there is no generalized thing in the Tiv idea which can be counted.

For Tiv, time is divided by natural and social events into different sorts of periods, but since the events often belong to different logical series, there is little attempt to correlate the different sorts of division of time. Tiv make no attempt to correlate moons with markets or either with agricultural activities, or seasons. If one asks how many "moons" there are in a year, the answer varies between ten and eighteen; if one asks the number of markets in a moon, the answer varies between three and eight; if the number of days in a moon, between ten and fifty. Tiv could, of course, observe these matters accurately if they chose to do so. We must assume, on the basis of this evidence, that they have no occasion for doing so.

There are other situations in which, on the surface, Tiv doctrine seems actually to contradict our notions of time. Age-sets (*kwagh*) are loosely organized when their members are about twenty years old. Tiv tell the investigator that all the members of an age-set were born in the same year. The ordinary European interpretation of this statement (at least, it was mine) is that an age-set is formed every year. However, when by careful study one determines that in point of fact a new age-set is formed about every three years, and points this fact out to Tiv, adding that if a new one were formed every year there would be more of them, most Tiv will say that you are quite right: nevertheless, they were born in the same year as all the other men of their age-set. The statement must be interpreted equivocally, referring to the nature of the relationship between age-mates, not as referring directly to time. Tiv do not make a correlation "one age-set: one year" just because everyone in the same age-set was "born in the same year." The two statements have reference to different aspects of the social life. So far as I am aware, Tiv do not use age-sets for purposes of time correlation or time reference as some societies in East Africa are said to do.

III

Tiv indicate most periods of time which exceed four or five years in length, but which are still contained within the life expectancy of a single man, by reference to the life-cycle of the individual. Again, time is indicated by direct correlation of two events: "That market hadn't yet moved when my eldest son was born, for I bought camwood there to rub on him" is made specific by the fact that one can see the son and so get some idea of the time involved. "The Europeans came after I had been circumcized, but before I married" is a typical expression of time indication over such a longer period of time.

Except in response to an ethnographer's "when" questions, the purpose of such sentences is not to indicate specific time, but to indicate lapse of time and more often to indicate sequence and relative duration by reference to a culturally accepted series of social events or to common human factors such as the rate of growth and maturation of the human being.

Furthermore, the mere fact that two events occurred within the lifetime of a single man is not *per se* any indication that we can accept his correlation of the two events, in what we would call a time milieu, as accurate. Most people can, I should judge, remember the order of several related events in a single series of events, even though none or not all of them are repetitive. That is, one can remember the series of events leading to one's marriage in the correct order; one can remember the events which led to an election, also in the correct order. The question is: can these two logically unrelated series of events, if they took place simultaneously, be accurately interdigitated from memory after a lapse of several years, in the absence of a formulated, calibrated time dimension? This is a problem for experimental psychologists—one of which they are not unaware, but one on which they seem not yet to have worked sufficiently. It lies, of course, at the basis of the ethnologist's problem of historical reconstruction.

Except for occasional references to dead parents, grandparents or friends, in which time is usually not in any wise important, Tiv refer to periods of time longer than a single life-span, or further removed than a single life-span, in only two contexts: that of genealogy and that of the myths and legends of migration, which include myths of origin of social traits and cultural items. Genealogies, intrinsically, bear their own time elements; myths and legends of migration and culture origins are timeless.

From the point of view of Tiv, there is comparatively little to say about such statements. Since, however, there is some likelihood that Tiv statements of this sort will be misunderstood by Europeans—since, in fact, some writers on the Tiv have misunderstood and mistranslated them—it is just as well to look more carefully into their content.

Tiv believe that their genealogies are true (*vough*). It is important in investigating Tiv time ideas, however, to realize that the operative "true" correlation of genealogical depth lies with Tiv political structure rather than with biologically countable generations of ancestors (L. Bohannan 1952): with social space instead of with time of any sort. That in genealogies the generations are not primarily time notions is demonstrated by the recent addition of a new ancestor—Adam. In the same way that ancestors such as Ishon and Takuluku were postulated prior to "Tiv," the ancestor (but never in so systematic a way as the descendants of "Tiv"), in order to place the neighboring peoples in a genealogical relationship with themselves, so when Tiv encountered Europeans and heard the creation story, they immediately accepted "Adám and Ife" as part of their cosmic doctrine, and thus were enabled to include Europeans, as a lineage, in the over-all lineage brotherhood of the human race. We have on several occasions been asked by ex-soldiers whether the Japanese, Burmese, and Indians are subordinate lineages of the Europeans, and if not how they fit in.

It is obvious that in recognizing Adam, Tiv have incidentally added a generation to their social time. This is incidental, and I believe irrelevant to them. The reason that the Adam story was accepted so quickly was that it allowed them to account for formerly unknown men and social groups, hence increasing their spatial horizons, in a familiar idiom.

Yet, intrinsically, an increase of time is concomitant with an increase in space. Tiv tell an investigator that they are more numerous today than they were in the past. If one challenges the statement that there were fewer people long ago, Tiv cite lineage genealogies to prove that you are wrong. We collected information which enables us to show how Tiv genealogies "collapse" (L. Bohannan 1952). It is a basic Tiv notion that, unless evil forces are at work, a child generation is larger than its parent generation. That Tiv say they increase with the passage of generations is primarily a cosmographical notion, and its spatial aspect is of vastly greater importance than its temporal aspect.

Tiv say that since they increase with the passage of time (and since every Tiv has a right to sufficient farmland in the territory of his minimal agnatic segment) the amount of territory which they occupy also increases.

None of these three ideas—increase of area, passage of generations, and population increase—is independent. Each is validated by the other two. A man knows that an event happened long ago because there was a different spatial distribution than is to be found at present and because "we were few." "We were few" obviously because of the fact that the different spatial distribution is said to have existed and because it was long ago. A different spatial distribution existed because "we were few" and because it was long ago. This is a circular argument from which there is no escape.

The more important fact, however, is that beyond a generation or two, neither a particular spatial distribution nor a specific event in the myths and legends of migration and cultural origins is commonly connected with a specific ancestor in the lineage genealogies. Though a few Tiv elders may make an occasional connection, there is certainly no general agreement, and the most amazing fact is that the "characters" in the myths and legends are *not* attached to a specific ancestor at a specific point in the genealogies.

It is difficult to realize why Tiv do not associate genealogies with myths and legends (for genealogies would be their only way of setting the mythical and legendary events in time) until we understand that the events and incidents in the legends and myths are told in explanation of social process, not as "history." The most common incidents all cluster about a standard situation which arises time and again in the dynamic of Tiv social process: particularly fission and fusion of lineage territories, which are the modal points in Tiv political process. As one collects more and more versions of the myths and legends in different parts of the country, it becomes evident that there are a relatively few stock incidents which can be applied to any instance of the social process to be illustrated. It is, of course, as impossible to prove that these incidents did not occur as to prove that they did. It can be stated with confidence, however, that they are applied to many different instances and that they are seldom correlated with specific persons in the genealogies.

The timelessness of the myths and legends is even more apparent when one realizes that a lineage name is the plural form of the given name of its apical ancestor. The grammatical number, here, is not so important as it would be in English; Tiv jump back and forth from singular to plural forms in these contexts with an ease and agility which at first bewilders the European mind which is used to precision in these matters. In recounting the adventures of a lineage, Tiv do not distinguish between the founder of a lineage and his group of descendants: it is impossible for them to tell an investigator whether a certain incident happened to "Kpar" (the man) or "Kparev" (the lineage made up of his descendants). Most will say, if pushed, that it does not matter—how could they know, since they were not there?

"Time" associations beyond the grandparents of living adults are utterly vague. Instead of referring an incident to a genealogy to pin down its time element, Tiv are content to say that it was "long ago" (*ngise*)—the same term with which they begin their animal folk tales. Although "long ago" can, in some contexts, mean day before yesterday, or even an hour past, most commonly it has no specific time referent at all, in the sense that we are accustomed to think of it. Its purpose is not so much to indicate that something happened long ago, as to indicate either that it is established and traditional, or else that it is outside the immediate purview.

The important point here is that Tiv, by and large, do not even correlate events over a period of time beyond a generation or two. There is only a dim "long ago" (*ngise*) which can be increased by saying "long long ago" (*ngise ngise*)—the more times you say the word, the longer ago or further removed it was. "Long ago" was filled with events and with people, but they are—from the standpoint of time reference—of much the same quality as the events which it is assumed will take place in future (*sha hemen*, literally "in front").

Tiv have not elicited the time element implicit in their lineage and political structure any more than they have elicited "time" from the course of a human life, the recurrence of the phases of the moon or of five-day markets. Time is implicit in Tiv thought and speech, but it is not a category of it.[10]

IV

We in Western Europe have elicited an idea, or a medium, which we call "time"—or better, "chronology"—and have calibrated it into a standard gauge against which we associate single events or a series of events. The presence of such a time gauge among our cultural apparatus means that in addition to time indication and time-lapse indication, we measure time.

A minute and a day are qualitatively as well as quantitatively different: the difference is that between measuring and counting. Days are natural events and can be counted without a special apparatus; minutes and hours are artificial events, if they be events at all, and can be counted only with the aid of special apparatus. Those Tiv who are acquainted with the idea of "hours" from Europeans seem to have changed the idea somewhat: Tiv servants and clerks use the word *ahwa* for "hour." Besides its obvious similarity to the English word, this is a plural form of *ihwa*, which means "mark" or "tally." One o'clock is "one mark" and six o'clock means "six marks." They are, in fact, counting the marks on a watch, I believe quite unaware that the watch is merely a device for counting standardized symbols for artificial units of time.

Thus, although Tiv indicate time by direct association of two events, and though they count recurrent natural units such as days, markets, moons, and dry seasons, they do not measure time. Because of the fact that they do not, by and large (and certainly not with any consensus) associate legendary incidents with genealogical ancestors (which supply the only "system"

---

[10] Evans-Pritchard has pointed out that to Nuer, the notion we call "time" is not a separate idea, but an integral part of social activities and ecological and meteorological phenomena (E. E. Evans-Pritchard 1940: 104–8).

which has immanent in it some sort of "natural time" to which long-period reference could be made), there is no device for indicating time in the distant past with any greater accuracy than in the future.

18 THE TEMNE HOUSE

James Littlejohn

I

AT THE BEGINNING of the sixteenth century Valentim Fernandes wrote of the Temne houses that "they are the best houses of all Guinea". They are probably still so. Sometimes stepping from the mottled light of the bush, where it takes an effort to distinguish single objects clearly, into the clearing of a village one has the impression of a powerful perhaps grim fortress. On it the lucid strong light falls like a benediction. This impression is particularly strong where the houses are round, a form which is giving way now to square or rectangular shapes. That the house is so stoutly built is all the more surprising in view of the relative lack of techniques at the disposal of their builders—techniques in the European sense of procedures derived from a scientific theory of reality. The European house as a structure is determined entirely by technique, mathematical calculation of area, height etc., physical calculation of stress and hydraulic calculation of pressure. It would be possible to describe the Temne village house in mathematical and physical terms, but the result would only be an exercise in ethnocentricity. A decision to build a Temne house is not followed by the production of a plan, but by a communion with the ancestors to secure their blessing for the project.

To build a village round house, two circles are marked off on the ground by pegging a length of rope and drawing out the circumference with a stick tied to the other end. The house consists of two circular walls, the inner higher than the outer, on which rests the roof. The space between the walls is partitioned into

Reprinted from *Sierra Leone Studies* (New Series) No. 14, December 1960, pp. 63–79, with permission of the author and of the editor, *Sierra Leone Studies*. The author has given permission for one diagram to be omitted.

bedrooms and store rooms. In gaps in the outer wall are placed kitchen and verandah. A wall is made from two circles of upright sticks about a span apart traversed by 8–12 horizontal rows of saplings lashed on. In the numerous squares so formed mud is roughly packed and allowed to dry. After that the wall is finished with supplementary packing and mud plastering inside and out. The main poles of the roof are lashed to specially stout uprights in the walls and held together at the top by a circlet of saplings. Several rings of saplings are lashed round them, smaller poles tied to these, and the whole thatched. A good strong house, say twenty-five feet high and about the same in diameter takes well over a year to finish. Naturally there are variations in design, but these are the essentials.

This is all done without machines and without a mathematical system of measurement. The only unit of measure is *an-fatm* which is the outstretched arms of any adult man. It was *Pa Nes,* The Spider, who showed men how to measure and older Temne say there is no other way. However, if need arise they will use the pace, the foot (actual human foot), the span and lengths between index finger knuckles. These measures have no names, are rarely used and do not form units in a system of measure. For the most part in housebuilding measuring is done by direct perception of "shorter/longer than" and "equal to", once a stick of the wanted length has been selected to serve as standard. There is no way whatsoever of measuring area. The area of a farm is the only one ever estimated and that is done by estimating the number of bags of rice it ought to yield.

In the space so created by this structure dwells the Temne household. Perhaps nothing distinguishes the Temne house from the European so much as the nature of this space, for it is *kanta-* closed. As well as being an adjective *kanta* is the verb, to close, the instrument for effecting the closure is *an-kanta,* and the space so closed can also be called *an-kanta.* The word is one of the few Temne terms known to most Europeans in Sierra Leone through the custom whereby a chief lives in *kanta* for up to a year prior to coronation. The closed space so inhabited by a chief is specially constructed for him at the time and is abandoned after coronation; thereafter he lives in his own house which like all others is closed. It is as essential to close the house as to roof it, and closing is generally begun soon after the floor space has been marked off on the ground. Farms are also closed in the same terms and in the same way. As there are numerous instruments for closing and this is not an analysis of *an-kanta*, I shall briefly describe the closing of a farm I witnessed. First there was a sacrifice (*sotka*) in which the ancestors were invoked and the farm handed over to them. *An-kanta* had been prepared beforehand. It consisted of a kola nut wrapped in a leaf and bound round with thread so that both were invisible. Two needles were stuck through the thread and four cowrie shells tied on by means of it. It was rusty orange in colour, probably chewed kola had been spat on it. It was put on a miniature tripod in the centre of the farm and a small shelter put over it. It was asked to ward off evil.

II

To return to the house, what is it closed off from, or against? To answer this it is necessary first to sketch in the nature of Temne space in general. From the account of measurement in house-building it is apparent that unlike European space it is not "hodological", not articulated through geometry and arithmetic. This is more clearly seen in measurement of distance. The only unit here is *an-wula* which means both the stretch between one village and another and also wasteland, i.e. if you ask how far it is to X the answer is so many intervals between villages, or simply the number of villages between "here" and destination. (I have been told by European administrators how infuriating it is on a hot trek to be told on asking how far to X—"only three more villages sir"). As villages are not evenly spaced over the ground this measure cannot be characterized mathematically, it is not in fact the application of a unit *to* distance but a meaning which arises *out of* the Temne landscape and human movement in it, just as the measure of short length is a meaning inherent in the Temne body. That the Temne landscape is neither absolute nature nor absolute culture goes without saying. There is not much primary forest left in Temneland; dry ground agriculture is of the shifting "slash and burn" type with an interval of 3–8 years between successive burning of any one area, so that most of the land at any time is covered with secondary bush out of which tower the stronger trees which escape burning, and out of which rear groves of primary forest left alone because they conveniently mark boundaries, are society meeting places, chiefs' cemeteries, and so on. Through this landscape run numerous rivers and streams, their course marked by a border of forest.

The qualitative organization of Temne space is apparent also in regard to the cardinal points. These are not mere co-ordinates for plotting position (the Temne have no maps) but directions of existence. Pre-eminent among them is East. The word for East is *Rotɔron;* ro = place of, tɔri = to disclose, tɔrine = to appear. Prayers are uttered to the East, animals' throats must point East before being slit at sacrifice, blood flows towards the East. "We think of East as rising up, like a hill, of everything going up to the East," say Temne. Correspondingly the word for West, *ro-pil,* is frequently used for "down" both in the sense of going down a slope and in the social sense as, for example, "down town." As facing East is where orientation is taken from, the word for North is that for "left hand" and for South that for "right hand". More details of this orientation are given below.

That space is articulated through meanings which have little reference to its geometrical and physical characteristics is also apparent from Temne wall paintings. These are never executed in conformity with the laws of perspective; they are two-dimensional. By the rules of perspective they incorporate distortion; it goes without saying that often the "distorted" outline of a subject carries more physiognomic meaning than when drawn in perspective. Some such wall paintings in the village of Katik convey with the utmost clarity and simplicity the pathos of Whiteman at the present day; firmly, perhaps a trifle arrogantly asserted on an earth he has mastered yet condemned to bear with him all the determinations of things (to paraphrase Kant, to make the object conform to his intellect instead of letting his intellect conform to the object).

This is not intended as a complete account of Temne space, only as a sketch to show that its determinations are not mathematical but are carried by meanings of a different sort. Before turning to these in relation to the closure of the house I wish to remark that determinations of space (like all knowledge) are not neutral factors in regard to other aspects of society and culture. They play a decisive role in the constitution of the world the society inhabits, which world in its turn plays a role in the constitution of the society. Without their geometrical space for example

Europeans would be unable to survey, navigate, calculate stress etc., as they do, and without such activities their economy would not be as it is. The conceptions which organize space not only partly determine technology and economics, but qualify experience in more general ways. European determinations of space are responsible for an initial dequalification of any landscape they take over. Surveying rests on this dequalification, space being reduced to "points" which are all alike. The best method of surveying is by beacons—"points of light"—on hilltops at night, when the qualities of intervening landscape are totally blotted out. On this initial dequalification is superimposed "economic interest", giving rise to the European categorization of landscape into the useful and the beautiful—beauty coinciding to a large extent with the useless. While the Temne are as sharp as anybody in marking out the useful, this categorization does not arise for them. They never climb hills to "look at the view". I have several times been laughed at for gazing at sunsets, once with the question "haven't you ever seen that before?" That there are accordingly possibilities of experience in the landscape which are open to Temne and not available for Europeans is demonstrated below.

The space which forms *kanta* can only be understood in the light of the two main regions of Temne *weltanschauung*. These are *Rosocki* and *Daru* (sometimes *Noru*); I shall clarify them as far as is necessary through *Rosocki*. *Ro* is the Temne prefix indicating a "where", accordingly features in numerous village names as e.g., Rosint (place of sand), Rogbane (meeting place), Robailey (Bailey's place) and so on. By itself it is the preposition indicating to, towards, in, at, into, or from, e.g., "I am going *ro pet*" (to town) or "*o der ro sith*" (he's coming from the house). Any question beginning with *reke* or *deke* (where?) contains the answer *Ro*-something. *Rosocki* is the "where" of *socki*. *Socki* by itself is both adjective and noun derived from the verb *sok* meaning to dawn both of daylight and the understanding, as in the phrase *pə sok mi*—it dawns me, I understand. *Socki* denominates or qualifies a creature as one with a special understanding as over against one who is not *socki*. If you join the Poro society you are *socki* as regards Poro things as over against one who is not a member. However, as a chief explained: "A society is a thing made by man so if you are *socki* for a society you are only second-class *socki*." A "first-class" *socki* is one who can see into *Rosocki*.

Usually in so doing he participates in the forms of existence found there. While anybody may be or become a real *socki,* the dead, twins, the child following twins and witches invariably are. The last three can see into Rosocki because each has four eyes. (The four cowries on the *kanta* described are its four eyes.)

Apart from these, Rosocki is invisible to people and that is how Temne first characterize it, in opposition to *noru* where things happen *"m' ma sə nənk yen"* (as we all or generally see). *Rosocki* has three sub-regions—*rokrifi* where the ancestors are, *roshiron* where witches are active ("a sort of town where witches start out from" as one man said) and another where the gods and demons exist, usually unnamed but sometimes called simply *rosocki.* It is largely through these sub-regions that the Temne deploy space around themselves. The measure *an-wula,* for example, does not derive its meaning entirely from the fact that there is "wasteland" there, for there are at any given time areas of crops, but partly in opposition to the space formed by a village. Parallel with this runs a classification of demons into bush-demons, river-demons, and town-demons. Bush-demons inhabit *an-wula* and become visible there sometimes as animals—most snakes are bush-demons who have undergone temporary metamorphosis into that form. Bush-demons are specially noted for destroying the human embryo in the womb. Town-demons on the other hand inhabit towns, are "more tractable" the Temne say, and if treated properly i.e. fed with rice, will secure fruitful pregnancies for women. Most women own one.

The pre-eminence of East over the other cardinal points arises not just through its being the direction of understanding and revealing but also because the first Temne, that is the ancestors, "came from" there. *Rotɔron* and *rokrifi* are practically the same. The operation of closing a space (in the sense of *kanta*) includes handing it over to the ancestors. East is "up" (as described) hence when a chief leaves *kanta* after coronation he is said to "come down".

To *kanta* the house is to place it within the bounds of *Rosocki.* But why should it be closed?

III

Here it is a question of contacts between *Rosocki* and *Daru*. These are various and by no means confined only to seeing as in the case of *socki* people. It is a typically European idea that knowledge and experience are got almost exclusively through the eye. As to contact with the ancestors through sacrifice the subject is too large to treat here. It is sufficient to say that it is the commonest ceremony of the Temne and is done by daylight mostly in the house or the yard at the back. By handing over (*lankili*) the house to the ancestors in the first phase of closing it the house becomes a temple to them. They become guardians of it and help to keep out the other creatures of *rosocki*.

There is one experience of *Rosocki* almost every Temne seems to have which, though it has nothing to do with closing the house, I wish to mention to illustrate my remark that different articulations of space offer and prohibit different possibilities of experience. This is an encounter with *Aronshon,* a demon who owns the forest. Though of *Rosocki,* he is not classed along with bush-demons partly because he is not a local deity, all forests are his; unlike bush-demons who have a local habitation and no name except to those few *socki* people they communicate with. Parents often send children into the bush on the edge of the village to collect leaves for wrappings. Sometimes "as you walk through the trees you begin to feel queer, your head becomes dizzy, you don't know where you are. You shout for your parents, then they come and find you". This spell the Temne say is *Aronshon's* work and nearly all seem to succumb to it at least once in childhood, and some in adulthood too; adults are said to receive a whipping from *Aronshon* so that they return cut and bruised. In the hodologic space of Europeans such an interpretation is impossible, disorientation being clarified as mere mistake or ignorance (i.e. of the "correct" direction) followed by panic.

However, there are visitations from *rosocki* which have much more serious results. According to the various counts I took about one third of illnesses are attributed to attacks from witches. Witches can also spoil crops and deprive a man of money. There is a special verb *tofi* meaning the action by which a witch causes you to lose money. While there is no end to the harm witches can do their most dreadful act is the killing and eating of children. Almost all children's deaths are attributed to witchcraft and it is usually a series of children's deaths in a village which starts off a witch hunt under the direction of one of the several societies who specialize in that. Bush-demons are sometimes responsible for the death of adults or children either by an attack on their own or in co-operation with witches, but what they are most feared for is spoiling pregnancies. All miscarriages occur through copulation with a bush-demon. The rate of miscarriage is extremely high and there are few women who do not wear a charmed thong or coils of wire round the hips to keep the demons off. Men fear the demons as much as their wives. One convert said "Though I am a Christian I fear the bush-demons. Three times they have come to my wife and she has lost her babies. Each time I sent her to the *alfa*" (a Mohammedan magician who makes charms to ward off demons).

The encounters occur at night in dreams. Night is the time when evil things "get up" (*yokane*) mostly. The dream in which a person encounters demons or witches is thought by Temne to be different from ordinary dreams; however the same verb is used for all dreaming—*i wərp oshir* (I dream a witch)—and as far as I could discover the only difference is one of content. The bush-demon appears to the woman in the form of a man and copulates with her; she then either miscarries or gives birth to a monstrosity. Witches appear in dreams in a variety of ways but usually as an animal. Witches themselves admit if asked that when witching their face turns into an animal's but do not seem to regard that as important or interesting. They usually mention co-operation between themselves and bush-demons. Here is an extract from the official confession of a witch (official in the sense of confessed before the *Ragbeŋle* society acting on behalf of chiefdom authorities). "During my first marriage to B. I worked hard. After working hard for him he got more wives then he became no longer mindful of me. He paid no attention to my parents either. I said I would spoil his work. I gave his farm to a demon, a bush-demon called Yebu who lives in a big tree called Kasaka. Then I left him and came to my present husband. As I was sleeping at night I dreamt I was going to the stream. As I returned there was a crowd in the middle of the town. They said 'you have no share here . . .' Then I found them slaughtering A's baby. They gave me some of its skin to eat. I ate the skin . . . About a month later the baby died."

To *kanta* the house is to close it against witches and bush-demons. It is in the house at night, sleeping, that people are near-est *Rosocki:* "In dreams you are often near *Rosocki,*" they say. At any rate it is in dreams that the evil creatures of Rosocki are mostly encountered. I wish to stress that it is not the case that the Temne do not distinguish between dream and wakeful percep-tion; they do. The point is that dreams count for as much as wake-ful perception. And not only in this context but in many others; doctors, for example, sometimes in dreams discover the exact leaf to cure a patient with. While experience neither in dreams nor wakeful perception can be said to be categorized with the Temne, both are subject to the same characterizations, both, for example, can have the character of "present reality", both can have the character of "forewarning" and no doubt both for the most part go to join the burden of forgottenness all men every-where accumulate in the course of their lives.

IV

It is always one's own house one closes while the description so far is of the house in general. To bring closer the Temne house and the existence of those who dwell in it I turn now to the house-hold. This is the anthropological area of social structure where arise the tensions such as were implicit in the witch's confession. I do not assume here that structure explains everything, but at least it gives direction to these tensions. The household can only be understood through a brief description of Temne society. The basic unit is the *bonshɔ*, an agnatic lineage varying in depth from three to twelve generations and in size from one person to several hundred. Generally speaking only a royal lineage is more than five generations in depth. There are two *bonshɔ* which are important in the life of each individual, that of his father called *makas* from *o-kas* (father) and that of his mother called *makara* from *o-kara* (mother). It is from the father's lineage that one derives one's ma-jor rights and obligations. All land is owned by *bonshɔ* and one is entitled to farm an area of ground by virtue of membership of a *makas*. From the *makas* one has the right to live in a house of the *makas,* and in a royal *makas* any adult male has the right to claim

chieftaincy of the chiefdom ruled by that *makas*. A village is normally composed of from 1–10 *makas* (plus any wives brought in
from other villages) each usually occupying adjoining houses.
Round the village stretches the land owned by them.

Within the *makas* the most striking feature of kinship is "the
unity of the sibling group". Brother and sister are denominated
by one term, *a-want,* and the identification of the two is carried
through all descending generations, *o-wan* being the term for both
son and daughter and *rɔk* that for grandson and granddaughter.
All a man's children by no matter how many wives are *o-wan*. In
the ascending generations the unity of the sibling group is cut
across by classification by sex, so that both father's and mother's
brother is *o-berin* and both father's and mother's sister is *ntene*.
"Unity of the sibling group" is a pressure from the generation
above broken by the emergence of a generation below, i.e. of
children.

The vast majority of *makas* are exogamous units, so that wives
have to be brought in from outside. The bride price paid to the
man's father-in-law varies from £2 to £100 plus (in the villages)
labour on his farm by the son-in-law. Whatever the price Temne
say "You always owe your wife's people . . ." ". . . even if you
pay father-in-law a thousand pounds you still owe him. Nothing
could pay for the services of your wife . . ." "You get your children from her." By payment of bride price children are got to
replenish the *makas,* but it seems there is no value equivalent to
a woman's fertility.

The unity of the sibling group is most outstandingly demonstrated through marriage, for one does not so much marry another person as attach oneself to a sibling group whose behaviour
towards one is only brought to a focus in the spouse. Terminology
is:—brother and sister-in-law are both referred to as *nasin;* a man
addresses his sister-in-law as *rani,* i.e., wife, while a woman addresses her brother-in-law as *awus,* i.e., husband; often a man
will address his sister's husband as "husband" and a woman her
brother's wife as "wife". Should a wife prove to be barren the
husband can get one of her sisters as an additional wife without
further payment of bride price. The husband is entitled to flirt
with his wife's sisters while they are entitled to "play with him".
"They will take down your trousers and play with you," say the
Temne. *Nasin,* asked why they behave this way say "he's taken

one of our *a-want,* he plays with her so why shouldn't we play with him?" Furthermore male *nasin* can enter their brother-in-law's house at any time and take away any small articles or food they find lying about. This is all done in a rough joking spirit and the husband has to respond with a show of good humour. They do not always feel good-humoured about it. One morning my interpreter was speechless with suppressed rage, when I asked him what was wrong he said a *nasin* had just come and taken away a new pair of trousers and a shirt. "You are always placating your nasin," he added, "they hold the marriage; they will take your wife away if you don't."

There is great variety in the composition of the Temne household, but the core of it is always a senior man and his wives and children and in addition there is usually a brother or a son (or several of them) along with their wives and children. The core of the household is a fragment of a lineage. From the point of view of the adult men each wife brought in is, as well as a source of children, the point of irruption of plundering *nasin* into the house. (Plundering is the word the Temne use of *nasin.*) Now in the dream of copulation with a pregnancy spoiling bush-demon, the demon almost invariably appears as a male relative of the woman with whom copulation is incest, and most often is her brother, is her husband's *nasin.* Incest for the Temne is typified by brother-sister incest, it is always this type they refer to when talking of the subject, and the only actual case I knew of during fieldwork was of this kind.

Not only does a wife, dreaming at night, attract bush-demons into the house. Hatreds among co-wives and between husband and wife is a major breeding ground of witchcraft. (It is not the only source but a very common one.) In the confession quoted the witch, a neglected co-wife, destroyed her first husband's farm and the baby she feasted on was one of her second husband's by a co-wife. Infants themselves, though less often witches than adults are the main victims of witchcraft. The Temne explain this as due to their being less "strong in the head" than adults are, they more easily succumb to witchcraft hence attract witches into the house. Most village children wear charms (*sɛbɛ*) to keep off witches, and sometimes these charms are said to *kanta* the body of the child. The space occupied by the body is of the same nature as that of the house.

V

A house is not just a structure filled with people but also a work place, both in the sense that it is the woman's main place of work and the place where men find rest from work. As such it has its own implements which only have meaning in the house. I wish to turn to these now partly because a house is not a house without them and partly to prevent a misunderstanding which is liable to arise through the cursory account I have given of the two regions of *Rosocki* and *Daru*. One is apt at first glance to equate these with European categories of spirit and substance or of their derivates—mind and matter, culture and nature, the ideal and the real, etc. To do so is to misunderstand the Temne, and while I cannot argue the point here a consideration of their household utensils should make this clear. For all of them sidle over from *daru* into *rosocki* or can be made to do so. Most of them have the character of *wanka*.

An-wanka is an instrument set up in vegetable plots and orchards to punish thieves. The vegetable plot is the woman's responsibility. The verb used for setting up a *wanka* is *pər*, which means "to persuade someone to harm a third party for one's own satisfaction". I shall describe one completely then list household utensils used to make *wanka*. This is a very powerful one, so powerful that it even attacks monkeys and its maker is famous for it. You take a small anthill, slice two sides and the bottom so that it has the rough outline of a human head, it then represents a head. Take some grass and make a head pad with it (i.e. the normal pad used to protect the head when carrying heavy loads on it), put it on top of the anthill and add six stones. In the vegetable garden make a small shelter of sticks and palm leaves on the ground and put the *wanka* in it. You have to face East and use the left hand only to lay it. Then you address *Kuru* (God) saying what you are doing. "I'm putting this *wanka* on this spot. As long as it is true you originated-and-own the earth . . . anybody tampering with these crops I'm handing over his nose, his lips and those of his children (according to the number of stones) to that *wanka*. Let all rot." Any thief then suffers a disease which rots away nose, lips and teeth, presumably yaws. The exposed galleries and chamber of the anthill resemble a face rotting from yaws. The one who lays the *wanka* of course has to protect himself with an ablution which both he and the owner of the plot must use later when the *wanka* is lifted at the end of the season. It has to be lifted with the right hand. *Wanka* on the whole inflict diseases which leave some disfigurement but at least the course of the disease can be halted. The cure for this one consists of the bark of three different trees taken from the East and West sides of the trunk. It costs 2/– to 5/– plus some kola nuts to have it laid and the same with a small gift of some of the crop for lifting. The cure for the disease is liable to cost several pounds. This particular *wanka* can be strengthened by objects belonging to the society which owns it; the maker who taught me, a most conscientious man, always adds to it a special potion to ensure that witches don't appropriate it and use it for their nefarious projects. The name of the disease inflicted by a *wanka* is also the name of that kind of *wanka* and often the name of the principal object used in the making of it, as for example *ralil* = leprosy = vine (in general) = type of *wanka* made with the vine *ratonk*.

Household utensils which figure prominently in the making of *wanka* are:—

a-pɛpɛ	Calabash, the commonest utensil. Take a piece of calabash, bore holes in it and stuff them with cotton. It gives sores.
anbata and *kalapat*	Mat and dead firestick. Cut a piece of mat and wrap round the firestick. The mat gives swellings down the ribs and the firestick itching pains.
ka-binthi	A basket with a small opening, used to keep food in. Attacks children mostly causing frequent stools and vomiting.
ankusɔ	Firestone. (A kitchen fireplace is always made from three round stones.) It hardens and swells the abdomen.
anete	Menstrual rags. They stop the menstrual flow of women thieves or else prevent it stopping.

Northcote Thomas in his *Report on the Temne-speaking Peoples* (1916) lists several others which do not seem to be known in the Port Loko District. They vary from district to district. Men's implements are employed too, for example the hoe, the fish trap and the vine *ratonk* mentioned above which is used to poison fish. Household utensils can have other characters besides *wanka*, for example the large wooden vessel in which rice is beaten can be used to catch witches who are as yet foetus in their mother's womb and so on. I do not wish to consider these other characters here. What is important at the moment is that all household utensils have the signification *wanka* because as one Temne said (in English) "they all maintain the household". The verb he translated as "maintain" is *bumr* which includes the meaning "protect", e.g., a dog, though it is not *wanka,* also *bumr*(s) the house by barking and chasing away strangers. The *wanka* described above which seems to have no bearing on utensils of any sort is actually one of the most useful of all—without the wheel or beasts of burden the human head with head pad is indispensable for carrying heavy loads.

That these utensils have the character of *wanka* because they maintain the household reveals the inadequacy of any attempt to explain *wanka* by the so-called principles of homeopathic magic. These principles are based on a notion of some kind of automatic association in the mind between things which are like and between things which have once been or are in contact. The association is automatic since the theory includes no reference to a human being who is to make the association. The theory would claim, for example, that since a firestone is "hard and round" it is associated with "hard and swollen" belly and mistakenly believed to cause it. The explanation is false because it cannot show why it should be a firestone precisely that is selected for *wanka* and not something else, and it cannot do this because the theory of homeopathic magic does not provide for the limiting of the flood of possible associations between things which are like. Temneland is full of "hard and round" objects, e.g., stones before they are used as firestones, but only the *fire*stone does for this type of *wanka.* Were the theory correct there could be organization of the things in the world by the Temne or any other people, because every solid object is like every solid object (in being solid) hence anything could be confounded with anything. The Temne utilize likeness between things in fashioning *wanka* but to be utilized for this purpose a thing must already have the signification "maintainer" or "protector" of the household. The character of *wanka* is not present in any of the household utensils in so far as these are objects in the scientific sense (i.e. display constant properties like extension, impenetrability and secondary qualities like colour, shape, etc.) but in so far as they play a part in maintaining the household. Moreover, as the Temne explained to me, the *wanka* acts by being transformed into *Rosocki* out of *Daru*.

If "maintainer of household" seems a strange index to seize upon for characterizing utensils that is perhaps because the European house is by no means a temple and its utensils are viewed under the character of efficiency and prestige, which alter from generation to generation or even in a shorter span of time. In a world organized by technique there can be no other characters, for efficiency there is not merely one "quality" among others but the ostensible goal of all production and use of utensils; while a people from whom the gods, demons and ancestors have departed can do little else with their possessions but compare them with each other.

For the Temne the house itself is not merely a shelter from the elements, etc., equipped with comforts of such and such a social standard. As "containing the household" it can resolve some of the pains of members of the household. A sore throat the Temne reckon is often caused by the grudge a female *nasin* bears towards one. This kind of sore throat is cured by her pouring water down the roof of the house whilst one catches a spoonful as it drips off the eaves and swallows it. One of my interpreters cured himself of a sore throat in this way.

The above is not intended as a complete elucidation of *wanka,* which I cannot undertake here.

VI

There is always an intimate connection between a dwelling and the kind of existence led by those who live in it. "Suburban semi-detached," "slum," "country house," "council house," etc., signify for Britons not just architectural styles but different positions in a social system and different "styles of life". The only distinction among permanent residences of the Temne is that between the chief's house (*kama*) and any other (*an-sith*). In a previous article in this *Journal* on the Temne *ansasa* (Littlejohn 1960), I pointed out that one of the principles on which it is based is the representativeness of the individual existence, as Temne see it. Rice and earth are constituents of *ansasa* because every man eats rice and tramps earth, hence man is represented by their presence there. In this sense few things represent man so much as a rubbish heap: like archaeologists, the Temne find man most heavily present in what he rejects. The rubbish heap (*amuruŋ*) in the yard with very little preparation is a deadly *ansasa* capable of killing not only a witch or unknown burglar but all his or her family. (Naturally, as the witch attacking one's children may be a member of the family one has to be careful about using *amuruŋ*.) It is a punishable offence to use it without first getting the consent of the chief.

The representativeness of existence allows the Temne easily to attack someone who has sinned against him, stands in the relationship of *a-teki* (sin) towards him (see the previous article cited). It also leaves him open to attack if he sins. There is one other situation where this is again the case though here there need be no *a-teki*. In civil disputes the Temne hold that the best way of winning your case (apart from a judicious distribution of gifts) is to damage the opponent's eloquence. This is done by *təmabɔro*. This is a small cylinder of earth and leaves wrapped first in chequered red and white cloth then in red cloth. To use it you must twist red and white threads tightly round the cylinder while uttering the opponent's name; he is choked, unable to talk seriously. When not in use *təmabɔro* should be buried under a doorway. When I was being initiated into it I queried the necessity for this on the grounds that not every man passed through my doorway. The answer to this objection was that every man must pass through *a* doorway. As one who has to do that, he is open to the spell of *təmabɔro*.

To represent in Temne is *təma ta* "stand for". There are numerous occasions on which one "stands for" another in Temne life. The head of a *bonshɔ* should stand for any of its members in dealings with the chief, or in certain court cases, i.e., he should represent them. The "unity of the sibling group" appears as a relationship in which sibs regularly stand for each other—children are exchanged between brothers for quite long periods, a dead man's children become his brother's children. Recently in one town a man was put in the stocks because his sister had been convicted of stealing but had fled. Quite reasonably he was punished for her.

VII

I have been considering the Temne house as a structure and set of activities in space. It is evident that a full account of the house would have to consider its position in time as well—the presence of the past in and around it in the form of the ancestors; the alternation of day and night over it, an alternation of good and evil, help to constitute the Temne dwelling. There are other customs not mentioned which show how time would have to be taken into account. For example, a first born baby who dies soon after birth is buried in the rubbish heap and returns as the second born. A second born who dies is buried under the verandah and returns. However, time and the house require a separate analysis.

Finally, this article is solely about collective representations, which should not be confused with anything like "intelligence".

BIBLIOGRAPHY

AMERICAN FOLK-LORE SOCIETY.
1904 *Memoirs* No. 8.
ASDELL, S. A.
1946 *Patterns of Mammalian Reproduction.* London.
AUGUSTINE, SAINT.
1958 Ed. *The City of God.* New York.
BANKS, E.
1949 *Bornean Mammals.* Kuching.
BARTSCH, H. W.
1953 *Kerygma and Myth: a theological debate.* London.
BEATTIE, J. H. M.
1957 "Nyoro personal names," *Uganda Journal* 21.
BEIDELMAN, T. O.
1961a "Hyena and rabbit: a Kaguru representation of matrilineal relations," *Africa* 31 (1).
1961b "Right and left hand among the Kaguru: a note on symbolic classification," *Africa* 31.
1961c "Kaguru justice and the concept of legal fictions," *Journal of African Law* 5.
1961d "Beer drinking and cattle theft in Ukaguru: intertribal relations in a Tanganyika chiefdom," *American Anthropologist* 63.
1963 "Witchcraft in Ukaguru," in: Middleton, J., and E. Winter (editors), *Witchcraft and Sorcery in East Africa.* London.
BERG, C.
1951 *The Unconscious Significance of Hair.* London.
BEST, E.
1924 *The Maori.* Wellington.
BIDNEY, D.
1953 *Theoretical Anthropology.* New York.
BIEBUYCK, D.
1953 "Repartitions et droits du pangolin chez les Balega," *Zaire* 7 (9).
BOHANNAN, L.
1952 "A genealogical charter," *Africa* 22.
BOSCH, F. D. K.
1960 *The Golden Germ: an introduction to Indian symbolism.* 's-Gravenhage.
BURRIDGE, K. O. L.
1954a "Cargo cult activity in Tangu," *Oceania* 24 (4).

1954b   "Racial tension in Manam," *South Pacific* 7 (13).
1956   "A note on Tangu dreams," *Man* 130.

CAPELL, A.
N.d. "Surveys of linguistic research," *South Pacific Commission Project S.6. Report No. 1,* Vol. I.
1952   "Languages of Bogia District, New Guinea," *Oceania* 22.

CARSTAIRS, G. M.
1957   *The Twice-born.* London.

CRAWLEY, E.
1927   *The Mystic Rose.* London.

CRAZZOLARA, J. P.
1933   *Outlines of a Nuer Grammar.* Vienna.

DEVEREAUX, G.
1939   "The social and cultural implications of incest among the Mohave Indians," *Psychoanalytic Quarterly* 8.

DIXON, R. B.
1916   "Oceanic mythology," in: Gray, L. H. (editor), *The Mythology of all Races,* Vol. 9, Boston.

DOUGLAS, M. M.
1954   "The Lele of the Kasai," in: Forde, D. (editor), *African Worlds,* London.
1955   "Social and religious symbolism of the Lele of the Kasai," *Zaire* 9 (4).

DUBOIS, C.
1944   *The People of Alor.* Minneapolis.

DURKHEIM, E.
1912   *The Elementary Forms of the Religious Life.* London, Glencoe (1947).

ELSHOUT, J. M.
1923   *Over de Geneeskunde der Kenja-Dajak in Centraal-Borneo in verband met hunnen Godsdienst.* Amsterdam.

ELWIN, V.
1939   *The Baiga.* London.

ETTER, C.
1949   *Ainu Folklore.* Chicago.

EVANS, I. H. N.
1923   *Studies in Religion, Folk-lore, and Custom in British North Borneo and the Malay Peninsula.* Cambridge.
1937   *The Negritos of Malay.* Cambridge.
1953   *The Religion of the Tempasuk Dusuns of North Borneo.* Cambridge.

EVANS-PRITCHARD, E. E.
1936   "Customs relating to twins among the Nilotic Nuer," *Uganda Journal.*
1940   *The Nuer.* Oxford.
1953a   "The Nuer conception of Spirit in its relation to the social order," *American Anthropologist* 55.
1953b   "The sacrificial role of cattle among the Nuer," *Africa* 23.
1960   *Kinship and Marriage among the Nuer.* Oxford.

FARON, L.
1956   "Araucanian patri-organization and the Omaha system," *American Anthropologist* 58.

1961a "The Dakota-Omaha continuum in Mapuche society," *Journal of the Royal Anthropological Institute* 91 (1).
1961b "On ancestor propitiation among the Mapuche of Central Chile," *American Anthropologist* 58.
1961c *Mapuche Social Structure.* Urbana.
1962 "Matrilateral marriage among the Mapuche (Araucanians) of Central Chile," *Sociologus* 12.
FATHAUR, G.
1961 "Trobriand," in: Schneider, D. M., and K. Gough (editors), *Matrilineal Kinship.* Berkeley.
FIRTH, R. W.
1951 *Elements of Social Organization.* London.
1961 *We, the Tikopia.* London.
FISCHER, J. L.
1963 "The sociopsychological analysis of folktales," *Current Anthropology* 4 (3).
FORDE, D.
1941 *Marriage and Family among the Yakö.* London.
FORTES, M.
1949 *The Web of Kinship among the Tallensi.* London.
FORTUNE, R. F.
1932 *Sorcerers of Dobu.* London.
FRAZER, J. G.
1915 *The Golden Bough.* London (New York, 1960).
1918 *Folklore in the Old Testament.* London.
FREUD, S.
1919 *Totem and Taboo.* London.
FROBENIUS, L., and D. FOX.
1938 *African Genesis.* London.
GIFFORD, E. W.
1916 "Miwok moieties," *University of California Publications in American Archaeology and Ethnology* 12.
GINSBERG, M.
1953 "On the diversity of morals," *Journal of the Royal Anthropological Institute* 83 (2).
GLUCKMAN, M.
1950 "Kinship and marriage among the Lozi and Zulu," in: Radcliffe-Brown, A. R., and D. Forde (editors), *African Systems of Kinship and Marriage.* London.
GRAVES, R., and R. PATAI.
1963 "Some Hebrew myths and legends," *Encounter* 114.
GRIANLE, M., and G. DIETERLEE.
1954 "The Dogon," in: D. Forde (editor), *African Worlds.* London.
GRODDECK, G.
1934 *The World of Man.* London.
HADDON, A. C.
1901 *Head-hunters, Black, White, and Brown.* London.
HARDELAND, A.
1859 *Dajacksch-Deutsches Wörterbuch.* Amsterdam.
HARRISON, J.
1912 *Themis.* Cambridge.
HELD, G. J.
1957 *The Papuas of Waropen.* The Hague.

HERTZ, R.
  1960   *Death and the Right Hand* (translated by R. and C. Needham). Glencoe.
HOCART, A. M.
  1950   *Caste.* London.
HOGBIN, H. I.
  1938   "Social reaction to crime," *Journal of the Royal Anthropological Institute* 68.
  1947   "Shame: a study of social conformity in a New Guinea village," *Oceania* 17.
HOLLEMAN, J. F.
  1952   *Shona Customary Law.* London.
HOMANS, G.
  1941   "Anxiety and ritual: the theories of Malinowski and Radcliffe-Brown," *American Anthropologist* 43 (5).
HOWELL, P. P.
  1954   *A Manual of Nuer Law.* Oxford.
HUBERT, H., and M. MAUSS.
  1897   "Essai sur la nature et la fonction du sacrifice," *Année sociologique* 2.
  1902   "Esquisse d'une théorie générale de la magie," *Année sociologique* 7.
  1909   "L'origine des pouvoirs magiques dans les sociétés australiennes," *Mélanges d'Histoire des Religions.* Paris.
HUTTON, J. H.
  1921   *The Angami Nagas.* London.
  1928   "The significance of headhunting in Assam," *Journal of the Royal Anthropological Institute* 58.
IYER, L. K. A.
  1928–35   *The Mysore Tribes and Castes.*
JAKOBSON, R., and M. HALLE.
  1956   *Fundamentals of Language.* The Hague.
JUNOD, H. A.
  1913   *The Life of a South African Tribe.* Neuchâtel.
KANE, P. V.
  1946   *History of Dharmaśāstra.* Poona.
KIRCHHOFF, P.
  1948   "Food gathering tribes of the Venezuelan Illancs," in: Steward, J. (editor), *Handbook of South American Indians,* Vol. 4. Washington.
KRAUSE, A.
  1956   *The Tlingit Indians.* Seattle.
KRIGE, E. J., and J. D. KRIGE.
  1943   *The Realm of a Rain-Queen.* London.
KROEBER, A. L.
  1947   "The Chibcha," in: Steward, J. (editor), *Handbook of South American Indians,* Vol. 2. Washington.
KUPER, H.
  1950   "Kinship among the Swazi," in: Radcliffe-Brown, A. R., and D. Forde (editors), *African Systems of Kinship and Marriage.* London.
LAWRENCE, P.
  1954   "Cargo cult and religious beliefs among the Garia," *International Archives of Ethnography* 47 (1).

LEACH, E. R.
1954 "A Trobriand Medusa?", *Man* 54.
1961a *Rethinking Anthropology*. London.
1961b "Lévi-Strauss in the Garden of Eden," *Transactions of the New York Academy of Sciences* 23 (4).
LÉVI-STRAUSS, C.
1949 *Les structures élémentaires de la parenté*. Paris.
1948 "The Nambicuara," in: Steward, J. (editor), *Handbook of South American Indians*, Vol. 3, Washington.
1955 "The structural study of myth," in: Sebeok, T. A. (editor), *Myth: a symposium*. Bloomington.
1962a *Totemism*. Boston.
1962b *La pensée sauvage*. Paris.
LEVY-BRUHL, L.
1938 *L'expérience mystique et les symboles chez les primitifs*. Paris.
LITTLE, K. L.
1951 *The Mende of Sierra Leone*. London.
LITTLEJOHN, JAMES
1960 "The Temne *Ansasa*", *Sierra Leone Studies* new series 13, June 1960: 32–35.
LUANG BORIBOL BURIBHAND and A. B. GRISWOLD.
1957 *Images of the Buddha in Thailand*. Bangkok.
MAC NEICE, L.
1949 *Collected Poems 1925–1948*. London.
MALINOWSKI, B.
1923 "The problem of meaning in primitive language," in: Ogden, D. K., and I. A. Richards (editors), *The Meaning of Meaning*. London.
1929, 1932 *The Sexual Life of Savages in North-Western Melanesia*. London.
1935 *Coral Gardens and Their Magic*. London.
MARETT, R. R.
1911 "Rudimentary ethics," in: J. Hastings (editor), *Encyclopaedia of Religion and Ethics*, Vol. 5.
MAXWELL, W. E.
1879 "The aboriginal tribes of Perak," *Journal of the Straits Branch, Royal Asiatic Society* 4.
MEAD, M.
1930 *Social Organization of Manua*. Honolulu.
MELLAND, F. H.
1923 *In Witch-bound Africa*. London.
MILLS, J. P.
1937 *The Rengma Nagas*. London.
MOONEY, J.
1902 *Myths of the Cherokee*. Washington.
MORGAN, K. W.
1953 *The Religion of the Hindus*. New York.
MURPHY, R. F.
1959 "Social structure and sex antagonism," *Southwestern Journal of Anthropology* 15.
NADEL, S. F.
1953 "Social control and self-regulation," *Social Forces* 31 (3).
1947 *The Nuba*. London.

1950 "Dual descent in the Nuba Hills," in: Radcliffe-Brown, A. R., and D. Forde (editors), *African Systems of Kinship and Marriage*. London.

NEEDHAM, R.
1954 "A note on the blood-pace in Borneo," *Man* 54.
1958 "A structural analysis of Purum society," *American Anthropologist* 60.
1960a "The left hand of the Mugwe: an analytical note on the structure of Meru symbolism," *Africa* 30.
1960b "Research projects in Southeast Asia," *Bulletin of the International Committee on Urgent Anthropological and Ethnological Research* 3.
1960c "Alliance and stratification among the Lamet," *Sociologus* 10.

NIEUWENHUIS, A. W.
1900 *In Centraal Borneo: reis van Pontianak naar Samarinda*, 2 vols. Leiden.

NILSSON, M. P.
1920 *Primitive Time-reckoning*. Lund.

NSIMBI, M. B.
1950 "Baganda traditional personal names," *Uganda Journal* 14.

OTTO, R.
1926 *The Idea of the Holy*. London.

PARRINDER, G.
1951 *West African Psychology*. London.

PARRY, N. E.
1932 *The Lakhers*. London.

PFEFFER, P.
1963 *Bivouacs à Bornéo*. Paris.

PLAYFAIR, A.
1932 *The Garos*. London.

POCOCK, D. F.
1955 "The movement of castes," *Man* 55.
1961 *Social Anthropology*. London.

RADCLIFFE-BROWN, A. R.
1933 *The Andaman Islanders*. London.
1952 *Structure and Function in Primitive Society*. London, Glencoe.

RADIN, P.
1927 *Primitive Man as Philosopher*. New York.
1933 *Method and Theory of Ethnology*. New York.
1945 *The Road of Life and Death* (Bollingen Series V). New York.
1949 *The Culture of the Winnebago:* as described by themselves. (Special publication of the Bollingen Foundation also published as a Memoir [2] of the *International Journal of American Linguistics* 1949.)

READ, K. E.
1952 "Nama cult of the Central Highlands," *Oceania* 23 (1).
1954 "Cultures of the Central Highlands," *Southwestern Journal of Anthropology* 10 (1).

RIDLEY, H. N.
1922–25 *The Flora of the Malay Peninsula*. 5 vols. London.

ROHEIM, G.
1950 *Psychoanalysis and Anthropology*. New York.

SCHAPERA, I.
1950 "Kinship and marriage among the Tswana," in: Radcliffe-Brown, A. R., and D. Forde (editors), *African Systems of Kinship and Marriage*. London.

SCHÄRER, H.
1963 *Ngaju Religion: the conception of God among a South Borneo people*. The Hague.

SCHEBESTA, P.
1929 *Among the Forest Dwarfs of Malaya*. London.

SELIGMAN, C. G., and B. Z. SELIGMAN.
1911 *The Veddas*. London.

SHANNON, C., and W. WEAVER.
1949 *The Mathematical Theory of Communication*. Urbana.

SKEAT, W. W., and C. O. BLAGDEN.
1906 *Pagan Races of the Malay Peninsula*. 2 vols. London.

SOUSBERGHE, R. P. L. DE.
1955 *Structure de parenté et d'alliance d'après les formules Pende*. Brussels.

SOUTH PACIFIC COMMISSION.
1952 *Bibliography of Cargo Cults and Other Nativistic Movements* (Technical paper No. 30). Noumea-Sydney.

SRINIVAS, M. N.
1952 *Religion and Society among the Coorgs of South India*. Oxford.

STAYT, H. A.
1931 *The BaVenda*. London.

STIGAND, C. H.
1923 *Equatoria, the Lado Enclave*. London.

TAYLOR, D.
1945 "Carib folk-beliefs and customs from Dominica, B. W. I.," *Southwestern Journal of Anthropology* 1.

TEMPLES, P.
1949 *La philosophie bantoue*. Elisabethville.

THOMAS, N.
1916 *Report on the Temne-speaking peoples*. London.

THOMPSON, S.
1961 *Motif-index of Folk-literature*. Bloomington.

TITIEV, M.
1951 "Araucanian culture in transition," *Occasional Contributions, Museum of Anthropology, University of Michigan* 15.

TOPLEY, M.
1954 "Chinese women's vegetarian houses in Singapore," *Journal of the Malayan Branch of the Royal Asiatic Society* 27 (1).

TURNER, V. W.
1953 "Lunda rites and ceremonies," *Occasional Papers of the Rhodes-Livingstone Museum, n.s.* No. 10.
1957 *Schism and Continuity in an African Society: a study of Ndembu village life*. Manchester.
1961a "Ndembu Divination: its symbolism and techniques," *Rhodes-Livingstone Papers* 31. Lusaka.
1961b "Ritual symbolism, morality and the social structure among the Ndembu," *Rhodes-Livingstone Journal* 30.

TYLOR, E. B.
1873 *Primitive Culture*. London.

VAN GENNEP, A.
1909 *The Rites of Passage,* translated 1960 by Vizedom and Caffee. London.

VIVAS, E.
1950 *The Moral Life and the Ethical Life.* Chicago.

WAGNER, G.
1954 "The Abaluyia of Kavirondo," in: Forde, D. (editor), *African Worlds.* London.

WARNER, W. L.
1930 "Morphology and function of the Murngin kinship system," *American Anthropologist* 32.
1937 *A Black Civilization.* New York.

WERNER, A.
1933 *Myths and Legends of the Bantu.* London.

WILKEN, G. A.
1886 "Über das Haaropfer," *Revue coloniale internationale.* Amsterdam.
1912 *Über das Haaropfer und einige andere Trauergebräuche bei den Völkern Indonesiens. De Verspreide Geschriften, verzameld door F. D. E. van Ossenbruggen,* Vol. III. 's-Gravenhage.

WILLIAMS-HUNT, P. D. R.
1952 *An Introduction to the Malayan Aborigines.* Kuala Lumpur.

WILSON, G.
1939 "Nyakyusa conventions of burial," *Bantu Studies* 13.

WILSON, M.
1951 *Good Company: a study of Nyakyusa age-villages.* London.